RETHINKING BILINGUAL EDUCATION

Welcoming home languages in our classrooms

Edited by Elizabeth Barbian,
Grace Cornell Gonzales, and Pilar Mejía

A Rethinking Schools Publication

Rethinking Bilingual Education: Welcoming home languages in our classrooms
Edited by Elizabeth Barbian, Grace Cornell Gonzales, and Pilar Mejía

A Rethinking Schools Publication

Rethinking Schools, Ltd., is a nonprofit publisher and advocacy organization dedicated to sustaining and strengthening public education through social justice teaching and education activism. Our magazine, books, and other resources promote equity and racial justice in the classroom. We encourage grassroots efforts in our schools and communities to enhance the learning and well-being of our children, and to build broad democratic movements for social and environmental justice.

To request additional copies of this book or a catalog of other publications, or to subscribe to *Rethinking Schools* magazine, contact:
Rethinking Schools
6737 W. Washington St.
Suite 3249
Milwaukee WI 53214
800-669-4192
www.rethinkingschools.org

© 2017 Rethinking Schools, Ltd.

Cover and book design: Nancy Zucker
Cover illustration: Ricardo Levins Morales
Proofreading: Lawrence Sanfilippo
Indexing: Marilyn Flagg
Production: Michael Trokan

ISBN: 978-1-937730-73-4

Rethinking bilingual education
Library of Congress Cataloging-in-Publication Control Number: 2017008183

Acknowledgements

We are indebted to the students and families who have shared the immense richness of their home languages and cultures in the schools and communities where we've worked. We are also deeply grateful for the bilingual education advocates who contributed articles and shaped the ideas in this book, and for the work of the many bilingual educators, scholars, researchers, and activists who have fought for and continually reenvisioned bilingual education over the years.

Many of the articles in this book went through *Rethinking Schools* magazine's rigorous editorial process. We are grateful for the critical work of the editorial board and editorial staff, which have included Wayne Au, Bill Bigelow, Melissa Bollow Tempel, Linda Christensen, Helen Gym, Jesse Hagopian, Stan Karp, David Levine, Larry Miller, Bob Peterson, Adam Sanchez, Jody Sokolower, Stephanie Walters, Dyan Watson, Kathy Xiong, and Moé Yonamine. We especially thank David Levine, Rita Tenorio, and Bob Peterson for taking the time to give detailed feedback on many aspects of the book production process.

Special thanks to managing editor Jody Sokolower who skillfully copyedited many of the articles and who, along with curriculum editor Bill Bigelow, provided invaluable mentorship, guidance, and perspective throughout the book editorial process. We are also thankful for the wisdom and guidance of Mike Trokan, production manager, and for the support of past and current Rethinking Schools staff members, including Tegan Dowling, Rachel Kenison, Valerie Warren, and Gina Palazzari.

We are much indebted to art director Nancy Zucker and proofreader Lawrence Sanfilippo. A huge thank you to artist Ricardo Levins Morales for his work on the cover, and to the artists and photographers who contributed their work throughout the book. We are also grateful to the Ruth and Herman Frankel Rethinking Schools Seeds for Sowing Fund for their generous support of our editorial work.

Finally, we thank our families and friends; without their patient support and encouragement over these last three years, this book would never have been possible.

Contents

Chapter 3: Welcoming Home Languages

Chapter 4: Equity at the Center

Chapter 5: Families and Communities

Chapter 6: Policy and Advocacy

Rethinking Bilingual Education

Introduction

What does it mean to rethink bilingual education? When we started to work on this book, we envisioned a collection of articles that would empower bilingual teachers to reflect upon their practice, position social justice pedagogy at the center, and tackle the tough issues of racial and linguistic equity.

Yet, as we gathered articles and did interviews, we were reminded just how much is at stake when it comes to language. Rethinking Schools editor Moé Yonamine shared her story of being hit and knocked to the ground by her teacher in Okinawa for the offense of speaking their shared native language. Educator and activist Debbie Wei described how her parents chose not to speak their Chinese language at home because of the climate of fear and discrimination when they immigrated to the United States from China during the McCarthy era. Debbie explained that, years later,

> I was the only person with my mom when she passed on. She passed at home and everyone but me was in another part of the house at that moment. I was just sitting, watching her, because we knew she was passing soon. Her final words were in her village dialect. I was the only person there to hear them, and I didn't understand what she said. No kid should have to go through that. I never want another child to not understand their mother's final words. Language should be seen as a gift, an asset, not a deficit.

As Debbie reminds us, education in one's native language is a human right. That is the central premise of this book. Many of the authors in this book show us how, over and over, people's fundamental rights to their languages have been suppressed— from boarding schools for Indigenous peoples in the United States, Australia, and Canada; to Deaf students forbidden to express themselves in sign languages; to elementary school students being physically beaten by teachers for speaking in their native tongues even today.

The classroom stories in this book provide a strong counter-narrative to the suppression of non-dominant languages and the repression of bilingual education. In them, teachers share the powerful work that they are already doing to welcome their students' languages into their classrooms and keep equity at the center of their teaching. As we compiled these articles, we identified some common principles that we believe should form the foundation of any bilingual program.

Social Justice Principles for Bilingual Education

Home Language Is a Human Right. Students have the right to learn in their native languages; this belief should be at the core of any model for bilingual education. When we view language as a right, it becomes clear that bilingual programs should not simply use students' languages as a bridge to English. Biliteracy should be valued along with bilingualism; students should have the right to develop academic literacy in all subject matters throughout their school careers.

Even if there is no official bilingual program, schools must ensure that home languages are welcomed and supported. This isn't just an individual right. As we learn from Indigenous educators and activists, it is often a matter of cultural survival. Moé Yonamine reminds us:

> If our *mirukuyuu* (youth) lose their language, they will lose their culture and their identity. Schools must be places where our youth are empowered to learn and nourish heritage languages, to use them and spread them to the next generation.

Culture and Language Are Inseparable. Teaching a language means teaching the cultures that are integrated and embedded in it. Language encodes a way of conceiving of and being in the world. In her article about helping found a Mi'kmaq immersion program in Nova Scotia, educator Starr Paul describes how "The language itself changed the way we taught:"

> "*Mukk pepsite'tekew*," or respect your Elders, became part of the day-to-day classroom environment. Respect and other Mi'kmaq values were embedded in everything we did. When I was growing up and studying in English-only classrooms, if I tripped or fell off my chair, everybody would laugh at me. But in my Mi'kmaw classroom, kids showed concern. They asked, "*Mu kesito'kewn?*" (You're not hurt?) You didn't hear anyone laughing.

Just as Paul does in her classroom, good bilingual programs weave culture into every aspect of teaching. They honor students' family stories and their heritages, and integrate them into the curriculum. They teach a language through the cultural traditions associated with that language. And they are multicultural—they seek out connections to other languages and other cultures.

Equity Between Students and Between Languages. Students need opportunities to think critically about the racism and bias they see in the world around them. Bilingual teachers should work hard to foster equity in their classrooms and schools by teaching anti-racist curricula, modeling respect for differences, and assuring that all students have the opportunity to see their language skills as an asset—and themselves as valuable members of the classroom and broader community.

Strong bilingual programs also promote equity between languages by working to honor the non-dominant language. It is important to analyze all the subtle ways—like language choice at assemblies or during P.A. announcements—that students might be getting the message that English is more important. As Deborah Palmer reminds us in "Why Are We Speaking So Much English?" we can also teach our students how to recognize language imbalances and become their own language advocates, challenging the hegemony of English in their classrooms, schools, and society.

Social Justice Curriculum. In the introduction to *Rethinking Our Classrooms*, Rethinking Schools editors wrote that social justice curriculum and practice must be grounded in the lives of our students; critical; multicultural, anti-bias, pro-justice; participatory, experiential; hopeful, joyful, kind, visionary; activist; academically rigorous; and culturally sensitive. The educators who contributed to *Rethinking Bilingual Education* show us many examples of social justice curriculum being taught in bilingual classrooms—from Deaf students learning about the genocidal roots of Native American boarding schools to 1st graders inquiring into the lives of farmworkers, from high school students investigating the legacy of Afro-Mexicans to young elementary school students having challenging discussions about race and skin color.

Education in one's native language is a human right.

The critical sensibility present in the development of social justice curriculum also applies to how we teach language. Bilingual programs encourage students to take risks, play, and experiment with language. Students should improve their first and second languages through active learning, meaningful content instruction, and critical pedagogy—not worksheets or grammar drills.

Deep Family and Community Involvement. Effective bilingual teachers create curriculum that brings families into the classroom. Teachers include family knowledge and stories into the academic instruction, as Peggy Morrison does when her 1st graders in Watsonville interview their parents about the life cycle of the strawberry, incorporating knowledge from their majority immigrant, farmworker community into the science curriculum. Families are also physically welcomed into the learning space. They participate in writing workshops, are featured as guest speakers, teach traditions and values, and work together to advocate for the schools they want for their children.

School leaders also have the responsibility to incorporate families as partners and allies to assure equity and overturn traditional exclusionary practices. This includes making sure that opportunities for parent involvement and leadership are accessible to all families, and that parent leaders represent the diversity of families at the school. It also includes bringing in community artists and other community members that reflect the varied school cultures and languages.

Critical Reflection. When founding and developing the social justice-based, two-way bilingual program at La Escuela Fratney in Milwaukee, Bob Peterson explains that he and his colleagues knew they didn't have all the answers. "But," he adds, "we try to ask the right questions."

This is a valuable reminder to seek out important questions and to ask them again and again. Bilingual programs must be responsive to the changing needs of students, families, and communities, while maintaining a focus on equity and language as a human right. Ongoing critical reflection is key to meeting the needs of all students. Schools must provide space for adults and children to ask questions, both within and beyond the curriculum, and be open to change.

Toward Models that Promote Sustained Bilingualism and Biliteracy

With so much variation across classrooms and schools, it is essential for educators, families, students, and community members to educate themselves about different types of bilingual programs and to carefully consider how best to fulfill the needs of their community. In this book, we have tried to highlight the stories of educators who teach in programs that promote long-term bilingualism and biliteracy, as these programs most support students' rights to maintain and develop their home languages.

Not all bilingual programs have sustained bilingualism as a goal. In transitional bilingual classrooms, students' home language is used as a bridge to English in the younger elementary grades, with the goal of transitioning students to all-English instruction by 2nd or 3rd grade. Such programs have been strongly criticized by proponents of bilingual education for not fostering sustained bilingualism and biliteracy.

Maintenance (sometimes called "developmental") bilingual programs aim to develop students' home languages with the goal of bilingualism and biliteracy. Some districts operate maintenance programs through only elementary school, while other districts have such programs through middle and high school. Often maintenance programs start with a high percentage of instruction in the home language and then, by upper elementary, have a balance of English and home language instruction.

Dual-language models generally aim to serve 50 percent native English speakers and 50 percent native speakers of the program's other target language, such as Spanish or Mandarin, although many dual-language programs also serve students with other home languages. In these programs, instruction is in both the target language and English, although the ratios vary with the program. For example, one popular model starts in kindergarten with 90 percent of the instruction in the target language and 10 percent in English, moving toward a 50/50 ratio by upper elementary. Another model maintains a 50/50 balance from kindergarten on.

> Teaching a language means teaching the cultures that are integrated and embedded in it.

Immersion programs, in which most or all instruction is in the target language, can involve native speakers of that language, heritage language learners, and/or other students who have a goal of learning the program's language. Other schools teach a heritage language as an academic subject; this is a language class geared toward students with a family connection to the language. Sometimes these students have familiarity with or are already fluent speakers of that language.

Maintenance programs, dual-language programs, immersion programs, and heritage language classes all aim to develop biliteracy and bilingualism, although they go about it in different ways. We believe a community's needs should determine the bilingual program model in a given setting—but we strongly favor programs that help students maintain their languages and have sustained biliteracy as a goal. We also believe that bilingual education should not be a means to track students who speak another language at home, separating them from their peers. And, regardless of the model chosen, the community's and staff's commitment to implementing language inclusion and equity is what ultimately determines a good program.

Welcoming Students' Languages When There Is No Bilingual Program

Of course, bilingual programs are not possible for all students and in all contexts. There might be too few speakers of a specific language, too few teachers of a particular language, or a large number of home languages at a particular school. When our schools cannot provide bilingual programs, we believe that we need to maintain students' right to their native languages as an ideal.

How can we honor our students' native languages, even when we don't teach in a bilingual setting?

Even if we don't speak our students' home languages, we can find books, music, recordings, and other resources that highlight students' languages and cultures. We can ask our children to teach us words and phrases, incorporating these into classroom routines. And, as Linda Christensen does in "Uncovering the Legacy of Language and Power," we can help students understand the "invisible legacy that privileges some languages—and people—and excludes or decimates others," through teaching the histories of language suppression, loss, advocacy, and revival around the world.

It is essential that we explicitly celebrate students' language knowledge. Too often in our classrooms, conversations—and labels—focus on the learning of English rather than the recognition or development of students' home languages. If we focus our conversations exclusively on English acquisition, we lose sight of the importance of simultaneous home language development and miss out on rich opportunities to bring students' home languages into the daily curriculum.

Overview of Chapters

Our hope is that this book illuminates the nuances and complexities of educating students in their native languages and poses some important questions: How do we bring social justice curriculum into our bilingual classrooms? How can we develop equity-centered bilingual programs at the school level? How can we honor our students' native languages, even when we don't teach in a bilingual setting? What can we learn from Indigenous language immersion about the integral relationship between language and culture? How do we involve diverse groups of parents in our classrooms and schools? How do we elevate the status of non-dominant languages when there is so much pressure to prioritize English?

We've organized the book so that it gradually expands outward from individuals' stories to classroom teaching to policy issues. In the first chapter, a small collection of poignant personal narratives by educators sets the frame for the book: What is at stake when language is lost? Why is bilingual education so important? In Chapter 2, educators share social justice curriculum they've taught in bilingual contexts ranging from Spanish/English and ASL/English settings to a Mi'kmaq immersion program in Nova Scotia. Chapter 3 tackles the question of how to make space for students' home languages, as well as support their critical understandings of language issues, in schools where there is no bilingual program.

> **How do we bring social justice curriculum into our bilingual classrooms?**

Chapter 4 is centered around equity—from promoting non-dominant languages, to teaching anti-racist curriculum to young children, to advocating for the resources our programs deserve. Chapter 5 focuses on family and community—educators share how they involve diverse groups of parents and create family-centered curriculum. Finally, articles in Chapter 6 address policy and history, looking at issues such as the Common Core State Standards and standardized testing, as well as struggles faced by some individual schools and programs.

We hope this book contributes to an important, ongoing conversation. As we continue to rethink bilingual education, we are thankful for all of the great educators, activists, and thinkers who have been engaged in this work for many years. We hope this book will ignite and deepen our commitment to honoring all students' languages. ☼

A Note on Terminology

As we compiled this book, we frequently found ourselves talking about the choices we make when we discuss bilingual education, and the ways labels limit students and families. When we use labels instead of descriptions, we too easily lose the nuances and complexities of the human beings behind them. As we talk about "English speakers," "Spanish speakers," or "Hawaiian speakers," it is easy to forget that we are referring to bilingual or multilingual individuals whose fluency in each language is developing to varying degrees.

Some terms also limit students' potential. The commonly used term "English language learner" describes political contexts more than students' abilities. Even if we use the increasingly popular "emergent bilingual" instead, we need to ask questions: Is it fair to use the term in educational contexts where there is no intention of simultaneously developing a student's home language at school? And "emergent" usually defines the lack of English—rarely do we hear the term applied to English-dominant students. Would it be better to simply use "bilingual" instead?

That said, it is hard to write about bilingual education without relying on imperfect labels; in this book, we trusted each author to use them with awareness and intention. We hope the articles in the chapters ahead will generate critical discussions about how the words we choose to describe programs and learners have the potential to foster equity and justice.

A Brief Look at the History of Bilingual Education in the United States

Throughout U.S. history, nativist groups and others who believed in the superiority of Anglo American culture have sought to repress and even annihilate non-English cultures and languages. As early as the colonial period, English slaveholders deliberately separated Africans from other members of their tribes—and children from their parents—in order to destroy their languages and reduce the potential for insurrection. There was a similar assault on Native American children. During the 1800s, German immigrant communities won the right to establish bilingual schools. However, their efforts were fiercely opposed by nativists keen to pass laws mandating English-only instruction.

In this context, it is not surprising that bilingual education in the United States has always been a battle. The bilingual programs that we have today emerged through the work of local activists and through sustained community struggle. Jeff Bale, in "English-Only to the Core," explains:

> Usually, when the story of bilingual education in recent U.S. history is told, that story tends to focus on the actions of Important People like President Lyndon Johnson and Sen. Ralph Yarborough. The narrative tracks formal policy, including the Bilingual Education Act of 1968 and the *Lau v. Nichols* Supreme Court case in 1974 as key plot points. However, this approach to history distorts as much as it reveals. Actually, it was the actions of Chicana/o, Puerto Rican, Native American, and Asian American activists in the 1960s and '70s that brought about bilingual education in the first place.

Bale points to many local struggles that laid the foundation for bilingual education, such as the Third World student strike in San Francisco in 1968 and the student boycotts in Crystal City, Texas, in 1969. In an interview with Rethinking Schools editor Bob Peterson, educator and longtime bilingual advocate Tony Báez cites the work of activists in the Southwest and Cuban immigrants in Miami, along with Puerto Rican activist Evelina López Antonetty in New York City and Chicano leader Rodolfo "Corky" Gonzales in Colorado, who worked to help bilingual/bicultural education be recognized as a key civil right.

In the years that followed, this grassroots organizing also brought more people from the local communities into the classroom, as paraprofessionals or teacher's aides who spoke the language of the students. However, the movement faced backlash from the Reagan administration, which led a major campaign against bilingual education and in favor of a "back to basics" approach in the 1980s.

The assault on immigrant families and bilingual education gained steam through the 1990s. Proposition 187 was passed in California in 1994, a policy that barred undocumented immigrants from accessing healthcare and social services and banned undocumented children from attending public school—although this illegal provision was never officially enforced. In 1996, the U.S. House of Representatives approved a measure designating English as the nation's official language and prohibiting the use of other languages by government agencies; however, the measure did not pass in the Senate.

Then, from 1998 to 2002, a handful of states passed legislation "banning" bilingual education—the result of a xenophobic policy that masqueraded as "English for the children." These laws—Proposition 227 in California, Question 2 in Massachusetts, and Proposition 203 in Arizona—revealed how much the public perception of bilingual programs has been shaped by fear and distrust of immigrant communities.

A lot has happened in the last 15 years—some of it inspiring hope, and some painting an even bleaker picture. In 2016, California's Proposition 58 was passed with 73 percent of the vote, repealing the English-only immersion requirement and other provisions of Proposition 227. At the moment, two-way bilingual, or dual-language programs, are growing in popularity across the United States. In these programs, native speakers of English learn alongside native speakers of the target language (whether Mandarin, Korean, or Spanish), with the goal of bilingualism and academic biliteracy. When implemented well, dual-language programs allow all students to bring their linguistic strengths to the table and have the potential to develop cross-cultural understandings and foster integrated, diverse public schools. However, in some cases, they are also influenced by and can speed gentrification—as more privileged families vie to get their children access to what they see as an enrichment opportunity. When not implemented with a focus on equity and social justice, dual-language programs can disproportionately benefit students of privilege—putting the needs of white English-dominant students and their families first.

Although proponents of bilingual education have won some recent victories, the current focus on increased testing and standardization undermines bilingual programs even without English-only rhetoric. This narrow focus on academic standards and high-stakes testing also takes place against a national backdrop of increasingly open racism and virulent anti-immigrant sentiment. As this book goes to press, it feels as if the fight for bilingual programs and language rights has never been so important.

Chapter 1

LANGUAGE STORIES

RICARDO LEVINS MORALES

Introduction

In a 2009 TED talk "The Danger of a Single Story," Nigerian writer Chimamanda Ngozi Adichie discussed how easy it is to reduce people to a single narrative, to turn one aspect of a person into a definition or truth. Adichie points out the limits and potential harm that can result from a monolithic view of a person, group, or even continent: "The single story creates stereotypes, and the problem with stereotypes is not that they are untrue, but that they are incomplete. They make one story become the only story." This book opens with a collection of teacher-writer narratives; we hope they will highlight the importance of diverse stories as we embrace students' languages in our classrooms.

Personal language stories help us reflect on the ways that our schools honor, value, and erode students' home languages. They give insight into how students' languages are intimately woven into their perspectives and identities. And, most importantly, they urge us to look more closely at our bilingual programs, and invite us to ask questions. What more might we do to develop and honor students' home languages at school and at home? How can we value all aspects of students' cultures and backgrounds—from their names to their traditions to their experiences of discrimination? How can we help students find their voices? How might we create spaces in our curriculum for students to tell and hear stories?

As we listen to stories, we can start to appreciate differences, nuances, and connections across them, and be open to the ways they might change our bilingual programs and classrooms. From Spanish to Tamil to Uchinaaguchi, the language stories in this chapter remind us to be wary of the ways that languages and minds can be colonized in school. As teacher-author Camila Arze Torres Goitia writes in her poignant essay:

> My mind was colonized by the English language in preschool. Ever since, it has been a constant struggle between accepting the privilege and responsibility that come with being bilingual, and fighting to keep my mother tongue alive in its original integrity.

The privilege and responsibility that Arze Torres Goitia talks about extend to our work with emergent bilingual students, regardless of whether or not we teach in a bilingual program. It is our responsibility to work beside our bilingual students in their fight to maintain—and develop—their home languages and cultures. And to provide ways for our students, parents, and colleagues to continue telling their many stories. ☼

Colonizing Wild Tongues

BY CAMILA ARZE TORRES GOITIA

FAVIANNA RODRIGUEZ

My brain is a constant battlefield: harsh *ch*'s and guttural *r*'s fighting against soft *ah*'s and rolling *rrrr*'s. My tongue tries to follow, catch up, code-switch to what my brain wants. As I suppress some words that come naturally for others that don't quite fit what I am trying to say, I speak, knowing that there is a better way to express myself. I continually ask myself, "Who am I talking to?" I can't say anything off the top of my head without running through it. When I write, I pick through the words in my head and constantly erase when I realize the "wrong" one slipped out.

The colonization began when I was 3. That was the year when *one, two, three,* and *four* staked their claim over my brain and tried to enslave *uno, dos, tres, y cuatro*—telling them they were no longer appropriate in public. It was the year when my favorite fruit became *grapes* instead of *uvas* and the year my *abuelita* couldn't understand when I told her "I love you" because she could only understand "*Te quiero*." My mind was colonized by the English language in preschool. Ever since, it has been a constant struggle between accepting the privilege and responsibility that come with being bilingual, and fighting to keep my mother tongue alive in its original integrity.

On my first day of school, I was all excitement. Not like my brother, who had trembled beneath my mother's skirt, trying to hold off entering the doors of education as long as possible. As soon as I was unbuckled from my car seat, I was flying through those doors too fast to hear my mom yelling, "*¡Espera, mi hija!*"

I greeted the teacher, "*Hola, ¿cómo está usted?*"—just like I was taught to politely address my elders.

She said: "NO. We say *hello*."

And just like that, a border was drawn across my mind—half of me was legitimate, appropriate, and civilized, and the other half was wild, inappropriate, and primitive. Living with the genetic memory of my Incan *ancestras/os*, whose tongues were cut for noncompliance, I obeyed. I let those unfamiliar words infect my brain, spread, grow, and exit out through my tongue—temporarily stunting the flourishing of my native language.

More than that, though, I let those colonizers make me believe that I was better than my own blood simply because my mother could not speak their words. I betrayed my people to claim a place for myself in the hierarchy of elementary school. And if learning those sounds and words was not enough, I had to make sure I could navigate them with convincing ease. When Debbie and Ashley—in blonde pigtails and corduroy overalls—told me I had a funny accent, I went home and talked to myself in my room for hours until I sounded just like them. That night at the dinner table, when my mom said "bold" instead of "bald" and "pass the carrrrrots," I gloated inwardly at my superiority. The next day, I made a point of speaking to Debbie and Ashley in my new Western sound, but they still moved on to their hopscotch and jump rope without inviting me.

> **Just like that, a border was drawn across my mind—half of me was legitimate, appropriate, and civilized, and the other half was wild, inappropriate, and primitive.**

This is what colonialism does. It makes you believe that you are better and smarter if you adopt the ways of the colonizers. It made me believe that, if I sounded like Debbie and Ashley, I could have their life and their opportunities.

But I wasn't Debbie and Ashley. I was Camila. Not Camille and not Camilla, even though that is what I let teachers call me. I would always be "other" in the United States. It was years later, when I truly understood this, through plenty of trial and error with the Debbies and Ashleys of the world, that I started my own revolution—a struggle for independence—promising to nourish my authentic self by never forgetting my birth language.

To talk about this colonization, though, without discussing the privilege that has come along with it would be unfair, because to be a survivor of colonialism is a privilege. Yes, bilingualism opens doors. Yes, I have opportunities that some people who look like me and have similar backgrounds do not have.

Still, these opportunities come with comments like "Oh, yeah, you got that job because you're bilingual." First of all, thank you for reducing me to one aspect of myself. I am sure I do not have any other positive qualities that could have aided in this achievement. Secondly, being given a job for being bilingual is like being handed broken pots as a Taíno in exchange for gold. Although multilingualism opens doors, it also serves as a gatekeeper—displacing me on the outside: somewhere between Latina and *Ah-muh-ri-can*. If I am speaking with a colleague and mispronounce *jew-el-ry* (one word my tongue has yet to conquer) then I am other. If I am speaking with my grandma and I pause, suck my teeth, and say "*¿Cómo se dice?*" she has an hour-long conversation with my mother mourning the death of my Spanish. My tongue becomes a casualty of war. I constantly find myself playing a losing game where I can never be Latina enough for the Latinas ("Where's your accent?" they say) or American enough to be accepted ("You're so exotic!" they exclaim).

> **Multilingualism opens doors, but it also serves as a gatekeeper—displacing me on the outside.**

And so the colonization continues. So the *sh*'s and *ll*'s try to coexist without slaughtering each other. And they will remain at a stalemate until I do not have to choose to use either when I'd rather use both, or until I can stop translating in my head, or until I can stop accommodating others by code-switching. My mind is colonized and it is up to me to resist, day after day, fighting to overcome the tradition of silencing wild, inappropriate, and primitive tongues. As Gloria Anzaldúa said, "Wild tongues cannot be tamed; they can only be cut out." ☼

Camila Arze Torres Goitia (msarze@gmail.com) teaches at Madison High School in Portland, Oregon.

Uchinaaguchi

The language of my heart

BY MOÉ YONAMINE

BRUNO CORDIOLI PHOTO—RYUKYU BINGATA/FLICKR/COMMUNITY COMMONS

"Don't you talk that dirty language," my teacher shouted at me after he punched me in the head. I got up off of the floor, dusted off the navy skirt of my school uniform, and put my chin up. I walked away as he continued to shout at me in Japanese with that unmistakable island accent. As I walked down the 8th-grade hall, I could still hear him. I walked straight out of the school building and out of the gates of our school.

I took a pledge that day: No one will ever stop me from speaking Uchinaaguchi, the Indigenous language of my homeland, Okinawa. I came to the United States as an immigrant when I was a small child. I returned to Okinawa as a 13-year-old with the hope of learning about our culture, language, and history. This was the lesson of my first week of school back on my home island.

In 1972, the Japanese government re-annexed the Ryukyu Islands—my beloved Kingdom of Dragons. Okinawa is the largest of the islands. My mother was 19, just starting college. She had grown up during the "American generation," when the U.S. military occupied all 55 of our islands. As students, my mother and father were taught both Japanese and English, as our Uchinaaguchi diminished—kept out of the schools even back then. So when I got home that day, my head still hurting, my father wasn't surprised by what had happened. He said: "It's a Japanese school. You're supposed to speak Japanese." I felt a flood of tears begin.

But my grandfather sat on the floor across the room and began to teach me the story: In 1945, our country was caught in the crossfire and destroyed. Occupied by Japan, we were the island that the Allies wanted as a stepping-stone to invade Japan. The two military forces staged their fight without regard for Okinawa's sovereignty. As many as 150,000 Okinawan civilians, many of them children, died over the three-month battle. My grandfather watched. He saw his own best friends killed by Japanese and U.S. soldiers during the bombings and battles. Yet he promised himself that war would never bully him into forgetting who he was. He said he needed me to remember: "Don't let anyone make you forget who you are." I told him I had walked away from my teacher and walked out of the school. "We all have to stand up," he said. "When it's wrong, we have to stand up."

Under Japanese government control, the public school system in Okinawa enforces the sole use of the Japanese language in curriculum and teaching. All of the textbooks and content emphasize the centrality of Japanese language and culture. Every teacher I had from early elementary and middle school upheld this in their teaching practices and classroom interactions. Being a good student meant assimilating, following the rule that Uchinanchu-speaking students of Okinawa speak Japanese at all times. My grandparents' generation proudly spoke Uchinaaguchi. Now, 70 years after the Battle of Okinawa, UNESCO has declared Uchinaaguchi a "severely endangered" language.

Today, most speakers of Uchinaaguchi are past the age of 50. My generation can't understand the elders who speak to us at the markets. The *minyō* lyrics and hummable melodies instantly bring me to tears, yet I'm unable to translate the words for my children. I wish they could feel the *kanasasoulmn*—that's a word that doesn't exist in English. It expresses the emotion that you love something so much that it brings you sadness. The aunties and uncles who animate their conversations with tone changes and arms swaying gather at our homes, maintaining our Indigenous oral storytelling ways. But our youth are deaf to this language.

I have friends who say they wish their skin were lighter, that their last name didn't make their island roots so obvious, that they will make sure their children speak without a hint of island accent.

They have forgotten. They have forgotten that we are the result of Indigenous beauty thousands of years old, the specific age unknown because we are a people of oral language, not written language. They have forgotten that our island dancers tell the stories of ocean waves with their hands, our resilience with their stomping, our friendliness in their eyes, and our humor in the way the lips curve to display sarcasm. *Tii*, the firm hand strikes of our Okinawan karate, reveal the powerful resistance developed long ago to fight against Japanese feudal occupation. And they have forgotten the respect given to the oldest woman of the family leading the *ūtōtō* of Indigenous prayer, connecting this world with loved ones in the spirit world. But I will not forget.

I will tell my children and my students about the day when my little sister, Aki, at the age of 6, danced in front of thousands of island people, mostly elderly grandparents, in a festival to honor our culture. Smiles of pride could be seen stretching to the very back row. Their shouts in our native tongue cued to rhythm so perfectly that it sent vibrations through my spine. Mesmerized by the taiko drumming and the red and gold streaming down the dancers' backs, one elder after another wiped their tears. When Aki and her friends finished their dances and walked off stage, one grandmother raised her wrinkled hand, beckoning Aki to come as I stood nearby waiting to greet her. Aki looked at me, unsure, and I gestured for her to go ahead. The grandmother took Aki's hand, rubbed it gently, and thanked her in Uchinaaguchi, saying *nihe-debiru* over and over as she wept. The grandmother's daughter draped a lei of candy around Aki's neck. The grandmother said to Aki, "Don't forget who you are. Don't ever forget," as she walked slowly away.

No Indigenous people should have to fight having their language taken away from the youth, because the youth are our future. *Mirukuyuu* is another word that doesn't exist in Japanese or English. Both languages translate it as "youth." But when we Uchinanchu hear *mirukuyuu,* it means "peaceful generation" at the same time as we visualize calm ocean waves. If our *mirukuyuu* lose their language, they will lose their culture and their identity. Schools must be places where our youth are empowered to learn and nourish heritage languages, to use them and spread them to the next generation. And this must begin today. My language is not dirty. My language is powerful. *Kanasasoulmn*, Uchinaaguchi, the language of my heart. ✿

Moé Yonamine (yonaminemoe@gmail.com) teaches at Roosevelt High School in Portland, Oregon. She is an editor of Rethinking Schools *magazine.*

The Death of My Mexican Name

BY EDITH TREVIÑO

MELANIE CERVANTES

My name was Maria Edith Espinosa Yepez. A beautiful name. Maria Edith is two names in one, and that is how I would write my name on all of my school papers as a young immigrant student in the United States. I would curve my *M*, and my *Y* took a very fancy shape as my handwriting improved throughout the years. I was always proud of the last name Yepez because no one had ever heard of it.

One day, my 5th-grade teacher Mrs. Sauceda called me over to her desk. As I approached, her voice turned preachy: "Ayyy, I already told you, your name is too long! We don't go by two names here and we don't go by two last names. Pick a name. Maria or Edith. And as far as last names, you are Espinosa. We don't use your mother's last name. So what's it going to be?"

I was a shy student and extremely embarrassed that my teacher was confronting me about this issue *again*. Mrs. Sauceda always spoke in a hurried pace. I felt rushed to reply. All of my classmates were looking at me. I hated that moment and wished the *tierra* would swallow me whole. Looking at the floor, I finally whispered, "Edith."

"OK, then in the United States, you are Edith Espinosa. Learn it. And no more Yepez!" Mrs. Sauceda concluded.

When my teacher changed my name, my life was altered in one instant. I remember walking back to my desk feeling ashamed of my beautiful name. There I was with my Mexican braids, my history being buried in the ground. My name was all I had left of my sense of home, *mi identidad perdida*.

> **I hated that moment and wished the *tierra* would swallow me whole.**

After that I never wrote Maria or Yepez again in any school setting. In fact, that same day, my teacher nicknamed me "Edie." To make me feel better, I assume, she took a multicolored map pencil and wrote the name "Edie" on a piece of college-ruled paper and gave it to me. The name had different colors like a rainbow. There was my new identity, written on college-ruled paper, the Mexican girl now "Americanized."

But I sure did not feel Americanized. After that day, I was ashamed of my real name in the United States. Yet when I crossed over to Mexico, I was Maria Edith again, and I felt like I was home.

Even today, I don't like to be called Edith. And I don't like to be called Maria. I want my complete name back. I want to be Maria Edith again, no matter where I am. ☼

Edith Treviño is a former bilingual teacher and now works as a digital learning specialist for Los Fresnos Consolidated Independent School District in South Texas.

Some Languages Are More Equal than Others

BY GEETHA DURAIRAJAN

CHRISTIANE GRAUERT

Monsoon rains were very heavy in those days in Madras, a city in South India now known as Chennai. In the early 1960s, when I was 10 years old, our school was located in a low-lying area and the grounds would get flooded if there was a heavy downpour. Sometimes a holiday would be declared for the afternoon, which meant that children had to be picked up earlier than usual. Telephones had just become popular in homes. There was one in ours, but we children were not very familiar with its use.

One afternoon, when the school had declared a holiday, those of us who had phones at home went to the school office to call someone to pick us up. I was standing in line to make that call, a little apprehensive because it was the first time that I was going to speak on the telephone in a public place. A girl who was ahead of me in the line picked up the phone, dialed a number, and asked in English:

"Is the car at home?"

I heard that query and said to myself, "So this is how you talk on the phone!"

When it was my turn, I dialed the number. It was my father who picked up the phone. Very smartly (I thought), I asked, "Is the car at home?"

In reply, I got an earful and a scolding, in Tamil. "What is that arrogance, have you forgotten Tamizh?"

This continued after I reached home. I did not have the language, guts, or ability to explain why I had done what I had done. I could not convey in words what the culture of my school was like: that if you spoke one word of Tamizh outside the Tamizh classroom, even during lunch break, your friends would look at you as though you were a worm. I kept quiet and took the scolding, not knowing what to say or do except cry and look remorseful.

This confusion would have continued if it had not been for another "holiday" gifted by the rain. How I bless those infernal monsoon rains!

Same place, same line, same call; this time, a few people ahead of me, was Mrs. Thailambal—a Tamilian, like me, who taught Hindi in our school. She picked up the phone and stated loud and clear: "*Naan Thaila peesareen. Romba mazhai peeyarithinnu schoolla leavu vittuttaa. Caar anuppamudiyumaa?*" (I am Thaila speaking. Since it is pouring, school has declared a holiday. Can you send the car?) She spoke in Tamizh, but in her dialect, which was a little different from mine. Flabbergasted and amazed, I stood there asking myself, "*Ippadikkuuda schoolla peesalaama?*" (You mean, we can even talk like this in school?) I was quite relieved to find that a teacher, of all people, actually spoke in her mother tongue in school.

> **Why was I ashamed of my own language? Where and how did English become acceptable and Tamil disallowed?**

That day, I bravely spoke on the phone in Tamizh, but I was careful not to be too loud. I was still scared of peer pressure and being reprimanded. Needless to say, there was no scolding.

Why was I, a Tamilian studying in Chennai, timid and scared to use my own mother tongue in school? What made my friends scoff at me, and feel the same way? Why was I ashamed of my own language? When and how did English become acceptable and Tamil disallowed?

Today, schools are still full of linguistic discrimination and English dominance. In early 2012, an incident made headlines in local newspapers in Hyderabad, India, where I live. A 9-year-old child in a small town in Andhra Pradesh (now in the state known as Telangana) in southern India had been mercilessly beaten by the school principal for having spoken in Telugu—her mother tongue—in school. The headlines and the protests that followed were all about the corporal punishment that was meted out. But, except for the stray blog, no one seemed very concerned about the reason for this beating. There were hardly any complaints or protests about the banning of the student's first language in school.

What are the reasons for this discrimination against our languages? Because of our colonial history, English, the language of the "imperial ruler," had pride of place. As a result, we Indians learned to look down on our own languages and see them as inferior. Regrettably, this mind-set continued even after India gained independence in 1947. The end result is that languages that live comfortably inside our heads, sharing mutual space and borrowing and learning from one another, are forced to quarantine themselves from each other in public spaces.

Linguistic discrimination reflects the economic outlook of English monolingualism. With that jaundiced eye, two languages are a nuisance, three languages are uneconomic, and many languages are absurd. But the norm in India is grassroots multilingualism at the individual and societal level. Speaking many languages is a fact of life. Children grow up using two, three, or even four languages.

We mix and borrow from other languages in our repertoire, not because we are deficient in the use of the other language, but for effect. In fact, it is our multilingualism that has kept our cultural and ethnic distinctiveness alive. To chant *slokas* in Sanskrit, talk to a *paatti* (grandmother) or a *thaattha* (grandfather) in Tamizh, an *atthai* (aunt) in Hindi or Telugu, and to friends in English is a reality for us. We also comfortably bring in one language while speaking the other. Tenglish (Telugu + English), Hinglish (Hindi + English), and Tanglish (Tamil + English) were all born that way. This does not mean that we do not master one language properly. It does not imply deficiency or gaps. We do it for effect, to create a rapport, or because we feel like it.

Having many languages implies having more than one tool at hand. Viewing languages as different tools means that English classrooms need to be imagined differently. There are many contexts where multilingual students are learning English as a second, third, or fourth language. In these classrooms, English must not only recognize and respect other languages, but also learn to share space with and nurture them. Some students may have receptive knowledge of English but respond only in their first language; others may respond in English but slip into another language when the content that is being discussed is cognitively complex. Students can be invited to think and plan in their more enabled language and then respond to the discussion or assignment in the language that is being taught. They can learn to see their languages as different tools to be kept in the same toolbox, to be pulled out and used as needed and desired.

Although I can fulfill my everyday needs in Tamizh, I use English for all educational and official communication. I often wish I might have been allowed to use my native language freely in school so that I might be more comfortable using it for academic purposes now. I regret that I cannot write this in Tamizh, my mother tongue.

What would it be like if every student could hear a Mrs. Thailambal speak their home language at school? We must find ways to design instruction so that students are comfortable using all their different languages in our classrooms, without fear or shame. Students have the right to have their native languages respected and valued in school, whether they are talking to peers, writing an essay, analyzing a poem, or calling home on a rainy day. ☼

Geetha Durairajan (geetha@efluniversity.ac.in) is a professor in the Department of Materials Development, Testing, and Evaluation at the English and Foreign Languages University, Hyderabad, India.

Chicago Stole My Mother's Yesterdays

BY PATRICIA SMITH

Chicago not only stole my mother's tongue, it also stole all her yesterdays. From the moment her battered shoes touched new ground, she wanted Alabama gone, she wanted nothing more than to scrub the Delta from her skin, rid her voice of that ridiculous twang, pretend and then adopt a city sophistication. She thought her *ain't gonnas* and *shoulda dids* and *ain'ts* and *been done hads* signaled ignorance, backwoods, branded her as one of those old-time Negroes. Even years later, after she had married my father, raised a daughter and had to know that her corner was not a promised land but no more than an obscenity of brick, she continued her relentless scrubbing. "I want to talk right before I die," she said, each of her words irreparably Alabama even after she paid an articulate white woman to please fix the mistake of her throat.

And how did my mother's insistence on a blank slate affect me? She slams shut when I ask about the faces in curled-corner Polaroids, when I urge her to tell me what kind of girl she was, when I am curious about her mother, father, grandparents, schooling, baptism, about the steamy hamlet of Aliceville, the stores, schoolhouse, was she fast, was she sullen, did she have the gold tooth then, did she sing? Before her confounding sense of shame, her "Don't know why you wanna know about that nasty ol' down South stuff no way," I was robbed of a history that should have been mine as well as hers.

My husband, on the other hand, has diligently traced his huge raucous family back to the early 1800s. He has remarkably preserved portraits, marriage licenses, death certificates, farm inventory, a rusted scale from his grandfather's store, even a yellowed handkerchief that has been passed gently from hand to hand for more than 100 years. As we pore over the few faded and sun-stained photos my mother reluctantly parted with, I sound like an impossibility, an orphan with a living parent.

> **Right now, if I close my eyes and concentrate, I can't hear my mother's voice.**

That is my mother, I say, pointing to a teenage stranger with an unmistakable gap-toothed grin. But in every picture she is surrounded by ghosts. I say, "I don't know who that is . . . I don't know who that is," because my mother claims not to remember.

In one shot, a ghost turned out to be an aunt I didn't know my mother had.

Right now, if I close my eyes and concentrate, I can't hear my mother's voice. I hear something that sounds like her, but it's a tortured hybrid of the voice she had and the one she wanted so much to have. I've told her story time and time again, and I hear other 50-year-old children tell the same stories of their parents, who spent whole lives trying to reshape their throats, to talk *right* instead of talking *wrong*, ashamed of the sound they made in the world.

How do we lose our own voices? My mother spent her entire life telling me how wrong I was, how my nose was too broad, my hair too crinkled, my skin—Lord, I wish you could be light like cream, like your cousin Demetria. Don't tell anyone your stories, she said, your shameful stories of a mama from Alabama, a daddy from Arkansas, an apartment where roaches dropped from the ceiling into your bed and mice got trapped in the stove, a neighborhood burned down by its own folks right after the riots when that nice Dr. King got killed. Don't tell anyone your stories, stories you should keep to yourself, stories of how your mama and daddy both work in a candy factory, how your auntie lives in those projects, how the apartment we live in's been broken into three times. Don't tell how you live on the West Side, the side everybody tells you to stay away from,

How do we lose our own voices?

and how the school you go to is one of the worst schools in the whole city. And for goodness' sake girl, talk right. If you want to get out of here, ever, you got to talk like white people, and you got to talk about things white people want to hear.

In other words, I was to become a clean, colorless slate, scrubbed of my own history, a slate where people could write my life any way they wanted—any beginning, any middle, any outcome.

How do we lose our own voices, how do we hand our stories over to other people to tell? ☼

Patricia Smith is the author of five volumes of poetry, including Blood Dazzler, *a finalist for the National Book Award, and* Teahouse of the Almighty. *Her most recent book is* Shoulda Been Jimi Savannah.

Note from the editors: "Chicago Stole My Mother's Yesterdays" is an excerpt from "Keepers of the Second Throat" in *Rhythm and Resistance: Teaching Poetry for Social Justice* (Rethinking Schools, 2015). "Keepers of the Second Throat" was originally delivered as the keynote address at the Urban Sites Network Conference of the National Writing Project, Portland, Oregon, April 2010.

Chapter 2

OUR BILINGUAL CLASSROOMS

RICARDO LEVINS MORALES / COURTESY OF HEADWATERS FOUNDATION FOR JUSTICE

Introduction

n *La mariposa*, Francisco Jiménez' autobiographical picture book about his 1st-grade year, young Francisco struggles because he does not speak English and cannot understand his teacher and many of the other students. At one point, the principal gives him a winter jacket from the lost and found because the days are getting colder. Out on the playground, Curtis—the biggest, most popular boy in class—yells at Francisco and knocks him to the ground to try to get the jacket. Later, Francisco learns that the jacket originally belonged to Curtis, who had lost it at the beginning of the year.

When asked why Francisco and Curtis got into a fight, Marijke Conklin's 1st graders could have talked about how both boys wanted the jacket, or how it wasn't fair that Francisco got punished when it was the principal who gave him the jacket in the first place. Instead, Kayla summed it up simply: "The boys don't understand each other. They have to learn each other's languages."

Kayla makes this connection because her teacher tackles social justice issues in her bilingual curriculum, like all of the educators who contributed to this chapter. These bilingual teachers root their teaching in the fertile ground of their students' lives, families, and communities. They recognize that—in order to give all students a chance to develop and use their voices—there must be a place in the classroom for them to share the details of their lives and cultures, their family traditions and values. These teachers don't shy away from discussions of difficult topics like deportations and family separations. And they don't listen when others tell them that their students are "too young" to talk about racism and discrimination.

The educators in this chapter also push their students to think beyond their classroom walls. Students are encouraged not only to learn about themselves, their cultures, and their family histories, but also to make connections to the struggles of those who are from a different culture, time, or place. In doing so, they deepen and broaden their concept of social justice.

There is another thing all of these bilingual teachers have in common: They support and scaffold language in every aspect of their teaching. This may mean annotating complex texts and highlighting academic vocabulary, observing student discussions and developing equitable discussion norms, or building a curriculum from scratch.

Despite their similarities, these educators differ widely. Some work with young children, others in high schools. Their programs range from dual-language classrooms and maintenance bilingual programs to heritage language classes and immersion schools. However the settings may vary, we can all learn from the respect that these educators show for their students, the value they place on language, and the desire they have to bring a focus on social justice into every aspect of their teaching. ☼

Cultivando sus voces

1st graders develop their voices learning about farmworkers

BY MARIJKE CONKLIN

MARIJKE CONKLIN

"**¡V**iva la huelga! ¡Viva la huelga! ¡Viva la causa de verdad!"
This was the energetic, ascending chant of my 24 1st graders, as they joyfully presented the United Farm Workers (UFW) protest song "Niños campesinos" to their families at our end-of-year expo night. We had just finished our study of farmworkers, and these 6-year-olds captured the passion of a protest movement that galvanized millions to march against injustice in California in the 1960s.

My students, part of a Spanish K–8 dual-immersion program at Melrose Leadership Academy, a public school in Oakland, California, learn in Spanish for five hours per day and in English for the remaining hour. They come from diverse racial and economic backgrounds.

Many of our students come to school with a strong sense of fairness and an interest in working together for a goal. By focusing on California farmworkers, I wanted to offer my students a platform in the classroom to share and develop those values. The whole study was in Spanish. Half of my students are Spanish language learners. That meant teaching vocabulary and concepts through songs, stories, trips, and discussions.

"How Do You Grow Fruit?"

In March, I gathered students together on the rug to kick off our study. "We've learned about wheat and fruit in California," I began, making a bridge to our previous studies. "Starting today, we'll learn about the people who grow the fruit we eat. We'll take a trip to a farm where you'll get to find out about some of these farmers."

The room brimmed with excitement, and right away I got a wave of questions: "Where are we going? How far away is it? How will we get there?"

I told them we'd be riding a bus for an hour to Brentwood Berry Farm. "A family owns and works on the farm. Today, you'll be working together in groups to come up with questions to ask them. Remember, questions can help us get more information about what we are learning. How do questions start again?"

Students called out "Who?" "What?" "Where?" "When?" "Why?" "How?" I charted their answers.

"Now let's use those words to start a question for the people who grow our fruit."

Coszcatl raised her hand. "Do they speak English or Spanish?"

Adam's hand went up next. "What is your favorite color?"

"All questions can give us interesting information," I said, wanting to validate Adam but also guide the class toward content-specific questions. "But we're especially looking for information about what it's like to be a farmworker."

Pablo asked, "What kind of fruit do you grow?"

The students then gathered in their groups. Loretta, the notetaker, got her group started by asking, "OK, what are our questions?"

Daniel posed the first one: "What do you like about working on a farm?"

Ethan: "How do you grow fruit?"

Sofia: "What don't you like about working on a farm?"

Loretta: "What different fruit do you grow?"

Daniel: "Where are you from?"

I signaled the end of the group work with my rain stick. Back on the rug, students shared with each other and decided which questions to keep. I charted their questions and asked them to consider which ones would help us get the most information.

"They Couldn't Get Water or Use the Bathroom?"

A few days later, we arrived at Brentwood Berry Farm after a long, humid ride in a rented yellow school bus. The sky was clear and the sun was blazing. The family who owned and worked on the farm greeted us, and we sat down to interview them.

"*Buenos días,*" Señor Roberto began, and the students looked at each other, smiling. Coszcatl's question had been answered, and the conversation continued in Spanish.

Sally started the interview by asking, "*¿Cómo cultivan las fresas?*" (How do you grow strawberries?) I was excited to hear Sally, who is learning Spanish as a second language, use a precise word—*cultivar*—that she had learned recently.

The farmer explained: "We have to cover the strawberries until the plants are big enough to have leaves to cover the fruit. We also have to be careful with the rain. Too much rain damages the plants."

Sofia's hand shot up. "What do you think about growing strawberries?"

"I love strawberries," Señor Roberto replied in a jolly tone. "In my opinion they are the best things in the world."

As the interview continued, it was clear from their eagerly raised hands how proud the students were to demonstrate their Spanish, whether acquired in school or at home.

Miguel's next question helped us explore the farmer's life: "Where are you from?"

"I arrived here in 1974. I'm Zapotec. My mother is Maya but I speak very little Maya. I crossed over the border."

Coszcatl perked up. "My family is Maya, too."

Loretta raised her hand. "What's hard for you on the farm?"

The farmer's tone grew serious. "Before, I worked on other farms for 20 years. We didn't get any rest breaks. There weren't bathrooms; we didn't have shoes. They gave all of us water in a big bucket with one glass. There were 32 of us and only one glass. There wasn't shade, and we had to work in silence."

"You must have been very thirsty," said Loretta.

The other students sat silently, curiously gazing at the farmer. Their silence made me wonder how they were understanding the hardships he described. What past experiences in their lives, if any, would they compare it to? How would they make sense of the harshness that the farmer described?

After a few more minutes of questions, we got up and wove our way through the rows of fruit to spend about 15 minutes picking ripened strawberries. The groans started immediately: "When are we going?" and "I'm so hot." Although still morning, the sun was beating down on the students, making them squint as they wiped sweat from their faces. It became a tiny window into the physical hardships of being a farmworker.

Later that day, back in the cool classroom, we reflected on the experience of being in the field. Loretta continued her earlier line of thinking: "I was so thirsty. I thought I was going to die."

"How long do you think we were out there?" I asked. "Was it shorter or longer than farmworkers have to be out there?"

"Shorter!" shouted a few students.

Loretta made the vital connection: "So they had to be out there all that time? And they couldn't get water or use the bathroom? I couldn't do that." Through hearing the farmworker's story, followed by her own brief experience, she was beginning to understand how inhumane the working conditions of farmworkers could be.

Lado a lado: Cesar and Dolores

After our trip to the farm, I wanted to make connections between the experience of farmwork and the ideas of fairness and working together. Our first text was a non-fiction narrative, *Side by Side: The Story of Dolores Huerta and Cesar Chavez/Lado a lado: La historia de Dolores Huerta y César Chávez.* This colorful book tells the stories of the two activists from childhood to when they met as adults, and how they organized a large-scale grape boycott.

"Who has heard of Cesar Chavez?" I asked, and a few hands went up in the air.

"He helped people," said Sofia.

"He marched with people," suggested Daniel.

I put their ideas on a chart. "You already know two important things about Cesar Chavez. We'll be learning more about him, and about the people he helped and marched with. What questions do you have about Cesar Chavez?

"What farms did he work on?" asked Jamil.

"Does he live in Oakland?" asked Patricia.

I charted their questions, knowing the students would answer them together as we read the book. Then I asked, "What about Dolores Huerta?" Only one hand went up—Coszcatl's.

After our brainstorm, I read the story aloud, checking for understanding by asking students to recall details and make connections. "Wait—" I paused. "Why did Dolores and Cesar say not to buy grapes? Why wouldn't we buy grapes?"

Afterward, students drew portraits of Chavez and Huerta and wrote down words to describe them. This prepared them for small-group conversations about the two leaders. Students gathered in groups of four or five at a table. In book club style, they were free to share ideas and ask each other questions about the text. I provided suggestions for questions or sentence starters if they needed support. One suggestion was to talk about how the two leaders were similar and different.

How would my students make sense of the harsh life that the farmworker described?

"I think Cesar and Dolores are different because one is from Arizona and the other is from New Mexico," Lila said at the outset, placing a talking piece in the middle of the group. Each student received five talking pieces to encourage them to monitor talk time and to participate equally.

"I believe the two are similar because they fought for justice," said Pablo.

"I think the two are similar because both said don't buy grapes because the farm owners use poisonous substances."

"*Estoy de acuerdo con Pablo porque Dolores era una . . . una . . .*" (I agree with Pablo because Dolores was a . . . a . . .) Lila paused as she sought out the right word. In my classroom, pauses are common for the children learning Spanish. The other children waited patiently for Lila to complete her thought. Whether in English or Spanish or both languages, they had all been there before—uncertain of which words to use.

"*Una* girl scout," Lila eventually said and then continued in Spanish, "and she helped people, and Cesar worked on a farm and helped people."

By using an English word as a bridge, Lila was able to get back to Spanish to elaborate her main idea: how the two people were similar. This persistence and creativity allowed her idea to flow and the conversation to continue. Later, she would ask, "*¿Cómo se dice* girl scout *en español?*" (How do you say girl scout in Spanish?) and together we checked the word the author had used.

The group conversations continued, as students remembered important details and the central message: People who are different can become conscious of unfairness in their own ways and then work together to address it.

Making Connections to Fiction

Now that students had an authentic experience on a farm and some nonfiction background, we were ready for some fiction.

I selected *El camino de Amelia,* by Linda Jacobs Altman, and *La mariposa,* by Francisco Jiménez, to deepen the students' connections to the inner lives of a farmworker their age. Both stories take place in California, and each of the protagonists is a 1st grader in a farmworker family. Amelia longs to stay in one place, but her family moves often to follow the harvest. When she discovers a secret path to a tree after school, she buries a box of things that are special to her as a way to feel rooted when she and her family must move on. In *La mariposa,* Francisco is the new boy who speaks only Spanish at a school where everyone else speaks English. He withdraws into an internal world, daydreaming and drawing. Though a misunderstanding gets him into a fight with another student, by the story's end Francisco wins an award for his illustration of a butterfly and begins to feel connected to school.

> **"I think the problem is that Francisco can't speak Spanish at school."**
> **—Victor, a student**

Over the course of two weeks, I read the stories aloud and the students responded to them in three ways: writing, art, and discussion. I asked them to explain in their writing journals what they thought the characters were feeling. To help them, I posted starter frames such as "Amelia feels _____ because _____." and "She would like _____." Manuel wrote: "Amelia feels bad because she did not want to pick apples because her arms and hands hurt. She wants a house with curtains and a shade tree and does not want a shack, but she doesn't have enough money. Amelia and her family work in the fields. At the beginning she felt sad because she didn't have a permanent home."

I asked students to imagine they were going to bury a box of special things like Amelia did. Sophia drew a picture of a box with seeds, her favorite CD, a toy, and a picture of her family and pet.

After we read *La mariposa,* I asked, "What do you think the problem is for Francisco at his new school?"

Daniel's first answer was "Francisco doesn't understand English."

Victor vigorously waved his hand. "I think the problem is that Francisco can't speak Spanish at school."

Coszcatl had a pensive look as she raised her hand. "Also, his teacher doesn't speak Spanish."

I found their discussion fascinating. Victor and Coszcatl had located the problem—and by implication the responsibility to solve it—not with Francisco, but with the structure of the classroom he attended.

"Does anyone have a connection to Francisco?" I prompted.

Adam nodded. "I also sometimes don't know what people are saying, but in Spanish."

Stella chimed in, "I was nervous when I came to school, but then, by the last day, I wasn't lonely anymore. And we have caterpillars in the classroom."

I then posed, "Why do you think Curtis and Francisco got in a fight in the story?"

For Kayla, the solution was simple—and profound: "The boys don't understand each other. They have to learn each other's languages."

Farmworkers + Imagination

Now, I decided, the students were ready to write their own stories. "Use your imaginations to write a story," I said, "about a child who works on a farm. Remember what we learned about the lives of farmworkers on the farm we visited, Cesar, Dolores, Amelia, and Francisco."

At this point, we had also started learning the UFW song "Niños campesinos" that they were to present at the expo. During our morning meeting, I introduced it stanza by stanza, posting an illustrated board of vocabulary and playing a recording. The song relates the daily difficulties of children farmworkers, including waking up early and laboring for long hours with no compensation. It ends with them participating in a strike. This song became another text model for sensory details and central conflicts for their stories.

The first day of our story writing project, I posed what I thought would be the most accessible, concrete question to get them started: "What is the name of your main character? What is he or she like?"

Students looked at me blankly. I was reluctant to provide my own example for two reasons. I wanted them to consider the lives of the people we'd read about, and I believed that by giving students open space to think and wonder, they would come up with their own ideas.

"Um . . . David?" Victor ventured tentatively, glancing at his classmates and then searching my face to get the OK. David was Victor's older brother.

"Fine," I said. The other students took a collective sigh and started raising their hands to share name ideas.

"All of us are going to have time to think about a name and share," I said, wanting to reassure those who didn't have a name yet and encourage those ready to share. "But first, how could we write the name of Victor's character in a sentence?"

Together they responded, "His name is David."

I charted the sentence and asked, "How else could we introduce him?"

Sally raised her hand. "David is a boy?" Her voice was uncertain. Like Victor earlier, Sally wanted to make sure that her idea was OK.

"Good," I said as I wrote her sentence. "What will your character be like? Let's think about how the character looks. What is the character wearing?" We had created posters of Señor Roberto, Cesar, Dolores, Francisco, and Amelia. Now, I pointed to the posters and reminded them to consider what their characters might wear or look like.

"You can write more than one name since we're just listing ideas right now," I said as I gave them paper with space for writing and drawing.

Students went to their desks to use crayons to create their characters. As I circulated, I encouraged them to write down all the ideas that came to their heads—even their own names. "You can draw your character first," I suggested over a low hum of students consulting each other when I realized some students were stuck.

Students spent 20 minutes working. As they were done, they came back to the rug. They shared in pairs and then in a larger group what they had drawn and written.

Each day after, we followed a similar process. I prompted students to brainstorm the details of the story: "What is your character's family life like? What is the setting? What will happen first? What is the most exciting part of your story going to be?" For each question, I elicited ideas from students, then offered sentence frames or starters if they were stuck. It became common for me to say: "Remember what the sun felt like when we went to the farm? What did the farmer say? What did Amelia do? Why did Francisco feel the way he did?" During each writing block, I encouraged students to go back to the work they had done with the model texts for ideas.

I wondered, "Was it essential for students to recreate the exact conditions we'd learned about to develop their ideas of fairness?"

Some of the children's stories successfully integrated a problem of unfairness into a realistic story about farmworkers. For example, Isabel told the story of a girl and her friends who couldn't celebrate a birthday because of their unfair boss:

> It was Coszcatl's birthday but they couldn't celebrate because they had to work in the field. Her friends were so sad. The saddest one was Coszcatl. Isabel went to talk to the boss to ask for a day off. The boss said, "You cannot have a day off because if you want your money, you have to work every day!" Isabel went to tell the bad news to her friends. But the other girls said, "But that is not fair. We must strike!"

Some stories maintained a focus on inequity, and to some degree farmworkers, but the students' imaginations often led them away from the real experiences of farmworkers. For example, Sofia's "Mágica" told of two sisters discovering a haunted house and a witch making a potion. The witch then enslaves the sisters to work for her. Ethan's "Los ratones" is set on a peach farm, where mice have hidden peaches in an electric box. Other stories included Pablo traveling by airplane to a lake filled with piranhas and sharks, Jane living on a farm in Japan and feeling lonely, and a strawberry that was so large the main character couldn't pick it alone.

The students were highly engaged in developing their stories; their ideas and words poured out of them. However, many were not realistic fiction about farmworkers.

Something interesting was happening: Students wanted, perhaps needed, to write their stories imaginatively, but not confined to the life of farmworkers. I wasn't sure what to do. I wondered, "Was it essential for students to recreate the exact conditions we'd learned about for them to develop their ideas of fairness?"

After reflection and a second, closer reading of the stories, I realized that although the stories did not always reflect our study on farmworkers, they did represent situations of systemic unfairness followed by coming together to address it.

For example, in "Mágica," the sisters stage a strike to escape the witch's control. Ethan's story ends with a little boy setting up a system to fairly share the peaches. Loretta's protagonist galvanizes her family to help with the large strawberry, which they cut up and sell at the market to support the household. It turns out Pablo's trip to the piranha-filled lake was to get food to share with his family because the harvest has failed. Finally, Jane's friend solves her loneliness by making a drawing for her—just like Francisco gives a picture to Curtis in *La mariposa* as a gesture of reconciliation after the fight. Each story had a message of agency and working together against an unfair situation. In narrative writing, I reflected, students need structure, but also the freedom to reimagine the themes they are studying.

"Niños campesinos"

We concluded our unit by publishing our stories, complete with each author's biography. The students bound and illustrated them. At the expo, they sang the UFW song, read their stories, and shared their illustrations with their families. All the students' ability to express complex ideas in Spanish had improved, thanks to all that conversation, the literature we read, and learning "Niños campesinos," which contains complicated vocabulary and language constructs.

But as I watched the students sing together that night, fists in the air, faces open and proud, I was struck by another change: Their voices had become powerful and confident. They had cultivated their ideas and developed their stories, and now, singing for their parents and their community, they radiated a sense of self and purpose. ☼

Marijke Conklin taught in Oakland for 10 years and currently works as a curriculum consultant with EL Education. All names have been changed.

Resources

Altman, Linda Jacobs. 1995. *El camino de Amelia.* Lee and Low Books.

Brown, Monica. 2010. *Side by Side: The Story of Dolores Huerta and Cesar Chavez/Lado a lado: La historia de Dolores Huerta y César Chávez.* Rayo.

Jiménez, Francisco. 2000. *La mariposa.* HMH Books for Young Readers.

"¿Qué es deportar?"

Teaching from students' lives

BY SANDRA L. OSORIO

was sitting around a kidney-shaped table with Alejandra, Juliana, and Lucia, 2nd graders who had chosen to read *Del Norte al Sur* (*From North to South*) by René Colato Laínez. I read the book's introduction out loud, which included the word *deportado* (deported). I asked my students: "*¿Qué es deportar? ¿Ustedes saben qué significa?*" (What is deported? Do you know what it means?) Lucia looked straight at me and said, "*Como a mi tío lo deportaron.*" (Like my uncle, they deported him.)

Our class was part of a developmental bilingual program with all native Spanish speakers. I had introduced literature discussions the previous year when I had the same students in 1st grade, but now I was carefully choosing books with themes I thought would resonate with my students' lives, including the complexities of being bilingual and bicultural. In *Del Norte al Sur,* José desperately misses his mother, who has been deported to Tijuana because she doesn't have the right papers to be in the United States. I knew that some of my students were also missing members of their families. One student's father had been deported back to Mexico and he had not seen him in years. Another student's father had separated from her mother and moved to a city more than three hours away. I hoped these two students would connect with José's problems and begin to talk about their feelings. I soon learned that many other students shared similar feelings and experiences.

Although immigration is passionately debated in the media, it is an issue often ignored in schools, even though it's central to the lived experiences of Latina/o children—even those born in the United States. This was something I didn't realize until I created space for students' lives in the curriculum.

I originally decided to teach bilingual students because of the struggles I had faced as a bilingual child myself. I attended a bilingual (Spanish/English) preschool, but when my parents enrolled me in a private, English-only kindergarten, they were told to immediately stop speaking Spanish to me because it would "confuse me." This was surprising to my parents—I had not even entered the classroom yet. My parents made the decision to continue to speak Spanish in our household; they wanted me to be able to communicate with our extended family in Colombia. I am grateful for this decision because it allowed me to grow up bilingual and maintain ties to my bicultural heritage.

At school, I don't remember ever reading a story with a main character who was bilingual or bicultural. Because Latina/o culture and people were invisible in the curriculum, I felt I had to keep my Spanish language knowledge at home and hidden from my teachers and classmates.

I did not want another generation of students to feel like I did. I wanted to help students build and nurture their cultural and linguistic pride. I wanted to make sure that bilingual students were held to the same high expectations as other students. And I wanted them to understand that they did not have to give up their home language to be successful.

So I fulfilled my dream and became a teacher. All of my students were emergent bilinguals who spoke Spanish as their home language and were born in the United States, many in the same town as the school. Of my 20 students, 16 were of Mexican descent, three were Guatemalan, and one child had one Guatemalan parent and one Mexican parent.

Bilingual Isn't Necessarily Bicultural

Our program was supposed to be one of academic enrichment, using both the students' native language and English for academic instruction. The primary goal was development of biliteracy. In 2nd grade, 70 percent of the school day was to be in Spanish and 30 percent in English. But since 3rd graders in the program were not "making benchmark" on state tests, I was pressured to introduce more English in my 2nd-grade classroom.

For the first couple of years, I was a rule follower. I implemented the exact curriculum passed down from the administration without question, including the required language arts curriculum. It was a scripted basal reader program—the exact same one used by the non-bilingual classrooms—only it had been translated into Spanish. Each week we read a story from an anthology and worked on the particular reading skill dictated by the manual.

This was convenient for me as a beginning teacher because it is challenging to find quality texts in Spanish. According to the Cooperative Children's Book Center, of an estimated 5,000 children's books published in the United States in 2014, only 66 were about Latinas/os. At least, I told myself, my students were reading in their native language on a daily basis.

Yet I began noticing that my students were not seeing themselves in the stories we read. The basal reader had more than 20 different stories, but only one that included a Latina/o-looking individual, and nowhere in the story did it talk about any of the complexities of being a bilingual or bicultural child.

My students were learning to read in Spanish that had been translated from English, with texts that were Latina/o culture-free. The basal reader conveyed a clear message: Diverse experiences don't matter. Every student was treated the same, given the same story to read, and taught the same skills. There was no differentiation. There was no mirror. There was no joy.

> **My bicultural students were learning to read in Spanish from texts that were Latina/o culture-free.**

I began to question whether what I was doing was in the best interests of my students. I realized that I had to be the one to advocate for them.

I decided to bring in more literature written by Latina/o authors about Latina/o children. I began to compile a list of books by award-winning authors on such lists as the Pura Belpré Award, the Tomás Rivera Mexican American Children's Book Award, and the Américas Award. I also looked for additional books by authors I already knew: Alma Flor Ada, Gloria Anzaldúa, and René Colato Laínez. In addition to *Del Norte al Sur*, the books I chose included *La superniña del cilantro*, by Juan Felipe Herrera; *Esperando a papá*, by René Colato Laínez; *Prietita y la llorona*, by Gloria Anzaldúa; and *Pepita habla dos veces*, by Ofelia Dumas Lachtman.

The greatest challenge I faced was getting multiple copies of the books I wanted my students to read in small groups. To clear this roadblock, I applied for and received a grant to purchase books. I also borrowed copies from colleagues and scoured the shelves of multiple public libraries around the area. One way or the other, I was able to get four to five copies of each book.

I centered the literature discussion groups around four themes: Family, Cultural Stories, Language, and English. For each theme, I gave students four or five titles to choose from. I started each unit by giving a book talk in which I shared a few passages from each of the book choices. Then I gave students time to browse through the books and fill out a ballot ranking their top choices. Each group of literature discussions was five days long, including two days of preparation and three days of group discussion that I facilitated. Students prepared for discussions by reading the story and marking the book with sticky notes. They used the sticky notes so they would remember what they wanted to say in the discussion group. To help with that process, I gave them a sheet with sentence starters.

When our classroom shifted from basal-based reading instruction to literature-based discussions, I noticed an immediate change in my students. They were more engaged in the stories. Through the personal connections they shared, I learned new things about them and their families. Our literature discussion groups became a place where we came together and shared our joys and the difficulties we were going through. It became a place where we learned that we were not alone, and that the curriculum could be a space for reflecting and holding our own experiences. Students who had been labeled with "low proficiency" in reading on the benchmark test at the beginning of the school year were often the ones talking the most during the discussions. Our conversations helped them feel more comfortable, see themselves in the curriculum, and explore their multiple identities. They were acquiring the tools and space to unpack complex issues in their lives.

Making Space for Students' Fears

In *Del Norte al Sur*, one of the books in our Family theme, we read about José going with his father to Tijuana to visit his mother, who is staying in a women's shelter while she tries to assemble the documents to return to the United States. José, who lives in San Diego, is able to go visit his mother on the weekends and help her with the garden at the shelter; his father pays for a lawyer to process the paperwork. Although the situation is challenging for José and his parents, it is far milder than the reality of most individuals who are deported. Most children are not able to see members of their families who have been deported for extended periods of time. Many who are deported are never able to return to the United States.

Even though the story wasn't a perfect match to my students' own experiences, they started making personal connections to the text. When Lucia shared that her uncle had been deported, I asked her to explain what that meant. "*Es cuando la policía para a una persona y les toman los fingerprintes y después se fija en una máquina si los deportan o no, pero deportar significa que los van a mandar a México.*" (It's when the police stop someone, take their fingerprints, and look on a machine to see if they will deport them or not, but deporting means they send them to Mexico.)

Although I was excited that my students were discussing this topic and I asked questions to further the conversation, I wanted to make sure I didn't push them into an uncomfortable or upsetting space. I paid close attention to everyone, looking for cues about how they were feeling. My ultimate goal in the introduction of these literature discussions was to get my students to develop their critical thinking skills, but first I had to make sure they felt safe enough to share their stories. Before we began the literature discussions, we had developed community norms. Two of our norms were "we feel safe" and "we respect and listen to others." When we created and reviewed the norms, my students and I talked about not making fun of each other, not laughing at individuals who were sharing, and not interrupting.

When Lucia shared her uncle's story, it opened up a group discussion. Alejandra told us about a time her father was stopped by the police while they were driving to a nearby city. She also told us about a time her family was driving and her mother spotted a police officer. Her mother said, "*Bájense porque ahí está la policía y qué tal si nos detiene.*" (Get down because the police are there and what if they stop us.) Alejandra demonstrated how she slouched down in her chair. Her mother told Alejandra and her sisters, "*No escuchen lo que está diciendo el policía.*" (Don't listen to what the police officer says.) Alejandra said, "*Entonces no escuchamos.*" (So we didn't listen.) As Alejandra talked, we just listened. I made sure not to ask questions because I wanted to allow Alejandra the opportunity to share just as much as she wanted to.

Staying silent took lots of practice. I was so accustomed to jumping in and guiding my students in a particular direction. The pressures I felt to cover the curriculum and raise test scores made me want to push my students along at a faster pace. I had to change that mentality. I wanted my students to do most of the talking because I wanted to open up space for their lives. I didn't want them to feel judged. I wanted our discussions to be a place where they felt safe discussing

> "My mom says if they are going to deport her, she won't know who to take."
> —Alejandra, a student

any topic. Too often, I found my students waiting for me to speak so they could agree and repeat what I said. I wanted to move away from the idea that teachers were the only ones with answers. My students had important things to share. I wanted them to realize that their experiences could help us understand each other and the book.

Alejandra finished her story by saying that the police officer followed them home and talked again to her father when they arrived. She explained that she and her younger sister were born in the United States, so they are allowed to stay, but her parents and older sister don't have this advantage. If they are stopped again by the police or ICE (U.S. Immigration and Customs Enforcement), her family might be split apart. I had never seen her so vulnerable.

I turned to Juliana and asked if she had anything she wanted to share, or if she knew anyone who had been deported. She fidgeted with her hands, staring at the table, before looking up and saying "*Sí, mi papá.*" (Yes, my dad.) Lucia nodded. "*Oh, sí, ella ya nos contó la historia.*" (Oh, yes, she already told us the story.)

Taking Time to Listen

At one point in our discussions Lucia announced, "*No me gustan los Estados Unidos para nada.*" (I don't like the United States at all.)

This caught me off guard. "*¿Por qué?*" (Why?)

Lucia said that here in the United Stated she felt enclosed, but in Mexico she was free to go outside every day.

Alejandra added, "*Mi mamá dice que no le gusta aquí.*" (My mom says she doesn't like it here.) She told us about a lady who helped her mother fill out some paperwork and told her mom to call her if she ever got stopped by the police. The lady told Alejandra's mom that the police had gotten harder and that they didn't want people from Mexico. They wanted to deport everyone.

Lucia jumped in. "*Sí, están mostrando mucho de eso en Primer Impacto, que tratan de sacar a los mexicanos.*" (Yes, on *Primer Impacto*, they are showing lots of that, that they are trying to get rid of the Mexicans.) *Primer Impacto* is a popular Spanish-language, daily news program. My students were watching the media alongside their parents. This is where they were getting a lot of their information about the current political context in the United States, including hostility toward immigrants, harsh deportation policies, and family separations.

Although I felt pressure to keep the students reading and to move things along so that they could answer specific questions about the text, I resisted the temptation and asked, "*¿Cómo se sienten ustedes con eso, ustedes siendo mexicanos y americanos?*" (How do you feel about this, being both Mexican and American?)

Alejandra answered: "*Yo me siento mal ser mexicana y americana porque mi mamá dice que si la van a deportar que no sabe a quién llevarse, porque le toca llevarse a Perla pero puede dejar a mi hermana y a mí. Y dice mi mamá que si llegan a pararla, que puede que ya nunca la veamos.*" (I feel bad being Mexican and American because my mom says that if they are going to deport her, she won't know who to take because she'll have to take Perla, but can leave my sister and me. And my mom says if they stop her, we might never see her again.)

Hearing Alejandra talk this way made me extremely sad. Why did a child this young have to deal with issues normally reserved for adults? When I was growing up, I didn't realize my parents were undocumented. They had overstayed the tourist visas they used to enter the United States, but I only learned about it

The children saw both positive and negative aspects to crossing the border illegally.

when I was 10 years old and my parents became U.S. citizens. Both of my parents were given amnesty under the Immigrant Reform and Control Act of 1986 signed by President Reagan. I can't even imagine what it would have been like to worry about my parents possibly not coming home.

My students' narratives shed light on the complex lived experiences they navigate on a daily basis. On the one hand, they want to be in Mexico or Guatemala with their extended families; on the other hand, they know how hard their parents are working to stay here. As a child, I had many of the same contradictory feelings. My entire family, other than my parents and brother, was in Colombia. I felt like I didn't belong here in the United States. At the end of one trip to Colombia, I cried and begged my father to leave me there to continue school. He said no, that there were more opportunities for me in the United States, but I'm not sure he realized the impact of the fact that none of my teachers or classmates acknowledged the difficulty of being in a learning environment that ignored and devalued my language and culture.

Embracing Complexity

While Lucia, Juliana, and Alejandra were reading *Del Norte al Sur*, the other literature groups were reading *La superniña del cilantro* and *Esperando a papá*. (So many students wanted to read *La superniña del cilantro*, we ended up with two groups working with that book.) Both of these books also raised issues of family separation and the border.

Students in the group reading *Esperando a papá* told personal stories about family members crossing the border. One day, I explained that, according to the U.S. government, it's against the law to cross the border without the right documents. I asked them what they thought about that—was it a fair law? Was it OK to break that law? Camila said, "*Mi mamá y mi papá nomás cruzaron, porque querían a lo mejor ver lo que estaba aquí, pero si tú matas a alguien y te vas entonces eso es como no seguir la ley.*" (My mom and dad only crossed because maybe they wanted to see what was over here, but if you kill someone and then you leave, then that's not following the law.) Camila was talking back to the dominant discourse that says it is "wrong" to cross the border without papers and expressing a more complex view of the moral issues involved.

When I brought up the same question to the whole class, the children saw both positive and negative aspects to crossing the border illegally. In terms of positive aspects, they knew and retold stories about family members coming over to find a better life or get a better job. But many of them experienced the constant fear of family members being deported, and they had heard stories about hardships in crossing the border. For example, one child said her female cousin had to cut her hair like a boy for fear of being hurt as she tried to cross over. When Eduardo talked about how hard it was for his dad to climb over the fence, Carlos looked confused. I pulled out my iPad and showed the class pictures of the fence along the U.S.-Mexico border.

Together, we read stories about immigrants to the United States from other parts of the world and the difficulties they faced, including *In English, of Course*, by Josephine Nobisso; *I Hate English!*, by Ellen Levine; and *No English*, by Jacqueline Jules. I wanted my students to understand that they shared experiences with people from other cultures, places, and times. I wanted them to see the injustices and prejudice they faced as part of a bigger pattern of power and marginalization. I tried to help them better understand these aspects by connecting them directly to the stories they shared.

For example, one day Camila told us about a conflict she and Lucia had during recess with English-speaking students from another class. Camila and Lucia were playing on top of the play structure when two girls started pushing them and calling them names. Camila said she told them "That's not right," but they continued. Then, Camila told us, "*Yo le dije a Lucia en español que mejor nos vayamos de ahí y nos fuimos.*" (I told Lucia, in Spanish, that it would be better if we left and we did.) After we gave Lucia and Camila support, we talked about the lack of integration between the bilingual students and non-bilingual students at the school. We discussed what they could do to make friends from other classrooms.

Soon these conversations influenced my planning across content areas. I realized I had to make space for students' stories beyond literature discussions—in writing, math, and social studies. In social studies, for example, students and their parents became experts as we studied their home countries.

My students' stories were different from my own. Lucia's, Juliana's, Alejandra's, Eduardo's, and Camila's stories have similarities, but also differences. I realized the importance of not grouping all Latina/o narratives into one stereotypical box. Giving my students voice and exposing them to a range of multicultural literature gave us the opportunity to dig deeper and see broader vistas. ☼

Sandra L. Osorio was an elementary bilingual teacher for eight years. She is now an assistant professor at Illinois State University. Student names have been changed.

*A Spanish translation of this article is available on the Rethinking Schools website at rethinkingschools.org/articles/que-es-deportar-ensenar-a-partir-de-las-vidas-de-los-estudiantes.

Resources

Anzaldúa, Gloria E. 2001. *Prietita and the Ghost Woman/Prietita y la llorona.* Children's Book Press.

Colato Laínez, René. 2004. *Waiting for papa/Esperando a papá.* Arte Público Press.

Colato Laínez, René. 2010. *From North to South/Del Norte al Sur.* Children's Book Press.

Dumas Lachtman, Ofelia. 1995. *Pepita Talks Twice/Pepita habla dos veces.* Arte Público Press.

Herrera, Juan Felipe. 2003. *Super Cilantro Girl/La superniña del cilantro.* Children's Book Press.

Questioning Assumptions in Dual Immersion

BY NESSA MAHMOUDI

CHRISTIANE GRAUERT

T he room was fairly quiet as my students worked on the first drafts of their stories in Spanish. Some were drawing sketches, others were re-reading what they had written the day before, and a few were showing their pictures to one another. I overheard Tamir retelling a story to Kareem in English about how his father had fallen off his skateboard at the park the previous weekend. Tamir spoke Spanish at home with his mother and English when he went to his father's home. He loved to read in Spanish, and his vocabulary was fairly large. I considered him a Spanish expert in the class.

I listened to them talk, considering whether or not I thought this conversation was off topic and if I should interrupt. Both boys seemed engaged, and the conversation was about their writing, so I kept walking. My mind began to wander to all the questions I had asked myself this year about writer's workshop. When could students sharpen pencils? Should I sharpen them myself in order to maximize writing time?

Should I choose where they sit? How much English should I allow in the first draft of their writing? I had decided this year that students could and should talk to each other during independent writing. After all, when students raised their hands and asked for help, the question was almost always the same, "*¿Maestra, cómo se dice* fireworks *en español?*" or "*¿Maestra, cuál es la palabra para* stroller?" I thought I had finally solved the problem. If the Spanish learners could ask the native Spanish speakers the *¿cómo se dice?* question, I might have more time to focus on individual writing conferences and small-group instruction.

I circled back around to Tamir and Kareem, wondering if they'd now be focused on their writing after their side conversation. I was satisfied to see that both boys had gone back to their writing and drawing. Moments later Kareem looked up mid-sentence and asked Tamir, "Hey, how do you say 'hide-and-seek' in Spanish?" I felt a tinge of excitement, hoping to see my new plan in action. Much to my dismay, Tamir shrugged his shoulders and went back to his work. Kareem turned toward me and raised his hand.

Observations like this force me to rethink the pedagogy and curriculum of my classroom. Six years ago I was hired at one of the two dual-immersion schools in Oakland. My school had just begun its program, and though we were committed to the idea, none of our staff were entirely sure what dual immersion would look like in our context. We all had experience working in maintenance bilingual programs with 100 percent Latina/o students, but none teaching Spanish to such a diverse group of children. Nevertheless, we threw ourselves headfirst into researching two-way immersion and how to best serve our population.

I was excited to receive a rather succinct description of two-way immersion. The Center for Applied Linguistics, an important database and resource for bilingual teachers, writes that two-way immersion is a program with "a balanced numbers of native English speakers and native speakers of the partner language that are integrated for instruction so that both groups of students serve in the role of language model and language learner at different times."

"Great," I thought. "The kids will all have an opportunity to teach and to learn from one another." The idea aligned well with my vision of a progressive, student-centered classroom.

Six years later, our district now has five dual-immersion programs and our staff has been learning about the complexities of this work through national and state conferences, practical experience, and teacher-led inquiry projects. My first mentor told me that the purpose of inquiry should be to reexamine my own assumptions: my assumptions about teaching and learning, about my students, and even about myself.

Over time, I have learned that my assumptions often oversimplify an inherently complex situation. In my first couple years at the school, doing home visits with families and getting to know them in a deeper way, I realized that the simplified definition of two-way immersion did not represent the true linguistic complexity of my classroom. I began to question two of the most commonly held assumptions about two-way-immersion:

- In two-way immersion, there is a dichotomy of language resources. Students bring one of two home languages as their primary resource for language learning.
- Two-way immersion inherently creates opportunities for all students to be language experts.

Who's the Expert?

Each year about half of the students in my class speak English at home, but they may speak different varieties of English, including African American and Chicano English. The other half of the class often has had some exposure to Spanish at home, but families speak multiple types of Spanish, with students from Spain, Mexico, Cuba, Puerto Rico, and so on. There are also students like Juan, who receive a lot of Spanglish input at home. Other students speak a language besides English and Spanish: Akili's father spoke to him exclusively in Swahili, and Soraya's first language was Arabic. In my classroom, there is no simple dichotomy of language resources.

I had the opportunity to teach this group of students over the span of three years, looping from 1st to 3rd grade with them. Over time, I noticed the English learners were becoming more proficient in English and the Spanish learners were becoming more proficient in Spanish. However, I also observed a disheartening trend. When I compared the academic Spanish-language proficiency growth of English-dominant students, particularly those from a higher socioeconomic class, to that of Spanish-dominant, low-income, Latina/o students like Juan, it was clear that the English-dominant students were beginning to surpass them academically, even in Spanish.

At the end of the year, I was left with more questions than answers. What did it mean for a student like Juan to be labeled as a Spanish learner, while he was also labeled by the state of California as an English learner? When did Juan get to be an expert? Did all students *inherently* have an opportunity to be language experts in my classroom? And most importantly, what would it look like and sound like in my classroom if they did?

Learning to Value One Another

With these questions in mind, the next year I wanted to more closely examine what was happening for my students when language "learners" were paired with language "experts." I decided to observe two pairs of students in English class and two pairs in Spanish class. I recorded their conversations with each other and listened to the conversations with my colleagues to make sense of what was happening.

One of my focal students in English class, English learner Tomás, went silent when paired with Xavier, an English-dominant student who was articulate and talkative. Then, I paired him with another English learner, Elena, and now he wouldn't stop talking! The same student with a different partner yielded dramatically different results. Pairing kids with students who were also learning the focal language seemed to be helpful.

There were so many factors to consider. I started following my focal students in all their conversations and looked for trends by gender, race, socioeconomic class, and personality. As I collected more recordings of Tomás in English class, I found that he would talk most in partnerships with females, regardless of language proficiency. I also noticed that all my focal students went silent in English when paired with one English-dominant student, Fred. I began to realize that creating a psychologically and intellectually safe space for language practice in a dual-language classroom is much more complex than simply considering language proficiency. Students need to know one another and value what each person has to share.

As I examined student conversations, I learned the verbal and nonverbal language that students were using to invite or shut down conversations. I decided to share the recordings with my students so that they could identify how to show someone you value what they have to say. This was the list they created and used for discussions:

Science Talk Norms
- Sit up.
- Lean in.
- Nod as they speak.
- Be patient: Wait time.
- Speak slow and clear.
- Clarify: What do you mean when you say_____?
  Can you repeat that in a different way?

One particular day in English class, after we had made tops, investigated spinning them, and read about motion and gravity, I asked students to discuss why they thought the top fell over after it stopped spinning. After reviewing the list of discussion norms they had created, I showed students who their first conversation partner would be for the day.

I partnered Anabel, an upper-middle-class girl whose mother was Black and whose father was Mexican, with Tomás, a first-generation Mexican American boy. Anabel's parents both spoke fluent English and she had access to a lot of experiences outside of school that made her confident about both her English and science knowledge, yet she was also easygoing and humble. Tomás spoke Spanish at home and had attended kindergarten and 1st grade in English. When he arrived in our dual-immersion program, his oral English was developing well, but he struggled with reading and writing in both languages. I thought that perhaps Anabel would help Tomás find his voice in the conversation. I wasn't sure what his background was with the ideas of gravity and motion.

"Why do you think the top fell over after it stopped spinning?" asked Anabel. She asked the question with a clear voice and looked at Tomás, waiting for his response with a smile.

Tomás started to respond tentatively. "I think the top fell over after spinning because it. . . ." There was a long pause. Anabel quietly waited for Tomás to gather his thoughts. Then he continued, "It couldn't spin no more so it fell." Anabel leaned in and nodded as Tomás finished his sentence. "What do you think?" he asked with a smile.

"Well, I think that maybe it fell over because of gravity," she said.

"Can you repeat that in a different way?" Tomás responded quietly, reading off the norm poster.

"Well, like it stopped spinning and then gravity pulled the top and made it fall over on the table."

"Oh, OK."

As the class evaluated conversations like this through fishbowls and recordings, we were able to clarify what respect looked and felt like in academic discussions. And, as students became more respectful and opened up more thinking space for one another, I realized that English learners were generating and practicing more language, an important step toward language proficiency.

I learned that just because a classroom is a two-way-immersion classroom, it doesn't mean that language learning across differences will automatically happen. Such learning is the outcome of a thoughtful and inclusive community taking intentional steps to respect each other.

We Are the Curriculum

I began to realize that my observations needed to shape the curricular content. Having my students identify elements of respectful discourse was only part of the whole picture. I noticed that the quality of conversation also greatly depended on the task at hand. I found myself thinking about how I could create curriculum that reflected and empowered my most marginalized students, those whose home language furthest replicated "school English" or "school Spanish." Such curriculum might give these students a genuine purpose for language and an entrance into the academic space. Working from this assumption, I created a unit of study with the guiding question "Who are we?"

> I realized that the simplified definition of two-way immersion did not represent the true linguistic complexity of my classroom.

I believe that an important part of building my classroom community is openly sharing who I am with students. In my schooling, I never had an opportunity to share with teachers or classmates about my first language inside the classroom. Intentionally, I try to model a space where we all share the important language resources we bring from home. We begin by looking at photos from my family. I talk to them about my family structure and the experience of growing up Iranian in a community that didn't look like me. I talk to them about the many ways in which I have learned about who I am, through talking with elders in my family, learning to cook Iranian dishes, participating in important cultural traditions, and attempting to maintain my literacy skills in Farsi.

During the first days of school I announce, "In the year ahead, we will be asking the question 'Who am I?' over and over to get to know ourselves and each other better. We're going to start by drawing self-portraits."

I begin the self-portrait activity by handing out mirrors. When we are ready to start drawing, I think aloud with the students as I draw my own face, focusing on the details that make me unique, trying to be as accurate as possible. When I was a child, I remember vividly wishing I had the straight blonde hair and bright blue eyes of my white classmates. Likely I drew my self-portraits as a child in their image. In front of my diverse group of students, I try to model the self-love that I have grown to have as an adult.

I happily embrace the opportunity to draw my full black eyebrows, and I make a big deal about finding the perfect olive-tan skin color, bringing a bowl of skin-colored crayons close and matching them up to my skin. As I circulate around the room, I check in on all students, particularly students of color, as they look at their hair, lips, skin, and eyes in the mirror. I encourage students to pull out multiple colors and try them against their skin.

One year, Keisha finished drawing her head, nose, mouth, and eyes and came running over to me. "*Ya terminé*" (I'm finished), Keisha said, showing me her drawing.

"*Noto que no has dibujado tus trenzas*" (I notice you haven't drawn your braids), I told her, seeing that the head of her portrait was bare.

"*No quiero*" (I don't want to), she said, dropping her head.

I thought that maybe she needed help drawing them, since I hadn't modeled that in my own portrait. As I looked in the mirror with her and helped her draw, other students noticed and came over. Soon students were helping each other draw glasses, braces, dreadlocks, and braids. I've learned the importance of not just modeling self-love in my drawing but also being acutely aware of how each child is responding to the activity since each of us has our own insecurities—whether it's our size, the shape of our nose, our skin color, or the texture of our hair.

I now only put out six to eight mirrors, encouraging the children to share and be aware of one another. Allowing the portraits to be collaborative has changed my practice and the tone of the classroom. I now consider this activity as much an introduction to who we are as an introduction to the importance of collaboration and conversation in our classroom. Students who might be silent at the beginning of the year in their non-dominant language find all kinds of things to talk about as they work on their self-portraits with their classmates.

Students need to know one another and value what each person has to share.

As we begin to move into deeper levels of who we are, we think, read, and talk about the school values of kindness and responsibility. In order to learn more about each of my students' families and their values, during the first month of school I meet with them through home visits or beginning-of-the-year conferences. These are not focused on academic results, but rather the families' hopes, dreams, and aspirations for their child. We talk about ways that they hope their child will show kindness and responsibility during the year. The conversations give me an opportunity to understand what kindness and responsibility mean to each particular family, so that I can try to support them in their goals for their own children.

Parents are also invited to the class to share their own values, including how kindness and responsibility are shown in their homes and communities. I especially encourage families who do not have a historically close relationship to schools and schooling to come in. Students generate and practice questions with each other in Spanish and English, and then use them to interview families, asking things like "How did you learn to be kind?" and "What is important to you?" Fathers, mothers, aunts, grandmothers, and grandfathers tell stories of their own childhood and share challenges and lessons they have learned. They share in English, Spanish, or any other language, and students help translate for their classmates. The pride that this activity generates is a powerful anchor for the entire year.

We All Have Family Traditions

Once students have identified, discussed, and written about our collective values as a class, as well as their own and other families' values, we shift the focus to family traditions.

I invite students to bring objects that represent who they are. As students bring in objects—coins from their home countries, recipes, photos of their grandparents, records their parents listened to as children—they share with the whole class and then, once everyone has brought something in, with partners. Through our conversations about the objects, we learn about our connections as well as what makes each of us unique.

We create a collective definition for culture, which each year ends up being rather similar. It generally includes food, holidays, dance, music, and stories. Normally there is a student who mentions the word tradition, and I use this as a transition into the family traditions part of our unit.

"*¿Qué es una tradición?*" (What is a tradition?) I ask.

Students often begin with giving examples from books, movies, and their personal lives.

"*Haciendo tamales*" (Making tamales), Veronica answers.

"My birthday," Joseph responds in English.

"*Muy bien, éstas son tradiciones. Entonces, ¿alguien puede explicar qué significa la palabra tradición?*" (Very good, those are all traditions. So, can someone explain what tradition means?) I add, trying to build on their ideas.

The children begin to come up with a list for our definition.

"*Algo que se hace con la familia*" (Something that you do with your family).

"*Es algo que es especial para ti*" (It's something that is special for you).

A common definition they come up with is "something special that you do with your family, and you do it regularly."

Once we have defined the word together, we look for books in our classroom library that showcase family traditions. Students find books such as *Sam y el dinero de la suerte* (*Sam and the Lucky Money*), by Karen Chinn, and *Un sillón para mi mamá* (*A Chair for My Mother*), by Vera Williams.

Students practice identifying traditions as I read the books aloud. They sort sentences from the stories, recalling details and comparing them to our collective definition of a tradition. Once they begin to understand that traditions do not have to be the celebration of a holiday, I send a note home to families to help demystify the term for them as well. The note is a request for a list of their family traditions, essentially anything they do with their children regularly that has some special significance to them, even if that is visiting the local public library each Tuesday afternoon.

> **We are learners, not experts, working together to discover ourselves and each other.**

Once students brainstorm a list of their own family traditions, they turn the traditions into short stories in Spanish. As students' ideas for their books begin to take shape, they also work together as peer editors. They identify the tradition in each other's stories, along with elements of a high-quality children's story such as descriptions of setting and characters, a fully developed problem, and a solution that teaches the reader a lesson. Through this process, they become excited to share their books in the school library, where many of their younger siblings will be able to read them and see themselves in their stories.

The culmination of this unit is a Family Expo night where the children share their tradition stories with another family in the class. I intentionally pair families that speak different languages, live in different neighborhoods, and haven't had a chance to get to know each other deeply. Earlier in the unit, I help them set up a joint home visit, but this final evening is the main opportunity for them dive deeply into a shared experience. The conversation norms and vocabulary that the students develop during the unit help them connect their families. As they read their books to one another and learn more about the traditions of another family, the children are given agency to be the transformative and connective power our dual-language program envisions for our community.

Investigation vs. Expertise

There are many different ways to create curriculum around the lives of our students—self-portraits, family values, and family traditions are just a beginning. As I think back on my early musings about two-way immersion and the role of language experts, I realize that my view of teaching and learning has shifted dramatically. I have become more and more focused on seeing my students and myself as investigators, rather than experts in a particular field. As Māori scholar Wally Penetito wrote, "Learning one's culture is a lifetime experience." In my classroom I strive to open space where knowledge is shared by every member. We are learners, not experts, working together to discover ourselves and each other.

In a dual-language classroom, issues of language status are critical. Dual-language classrooms can be particularly oppressive if we are not finely attuned to the intricacies of power between our students. We cannot expect dual-language programs to automatically interrupt systemic racism and other inequities. But we can question our assumptions and create a curriculum that helps students find their voices and that promotes equity.

We must ask ourselves who is dominating the rich discussions that are supposedly happening in our classrooms in both English and Spanish. We must be aware of how language politics play out between our students. And, most importantly, we need to be aware of what our own role is in facilitating or interrupting the patterns of inequity that permeate not only the world outside our classrooms but also the world within them. ☼

Nessa Mahmoudi teaches at Melrose Leadership Academy, a public TK–8 dual-immersion school in Oakland, California. Student names have been changed.

Reference

Center for Applied Linguistics. "Two-Way Immersion." Accessed April 17, 2014. cal.org/twi/.

Resources

Books for teaching self-portraits:

Arzu-Brown, Sulma. 2014. *¡Pelo malo no existe!* Afro-Latin Publishing.

Carlson, Nancy. 1997. *¡Me gusto como soy!* Viking Books for Young Readers.

Guerra Burger, Jill. 2016. *Long Hair Don't Care: A poem about boys with long hair.* Jill Guerra Burger.

Liu-Trujillo, Robert. 2016. *Furqan's First Flat Top/El primer corte de mesita de Furqan.* Come Bien Books.

Tarpley, Natasha Anastasia. 2001. *I Love My Hair!* Little, Brown Books for Young Readers.

Books for teaching traditions and values:

Chinn, Karen. 2002. *Sam y el dinero de la suerte (Sam and the Lucky Money).* Demco Media.

Gonzales Bertrand, Diane. 2015. *A Bean and Cheese Taco Birthday/Un cumpleaños de tacos de frijoles con queso.* Arte Público Press.

Haeger, Erich. 2013. *Paquito y Abuelito (Paquito and Grandpa).* Muertoons.

Soto, Gary. 1996. *¡Qué montón de tamales! (Too Many Tamales).* Puffin Books.

Velasquez, Eric. 2006. *Los discos de mi abuela (Grandma's Records).* Lectorum.

Williams, Vera. 1994. *Un sillón para mi mamá (A Chair for My Mother).* Reading Rainbow Books.

"Kill the Indian, Kill the Deaf"

Teaching about the residential schools

BY WENDY HARRIS

s students in my middle school social studies classes examined American Indian and Deaf boarding schools at the turn of the 20th century and began to imagine themselves in similar situations, the reactions were visceral.

"I would refuse to go to school!"

"I think students and families would destroy the schools."

At Metro Deaf School—a bilingual school in St. Paul, Minnesota, for Deaf students from ages 2½ to 21—our primary language of instruction is American Sign Language (ASL). Alongside ASL, we teach written English as a second language. In addition, some students work on oral English in speech therapy.

Many Deaf students come from hearing families that don't know or aren't fluent in ASL. This means some students at our school don't have access to the language their family uses at home (English, Hmong, Spanish, and Somali, among others), so their primary exposure to information and language happens at school in ASL and written English.

Developing Deaf Identity

As a white, hearing person who learned ASL as an additional language, my experiences with ASL and Deaf culture are different from those of my students. Knowing how important it is for Deaf students to connect to the broader Deaf world, I work to explicitly develop Deaf cultural consciousness. This ranges from knowing one's right to have access to information, to feeling part of a larger Deaf culture. In Deaf studies lessons, ASL lessons, and my social studies lessons, students are immersed in the process of developing Deafhood—defining their place and identity as Deaf people within the intersections of multiple cultures, identities, and languages in their homes, communities, and school. I want my students to understand how these worlds fit together, and how they fit within these worlds.

As part of this process, I work throughout the year to honor the missing voices and history of Deaf, hard of hearing, and Deaf-Blind people. I decided it was important to teach the English-only and oralist policies at the turn of the 20th century and the impact this had on Deaf people.

In accordance with Minnesota middle school standards, I was already teaching local Native American history, focusing on the Anishinaabe and Dakota peoples. Because of the similarities in the way education was used to oppress Native Americans

First oral education class at the Minnesota School for the Deaf. Students are fingerspelling English rather than speaking American Sign Language. Faribault, Minnesota, 1906.

and Deaf people in the late 19th and early 20th century, I developed curriculum that helps students compare and contrast the goals and impact of Deaf and Native American schooling in this period.

Historical Photos as Text

I decided to start the unit with photographs. To do this, I selected images from the American Indian Boarding Schools collection at the Library of Congress website (see Resources). I chose photographs from the "Native Ways" and "Boarding School Ways" sections in the three categories suggested by the Library of Congress: Appearance, Homes, and Daily Life. Then I prepared a two-column graphic organizer.

"Remember how we talked about the experiences of different groups in Minnesota when white people started to come in large numbers in the 1860s?" I reminded my students. "Today we will be talking about life for Native Americans at the end of the 1800s." I explained that we would be looking at education, an issue that affected many different Native American cultures, not just those in Minnesota. Then I distributed copies of the graphic organizer and the photographs.

I wanted students to pick a "Native Ways" image and a "Boarding School Ways" image to analyze for each category. We did the Appearance category together. I chose a pair of portraits of three Lakota boys from the Carlisle Indian Industrial School in Pennsylvania. In the "Native Ways" photo, two of the boys sit on the floor, one stands; the boys are wearing leggings, moccasins, and shirts; two have feathers in their hair, which hangs past their shoulders. In the "Boarding School Ways" photo, two of the boys are seated and one still stands. They are wearing military-style school uniforms: European-style pants, jackets with metal buttons, European-style shoes, and short haircuts.

"What differences do you notice between 'Native Ways' and 'Boarding School Ways'?" I asked.

One student said, "At the school, the clothing is fancy."

"What do you mean by fancy?"

"You know, normal."

Another student added, "The Indian clothes are dirty."

I paused, wondering how to discuss cultural relativism. I also thought of the comparison to Deaf students, who see other people refer to hearing people as "normal," implying that they are not. Not wanting to squash students' reactions but also not wanting to let the issue go, I asked, "If your family was sending you away to school, do you think they would send you in your best clothes, or in dirty, old clothes?"

"Best clothing," someone said. Others nodded in agreement.

"Do you think these students' families sent them to school wearing dirty, old clothing, or their best clothing?" The students agreed it was likely these students had been wearing their best clothing when they got to the schools.

As we continued to discuss the radical change in students' appearance, a student referred to "the picture with the girls" (Native Ways) and then the one with "the boys" (Boarding School Ways). I pointed out that it was the same three youth in both photos. The students didn't believe me until I showed them the two photos again, named the students, and pointed out that two had swapped positions, but that they were the same students.

Then students completed the graphic organizer, picking images to compare in the Homes and Daily Life categories. They wrote paragraphs summarizing what they had noticed. One student's work repeatedly referred to "Indians" and "people." I asked her what she meant by "people," and it became apparent she thought the boarding school images were white people and the other photos were Native Americans. I clarified that they were all Native Americans, and pushed her to think about what made her decide the boarding school students were white. "Perhaps," I suggested, "those factors are part of white culture. What do you think? How could you describe that?"

Home to Medicine Mountain

Next, we read the picture book *Home to Medicine Mountain*, by Chiori Santiago, based on illustrator Judith Lowry's family history. The book describes experiences at the American Indian boarding school in Riverside, California, in the 1930s.

First, I gave students some context: "We've looked at photographs of Native Americans in schools and at home. This book is another look at Indian boarding school life. It is the true story of two brothers and their experience in the 1930s. While I read, I want you to think of ways that things in this book are similar or different from the photos you analyzed."

At our school, reading aloud an English text requires translation into ASL. There are a variety of ways I do this. Depending on students' levels of fluency in written English, I might have them read passages independently and then discuss them in ASL (translanguaging). Or I might have students work through the text together, producing an ASL equivalent of each sentence (translating). Or, as I did with this particular book, I might translate the text into ASL as I read aloud. I wanted students to focus on the content.

I read the preface and showed the students the map to help them place the story in time and space. As I read the story in ASL, I paused every few pages, asking the class if they had noticed anything similar or different from the photos.

"They aren't wearing shoes."

"They have uniforms."

"School is very different from home."

As our third glimpse into American Indian boarding schools, I turned to three excerpts from "The School Days of an Indian Girl," by Zitkala-Sa. Zitkala-Sa (also known as Gertrude Bonnin) was a Lakota woman from South Dakota who went to Carlisle Industrial Indian School and seemed to assimilate, even becoming a teacher there for a while. But later she changed her perspective and wrote a short memoir about her experiences. She was well-known as a writer and political activist in the early 20th century. This piece was originally published in *Atlantic Monthly*.

I created a glossary for each selection and also had the students watch an ASL translation, with copies of the English text available for reference afterward. The first excerpt described the moment Zitkala-Sa learned her hair would be cut, the second the actual experience of the haircut, showing her resistance, and the third talked about her struggle to fit in at school and at home.

> **"I felt the cold blades of the scissors against my neck, and heard them gnaw off one of my thick braids. Then I lost my spirit." —Zitkala-Sa**

To help them process Zitkala-Sa's story, I asked students to pick an excerpt and draw a picture showing all the details in the scene. This is an approach I often adopt to see if they understand a complex concept, one that would be difficult for them to explain in written English. One student, who herself has long hair, chose to illustrate Zitkala-Sa's description of her haircut experience:

> I cried aloud, shaking my head all the while, until I felt the cold blades of the scissors against my neck, and heard them gnaw off one of my thick braids. Then I lost my spirit. Since the day I was taken from my mother I had suffered extreme indignities. People

had stared at me. I had been tossed about in the air like a wooden puppet. And now my long hair was shingled like a coward's! In my anguish I moaned for my mother, but no one came to comfort me. Not a soul reasoned quietly with me, as my own mother used to do; for now I was only one of many little animals driven by a herder.

The student chose to present the scene in two images—the first with Zitkala-Sa sitting, facing the viewer with long braids over her shoulders, and the second with tears flowing and one braid cut chin-length.

Getting Rid of the "Indian"

Next, to help students generalize what they had learned about the boarding school experience so far, I assigned them to groups of two or three to put their information into a three-part Venn diagram made on chart paper. Most of the students were experienced with two-part Venn diagrams, so I introduced a three-part diagram using fruit—apple, orange, banana—and asked the students to help me start to fill it out. Then I encouraged them to refer back to their graphic organizers for the photographs, *Home to Medicine Mountain*, and "School Days of an Indian Girl" while working.

In one group, gender identification came up again. It happens that I identify as a woman and have very short hair; Roger, the paraprofessional in my room, identifies as a man and has long hair. I asked, "Short hair means boy?"

"Yes," the student confirmed.

"So I'm a boy? And Roger is a girl because he has long hair?" The student paused and then finally suggested, "Maybe I could use 'long hair' and 'short hair' to describe them instead."

I wanted to encourage students to think about the motivation behind establishing Indian schools. Earlier in the year, we had studied Anishinaabe and Dakota experiences in Minnesota with missionaries and settlers, their loss of land due to treaties, and the U.S.-Dakota War. I hoped my students would see the connection between destroying Native American culture—by forcing children to live apart from their families and communities, adopt U.S. clothing and hairstyles, and speak only English—and their loss of land and human rights. In other words, to see the push for assimilation as part of a genocidal strategy.

"What details did you note in the overlapping parts of the diagram? I'll record them here in a class list."

After the groups had taken turns sharing their notes, I asked: "Are any of these similar? Could they be grouped as a category? Let's work as a class to group what you think is similar."

Once they had reduced the list to a few general themes, I asked, "OK, now that you have themes, can you think of a hypothesis? Why do you think the schools were established? What did the founders want to happen?"

"The schools want Indians to be American," they wrote.

"What is 'American'?" I asked. "Were the Indian schools Mexican American? Hmong American? Did they value Spanish or Hmong as languages at the school? Did they value the home languages of the Native American students who attended?"

"The people who made the school wanted the students to have white culture," they decided.

In another class, I worried that analyzing data to find a motive would be too difficult, so I provided them with a sentence starter: *Indian schools want American Indian students to _____.*

After a long wait, one student suggested, "The higher-up people, the white people, wanted them to cut their hair." I added the words "white people" above "cut hair" to our list, and asked students which other items would be "white." They chose "English-only," "uniforms," and "don't like school food." Then we went back to the sentence starter and the class created a hypothesis: "Indian schools want American Indian students to become like white people."

To test their hypotheses, I had students watch an ASL translation of two quotes from Captain Richard Pratt, who founded Carlisle. I projected the quotes in English on the board:

> All the Indian there is in the race should be dead. Kill the Indian in him, and save the man.

> Carlisle fills young Indians with the spirit of loyalty to the stars and stripes, and then moves them out into our communities to show by their conduct and ability that the Indian is no different from the white or the colored, that he has the inalienable right to liberty and opportunity that the white and the Negro have. Carlisle does not dictate to him what line of life he should fill, so it is an honest one. It says to him that, if he gets his living by the sweat of his brow, and demonstrates to the nation that he is a man, he does more good for his race than hundreds of his fellows who cling to their tribal communistic surroundings.

Students worked in groups to make sense of the formal language and determine Pratt's purpose. Then I called the class back together. "Why did Pratt set up the school?"

"He wanted them to be like white people."

"Yeah, he wanted them separate from their group."

"He wanted to take out everything Indian from them."

"A Deaf Variety of the Human Race"

Next, we moved to a discussion of Deaf schools of the same period. Carlisle Indian Industrial School was established in 1879. The following year, the second International Congress on the Education of the Deaf was held in Milan, Italy. The participants were nearly all hearing and voted overwhelmingly to endorse only oral (not signing) education for Deaf students. Schools in the United States—which had been producing well-educated and successful graduates for years and were largely run by Deaf people—resisted this move until the early 1900s, when Deaf leaders were gradually replaced by hearing people, largely with oralist perspectives.

Once again, I used photographic images, this time scanned from a history of the Minnesota School for the Deaf and from *Minnesota Reflections*, the Minnesota Digital Library online database. One of the photos we looked at, in a style popular in that era, showed Deaf students signing a message, each person with a different sign. Another photo showed a class of students spelling out "First Oral Class 1906." I pointed out the difference between using ASL and fingerspelling English, which some schools used at the time.

As I projected each image, I asked: "What are they doing? What clothes are they wearing? Where was the picture taken?"

As the students responded, I asked: "Is that similar or different to what we saw in pictures from American Indian boarding schools? How?"

Students noted similarities: "English-only," "military drills." And differences: "sewing class," "farms," "Deaf students didn't have uniforms." I had hoped that students would see similarities of preparation for manual labor and servant-type jobs as well. They didn't seem to be able to generalize about the career preparation. I realized that this is something I need to draw out from the beginning the next time I teach this unit.

As our final historical comparison, students watched an ASL translation of quotes from Alexander Graham Bell's *Memoir upon the Formation of a Deaf Variety of the Human Race*. Bell had a Deaf mother and Deaf wife, and was involved in Deaf education. He was also a staunch oralist and an early supporter of the eugenics movement, who wanted to end inherited Deafness by stopping Deaf people from becoming couples and having children together. I chose four quotes, including these:

> Those who believe as I do, that the production of a defective race of human beings would be a great calamity to the world, will examine carefully the causes that lead to the intermarriages of the deaf with the object of applying a remedy.

> The immediate cause is undoubtedly the preference that adult deaf-mutes exhibit for the companionship of deaf-mutes rather than that of hearing persons. Among the causes that contribute to bring about this preference we may note: 1. segregation for the purposes of education, and 2. the use, as a means of communication, of a language which is different from that of the people. These, then, are two of the points that should be avoided in the adoption of preventive measures. Nearly all the other causes I have investigated are ultimately referable to these.

I asked students to write a one-sentence summary for each of the quotes and we discussed them. Then I asked: "How were Richard Pratt's and Alexander Graham

Bell's motivations similar or different?"

"They wanted them to go away."

"Yeah, they had to speak English."

I tried to push the issue: "What about where Pratt and Bell wanted the Native American people and the Deaf people to live?"

There was a pause. Finally one student said, "With hearing people."

"With white people," another student added.

I wanted to guide students into seeing the removal of culture and identity, often by violence, as a connection between the experiences of Native people and Deaf people in this era. I wasn't sure if my students understood the connections to the depth I'd hoped, but clearly they saw similarities. And they were angry about what they were learning. "I would refuse to go to school!" and "I think students and families would destroy the schools" were just two examples of that anger. I wanted to make sure they knew that there was resistance by Native Americans and Deaf communities and individuals then, and that resistance continues to the present.

Resistance by Deaf and Native American Communities

I asked the students to brainstorm possible acts of resistance that students, families, or communities could take. It took a while for students to offer suggestions.

In one class, someone suggested that students could "refuse to take oral classes," which opened the floodgates to ideas of how to resist. With my prompting to refer back to the stories we had read and things we had learned, students came up with additional ways to resist: run away, yell/cry, refuse to speak English, use sign language, tell the teacher they want another language, refuse to eat or sleep, destroy the school.

Then I shared photos and information about ways students, families, and communities have resisted assimilationist policies. I included the formation of Deaf organizations, including the National Association of the Deaf (established in 1880), Deaf sports teams, and clubs. I told the stories of Hopi leaders who were sentenced to a year at Alcatraz for refusing to send their children to government schools, students rioting at Haskell Indian School, and kindergarteners at Fort Mohave using a log to break down a locked door to let out their classmates.

To connect our historical study to the present, students analyzed the National Association of the Deaf position paper on schools for the deaf. The first paragraph states: "Deaf schools are critical to the education of deaf and hard of hearing children, and every effort must be made to preserve them." We looked at recent statistics on educational placements for Deaf students in the United States (mainstream, partially mainstream, separate schools) and discussed the implications.

We also read a 2012 article about a 12-year-old Menominee student who was reprimanded for speaking Menominee in the classroom. The article focuses on the family's perspective. I asked students to work in pairs to think of two reasons why the family is mad and two reasons why the teacher is mad, deciding which side they think is right and why.

"I think the student is right because you have to respect language."

"It's her culture."

Thinking Ahead

The next time I teach this, I would like to incorporate more analysis of how language policies and course programming affect students' self-identities and ability to learn successfully. What did it mean to generations of students who were punished for speaking their Indigenous languages? How does what courses schools decide to offer affect what students learn? What does it show about expectations for students?

I was hoping the students would be able to make deeper connections between the material we were learning and their own lives; I struggled to get them to express a personal connection. I saw righteous indignation, so I know I struck a chord, but in discussion, they replied more simplistically than I would have liked.

Pressured by the school year timeline, I jumped from the turn of the 20th century to current issues, without making the connection of organizations like the American Indian Movement (started in Minneapolis) and the 1988 Deaf President Now movement at Gallaudet College. I also missed the opportunity to discuss the shift in language policies for Deaf students: the increasing acceptance of the use of signing in the 1970s, and the development of bilingual programs in the early 1990s—including Metro Deaf School—that were designed to value ASL and English equally.

Since I work with these students over multiple years, I can take advantage of the opportunity to weave discussions of linguicism, racism, and audism into other lessons. Developing Deafhood is not something done in the course of one unit; it needs to be at the core of everything I teach. ✿

Wendy Harris teaches at Metro Deaf School in St. Paul, Minnesota. Student and staff names have been changed.

Resources

Bell, Alexander Graham. 1884. *Memoir upon the Formation of a Deaf Variety of the Human Race.* National Academy of Sciences. archive.org/details/cihm_08831.

Indian Country Today Media Network. March 2, 2012. "Apologies Not Enough for Native Language Debacle." indiancountrytodaymedianetwork.com/2012/03/02/apologies-not-enough-native-language-debacle-101084.

Library of Congress. "Indian Boarding Schools." loc.gov/teachers/classroommaterials/lessons/indianschools/appear.html.

National Association of the Deaf. "Position on Deaf Schools." nad.org/issues/education/k-12/position-statement-schools-deaf.

Santiago, Chiori. 2002. *Home to Medicine Mountain.* Children's Book Press.

Zitkala-Sa. 1921. "School Days of an Indian Girl." *American Indian Stories.* Hayworth Publishing House.

Carrying Our Sacred Language

Teaching in a Mi'kmaq immersion program

BY STARR PAUL AND SHERISE PAUL-GOULD,
WITH ANNE MURRAY-ORR AND JOANNE TOMPKINS

"FRIENDS" BY MARCUS GOSSE

Mi'kma'ji'j
by Mi'kmaw linguist Bernie Francis

Mi'kma'ji'jk, ninen na Mi'kma'ji'jk
Ninen na mi'kma'ji'jk
Kekina'masultiek
Ta'n teli-l'nuwu'ltiek
Ula wiki'tiek
Mi'kma'ji'jk, ninen na Mi'kma'ji'jk
Attikne'taiek
L'nui'sultinen

Mi'kmaq children, we are the Mi'kmaq children
We are the Mi'kmaw children
Who are learning
About our Nativeness
Here where we live
Mi'kmaq children, we are the Mi'kmaq children
We are working hard
To speak our language

My Mi'kmaq immersion students first performed this song, along with *ko-jua* (an ancient Mi'kmaq dance), for the community at our kindergarten graduation during the first year of our immersion program. This was a special event for the first graduates of the program and their families. This powerful song is about Mi'kmaq children taking pride in who they are and in their language. A later verse urges adults to guide and teach the children because they are future Mi'kmaq leaders.

I (Starr) grew up speaking my mother tongue, Mi'kmaw, an Eastern Algonquian language. I live in a rural Mi'kmaq community in Eastern Canada, the traditional territories of the Mi'kmaw. With more than 3,800 people, it is the largest of the 30 Mi'kmaq communities spread over Nova Scotia, New Brunswick, Prince Edward Island, Quebec, Newfoundland, and Labrador. Our village faces unemployment and poverty, but there are also more economic opportunities than in many Mi'kmaq communities. There is a thriving community-owned fishery, tourism, a large supermarket, a First Nations health center, and a K–12 community-operated school, where I teach.

Despite several hundred years of European colonization and the devastating effects of the residential school system, there is still a strong Mi'kmaw language base. Most Elders in the community speak the language fluently, and a significant percentage of younger adults do as well. However, this percentage is decreasing at an alarming rate and the need for language revitalization is urgent. More and more parents of children in our school do not speak the language, even though they may still understand it. Increasingly, children come to school not speaking or understanding Mi'kmaw.

I was a fluent speaker as a child, surrounded by a family that constantly reminded everyone to speak Mi'kmaw, especially children. If I secretly spoke English and my aunt or uncle overheard me, she or he would say, "*L'nui'si!*" (Speak Mi'kmaw!) I heard that phrase a lot growing up; I believe this was a key factor that kept me speaking Mi'kmaw.

My best friend Sherise spoke English. I believed that she was smarter than me because she spoke English very well and English seemed to be more valued by the larger community. I attempted to speak English with her, yet what came out of my mouth was broken English. Gradually, I realized that I was smart in the Mi'kmaw language because I could converse with fluent speakers, especially Elders, the keepers of knowledge. I also realized that Sherise was trying to learn to speak the Mi'kmaw language fluently. Sherise was envious of my fluency in Mi'kmaw. She and I both began to see the value of each language.

Who would have ever thought that today we would be struggling as a nation to sustain our Mi'kmaw language? When I was young in the 1980s, sitting in a classroom, the Mi'kmaw language surrounded me. The majority of my peers spoke it. Back then, people in my community took it for granted that our language was secure and thought it was more important to learn English in order to succeed.

Now we are beginning to realize how important it is to maintain our language. The number of fluent speakers is dwindling, and few among even the fluent Mi'kmaw speakers can write the language. Luckily there were some educators and linguists who preserved the Mi'kmaw language in written form, including my own mother, Elizabeth Paul.

Starting a Mi'kmaq Immersion Program

After teaching for several years at the high school in my community, in 2000 I was excited to learn about a new Mi'kmaq immersion program being started the next year. This program arose because of concerns regarding the increasing number of children entering school speaking only English. I was hired to teach all kindergarten subjects using Mi'kmaw as the language of instruction. I split the 40 immersion students with Ida Denny, the other immersion teacher. Due to a lack of Mi'kmaw-speaking specialists in physical education, art, and music at that time, the immersion teachers taught these subjects as well. I went on to teach most of my students for several years, from kindergarten to 2nd grade.

Students' families, from both working-class and professional backgrounds, were excited about our program. Most were Mi'kmaw speakers, but their children did not necessarily speak Mi'kmaw. Parents were very supportive, and the immersion enrollment was higher than expected.

Developing Curriculum and Materials

With parent permission, we devoted half of every Friday to planning our curriculum and creating classroom materials. Our school is community operated and federally funded as a result of our treaty rights with the government of Canada. Because we weren't part of the provincial public school system, we had the flexibility to use time for curriculum development. The existing English program at the school was modeled after the public school program for the province of Nova Scotia, so when our Mi'kmaq program was established, it borrowed from the provincial program.

Mi'kmaq materials were scarce. It was daunting to see all the colorful posters and books in the English instruction classrooms. We did not want our students to feel like our program was inferior, so Ida and I worked hard to create posters, alphabets, and children's books. Making books in the Mi'kmaw language was especially challenging. We had to type, print off, cut, and paste the Mi'kmaw text over the English text.

We were not entirely alone in curriculum building. One great resource was the Centre of Excellence, an organization run by a group of former teachers who worked to make Mi'kmaq curriculum with the help of teachers, Elders, and other community resource people. They were expert linguists. We took ideas to them and they helped us develop books. They also helped us with vocabulary by translating words that we wanted to use in our lessons. I developed flash cards, songs, poems, and chants. For health, I labeled parts of the body and the Centre of Excellence translated a book that described body parts. Ida created several songs based on nursery rhyme melodies. She also made thematic songs and poems for different holidays and other events. As we sang nursery rhymes and chants in Mi'kmaw, we used hand gestures to help the students understand.

The need for language revitalization is urgent.

Culture and Traditions Embedded in the Curriculum

The initial purpose of the Mi'kmaq immersion program was to keep the language alive. Once the program was under way, we realized that the purpose extended to embedding our culture and traditions in the curriculum. The language itself changed the way we taught. For example, the concept of animate and inanimate, an important organizing principle of Mi'kmaw language, is very different from English. For instance, when you see something, in English you say "I see a chair" or "I see a bird." When you say it in Mi'kmaw, you say "*Nemitu kutputi*" (inanimate) for "I see a chair." You say "*Nemi'k jipji'j*" (animate) for "I see a bird." *Nemi'k* and *Nemitu* both mean "I see," but you know the animate from the inanimate by saying the sentence and what the object is. This feature of Mi'kmaw language reflects a Mi'kmaq worldview of relationality with the natural world. Natural objects, such as animals and mountains, are considered animate or living, but human-made objects, like a chair or a computer, are not.

Music and drumming also deepened students' sense of being Mi'kmaw. Ida drummed and sang a song about a little bumblebee in Mi'kmaw that included the students' names in the lyrics: *Amu amu alaqsink, tlmi ta'n teluisin?* (Bee, bee flying around, tell me what is your name?) Ida would point at a child to solicit that child's name, and the children would sing along; they were often still singing long after she had ended the song. Other times the drum would signal a transition and help the children move to another activity, or it would be used to produce a calming effect in the classroom. Frequently when children were engaged in learning activities, we played powwow or drumming music softly in the background.

"*Mukk pepsite'tekew*," or respect your Elders, became part of the day-to-day classroom environment. Respect and other Mi'kmaq values were embedded in everything we did. When I was growing up and studying in English-only classrooms, if I tripped or fell off my chair, everybody would laugh at me. But in my Mi'kmaw classroom, kids showed concern. They asked, "*Mu kesito'kewn?*" (You're not hurt?) You didn't hear anyone laughing. If somebody made fun of somebody else, I just stopped and said, "*Tal-lukwen?*" (What are you doing?). And the students thought, "*Tal-lukuti'k?*" (What are we doing?)

Addressing Parental Doubts

I can see that the students in our Mi'kmaq immersion program are thriving academically and developing strong Mi'kmaw identities. Unfortunately, for a variety of reasons—many related to the effects of colonization and the legacy of the residential schools—there are still people who are not convinced that immersion is a good path. This shows how strong the legacy of colonial oppression is in our community. Generations of our people were taken from their families and placed in residential schools where they were punished for speaking their language and were treated with cruelty and contempt. The Mi'kmaq immersion program is one important way the community addresses this lasting legacy of suffering and assimilation.

Early in the second year, one of my students was experiencing some difficulty. I had a conference with her mother. She was upset, and told me that her older children already knew how to read (in English) when they were the same age as her daughter now. Often the children in Mi'kmaq immersion do not learn to read in English as early because of their immersion in Mi'kmaw. Due to colonization, many Aboriginal people have internalized the message that English is best and Aboriginal knowledge, ways of being, or language are inferior. This can make it difficult for parents to accept the different path that literacy development takes in our immersion program.

There were other reasons parents removed their children from the program. Some felt it was too difficult for their children and for themselves as well. Some students continued to speak English no matter how hard we tried to have the child speak Mi'kmaw. Parents sometimes said that their child did not understand the Mi'kmaw-speaking teacher.

We worked hard to help parents understand the benefits and process of learning to read first in Mi'kmaw and later in English. We had evening language classes for parents and invited them to come into the classroom and to let us know if they had questions or concerns. Some parents did not know how to help their child with homework because they could not read or write Mi'kmaw. So I started writing the translation for what was written in Mi'kmaw at the bottom of the page. I also put literal phonics in the English language on the side of a word so the parent would know how to pronounce the word.

One year I invited a group of former Mi'kmaw immersion students who were in higher grades to write essays about the immersion program. Then students recorded their essays at our local radio station. These students expressed how much they enjoyed the Mi'kmaq immersion program and how they would recommend the program to others. They also talked about the importance of speaking the Mi'kmaw language.

Continuing to Build the Program

Several partnerships have helped our immersion program to grow strong over the years. In 1996, St. Francis Xavier University (StFX) signed an agreement with Mi'kmaw chiefs of Nova Scotia to prepare educators to teach Mi'kmaq students in Nova Scotia. Since the start of the StFX certification program, more than 100

Mi'kmaw teachers have graduated; this was vital for the development of the immersion program. More than 20 Mi'kmaq teachers have gone on to complete graduate education and several of us have done or are doing research about Mi'kmaw language revitalization.

Our local school board also played an important role in providing leadership to create specific inservice education about immersion teaching. Dorothy Lazore from the Mohawk Nation and Andrea Bear Nicholas from the Maliseet Nation traveled to our community on weekends and in summers to work with the immersion teachers. In 2009, StFX, in partnership with the community, created a part-time 30-credit Mi'kmaq Language Certificate Program to increase the capacity for immersion teaching. More than 23 Mi'kmaq teachers from various Mi'kmaq communities graduated from this program between 2009 and 2016.

Since 1998, StFX has also hosted the biannual L'nui'sultinej (Mi'kmaq Language Conference), which has brought together community members, educators, Elders, and researchers interested in language revitalization from all over the Mi'kmaq nation. This conference has allowed communities like ours to showcase what is being done and has built language capacity and sharing across Mi'kma'ki.

Our Future

Those of us who can see the results of the program on a day-to-day basis know its positive effects, but these are not evident to some families in the community. We need to keep sharing the positive results we are finding.

There are many stories about the successes of our program. Many students sing in Mi'kmaw, recite or read in Mi'kmaw, or are masters of ceremonies. One of our previous immersion students sang the national anthem in Mi'kmaw at the closing of the 2011 Canada Winter Games. Our children are proud of who they are and they are not afraid to show it.

Immersion students do very well academically after they leave the program at the end of 3rd grade. Sherise Paul-Gould, my childhood friend who now teaches grades 7 to 9, has consistently noticed that immersion graduates often lead the class in both English language arts and other subjects. As part of the joint MEd thesis we wrote (Paul-Gould, 2012; Sock, 2012), Sherise assessed reading levels of our 81 7th-grade students and found that the former immersion students had the highest reading levels, with the students who had been in the English program since kindergarten scoring lower on average.

Who would have ever thought that today we would be struggling as a nation to sustain our Mi'kmaw language?

This year the immersion program was able to move into a separate school building from the English program, thereby increasing the amount of Mi'kmaw that is spoken on the playground and in the hallways. A cafeteria has been added to the school, allowing the children to stay for lunch and use Mi'kmaw in another informal context in the school. Ta'n L'nuey Etl-Mawlukwatmumk (TLE), a resource center that has provided curriculum support for the Mi'kmaq immersion program, is now housed in the Mi'kmaq school. There are Mi'kmaw-speaking specialists in physical education and music who use Mi'kmaw as a language of instruction. The program has been extended to grade 4 with plans for a grade 5 class next year. More culturally responsive teaching is bringing an increasing number of community members into the school to teach traditional arts

> Once the program was under way, we saw that the purpose extended to embedding our culture and traditions in the curriculum. The language itself changed the way we taught.

such as beading and birch bark biting. Overall, the amount of time children hear and speak Mi'kmaw is increasing.

I am happy about what we have accomplished in the Mi'kmaq immersion program. It has not been an easy ride, but it has been a path worth taking. I am honored and humbled to take part in keeping the Mi'kmaw language alive. I will continue to advocate to our community, to our people, to our government, and to whoever will listen, because this is my purpose as a Mi'kmaq educator. This is our future for our children and our children's children—to carry on our sacred language. ✿

Starr Paul teaches grade 2 in the Mi'kmaq immersion program in Eskasoni Mi'kmaw community in Nova Scotia. Sherise Paul-Gould teaches grade 9 at Essissoqnikewey Siawa'sik Kina'matnewo'kuo'm (Eskasoni Elementary and Middle School) in Eskasoni Mi'kmaw community in Nova Scotia. Anne Murray-Orr and Joanne Tompkins are teacher educators and researchers in the faculty of education at St. Francis Xavier University in Antigonish, Nova Scotia. They have worked with Starr and Sherise on a research project exploring Mi'kmaq and Maliseet immersion programs in Eastern Canada.

Note from author Starr Paul: There are two common spellings for the name of our people and our language, Mi'kmaw and Mi'kmaq. Although Mi'kmaw is sometimes understood as the adjective form and Mi'kmaq the noun, there are many exceptions to this rule. I use each of them as my mother taught me.

References

Paul-Gould, Sherise. 2012. *Student Achievement, Fluency and Identity: An In-Depth Study of the Mi'kmaq Immersion Program in One Community.* Unpublished Masters Thesis. St. Francis Xavier University, Antigonish, NS.

Sock, Starr. 2012. *An Inquiry into the Mi'kmaq Immersion Program in One Community: Student Identity, Fluency, and Achievement.* Unpublished Masters Thesis. St. Francis Xavier University, Antigonish, NS.

Aquí y Allá

Exploring our lives through poetry—here and there

BY ELIZABETH BARBIAN

Allá en las montañas,
para entrar no necesitas
papeles, estás libre.

There in the mountains,
to enter you don't need
papers, you are free.

Adriana's steady gaze accompanies her sharing of her poem during our *Aquí/Allá* (here/there) poetry unit. Her words are met with silence and sighs, nods and bright eyes. She gets it, I think. In this verse of her poem, Adriana suddenly pushes beyond a contrast of the smells of pine and the cars of the city streets. She voices her critique of the world through her poem, contrasting two important places in her life—the city and the mountains.

The opportunity and space to find our voices—to see, name, analyze, question, and understand the world—is an invitation I work to create again and again in our 5th-grade dual-language classroom about 30 minutes south of Portland, Oregon. Labels and statistics define our school as 80 percent Latina/o, 70 percent English language learners, and more than 90 percent free and reduced lunch. My students spend 50 percent of their academic day in Spanish and the other half in English. Cultures, however, are not so easily equalized. The dominant culture—one in which much of my own identity was formed—can too easily shutter and silence the multifaceted, complex cultures of students' lives. My daily challenge is to pull up the details and experiences of their lives so that they become the curriculum and conversation content of our classroom.

Our *Aquí/Allá* poetry unit did just that. It surfaced the layers and parts of lives often overpowered by a common classroom curriculum. It created spaces where students could analyze and name the details of their lives.

The bilingual poetry and stories of Salvadoran writer Jorge Argueta have been an invaluable resource in my classroom. I've used poems from *Talking with Mother Earth/Hablando con madre tierra* for homework and class analysis during a study of ecosystems, the story *Xochitl and the Flowers/Xóchitl, la niña de las flores* to lead into persuasive writing, and *Sopa de frijoles/Bean Soup* to teach personification, similes,

FAVIANNA RODRIGUEZ

and beautiful poetic language. As I scanned books for a poem that would raise the level of vivid imagery in my students' narrative writing, I returned to this trusted source. Argueta's poem "Wonders of the City/Las maravillas de la ciudad," from his book *A Movie in My Pillow/Una película en mi almohada*, has the potential to pull the everyday details of students' lives into a place of power. It is a tightly packed representation of the tension of bridging cultures and places, something most of my students negotiate on a daily basis.

"Wonders of the City" has a simple and accessible structure, particularly for language learners, a category that fits all of my students at one time or another during our 50/50 day (see p. 72). The introductory stanza hints at the irony of the poem: "Here in the city there are/wonders everywhere." The second stanza surprises the reader with a puzzling observation: "Here mangoes/come in cans." As the reader wonders why someone would eat a mango from a can, the third stanza calmly counters, "In El Salvador/they grew on trees." The repetitive contrast pattern and concrete details are simple windows to the profound dissonance of longing for one place while living in another.

Breaking Down a Model, Building Up a Draft

After reading the poem out loud a few times and discussing the meaning, we read the poem again, this time as writers. I prefaced this reading with our usual writers' questions: "What do you observe or notice about the writing?"

"The author is contrasting two places."

"There is repetition, a pattern—here, there."

One Spanish language learner, Ben, surprised me by noticing the parallel language structure: "When the author talks about 'here,' he writes in present tense. When he talks about 'there,' he uses past tense."

When the responses to the open-ended question began to dwindle, I probed for more. "What does Jorge Argueta do to show the contrast? What details does he choose to compare?"

"He contrasts food." Students had a harder time naming the author's content choices. I pointed out the use of everyday details, like the comparison of the packaged wonders of the city with mangoes and chickens in a more natural environment.

We ended our discussion of the poem's meaning with the questions "What do you notice about the author's attitude toward the two places?" "What feelings does Jorge Argueta convey in the poem?" "Does he seem to like one place more than the other?"

Students noticed the irony: "He likes El Salvador more." We talked about how the culture that is labeled by the world as "more advanced" and full of technological wonders is often missing the richness and connections to the natural world.

After discussing the poem's irony, I asked students to think about contrasts in their own lives, suggesting possibilities that would open the assignment to all: home/ Grandma's house, the United States/another country, school/nature, Oregon/another state. Miguel's eyes lit up when he received an affirmative answer to his question "Can I contrast life in school and video games?"

Once students had chosen their topics, they created a two-column *Aquí/Allá* list to generate ideas for their poems. We looked back at the poem to notice how the author contrasted mangoes in both countries, how he compared mango to mango, and not mango to melon. I shared my own list of ideas comparing school with nature. Although I, too, wanted to write a poem contrasting two countries, I knew that many of my students had lived their whole lives in our community.

There is nothing "mini" about a brainstorming session in my classroom. I find that the more ideas we share during the prewrite stage of the writing process, the more excited, confident, and successful my students are as they begin their writing. We shared lists once students had a few ideas down. "Here in the United States we celebrate Halloween; there in Mexico they celebrate Day of the Dead," read Juliana. Although validating the observation (especially since we were listing ideas on Oct. 29), I realized that our challenge to show, not tell, had followed us across genres.

"How might you show the reader how people are celebrating Halloween or Day of the Dead so that the reader can see the difference? What do you see on Halloween? What do people do to celebrate *El Día de los Muertos*?" I asked. Students eagerly shared their experiences of families gathering to honor ancestors and loved ones.

Ana Maria suggested, "Maybe you could say, 'Here we knock on doors in our costumes/There families gather at the cemetery.'"

As students shared some of their ideas, I tried to push them to critique and value. I tried to explicitly value the *allá*: "I wish more people here celebrated Day of the Dead. What a powerful way to remember loved ones."

Students continued to share ideas: "The money is different," said Carlos. "You play different games." "The stores are different," Mayra observed. "Here I need to speak two languages to be understood, and there only Spanish." "In Florida it is hot, and in Oregon it is rainy."

I responded with questions that would generate word pictures: "What does the money look like? How could you show the reader the difference in appearance or value?" "How are the toys different? Where and what do children play?" "How do people dress or what do they do that might show us the difference in weather?" "What do you see and hear in the market?" As students headed off to write their drafts, I reminded them to write with vivid images instead of generalities.

> My daily challenge is to pull up the details and experiences of their lives so that they become the curriculum and conversation content of our classroom.

Some days during writing workshop you can hear pencils scratch and thoughts flow directly from the brain to the page. Not on our first *Aquí/Allá* drafting day. The clamor of questions and conversations continued as pencils carved thoughts in the white spaces between blue lines. "Alejandra! What do you call the toys the kids play with in Mexico?" asked David. "Which toys?" "The ones that you spin, the ones . . ." "Oh, yeah," I heard Roberto murmur from across the room.

Noticing, Naming, and Applying

At the end of the initial drafting session, we gathered in a circle on the floor. Students read a few of their favorite lines or their entire poem to the class. This in-progress read-around motivates students by providing an immediate audience, allows them to borrow and adapt ideas from others, and helps me develop revision mini-lessons. We all work together to notice and name what students are already doing so that others can try the technique in their own writing.

The bulk of my teaching about writing happens once students have a working draft that can be revised. Although all the students had easily applied the "here/there" structure to their poems, most students were struggling to show details instead of telling them. Their energy until this point had been focused on identifying the contrasts instead of crafting an image.

The next day began with a series of revision invitations that I listed on the board as I introduced them. "When Erica writes, '*Aquí dicen* trick-or-treat,' she inserts dialogue in her poem. You might try the same technique in your own writing today."

Next, I used a student poem as a revision possibility. "Dalia uses personification in her poem when she says, 'Over there in Mexico there is brilliant yellow lightning/

that cuts the sky like a cake.' Go back and find a place where you might add personification."

Later, as I conferenced with individuals, I noticed David's "*Aquí dicen* hello, good-bye/*Allá dicen hola, adiós*." He also wrote that children play with "wooden tops that dance."

Eva revised her lines about *paletas*:

Aquí venden
paletas dulces y sabrosas
"ay que ricas, que deliciosas"
Allá en México
hay paletas picosas
con chile
color fuego ardiente
"ay, ay, ay, me pica me pica
quiero agua"

Here they sell
sweet and tasty *paletas*
"oh, how yummy, how delicious"
There in Mexico
there are spicy *paletas*
with chile
burning fire color
"oh, oh, oh, it's hot, it's hot
give me water"

Fernando moved from "They are different" to:

Aquí los zapatos son famosos
por la marca y cómo se mira
Allá no les importa mucho
de cómo se mira
nomás les importan
si duran y están baratos

Here shoes are famous
for the brand and look
There it doesn't matter a lot
what they look like
it only matters
if they last and are cheap

Luis used a subtle form of personification:

Aquí hay trabajos de sudando
y de dolor de pie a cabeza

Here there are jobs of sweating
and ache from foot to head

Toward the end of our work on the poems, students met in small response groups. They shared their poems with one another, writing down favorite lines and images, describing cultural contrasts, trying to name what they noticed. In one group we paused to think about how much more sense it makes to play with a top or a ball than it does to buy a $200 video game system. In another we marveled over the personal relationships and interactions involved in buying tomatoes and onions in the market.

Students read their favorite lines from others' poems during a whole-group share. As I passed from one group to the next, Alex exclaimed, "Wow, you should read Juliana's poem. It is really good":

Aquí cuando llueve
sólo caen gotitas pequeñas
que bailan en el piso
Allá los truenos caen
y casi te desmayas del miedo
los relámpagos caen
pueden romper a la mitad un árbol

Here when it rains
only tiny drops fall
that dance on the floor
There the thunder falls
and you almost faint from fear
lightning falls
it can break a tree in half

Taking It Beyond Our Walls

Alex wasn't the only one who thought our poetry was "really good." When I shared our poems with Catherine Celestino, a 2nd-grade teacher whose class my students knew as "reading buddies," she responded with an invitation: "Could your 5th graders teach the poem to my 2nd graders?"

The plan to teach our reading buddies to write *Aquí/Allá* poems blasted fresh energy and relevance into our work. "When I plan a lesson for you, I always think about the goal of expressing our lives and views through the writing of a poem, as well as the skills I want to teach you in your writing. What are our goals as we teach our reading buddies?" I asked.

Students broke into groups of three or four to create a list of the important skills they had learned while writing their poems. We shared ideas with the whole group and then, together, determined which were most important. We decided that the prewriting and revision goal would be to use a list with commas, sensory details, and similes. The students defined the most important editing goals as taking out unnecessary words and deciding where to use line breaks.

"Who doesn't have a partner? Raise your hand." As we entered Mrs. Celestino's 2nd-grade classroom, students formed pairs and settled into work.

As students shared some of their ideas, I tried to push them to critique and value.

"What does your grandma's house look like? What kinds of things do you find there?" I heard Adriana ask her partner.

I saw students develop new strategies to scaffold learning: "We've decided that I will write one line for my partner and he will write the next." "I'm writing down whatever she tells me on this paper, and then my partner is copying the words onto hers." Jessica, Michelle, and Alex were dividing the *Aquí/Allá* columns horizontally and adding categories: food, names, toys, activities.

"*Aquí* we speak Spanish, *allá* we speak another language," I heard 2nd grader Alma explain to Mayra. Most students who had compared the United States and Mexico focused on the English in the here and the Spanish in the there.

"Can you teach us some words in your other language?" I asked in Spanish as I lowered myself to the rug to join the conversation. Alma smiled with the confidence of an expert as she told us the words for tortilla and water. Mayra and I repeated the new words, practicing and trying to learn the sounds. I moved across the room, and Mayra helped Alma move from oral idea to a new line in her poem: "Here we say *tortilla* and *agua*, in Mexico we say *sheck* and *nda*," she wrote.

When we returned to the room after our first teaching session, I heard about successes and frustrations. "My partner picked Mexico and she can't remember what Mexico is like." We talked about the importance of picking a place you know and remember well, and brainstormed some possible local choices. "My partner just sits there." "We've already written a whole page!"

Stepping Back and Learning Forward

I feel fortunate each time we shake to the surface parts of students' home lives, traditions, languages, and cultures, as well as their views of the world around them. I can't completely know and understand the *allá* of every student's life, but I can join Jorge Argueta in his critique of the "wonders" of *aquí*. I can create space for students to name the details and cultures of their lives in the classroom curriculum. I can help students question the *aquí* and value the *allá*. Next year I will ask even more questions, probe for more details, and leave more spaces for talking and sharing and critiquing the contrasts of our lives.

Students often follow me as we head out to the playground, eager to share a thought or experience that they weren't comfortable enough to share in class. We head out to midmorning recess after drawing and labeling detailed diagrams of crickets during a study of ecosystems. Andrea hesitates for a moment as some of her classmates sprint off, eager to join the game of tag or secure the best swing.

"We eat crickets at home. You know, they are really good with a little bit of lime and salt," she tells me, staring off in the distance as she stands at my side. "Really?" I ask, turning to face her. "What do they taste like? How do you catch them?" Andrea continues to talk, and, as we line up to head back to the classroom, we share her cricket connection with the class.

How can I continue to open spaces so that rich moments of linguistic and cultural revelation are not chance conversations on the peripheries of the playground and hallway, but a central core of the classroom curriculum? How can I help students bridge the conflicting cultures of their lives? ☼

Elizabeth Barbian (formerly Schlessman) has taught bilingual students and worked with teachers in the United States, Bolivia, Tanzania, and South Africa. She currently lives in the Denver area. Student names have been changed. All conversations and student work in this article were originally in Spanish.

Note from the author: The words *sheck* and *nda* come from the Oaxaca Amuzgo language, spoken in the village of San Pedro Amuzgos in Oaxaca, Mexico. The spelling of the words is taken directly from 2nd-grade student work.

Resources

Argueta, Jorge. 2009. *Sopa de frijoles/Bean Soup*. Groundwood Books.

Argueta, Jorge. 2006. *Talking with Mother Earth/Hablando con madre tierra*. Groundwood Books.

Argueta, Jorge. 2003. *Xochitl and the Flowers/Xóchitl, la niña de las flores*. Children's Book Press.

FAVIANNA RODRIGUEZ

Wonders of the City
Jorge Argueta

Here in the city there are
wonders everywhere
Here mangoes
come in cans
In El Salvador
they grew on trees
Here chickens come
in plastic bags
Over there
they slept beside me

Las maravillas de la ciudad
Jorge Argueta

Aquí en esta ciudad
todo es maravilloso
Aquí los mangos
vienen enlatados
En El Salvador
crecían en árboles
Aquí las gallinas vienen
en bolsas de plástico
Allá se dormían
junto a mí

"Wonders of the City," by Jorge Argueta, is reprinted from *A Movie in My Pillow/Una pelicula en mi almohada* with permission of the publishers, Children's Book Press, an imprint of Lee & Low Books Inc.

Not Too Young

Teaching 6-year-olds about skin color, race, culture, and respect

BY RITA TENORIO

ALL THE COLORS OF THE EARTH BY SHEILA HAMANAKA

Children come in all the colors of love,

In endless shades of you and me.

sat down one day with seven of the children in my 1st-grade class. It was early in the year and we were getting to know each other. We talked about how we were alike, how we were different. "Our skin is different," one of the children said. I asked everyone to put their hands together on the table, so we could see all the different colors.

One African American student, Dana, simply would not. Scowling, she slid her hands beneath the tabletop, unwilling to have her color compared to the others.

It was a reaction I had seen before. I was teaching at La Escuela Fratney, an ethnically diverse dual-language school in a racially mixed working-class Milwaukee neighborhood. My students typically included Black kids, white kids, and Latinas/os; Spanish speakers and English speakers. They had many things in common. Recess was their favorite time of day. Friendships were a priority. They wanted to "belong" to a group and they were very conscious of where they fit in a social sense.

And they all "knew" that it was better to be light-skinned than dark-skinned, and that English was better than Spanish.

Even though my students had only six years of life experience by the time they reached my classroom, the centuries-old legacies of bias and racism in our country had already made an impact on their lives. I would see fair-skinned children deliberately change places in a circle if darker-skinned children sat down next to them. An English speaker wouldn't play with a Latina/o child because, he said, "He talks funny." On the playground, a group of white girls wouldn't let their darker-skinned peers join in their games, explaining matter-of-factly: "Brown kids can't be in our club."

Dealing with issues of bias against language or race is perhaps the most complicated problem I encountered as a teacher. For many years, the problem didn't seem to "exist," and was glossed over by teachers as part of the view that "all children are the same—Black, white, or Brown." Yet I've learned that it is not the awareness of racial and cultural differences that leads to prejudice and racism, but how people respond to those differences.

I realized I needed to do two things. First, I had to immediately respond to unacceptable behavior by children, such as racist put-downs or slurs. Second, I had to develop a curriculum that included anti-bias lessons that help students recognize and respond to stereotypes and prejudice.

An Anti-Racist, Multicultural Focus

When I began my career, I worked in a specialty school where the students were learning Spanish as a second language. Moving from holiday to holiday, we learned about cultures all over the world. I changed bulletin boards and literacy activities to correspond to the holidays, and proudly integrated the activities into our daily lessons. We learned about our "differences" and celebrated our "similarities." I insisted that "we can all live together" and forbade words or actions that would "hurt" anyone.

It worked. At least I thought it worked.

But as I learned more about multicultural, anti-racist teaching, I began to recognize that just because the atmosphere was calm and children were not overt about their biases did not mean that bias and prejudice were not present. I began to observe and listen more closely to my students, especially in situations where they interacted independently with their peers both in and out of the classroom.

Later, I was part of the founding staff of La Escuela Fratney, a two-way, Spanish/English bilingual elementary school. Our vision was to explicitly explore issues of race and language. The language component was part of a broader framework that had a multicultural, anti-racist curriculum at its core. We wanted our multicultural, multilingual students to not only learn about the history and culture of major ethnic groups, but also to understand racism's influence on all of us. We developed a series of activities and projects that helped us discuss issues of language, race, and social justice in meaningful, age-appropriate ways.

We built classroom community by learning about each other's lives and families; students collected and shared information about their families and ancestry. We talked about how they got their names, how their families came to live in Milwaukee, and which holidays they celebrated and how.

Together we defined our classroom rules and discussed what "fairness" meant to each of us. Playground problems became the topics for class discussions or role plays during which students heard from each other how they might more peacefully resolve their disputes. We learned about people who have worked for fairness and equality. At every step we helped the children explore the nature of racial and cultural differences and overcome simplistic notions of who is "better" or who is "like us" and who isn't, whether it related to language, color, or culture.

Responding to Students' Comments

Even in a school with a social justice focus, I sometimes observed frustrating conflicts. Sometimes these centered on a verbal put-down or involved body language. Even the children's "make-believe" stories were at times defined by race or language. Comments like "You can't be the queen; there are no Black queens" or "If you want to play with us you have to speak English" caught me off guard. Equally disturbing, the children often accepted these statements without complaint. Interactions where children put each other down or where children reflect the discrimination that is so prevalent in our world provide opportunities for strong lessons in counteracting stereotypes and racism. They are as much a part of the curriculum as teaching a science lesson or reading a story.

When these incidents arose, I first put a stop to the behavior and made clear that it was inappropriate. Then I tried to explain why it was inappropriate and acknowledge the feelings of the targeted child.

Often the remark was unrelated to the conflict at hand, and I tried to help the parties focus on the real problem. The child who told her classmate that "there are no Black queens," for instance, needed to understand not only that her remark was incorrect, but also that she has insulted her friend. Next, she had to see that her real motivation was that *she* wanted to wear the rhinestone crown and sequined dress that were part of the playhouse scenario. Beyond that moment, it would also be good to have discussions of the queens throughout African history, perhaps using a piece of literature like *Mufaro's Beautiful Daughters*, by John Steptoe, or *Ashanti to Zulu*, by Margaret Musgrove.

It is not the awareness of racial and cultural differences that leads to prejudice and racism, but how people respond to those differences.

Some of the stereotypes at Fratney were related to our two-way bilingual program and the fact that some students were hearing Spanish for the first time. For example, I remember when an English-speaking student, Sean, referring to Miguel, a Spanish-speaking student, said, "I don't want to sit next to him. He talks funny."

One response might have been "Miguel is very nice, Sean. In our room we take turns sitting next to all the kids." But such a response would not have addressed Sean's bias or curiosity about a different language. It may have merely caused Sean to be less verbal about his feelings while still avoiding Latina/o classmates. In my view, Sean's remark was really a question to the adults as he tried to understand and get used to an unfamiliar situation. Most Spanish-speaking students come to school having experienced being in situations where everyone around them is speaking English. In our society, most English-speaking students have little or no experience being in a situation where they don't understand the language being spoken.

A more appropriate response might be "Miguel is speaking Spanish like the other people in his family. You and I are speaking English. In our classroom, we'll be speaking in both Spanish and English. It's fine for you to ask questions about what Miguel is saying, or say that you don't understand. But it's not OK to say that he talks funny. That's a put-down to all of us who speak Spanish. You'll be learning to speak in Spanish, too, so you can learn a lot from Miguel."

Another constant source of comments is skin color. A child may say, for instance, "Jonathan is too brown. I'm glad I'm lighter than him." One response from the teacher might be "We're all the same. It doesn't matter what color you are." Although meant to promote equality, it doesn't address the child's view that "being lighter is better." In addition, it might send Jonathan a very negative message. Such a comment from a child indicates that that child is quite aware that we are not all the same.

At first I found it difficult to respond to these types of insults, particularly because an explanation of why society views lighter skin as superior to darker skin, or one language more positively than another, is rooted in our history and may be developmentally difficult for young children to conceptualize. Yet it's important to intervene immediately to contradict the notion of "brown is bad" or "English is better." In this case, I would ask Jonathan how that comment made him feel. I would remind the other child that what was said sounds like a put-down to me and is not OK. Then, I would address the issue of skin color through specific curriculum activities—stories, interviews, and projects offer opportunities for children to learn and respond to these issues.

Activities

Over the years, I've gathered a variety of teacher-developed activities that can be used to address some of these issues with students. Although it's vital to respond to student comments in the moment, developing curriculum activities to address racial and linguistic prejudice is also essential. With young children, this can begin with activities to get to know each other and learn about similarities and differences. It can then progress to a more explicit exploration of skin color and privilege.

Me Pockets. This is always a class favorite. Each child takes home a letter-sized clear plastic sleeve, the kind used to display baseball cards. I ask students to fill the pockets with photos, pictures, drawings, or anything else that will help us know more about them and the things that are important in their lives. They return the pockets within a week and each child presents their work to the class. I put them into a three-ring binder that becomes the favorite classroom book to read and re-read. Students learn about the home language and culture of their peers.

The individual pockets reflect the cultural and socioeconomic diversity of the families. Some students put lots of photos in their pockets. Others cut pictures out of magazines or make drawings. My experience is that every family is eager to share in some way, and family members take time to help their children develop the project.

If someone doesn't bring their Me Pocket sheet back, the teachers step in to help him or her find pictures or make the drawings they need to add their page to the binder.

I'm always amazed at how quickly children learn the details about each other's lives from this project: who has a pet, who takes dance classes, who has family in Puerto Rico, who likes to eat macaroni and cheese. The children know there are differences among them, but they also love to share the things that are alike: "Look, Rachel has two brothers, just like me." "I didn't know that Jamal's family likes to camp. We do, too!"

Each of the teachers also completes a Me Pocket sheet. The students loved looking at the picture of me as a 1st grader, seeing my husband and children, and learning that chocolate cake is my favorite food.

Partner Questions. Each day I take time to teach the social skills of communicating ideas with others and listening to another person's perspective. I practice those skills with role-playing activities and problem-solving situations students or teachers bring to the group. This activity is done in both English and Spanish, with those learning the target language of the day getting support and scaffolding from the teachers and their peers. For example, I might ask such simple questions as "Do you like to speak Spanish? Why or why not." Or other more difficult questions: "What is the meanest thing anyone has ever said to you?" "Why do you think some people like to use put-downs?" The children take a few minutes to talk with a partner. Afterward, some are willing to share with the whole group. We might then role-play the situation as a group and look for ways to respond, such as speaking back to insults.

> **"Grandma says that everyone should speak only English."**

Someone Special. By the end of October, during the time of Halloween, *Día de los Muertos*, and All Souls' Day, we learn about how people remember their ancestors and others who have died or who are far away. I set up a table and students are encouraged to bring in pictures or artifacts to display. They bring a remarkable variety of things: photos, jewelry, a trophy won by a departed relative, a postcard that person sent them, or perhaps the program from a funeral. And they bring many, many stories. Again, the teachers also participate and share stories of those who have gone before us.

Let's Talk About Skin Color. Another important conversation I have with my students focuses on the varieties of skin color we have in our group. Usually when we begin this discussion, some children are uncomfortable about saying "what they are" or describing the color of their skin. In particular, children with very dark skin—like Dana, who would not even put her hands on the table—are often reluctant to join in.

Meanwhile, the white kids often boast about being "pink." Though we've never talked about this in class before, there is definitely a strong implication that it is better to be lighter. Many children are amazed that this topic is put out on the table for discussion. The looks in their eyes, their frequent reluctance to begin the discussion, tell me that this is a very personal topic.

As part of the lesson, I ask the students if they have ever heard anyone say something bad or mean about another person's skin color. The hands shoot up.

"Grandma says that everyone should speak only English."

"My mom says that you can't trust Black people."

"My sister won't talk to the Puerto Rican kids on the bus."

"Mara said that I couldn't play, that I was too black to be her friend."

They continue to raise their hands and this conversation goes on for a while. We talk about ways we've heard others use people's language or skin color to make fun of them or put them down. We talk about what to do in those situations.

As we continue to discuss issues of race, I often introduce my personal experiences. I tell them about the first time I realized that Black and white people were treated differently. I share my experience being one of the few Latinas in my school. And we try to ask questions that really intrigue the students, that invite them to try to look at things with a different perspective, to learn something new about the human experience and be open-minded to that idea: Do people choose their first language? Where do you get your skin color? Is it better to be one color than another? Lots of our conversations revolve around a story or a piece of literature.

> **"We put black, white, red, and yellow together. I like the color of my skin." How far Dana had come since the day she would not show us her hands.**

With a little work, this discussion can expand in ways that incorporate math lessons, map lessons, and other curricular areas. I ask children to interview their relatives to find out where the family came from. We create a bulletin board display that we use to compare and learn about the huge variety of places our students' relatives are from. We graph the data of where families come from and the languages that are spoken there.

Skin Color and Science. Our class discussions of skin color set the stage for lots of "scientific" observations. For example, I bring in a large variety of paint chips from a local hardware store. The students love examining and sorting the many shades of beige and brown. It takes a while for them to find the one that is most like their own skin color. *All the Colors We Are/Todos los colores de nuestra piel* by Katie Kissinger is an excellent resource.

In *The Colors of Us*, by Karen Katz, Lena learns from her mother that "brown" is a whole range of colors. Like the characters in the story, we take red, yellow, black, and white paint and mix them in various combinations until we've each found the color of our own skin. Then we display our "research" as part of our science fair project.

In another exercise, inspired by Sheila Hamanaka's *All the Colors of the Earth*, students are asked to find words to describe the color of their skin, and to find something at home that matches their skin color. Then we display the pieces of wood and fabric, the little bags of cinnamon and coffee, the dolls and ceramic pieces that "match" us.

As we continue these explorations, dealing concretely with a topic that so many have never heard discussed in such a manner, students begin to see past society's labels. It is always amazing to children that friends who identify as Black, for example, can actually have very light skin. Or that children who identify as Puerto Rican can be darker than some of the African American children.

Writing About Our Colors. As children begin to understand the idea of internalizing another's point of view, they can apply that understanding by examining different ideas and alternatives to their own experiences. As they learn to express themselves through reading and writing in two languages, they can learn to challenge stereotypes and speak back to unfair behavior and comments.

Once students have had a chance to reflect on skin color, they write about it. Annie wrote: "I like my skin color. It is like peachy cream." James wrote: "My color is the same as my dad's. I think the new baby will have this color, too." And Keila wrote: "When I was born, my color was brown skin and white skin mixed together."

When Dana wrote about mixing the colors to match her skin, she said: "We put black, white, red, and yellow together. I like the color of my skin." How far she had come since the day she would not show us her hands.

These activities have an impact. Many children have taken steps toward awareness of race. They are not afraid to discuss it. They now have more ways in which to think about and describe themselves. The activities challenge my consciousness, too.

Such activities are powerful, but it is also important to remember that there are no guarantees that children have internalized anti-racist ideas. So much still depends on the other forces in their lives and on the other ways that we deal with race in our classrooms.

Are They Too Young for This?

We rely on our schools to be the place for a multicultural, multiracial experience for our children. We want to believe that learning together will help our students to become more understanding and respectful of differences. Yet so often we do not address these issues head-on. Without specific instruction, it is unlikely that sensitivity and tolerance will develop, that children will bridge the gaps they bring to school from their earliest days.

Many people would say that 6-year-olds are too young to deal with these serious issues. I, too, had real questions at first about what was actually possible with young children. Can you have "real" conversations with 6-year-olds about power, privilege, and racism in our society? Can you make them aware of the effects that racism and injustice have in our lives? Can they really understand their role in the classroom community?

The answer to all of these questions is "yes." Even very young children can explore and understand the attitudes they and their classmates bring to school each day. They have real issues and opinions to share, and many, many questions of their own to ask. In this way, they can begin to challenge some of the assumptions that influence their behavior toward classmates who don't look or talk the same way they do.

In more than 30 years of teaching, I have learned that—contrary to what adults often believe—young children are not "blank slates." Instead, they have an unstated but nonetheless sophisticated understanding of issues of race and power. One of our most important roles as teachers, I believe, is to recognize society's effect on children, address the issue directly, and give students the beginning skills and strategies they will need to combat racism and bias in their lives.

Early childhood educators hold an incredible amount of influence over the minds of the children they teach. As the cliché goes, "All I really need to know I learned in kindergarten." For today's students, "all they need to know" goes beyond the traditional formula of playing fair and putting things back in their place. It includes developing the skills and strategies to counteract the racism in their lives. ✺

Rita Tenorio is a retired bilingual early childhood teacher. She is one of the founding editors of Rethinking Schools and taught at La Escuela Fratney for 24 years.

Note from the editors: This article was adapted from two previously published pieces by Rita Tenorio—"Race and Respect Among Young Children" (*Rethinking Our Classrooms*, Volume 1, 2007) and "Brown Kids Can't Be in Our Club" (*Rethinking Schools* magazine, Spring 2004).

Resources

Hamanaka, Sheila. 1999. *All the Colors of the Earth*. HarperCollins.

Katz, Karen. 2002. *The Colors of Us*. Square Fish.

Kissinger, Katie. 2002. *All the Colors We Are/Todos los colores de nuestra piel*. Redleaf Press.

Musgrove, Margaret. 1992. *Ashanti to Zulu: African Traditions*. Puffin Books.

Steptoe, John. 2008. *Mufaro's Beautiful Daughters: An African Tale*. Puffin Books.

Rethinking Identity

Exploring Afro-Mexican history with heritage language speakers

BY MICHELLE NICOLA

ENCUENTRO DE LOS PUEBLOS NEGROS BY MARIO GUZMÁN FOR ASARO.

66 "This is the country of my ancestors. It includes the fandango—music that takes Spanish instruments and plays them with African style, songs like 'La Bamba' that trace their way back to slavery and still influence music today, and a Mexican president with both Spanish and African ancestry. This is my history, but no one is talking to us about it," wrote Daniel as he reflected on the Afro-Mexican unit our class had just completed.

Several months earlier, I was searching for a way that my Spanish class could support African American Heritage Month activities at our school. At De La Salle North in Portland, Oregon, students organize month-long activities to celebrate and critically consider the histories of the many heritages represented in the student body. I wanted to support these student-led projects with lessons in my classroom, but how? Driving home one night, the solution hit me: Nicholas Marshall.

Nicholas was a memorable student from my first year of teaching. One day he looked at me, eyes wide, and said: "Wait, Señorita! There are Black people who speak Spanish?"

"Yes," I had said. "There most definitely are." I developed a whole unit for my Spanish World Language class based on Nicholas' question. I decided to adapt that unit to meet the needs of my current students. I hoped that, by the end of the unit, they would be able to identify ways that enslaved Africans and their descendants shaped Mexican culture, and describe the historical and political forces that led to Afro-Mexican invisibility. I wanted students to complicate their narratives about Mexican identity and realize that Afro-Mexican resistance weaves through the fabric of that heritage.

My students at De La Salle were heritage language speakers. Heritage students have both a cultural and a linguistic connection to a language other than English. Our class of 23 juniors and two seniors each shaped the definition of heritage Spanish speaker in their own way. For example, Marta didn't consider Spanish her native language—she favored English, although she spoke Spanish with her parents. Ana Maria emigrated from Mexico at the age of 10. She learned to read and write in Spanish, and then learned to do the same in English. Daniel grew up in the United States but spoke Spanish at home and often with his friends. Itzel was from Guatemala and English was her third language, after a Mayan language and Spanish. Alex's father was from Ecuador and his mother from Chile, so his Spanish was peppered with words that differed from those of his peers.

They all spoke, read, and wrote with high levels of fluency in Spanish, yet most of their formal schooling had been in English. They switched between cultures and languages and, in Daniel's words, sometimes felt "stuck between two countries I'm not wanted in." In that sense, the definition of a heritage speaker is not just about language; it also includes socio-emotional factors.

Where Did the Africans Go?

On our first day, I announced that we would be uncovering the history of Black Mexicans. "Does anyone already know anything about this topic?"

My students' faces were blank.

"When I was preparing this unit for you, I found out that many people believe the first Africans arrived with the first conquistadors. By the 16th and 17th centuries, one out of every two Africans who were enslaved and taken to the so-called 'New World' was sold in Mexico. In fact, until 1650, the number of African-heritage Mexicans equaled the number of Spanish-heritage Mexicans. Yet today, no one seems to know much about the story of Afro-Mexicans and their descendants. So where did they all go? How did they become invisible?"

"Maybe they left the country," Josué called out.

"It's possible," I replied. "Any other ideas?"

"Maybe they got kind of mixed," Lalo ventured.

I pulled out my trusty teacher phrase: "Tell me more."

"You know, Ms. Nicola, the birds and the bees, and then the kids got lighter skin or something." The class laughed.

"You may be on to something, Lalo. I want you to keep these ideas in the back of your minds throughout the unit. Keep asking the question: How does a history, a culture, and a people become invisible? I want you to collect stories of things you didn't realize had a connection to Africa, but that are deeply rooted in African cultures and that have shaped what we think of as 'Mexican.'

"Now grab your bags," I said. "We're going to the computer lab."

Once in the computer lab, I gave my students a piece of paper with the URL for the Afropop Worldwide website "La Bamba: The Afro-Mexican Story" (see Resources). "*Chicos*," I called out, moving to the center of the lab. "Remember that even though the website is in *inglés*, your notes need to be *en español*." Although I wanted our class to read, write, think, and speak in Spanish 100 percent of the time, the reality

Until 1650, the number of African-heritage Mexicans equaled the number of Spanish-heritage Mexicans. Where did they all go?

was that my students don't live in a 24/7 Spanish-speaking world. Too often, I ended up resorting to English-language resources.

The website contained a wealth of information, and I wanted to give students the autonomy to explore what they found interesting. So the only instruction I gave them was to spend time reading and writing down what they found interesting. At the end of the unit, students would need their notes for their essays, but I didn't bother them with that detail for the moment. Instead, I gave them time to let their curiosity lead the exploration. As they clicked from page to page, I wandered around the room, checking on their notes and gathering snippets of their conversations.

"Whaat? The fandango is African?" I heard Eduardo exclaim.

"Eduardo, don't forget to write down what you are learning," I reminded him.

"*Estamos hablando de cómo el son jarocho tiene raíces africanas*" (We're talking about how *son jarocho* music has African roots), Evelyn commented to me as I walked by.

"*Maestra*, what is this about the 'third root'?"

"*Bueno*, Alex, read it and you will see. That part is important, so write it down."

Alex jotted notes on *la tercera raíz* (the third root). In 1992, as part of the 500th anniversary of the arrival of the Spanish in the Americas, the Mexican government officially acknowledged that African culture in the country represented *la tercera raíz* of Mexican culture, along with Spanish and Indigenous peoples. Since then, many Mexicans (especially those living on the west coast) have reconnected with their African heritage through dance, theater, radio, and political mobilizations.

Daniel called out to me. "I'm interested in this guy Vicente Guerrero. He was a hero in the war for independence, and it says here that he was Mexico's first Afro-Mexican president—the Barack Obama of 1829!"

I smiled. My students were already rethinking some of their ideas about Mexico. They were collecting stories of things that they had taken for granted as "just Mexican" and uncovering a more complex version of those stories.

By the time we had finished our first lesson exploring the Afropop site, students were hooked and energy was high. It was a good launching pad for our next question: If Afro-Mexicans have been living in Mexico since the days of the slave trade, why wasn't anyone talking about it?

"The Black Grandma in the Closet"

If the goal for the first part of the unit was to challenge students to rethink Mexican identity, and specifically Black Mexican identity, parts two and three were about discovering the historical and political forces that led to the invisibility of Afro-Mexican roots, and the activism and resistance that occurred throughout history and into the present.

I decided to show an episode from the Henry Louis Gates series *Black in Latin America* titled "Mexico & Peru: The Black Grandma in the Closet." Gates documents the ways that Black Mexicans were oppressed and made invisible, and how they have fought against Spanish oppressors and modern-day discrimination. I gave students lots of freedom to explore the Afropop Worldwide website however they wished, but I took a different tack for this next activity.

"Mexico & Peru: The Black Grandma in the Closet" is full of information about why we don't often hear about Black Mexicans. Before students viewed the documentary, I created a note-taking template so they could work together to capture the relevant facts. I listed important names, dates, and ideas in the order they were mentioned in the documentary. Then I chose four items for each 15-minute segment of the documentary. I made a copy of the note-taking template for each student, and had students get into groups of four.

"*OK, clase, vamos a ver el documental,*" I said, moving about the room. "We've already discussed some ideas about why no one knew the African roots of the fandango, or that Mexico had important military and political leaders who were Black. Josué suggested maybe all the Afro-Mexicans left the country, and Lalo talked about interracial relationships. Now we're going to dig a little deeper and see what Mexican anthropologists and historians have to say. You can see on your papers that important terms from the documentary are divided into sets of four. Each person in your group will be responsible for taking notes on just one term. When we've heard all four terms, I'll stop the documentary and as a group you will write one summary that includes all of those terms. OK?"

Students decided how they wanted to divide the terms and ideas among themselves, and I hit *play*. By the time we finished, I was happy with my decision to have students share the work of understanding and synthesizing the reasons behind Mexico's hidden Black culture. They collectively gathered and analyzed more information than students working on their own. And, because each person was responsible for one term per video segment, everyone had a responsibility to listen and share.

In one of their summaries, Lalo, Ana Maria, Itzel, and Evelyn wrote: "Tlacotepec is the city where the documentary opens. They say that if the 'one-drop' rule were applied to this city, everyone would be Black! The fandango uses Spanish instruments but played in an African way. The documentary says that slaves were singing 'La Bamba' in 1683!!! (So, does that mean that Ritchie Valens broke copyright? LOL)"

Marta, Alex, Daniel, and Miguel wrote: "Vicente Guerrero, Mexico's first Black president (1830), said, 'The country comes first,' a common saying in Mexico. After that, they abolished racial categories on birth certificates and other official documents."

This act, though progressive in purpose, contributed to the systematic erasure of Afro-Mexican history. The simple act of eliminating racial categories did not eliminate racism, and some present-day activists are seeking to reinstate racial categories into the Mexican census so that Afro-Mexicans can benefit from public policy. Miguel in particular was uncomfortable with the idea that a reintroduction of racial categories would fix the problem: "Father Hidalgo started our nation's independence with *El Grito de Dolores*, and he believed that we should not have racial categories. Activists like Israel Reyes, a teacher in Mexico, are trying to boost Afro-Mexican pride with their radio shows and activism to reintroduce racial categories. I think the radio show is a good idea, but new census categories will divide the people."

Eduardo's group focused on the story of Sagrario Cruz Carretero, professor of anthropology at the University of Veracruz. Cruz Carretero did not discover that she was Black until she was 19, when she traveled to Cuba and started recognizing herself and her family in the faces of the Cubans she met. The foods they made were the same foods—like fufú—that Cruz Carretero's grandma made, foods that can be traced back to Africa. When she returned to Mexico, she asked her grandfather why he had not told the family that they were Black. Her grandfather responded that they were not Black, they were *moreno*. According to Cruz Carretero, "This happens in most families—you hide the Black grandma in the closet."

Camila, Sofia, and Adán wrote: "Yanga is a town and a man. The town of Yanga is named after a slave who freed himself and lived for 30 years in the mountains fighting off the Spanish and defending his community. If the TV show *Survivor* had existed in the 16th century, he definitely would have won. And he did win against the **Students were asking important questions about race and what it means to be Mexican.**

Spanish—in 1609 they finally grew tired of fighting him and gave him the land. Yanga became one of the first towns in Mexico where Blacks could live free!"

Lalo snapped to attention when the film started talking about interracial relationships. The Catholic Church allowed marriage between races and so, from early on, Africans, Europeans, and Indigenous Mexicans mixed bloodlines. The Spanish already had a heritage that was more open to interracial relationships than other European countries, thanks to the centuries-long dominance of the Moors in Spain, so those relationships weren't as taboo as they were in the United States. Interracial marriages continued over time, to the point that one's African roots could only be heard in the dropped *d* from the word *helado*, a certain hue in skin tone, or the taste of an old family recipe. "See?" Lalo said with a smug smile. "I told you they were making babies."

Pros and Cons of Racial Statistics

By now, I had a degree of guilt about the resources I was providing them with—our two main sources had been in English. I needed to get my students back to reading in Spanish. So next we looked at *Afrodescendientes en México*, by the Consejo Nacional para Prevenir la Discriminación (National Council for Preventing Discrimination).

This document describes the problems, including the difficulties connected with the lack of racial statistics in Mexico, and offers concrete actions that both the Mexican government and its citizens should take to counteract this history of invisibility and oppression. Specifically, it calls for more research and a way to document the numbers and experiences of Afro-Mexicans.

Once again, I had a resource full of important information that I wanted my students to capture. Therefore, I annotated the text before making copies for my students. I starred main ideas, wrote definitions and synonyms for high-level vocabulary in the margins, and added footnotes with questions for students to consider. I noted a few questions that I had while reading. Some students did not need this extra support, and for easier texts students would do this annotation work themselves. However, because this was a complicated government document, I wanted to make sure all my students had access to the information presented.

Then I divided the class into heterogeneous groups so that students could help each other as needed. I told them that each group would decide who would be the reader, summarizer, director, and question-asker.

"One person is going to read aloud," I explained. "Another is going to write a summary of the main ideas from the text. The director is in charge of watching the clock, and also making sure that everyone speaks and no one dominates the conversation. The question-asker will jot down questions that the group has while reading."

Students got busy reading and writing, and I walked around the classroom, listening in and answering questions.

Questions such as *"Maestra, ¿qué es el racismo interiorizado?"* (Teacher, what's internalized racism?) were an indication that students were being exposed to a broader understanding of systems of oppression.

The text did not have hard data in the form of statistics on achievement gaps, poverty, or access to services—how could they provide this when the Mexican census had no system for identifying those of African heritage? But the authors described the myriad ways that the ideology of racial superiority has spread into the language, education policy, and throughout Mexican society.

Mateo focused in on *Memín Pinguín*, a popular cartoon from the 1940s based on racist caricatures that could be compared to Sambo in the United States. The text reinforced information we had learned in the documentary. Mateo took notes on how the government had issued a commemorative stamp featuring *Memín Pinguín* in 2005 that had caused such an international stir that Jesse Jackson flew to Mexico

City to speak with then-President Vicente Fox. Mateo told me that he wanted to write his final essay on this character.

Sofia and Camila were curious about the experience of Afro-Mexican women. They began to write down questions about how basing beauty standards on *lo blanco* (whiteness) affected women. They were also struck by the information that Afro-Mexican women are the most vulnerable targets of racism in Mexico, to the point that many of them leave the country, primarily heading to the United States.

Miguel called me over. "They're saying that they want to reintroduce racial categories in Mexico. I think that will divide the people more." He shook his head. Miguel, a senior, had often encouraged the juniors to step out of their comfort zone and hang out with students of other races at our school. I admired his willingness to challenge his peers and the text. I also wanted him to consider multiple perspectives before solidifying his view.

"Miguel, I hear your concern about dividing people, but can you think of any ways that Black Mexicans would benefit from reintroducing racial categories? What does the article say?" Miguel returned to the text, searching the document for answers.

My students were asking important questions, and it was time for them to give voice to what they were learning. For their end-of-unit project, I asked them to write an explanatory essay, either highlighting an unsung Afro-Mexican historical figure or explaining how African ancestry has shaped the Mexico of today.

Eyes Wide Open

Before this unit, my students had little to no knowledge of the African presence in Mexico. By the end of the unit, students were asking important questions about race, defining racial categories, and what it really means to be Mexican. Many walked away with a different view of their family's country of origin, one whose history and cultural identity was infinitely more complex than they had previously imagined. Their final essays demonstrated that we had met our goals of rethinking identity, identifying ways that Afro-Mexicans helped shape the nation, and reflecting on the present-day implications of Afro-Mexican invisibility.

"Many people do not know the history of Afro-Mexicans," wrote Ana Maria, "but it's thanks to them that we have various walls, cities, food, and dance. It may be that you have to look with eyes wide open to see it, but their presence is there for those who wish to see it."

Miguel's paper was a response to the position of *Afrodescendientes en México*. He decided to stay true to his original stance: "I fear that reintroducing racial categories in Mexico will have the opposite effect of what they want. I don't think that they should divide people in this way because they may start to divide the country."

As sometimes happens, this six-week unit evolved into about 10 weeks of learning. There were a few things that I ended up cutting, and others that I will do differently next time. For example, I'll build in more time for small-group discussion, and plan for students to struggle with the questions present-day activists are facing: how to undo the legacy of invisibility and oppression. In addition, I will provide some more journaling time for students to self-reflect. For high school students deep in the throes of identity development, extra time for journaling may have allowed them to question assumptions they had about themselves, and the groups they identify with.

There is more work to do—more counter-stories to offer, more questions to ask, Afro-Latina/o history from countries other than Mexico to explore. Yet, my students began to understand that national identity is something we construct together and that, just like in our classroom, everyone has something to contribute. ☼

Michelle Nicola currently teaches middle school language arts and Spanish at Bridger School in Portland, Oregon. She was one of five 2014 recipients of the Excellence in Education Award from Teaching Tolerance. Student names have been changed.

Resources

Afropop Worldwide. 2013. "La Bamba: The Afro-Mexican Story." Public Radio International. afropop.org.

Velázquez, María Elisa, and Gabriela Iturralde Nieto. 2012. *Afrodescendientes en México: Una historia de silencio y discriminación.* Consejo Nacional para Prevenir la Discriminación.

"Mexico & Peru: The Black Grandma in the Closet." Dir. Ilana Trachtman. 2011. PBS. Available on YouTube: youtube.com/watch?v=6uol3pPmdVE

Chapter 3

WELCOMING HOME LANGUAGES

RICARDO LEVINS MORALES

Introduction

I n Tanzania, a visit—to a store, a friend or stranger's house, a classroom, a market stand, or the school office—starts with the host or owner's enthusiastic greeting, and usually goes something like this:

Host: "Karibu" (Welcome)
Visitor: "Asante" (Thank you)
Host: "Karibu *sana*" (*Very* welcome)
Visitor: "Asante sana" (Thank you very much)

The conversation in Swahili continues, but it is the warm welcome that frames the interaction.

Welcoming evokes images of open doors, outstretched arms, guiding signs, a prepared meal, an extra place set at the table, an unexpected invitation to enter a new space. In non-bilingual classrooms where the instruction is in English, students' home languages are welcomed when a teacher takes the time to incorporate a few home language words into the classroom routine, when a student is invited to write a poem or journal response in their home language, when students' cultures and ways of speaking become a part of the curriculum. But, as Linda Christensen points out in "Uncovering the Legacy of Language and Power," welcoming students' home languages also means challenging English dominance. When our schools or classrooms are de facto English-only spaces, we need to create curriculum and build spaces that urge students to question and critique the hegemony of Standard English.

The authors in this chapter welcome home languages in a variety of ways—asking a parent to record herself reading a children's book in Marshallese, teaching the grammar and syntax of Ebonics, having students translate Shakespeare into Jamaican Patwa, creating dual-language opportunities for high school students, facilitating a space where Latina/o middle school students are mentored by MECHA college students and are free to express themselves in either English or Spanish.

As we explicitly honor languages other than English, we need to question and critique the status of English and give our students the tools to do so as well. They deserve to know that their home languages are *karibu sana* in our classrooms and schools. ☼

Welcoming Kalenna

Making our students feel at home

BY LAURA LINDA NEGRI-POOL

When I was a child, our home was filled with the sounds of Spanish, mariachi music, and boisterous conversations. At home, my Nana cooked enchiladas, menudo, and tamales. During family celebrations we broke piñatas, danced, and hung *papel picado*. I was surrounded by six siblings, multiple cousins, *tíos*, and *tías*. My home was filled with light, color, art, texture, and love.

My school, in contrast, was drab, white, and unappealing.

I recall only one time when my Mexican American identity was validated during elementary school. When I was in 3rd grade, my mother organized a *Cinco de Mayo* event at our school.

My father, siblings, and I cut out the *papel picado*, made the piñatas, formed the papier-mâché sculptures, and created paper flowers. Seeing my culture represented at school made me feel at home there for the first time.

I want my students to have more than one memory like that. I've worked in early childhood education for more than 30 years, and I feel passionate about embracing families from nondominant cultures into the early childhood communities I work in.

As the result of a personal process of identity and cultural reclamation, I came to understand how my personal experiences influence this passion.

My experiences inspired me to find ways to make sure that other marginalized children and families see themselves and their lives reflected in our classroom community.

Welcoming Kalenna

One fall day, I held an open house to welcome the new children and families enrolled in our preschool program. When Kalenna entered our classroom, I immediately felt an affinity with her. Kalenna's dark, thick hair and chocolate brown skin set her apart from most of the other 14 children in the class. Our community college lab school served predominantly European American children whose parents were taking classes. Her mother, Diane, spoke with an accent that made me wonder if English was not her first language.

"Do you speak a language in addition to English?" I asked Diane.

She smiled and answered, "Marshallese." Our journey had begun.

I sensed Diane's feeling of relief and surprise when I asked about her language history. I knew from my own experiences what it was like to not be seen, to be treated with a question mark. I wondered how many times others had asked her, as they had me, "what she was" rather than respectfully and authentically inquiring about her. My question was an open and honest acknowledgment of her differences.

Over the next few months, I tried to infuse our classroom environment with the sounds, textures, and objects that surrounded Kalenna in her home.

First I had to learn about the Marshall Islands. I had no idea where or what the Marshall Islands were, let alone anything about the Marshallese language and culture. I started with a map, where I learned that the Marshall Islands are a collection of 1,225 islands and islets in Micronesia. From the internet, I learned about the ongoing struggle of the Marshallese people to maintain their language and culture given their history of domination by Germany, Japan, and the United States. Following World War II, the United States conducted nuclear tests on the islands—including Bikini Atoll. These tests exposed many inhabitants to high radiation levels.

> I wondered how many times others had asked Diane, as they had me, "what she was" rather than respectfully and authentically inquiring about her.

After gaining some knowledge of her origins, I was able to begin to speak more confidently with Kalenna's family. I began regular conversations with Diane, each of us sharing information about our family and culture.

I discovered a website with Marshallese music and language. I printed a list of simple words and phrases and brought it to the classroom. I showed Diane what I had found and asked her to translate a song into Marshallese. Each morning the children, student teachers, and I sang a greeting song utilizing the home languages of the children and adults present in our classroom, including Spanish, Chinese, and Afrikaans. Diane taught us how to sing our good morning song in Marshallese.

I asked Diane if she could help me locate items from the Marshall Islands that the students might use in the classroom. She brought in a hat, a basket, clothing, a hairpiece, and a necklace. We incorporated them into our dramatic play area. The children frequently wore the hairpiece and hat. The large basket with shells held an assortment of classroom materials throughout the year. The children loved wearing the seashell necklaces. They knew that the items belonged to Kalenna and treated them with care and respect.

I invited Diane to make an audio recording of the book *No, David!*, by David Shannon, in Marshallese. The book was a favorite in our classroom due in part to the artwork, the simple text, and message of unconditional love. In the story, a little boy repeatedly gets in trouble for typical misbehaviors, including making a mess, overfilling the bathtub, and playing with a baseball in the house. The story concludes with the mother expressing her enduring love for him despite his antics. The children already could "read" each page in English. I partnered Diane with a mom who spoke Spanish. Together they recorded the book in their home languages. The mothers joined us at circle time to read the book aloud and to allow us to hear their voices on tape. From then on, Kalenna listened frequently to her mother's voice reading *Jaab, David!*

Bridging Cultures

One of my best memories of Kalenna is of the day she brought some of "her music" to class. I had invited her mother to share music that they listened to at home, in part because I was having difficulty locating Marshallese music.

Kalenna and I began to listen. At first we listened to it as background music while the students played. Later Kalenna went to the large rug area. I began to move to the music and told her how much I liked it. Then she began to dance. As she danced, a magnificent smile appeared on her face. She clearly had a specific routine that she'd learned for that particular song. I began to mimic her movements. When the song ended, I rewound the tape and started it again. She began to teach me the moves. We laughed and moved, reveling in our intimate shared enjoyment. The other children watched, pausing in their own play to see our scene unfold. Later, some came and joined us. Kalenna's delight was evident as our dance continued. I had finally touched her where she lived.

A few years ago a former teacher of mine told me that he always pictured my face while reading of a young Mexican woman in the novel *The Pearl*. I was shocked. I never knew that he saw me as Mexican, that he associated me with the language, the culture, and the stories. I was touched, yet felt a loss. The loss was about not having my identity validated some 25 years earlier.

How I yearned to have a teacher who could see me, hear me, and dance with me.

Tips for Teachers

My own experiences of marginalization, invisibility, and outsider status propelled me to find ways to implement curricula and environments that embrace, validate, and honor the life experiences and cultures of children like me—those who are not white and not surrounded solely by the English language. Here are some simple ways teachers can help young students from marginalized communities to feel, hear, and see themselves reflected in the classroom:

- Spend time talking with and building relationships with parents and other family members.
- Learn to greet children in their home languages.
- Pronounce children's names correctly and with as much of an authentic sound as you can.
- Use fabrics and materials familiar to the children in the classroom for tablecloths, wall hangings, containers, and clothing.
- Play music from the children's culture during play periods, rest time, and meal time.
- Invite parents to cook family recipes with the class.
- Take and post pictures of the children and their families and their homes in the classroom. ☼

Laura Linda Negri-Pool was an early education teacher for many years. She currently works as the education coordinator at the Nike Child Development Program.

Uncovering the Legacy of Language and Power

BY LINDA CHRISTENSEN

(Above) Chiricahua Apaches as they looked upon their arrival at the Carlisle Indian School, an institution dedicated to inducing Native Americans to abandon their traditional ways. (Right) Chiricahua Apaches after four months at the Carlisle Indian School.

"You will never teach a child a new language by scorning and ridiculing and forcibly erasing his first language." —June Jordan

Lamont's sketch was stick figure simple: A red schoolhouse with Brown students entering one door and exiting as white students at the other end of the building. Kahlia's illustration depicted a more elaborate metaphor: She drew a map of Africa hanging from a tree; tightly closed red lips cover the heart of the map. A U.S. map flies over the tree, and sentences swirl around it: "I cannot speak my language. My identity is gone. My African language is gone. The language I grew up with has been taken from me."

Over the years, students have drawn mouths sewn shut, tongues nailed to the ground, languages squeezed out or buried under stacks of English grammar books, a Spanish voice box removed, graveyards for Indigenous languages, a mouth rubbed out by an eraser with the word English written across the top, and language trees with the withered leaves of Korean, Spanish, Russian, African languages dropping off while the red, ripe English fruit flourished. As my students' drawings depicted over and over in a variety of ways, schools and societies erase language and culture.

> **According to my students who study the linguistic history of the colonized, too often the job of the teacher is to "whitewash" students of color or students who are linguistically diverse.**

English-only laws in many states have banned Spanish and other languages from some classrooms. Ebonics was used as fodder for racist jokes after the Oakland School Board proposed teaching Ebonics. Native American languages were decimated in boarding schools during a time when "Kill the Indian, Save the Man" directives gave straightforward instructions to teachers. Although I intentionally invite and acknowledge the variety of languages and voices from our community into the classroom, I learned this wasn't enough. Without examining the legacy of language supremacy, I maintain the old world order because I haven't explored why Standard English is the standard and how it came to power, and how that power is wielded to make some people feel welcome and others feel like outsiders.

After years of teaching and tinkering with this language unit, I finally realized that I needed to create a curriculum on language and power that examined the colonial roots of linguistic genocide and analyzed how schools continue to perpetuate the myths of inferiority or invisibility of some languages. (See "Putting Out the Linguistic Welcome Mat" on p. 113 for more details on the development of this curriculum.)

Linguistic Genocide Through Colonization

Max Weinreich, a Yiddish linguist, wrote, "A language is a dialect with an army and a navy." In other words, it's about power. For students to understand how some languages came to be dominant, they need to understand how and why Indigenous languages were wiped out or marginalized. According to the Living Tongues Institute for Endangered Languages, more than half of the world's languages have become extinct in the last 500 years. In fact, David Harrison, a linguistics professor at Swarthmore, says, "the pace of their global extinction exceeds the pace of species extinction." Students need to understand how this invisible legacy that privileges some languages—and people—and excludes or decimates others continues to affect us today.

Teaching about language and power is huge and complex and messy because language policies and colonial practices played out in different ways across the globe. In some places, the languages died with the people who spoke them, as colonial powers took both the land and the lives of the people they "encountered." In some instances, Indigenous groups were pitted against each other. In many places, colonists renamed every nook and cranny, banned native languages, and created governments, schools, and economic systems using the language of the colonizer's home country.

Today, language is still contested territory in many parts of the world. Because most political, educational, and commercial interactions take place in the language of the colonizer or the primary language, many Indigenous languages have become marginalized or extinct. Parents are frequently forced to choose between teaching their children in their home language or pushing them to study the language of the dominant social groups. In a workshop in San Francisco, a teacher talked about how the educational and economic necessity of learning English pressed her to put her Vietnamese language aside. "I didn't feel like I had a choice." Ultimately, this forced choice causes a disconnect between generations of language speakers and a loss of family ties, traditions, and cultural memory.

Because of time, my classes didn't study each language situation in depth; instead, we looked for patterns across the stories. In many places, the colonizers taught people shame about their "primitive" or "backward" language and cultural practices. As Ngugi wa Thiong'o, a Kenyan teacher, novelist, essayist, and playwright, wrote in his essay "The Language of African Literature":

> The real aim of colonialism was to control the people's wealth . . . [but] economic and political control can never be complete or effective without mental control. To control a people's culture is to control their tools of self-definition in relationship to others. For colonialism, this involved two aspects of the same process: the destruction or the deliberate undervaluing of a people's culture, their art, dances, religions, history, geography, education, orature, and literature, and the conscious elevation of the language of the colonizer. The domination of a people's language by the languages of the colonizing nations was crucial to the domination of the mental universe of the colonizers.

Ngugi stopped writing in English and started writing in his native tongue—Kikuyu—as a protest against the devaluing of his mother tongue, but also as a way to revive and celebrate literature in his language. This "conscious elevation of the language of the colonizer" and the parallel domination of the "mental universe" that Ngugi wa Thiong'o describes is echoed in stories from Kenya to Ireland to Australia to the United States.

The "domination of the mental universe of the colonizers" continues today in the daily interactions that "non-standard" language speakers must negotiate when they enter the halls of power—schools, banks, government and employment offices. Whether it's the marking down of essays because of "poor" grammar or the conscious or unconscious way that lack of linguistic dexterity marks a speaker or writer as "unfit" for a position—a job, a college, or a scholarship—language inequality still exists. The power of the standard language is so pervasive and so invisible that students need to uncover what they take for granted and internalize as personal failure. But I also need to teach them how and why some languages have power and others don't.

The Linguistic Tea Party

To familiarize students with the context and characters they will meet during our journey into language and colonialism, I wrote a tea party to introduce the personalities and events they will encounter as we read stories or watch movie clips. The roles also alert students to the patterns that emerge in the unit—loss of languages, humiliation, shame, and beatings, as well as the heroic efforts to save dying tongues. I tried to make the tea party entice students into curiosity about language study—admittedly, not a subject that most students initially rate as the No. 1 topic they want to learn about.

In constructing the tea party roles, I write in first person, so students feel more comfortable introducing themselves as the person. Bud Lane's role, for example, gives students a sense of the urgency around the issue of language preservation. Although Oregon was once among the most linguistically diverse places on earth, it is now infamous as a language-death hot spot according to the Living Tongues Institute for Endangered Languages, because there are few remaining first speakers—people who learned the language as children:

> Some people already count my language as dead. I speak Oregon Coastal Athabaskan. At 50, I am one of the youngest speakers of my language. Here in the Northwest, we are a hot spot for language extinction. I'm hoping to change that. You see, I think that the language and the people are the same. I didn't grow up speaking my language either, but I found an elder Siletz woman who knew the words, but who never spoke them in public. She'd been taught shame of her native tongue by white society. But Nellie Orton found her voice and taught me my language. Now I teach our language at the local school, so that our children can save our native tongue.

Each character can answer at least one question on the tea party question sheet. For example, Lane's character answers the question "Find someone who started or joined an organization to preserve his or her language. Who is the person? Why did the individual decide to take this action?" Most of the tea party questions can be answered by more than one person.

Students meet a spectrum of characters, including Distinguished Professor Geneva "Dr. G." Smitherman; Irish poet Gearóid Mac Lochlainn; Hawaiian writer Lois-Ann Yamanaka; Carmen Lomas Garza, a Mexican American artist; Hector Pieterson, a 12-year-old boy killed in the Soweto Uprising; and Neville Alexander, a South

African linguist who worked to restore mother tongue literacy in Africa.

After I distribute a role and tea party questions to students, I ask them to read the role and underline key facts that their classmates need to know: Where is this person from? What is his or her experience with language? I also tell them to highlight any piece of information they find particularly compelling. Then I tell them to turn the role sheet over and write those key facts on the back. Students are more likely to remember the facts if they read them, write them, and recite them.

After the tea party, I ask students to write a paragraph about what they learned about language and power and then we talk. During our post-tea party discussion, Deandre said, "[The society] tried to take people from what they were raised to believe in, and I don't believe that was right." When I pressed him, "Who was one person you met who had something taken away from them?" he talked about his own character, Joe Suina. He said, "Well, myself. My name is Joe Suina. I am currently a professor of curriculum and instruction at University of New Mexico. I was punished at school for speaking my language, and they tried to teach me that my language was not right. They tried to turn me into what was the dominant culture. They tried to make me believe what everyone else believed in."

Reading the School Stories: Finding the Patterns

After the tea party, we dive into the readings and movies. I want to saturate students in the stories—memoirs and fiction—about language. We begin by examining five memoirs about language and boarding schools—two from the United States, one from Australia, one from Kenya, and one from Canada. These are short two- or three-page excerpts from longer pieces and two video clips. In addition to reacting to each piece about language and boarding schools through writing and discussion, students keep track of each person's experiences on a story retrieval chart, including a description of the race and class of each main character. I tell them to record who is forced or encouraged to change their language, who doesn't have to change, and who forces the change. Because the unit is long, the charts help them collect evidence over the span of the unit, so they can quickly go back and retrieve evidence for the culminating essay or project.

I begin by examining what happened to Native Americans. The video *In the White Man's Image*, a documentary about Native American boarding schools, shows the Carlisle Indian Industrial School established by Captain Richard Pratt, who attempted to assimilate Native American children into white society from 1879 to 1918. Today Pratt's mission is widely viewed as cultural genocide. Pratt's motto was "Kill the Indian, Save the Man." In order to "kill the Indian," he punished children for practicing their religion and speaking their language. He renamed them, cut their hair, and took away their clothes. Native students resisted Pratt's attempts to "deculturize" them, as my student Harold put it. Many died, others ran away, few graduated, and ultimately, most maintained their Native American identity. Pratt used before and after photographs of the students to sell white audiences on the success of his school.

In the White Man's Image portrays the boarding school system at work, but doesn't focus as much on the individual stories, except for Ernest White Thunder, who resisted the campaign to take away his culture by running away from the school and refusing to eat. Ultimately, he died. His resistance was a touchstone for some students who referenced White Thunder and later wanted to review his section of the video for their essays and projects. Dee said, "If you kill the Indian culture, you might as well kill the Indian because nothing about him is really him."

Joe Suina's essay "And Then I Went to School: Memories of a Pueblo Childhood" describes his experiences at a boarding school where he learned to be ashamed of his language and his home:

> My language, too, was questioned right from the beginning of my school career. "Leave your Indian at home!" was like a school trademark. Speaking it accidentally or otherwise was punishable by a dirty look or a whack with a ruler. This reprimand was for speaking the language of my people that meant so much to me. It was the language of my grandmother. . . . [I]t was difficult for me to comprehend why I had to part with my language. . . . I understood that everything that I had, and was part of, was not nearly as good as the whiteman's. School was determined to undo me in everything from my sheepskin bedding to the dances and ceremonies that I had learned to have faith in and cherish.

Because the video clips are only about 15 to 20 minutes each and the stories are short, we mostly read them aloud in class together, filling in the chart individually, then discussing each piece as a class, as we move through the stories. The boarding school stories, videos, and discussion take about a week. As we read one story after another, students see the pattern of punishment and shame that permeate the stories. When I asked, "What do these stories have in common? What do you learn about language and power?" Josh said, "When people weren't allowed to speak their own language, and when they were punished for speaking it, people felt inferior and stupid. It crumbled the community."

I need to teach students how and why some languages have power and others don't.

After learning about language policies in Native American boarding schools, we look at similar practices in Australia and Africa. Molly Craig's experiences in Australia, recounted in the film *Rabbit-Proof Fence*, parallel Suina's experience in Native American boarding schools. Molly was part of Australia's "stolen generation" of mixed-race children who were taken from the "bad influence" of their families and isolated in boarding schools where they were trained as maids and day laborers—another forced assimilation into the white society. Part of the process of merging "half-caste" children into white culture was separating them from their language as well as their religion. After watching a video clip from *Rabbit-Proof Fence*, I asked students to respond to Molly's story in an interior monologue or poem. Throughout these stories, students connected with loss of culture and heritage, but they also connected with Molly's resistance. In the following poem, Jennifer Overman takes on Molly's point of view, expressing her resistance:

> Write that I was a half-caste,
> taken away from my family and my home to be cleansed of my aboriginality,
> to be a slave.
> When you speak of me,
> Say that I refused to be erased,
> That my blood would stay the same,
> That I would not serve my other half.

Maria succinctly captured this resistance to "whitewashing" in her piece from Molly's perspective when she wrote simply, "You can never wipe the brown from my skin."

When I asked students to make connections between the stories, they pointed out both the enforced changes as well as the changes that students in the readings adopted to avoid embarrassment. Although students initially laughed at Denzell Weekly's comparison of the boarding schools to the movie *Men in Black*, ultimately, they agreed with his explanation. He said, "This is like the movie *Men in Black*. For anyone who's seen *Men in Black*, there is a flashlight. They're looking and they're flashing and they erase all of your memory. They tried to come in and just brainwash, basically take away their language and their culture." When students become passionate about a subject, this is what they do: search their own experiences to make original, unusual connections to the curriculum.

A number of students wrote their essays about assimilation. While some students merely summarized the series of events, Dennise Mofidi focused on children who resisted assimilation. "The children who did not fear punishment were the ones who fought for their culture. They were the ones who suffered horrible consequences, including the loss of their lives." She went on to relate this to her relationship with her grandmother and Farsi:

> Today assimilation is still happening. Children go to school and see that everyone else is speaking English and feel different if they are the only one who does not speak English at home. My family came here from Iran and speaks both English and Farsi. My mother and father taught me to speak Farsi, and I do at home and when I'm with my family. My younger brothers, on the other hand, do not speak Farsi. I asked them why and they told me, "I don't want people to know that I speak another language or ask me how to say a word in Farsi because then they will want me to talk in Farsi all the time and we live in America, not Iran." I couldn't believe that

being different at school was so hard that they would not want to be able to talk to their family. . . . My grandmother and I talk all the time in Farsi. She tells me about Iran and what it is like there. She also shares stories of life when she was younger. I love talking with my grandmother and couldn't imagine being like my brothers and needing someone to translate.

In his final essay, Daunte Paschal wrote about Carmen Lomas Garza's experience in school. "In 'A Piece of My Heart/Pedacito de mi corazón,' Garza wrote about her life growing up as a full-blooded Chicana in a predominantly white school. . . . Because of those girls at her school making fun of her, she started to feel ashamed about her food that her mother had made. Garza was verbally assaulted, and she eventually felt as if she was born in the wrong race and wrong culture. Assimilation will do that to you."

Metaphorical Drawings

Once we've read the memoirs and watched the video clips about boarding schools in the United States, Australia, and other countries, I bring boxes of crayons and colored pencils and large pieces of blank paper to class. I ask students to create a visual representation of language and power, telling them, "Don't worry about your drawing ability. I'm looking for the quality of your ideas, your ability to work with all of that information you've collected over the last quarter."

After the initial excitement of using crayons in a high school class and the groans that they can't think of a single metaphor, the ideas start rolling. We begin the conversation by recalling the definition of a metaphor and brainstorming a few examples. I walk a fine line of giving them enough models to jump-start their imagination, but not so many that my ideas crowd out theirs. I show them a couple of drawings from former students, including stick figure sketches, so they can see a range of possibilities, but also because I don't want their drawing skills to get in the way of their ideas. When they complete the drawing, they write a paragraph explaining their metaphor.

Students' metaphorical drawings are evocative. Michael Moser drew three boxes, each locked with a padlock. The writing on the first one said "Freedom of thinking, knowledge, freedom of speech"; the second box had a heart with the words "family, name, culture, homeland" on the exterior; the third one said "religion, soul, language, culture." Michael wrote:

> To assimilate someone you take away their mind, heart, and soul. Their mind is the right to think and their freedom to speak their own language. To take away their heart is to take the things they love, like their family and their home. The third is how the boarding school kids were taken from their families and forced to adopt a new religion and new language. And to take someone's soul is to take everything they stand for.

Kirkland Allen drew a picture of a dark-skinned woman with her black hair pulled straight by a comb with the word "school" across it. On the side of his picture, he drew a series of cans and jars labeled "Proper English Magic Grease," "Plan B Insurance," and "After School Bands." The title on his drawing read "If You Can't Achieve It, Weave It." He wrote:

> In this piece a nappy-headed woman is getting her hair done. Proper English Grease moisturizing it, a school comb working with the grease, forming it into a white version. After-school rubber bands hold the hair together, giving her the thought that going back is bad.

Deandre, a talented rapper, excelled in assignments that allowed him to bring his gifts of rapping to bear on the content of a unit. He drew a stage with two flags, a U.S. flag and a flag with "Africa" written on it. A microphone stood in front of each flag. The U.S. mic was plugged in. A hand unplugged the African microphone. He said, "It's about unplugging our voice."

When students shared their drawings with the class, I pushed them to fuller explanations. "What's that tell us about language and power? What's your explanation? What does your drawing illustrate?"

Although the student drawings demonstrated understanding, their discussion of their drawings bordered on generalizations, littered with indeterminate pronouns. For example, a number of students said, "They beat students for speaking their language." I pushed them to identify who "they" were, to name names. "Who beat them? Where did this happen? Locate it." At one point, I said, "Let's name them together. Whose languages and cultures were taken away? Who took them away? You need to be specific." This is an important part of the activity because too often students describe or recite events, but in the past I've failed to

Dee said, "If you kill the Indian culture, you might as well kill the Indian because nothing about him is really him."

push them to analyze their drawings. Students know things in their bones, and the metaphorical drawings tap this "bone knowledge." But without pressing kids to precisely articulate their analysis, the brilliant insights revealed in their drawings may stay in their bones.

Although the drawings might seem like a day of child's play—and we do have fun on those days—they also serve a critical purpose: They help students rehearse the creation of a thesis and support for their upcoming essay. Even if the students do not use the drawings and metaphors in their language essays, creating an image that summarizes their understanding about language pushes them to think more deeply about the patterns they saw across the readings and to start articulating those understandings as they draw, as they write their explanation, and as they present their piece to their peers. This class talk about the topic, the use of specific and varied examples, the building on each other's ideas, helps them later as they construct their essays.

Language Restoration

Because of time limitations, we never spend as much time on the language restoration movement as it deserves. But after all of the death and destruction, I want students to become familiar with some of the current work across the globe to save Indigenous languages. Students need to critique, but they also need to learn how to build and rebuild. The inspiring stories of language preservation from Ireland to Kenya to South Africa to Hawaii and the Oregon coast provide great models of how grassroots people—from grandmothers to youth activists—are creating language schools as well as lobbying for legislation to keep languages alive.

For example, Neville Alexander, the late director of the Project for the Study of Alternative Education in South Africa (PRAESA), created the National Language Project to bring "mother tongue" literacy back into the lives of African people across the continent. He recognized that because of colonization many people had become illiterate in two languages—their mother tongue and the colonial language. As the Language Plan of Africa states,

> Colonial conquest, imperialism, and globalization established a hierarchy of standard languages, which mirrors the power relations on the planet. The overall effect of this configuration has been to hasten the extinction of innumerable language varieties and to stigmatize and marginalize all but the most powerful languages.

PRAESA promotes a culture of reading and writing in African languages, and works with publishers to develop a market for African language writing and literature. It has also initiated programs with teachers to help develop materials and strategies to bring back mother tongue literacy in the schools.

In the United States, language activists, including Esther Martinez, pushed for legislation to keep the remaining 150 of the original Indigenous languages alive. The Esther Martinez Native American Languages Preservation Act, H.R. 4766, was passed in 2006. This legislation provides money to support Native American language immersion programs: language nests, survival schools, and language restoration programs. To bring the point home, we read our local paper's article, "Last of the Siletz Speakers," about Bud Lane's work to keep the Oregon Coastal Athabaskan language alive by teaching at Siletz High School. He recorded the elders in the community and developed a dictionary for the language. Now he teaches the language to students at Siletz High School and works with researchers at the Living Tongues Institute in Salem, Oregon, to preserve his language.

In retrospect, I should have spent more time on the incredibly exciting language preservation work, perhaps by assigning student groups different language projects to research and report on as part of the unit. Next time. ☼

Linda Christensen is the director of the Oregon Writing Project at Lewis & Clark College in Portland, Oregon, and a Rethinking Schools editor. Previously, she taught language arts in Portland Public Schools for 30 years. She is the author of Reading, Writing, and Rising Up: Teaching About Social Justice and the Power of the Written Word *and* Teaching for Joy and Justice.

Note from the editors: This is a shortened version of "Uncovering the Legacy of Language and Power," originally published as a chapter in *Teaching for Joy and Justice*, by Linda Christensen (Rethinking Schools, 2009). Materials from this unit, including the tea party roles and question sheet, the school stories, and the story retrieval chart, can be found online at rethinkingschools.org/rbe/materials or pp. 218–247 in *Teaching for Joy and Justice*.

References and Recommended Background Information

Anzaldúa, Gloria. 1987. "How to Tame a Wild Tongue." *Borderlands/La Frontera: The New Mestiza.* Spinsters/Aunt Lute.

Crawford, James. 1992. *Hold Your Tongue: Bilingualism and the Politics of "English Only."* Addison-Wesley Publishing.

Delpit, Lisa D., and Joanne Kilgour Dowdy. 2002. *The Skin that We Speak: Thoughts on Language and Culture in the Classroom.* The New Press.

Delpit, Lisa D., and Theresa Perry. 1998. *The Real Ebonics Debate: Power, Language, and the Education of African-American Children.* Beacon.

"In the White Man's Image." Dir. and writer Chris Lesiak. 1992. PBS: *The American Experience* [Television Series, Feb. 17 (Season 4, Episode 12)]. Available from WGBH Education Foundation.

Lippi-Green, Rosina. 1997. *English with an Accent: Language, Ideology, and Discrimination in the United States.* Routledge.

Martinez, Esther, Jacobs, Sue-Ellen, and Josephine Binford. 2004. *My Life in San Juan Pueblo.* University of Illinois Press.

Mac Lochlainn, Gearóid. 2002. *Stream of Tongues: Sruth Teangacha.* Cló Iar-Chonnacht.

Our Spirits Don't Speak English: Indian Boarding School. Dir. Chip Ritchie. 2008. Rich Heape Films. Available at richheape.com.

wa Thiong'o, Ngugi. 2003. *Consciousness and African Renaissance: South Africa in the Black Imagination.* Fourth Steve Biko Annual Lecture. Retrieved from ccs.ukzn.ac.za/files/NGUGI-BIKO.pdf.

Yamanaka, Lois-Ann. Undated. *The Politics of Pidgin.* Promotional material. Straus & Giroux.

Language Is a Human Right

An interview with Debbie Wei, veteran activist in the Asian American community

BY GRACE CORNELL GONZALES

In addition to her many years teaching English language learners and as a curriculum specialist, Debbie Wei is a founding member of Asian Americans United and the founding principal of Folk Arts-Cultural Treasures Charter School in Philadelphia. She is currently elementary school director at Crossroads School for Arts & Sciences in Santa Monica, California.

Grace Cornell Gonzales: Let's start by talking about your background as an educator.

Deborah Wei

Debbie Wei: I never envisioned myself as a teacher because I didn't have great school experiences. I fell into teaching by accident. I wanted to be a community organizer. In Philadelphia's Chinatown in the late 1970s, a lot of people were immigrants from Hong Kong and they spoke Cantonese. So I got a college fellowship to go live in Hong Kong for two years to learn Cantonese.

But this was right after the Vietnam War. When I returned to Philadelphia, there were many refugees from Vietnam, from Laos, from Cambodia. There were also some Haitians and Cubans. There was no longer a dominant language among immigrants in the communities where I was working and living, and I didn't speak any of their languages. But I could communicate with the kids because they were going to school and acquiring English. I thought, "Well, if this is the group that I'm going to be working with to try to change conditions in the community, why don't I become a teacher?"

I got certified through a program where you could work in a school and get your certification at the same time. I became an ESL (English as a second language) teacher and I fell in love with teaching. A few years later, the School District of Philadelphia published a pretty horrific diversity handbook. It included statements like "Puerto Ricans like to eat tacos." There was already an African American studies department within the district, so the Latina/o and Asian communities organized to demand that the district hire a multicultural specialist for each of these two constituencies. Many community members asked me to apply for that position. I became a curriculum specialist in multicultural studies for the next 13 years.

I was still organizing for educational justice during that time and working with an organization called Asian Americans United. We talked about how to make schools immigrant-friendly, and we decided after many years that we needed to create a model school. Starting the charter process was not an easy decision because politically we were concerned about the role of charter schools in public education. However, after a multiyear decision-making process, we decided to go ahead and start Folk Arts-Cultural Treasures Charter School (FACTS). I was the founding principal. I held that position for five years and then I stepped aside, knowing that I'd still be around if they needed me.

GCG: Why did you choose the focus on folk arts?

DW: We were always moved by the vernacular cultural forms in our communities—for example, the lion dancers in Chinatown each New Year. These forms usually aren't part of "popular" culture and the artists don't make a ton of money. You won't see them on MTV. But the form they practice is something they treasure, a gift that was passed on to them, and that they in turn feel a need to pass on. We saw folk art as an important vehicle to present an anti-materialist message to kids. It shows that you can value things deeply that don't have monetary value. It also shows that tradition and culture are things you can choose to keep and to pass on. It isn't easy. Sometimes you have to fight for it.

We knew the school was going to be serving a large and diverse immigrant community. We thought about language and how you bring non-English-speaking elders into a school so they are respected, so that they don't necessarily need to know English or speak it well, or have college degrees in order to be able to teach you something. Our Chinese opera teacher, Li Shuyuan, is a fifth-generation Chinese opera artist. She doesn't speak any English. But she taught kids how to do the martial arts roles in some of the operas (e.g., *Monkey King*) and the kids loved it. We wanted them to get this message: Adults don't need to know English and don't need to be recognized by "institutions" to be valuable resources. Our kids have learned so many different things from so many different traditions.

GCG: Why did you include Mandarin in the FACTS curriculum?

DW: From the beginning, we wanted to locate the school in a place where the kids would feel safe. There were a lot of anti-immigrant tension spots around the city. We thought Chinatown was a pretty safe community and we were well known there as an organization, so we decided to place the school in Chinatown. Chinatown lacked any public services, so the school would be an important resource and a political statement, too.

Since we would be in Chinatown and a lot of our kids (although certainly not all) would come from a Chinese heritage background, we decided to add the Chinese language program. There was disagreement among the founders; we wanted diversity among our students and families, and some founders worried that if we singled out Mandarin Chinese as a language, it would have an exclusionary effect. My feeling was that it didn't matter what language background kids were coming from—we wanted the school to show respect to the community in which we were located. We wanted the school's curriculum to address linguistic human rights and reflect on the importance of being bilingual and honoring languages. And you can't do that unless you teach a language. The language that made the most sense, given our population, was Mandarin.

We started with just one teacher for K through 5th grade, and just one or two periods a week of Chinese. We used a Foreign Language Acquisition Program Grant to split the Chinese language program between heritage and non-heritage language learners. The heritage language kids often already understood and spoke Chinese and, even if it wasn't Mandarin, they understood the structure of the language. (Mandarin, Cantonese, and Fujianese are different languages orally, but the written language is the same.) Another piece of the grant funded the kids' work on oral histories in the community so

The kids did oral histories in the community so we could identify folk artists. We used a Chinese chop (stamp) as the logo for our school, and we found the chop maker working as a waiter in the neighborhood.

that we could identify folk artists. For example, we used a Chinese chop (a stamp with calligraphy on it) as the logo for our school, and we found the chop maker working as a waiter in a restaurant in Chinatown. Initially, I envisioned students using their Mandarin language skills to interview folk artists, but there was concern that this would exclude many folk artists in the city, so we took out the explicit language component of the oral histories project.

GCG: Why is heritage language study important?

DW: Language is a human right. What you get from language is not just language. You get culture. You get history. It's a way to include non-English-speaking parents. In the United States, kids get the message pretty early on that it's not cool to be bilingual. That mind-set was there, even at FACTS. Sometimes I would see kids talking to their grandparents in Chinese. But when I talked to them in Chinese, they would claim that they didn't know Chinese and answer me in English.

I didn't grow up bilingual. My parents spoke Chinese but came to the United States during the McCarthy era. We weren't in Chinatown, and we weren't in a Chinese-speaking community. I didn't find out until my 30s that my parents were undocumented for the first few years that they were here. In hindsight, I understand why they didn't want us to speak Chinese. They were afraid. That is really sad. I don't want families to feel that way. If we value children and we're really about whole-child education, it's wrong not to support a heritage language.

I was the only person with my mom when she passed on. She passed at home and everyone but me was in another part of the house at that moment. I was just sitting, watching her, because we knew she was passing soon. Her final words were in her village dialect. I was the only person there to hear them, and I didn't understand what she said.

No kid should have to go through that. I never want another child to not understand their mother's final words. Language should be seen as a gift, an asset, not a deficit.

GCG: Is there a specific significance to heritage language study for Asian American communities in the United States?

DW: That's tough to say specifically, because I think my theoretical underpinning would apply to anyone. There's a pedagogical reason: There's so much research on the importance of first language (L1) development on English (L2) acquisition. And then there's race. One thing that's tough for Asians is that we are always perceived as foreigners because of our appearance. Because of restrictive immigration laws, Asians couldn't immigrate for a long time. So until recently there weren't many multiple generations of U.S.-born Asians. The racism of immigration laws, coupled with our faces, puts Asian American kids in a space where they're always having to prove that they're not foreign. That has a particular psychological effect on children and their heritage language. I think that's why so many of my kids at FACTS pretended that they didn't know Chinese.

Things are shifting now because Chinese has become "sexy." Now everybody wants their kids to speak Mandarin. What really galls me is when people say, "It's good for business. It's going to be a big market!"

That is not why you learn a language. I'm sorry, but that's really not a good reason. Be that as it may, for Chinese Americans now, there's not as much pressure to lose their heritage language. But racism can still have a strong psychological impact. If you are made to feel shame for who you are through implicit or explicit messages, you'll want to lose pieces of yourself.

Because of changes in the immigration laws, we can begin to find a community, be together, and find pride in who we are. So I think that things may be changing slowly, but only for Mandarin-speaking folks—not, for example, those who speak Tibetan or Lao or Vietnamese.

GCG: What factors affect the availability of bilingual and/or immersion programs in Asian languages?

DW: I think the trends mirror the national trends in bilingual education. Pennsylvania does not have a history as the starship state for supporting language acquisition. So bilingual education has not been well developed there, even in Spanish. People are working hard now to try to make that happen, but it's complex. In Pennsylvania there's no certification in bilingual education. If the colleges of education don't have a program that focuses on it, then you're not going to produce teachers who can do it. Even if you have a bilingual program in a school, who's going to teach it?

Another thing that hurts Asian language acquisition is the relative "obscurity" of many of the languages. When language is only looked at as a market force, what use is it to learn Khmer? Asian Americans are Asian Americans because of the racialization of who we are, but ethnically we're very different. There's no one common language. With a few exceptions, you'd be hard-pressed to find bilingual programs in Asian languages other than Chinese, Japanese, or Korean.

GCG: How can we support linguistic diversity in our schools when we don't have bilingual programs?

DW: It's important to create an environment where people honor the concept of bilingualism, even if they aren't bilingual themselves. It's also important to honor folks who don't speak English, as we did with the folk artists at FACTS, for example.

Another way schools can value language is to value everyone, especially speakers of languages other than English. Because we were committed to being multicultural and accessible multilingually, we hired support staff to be as representative of broad communities as possible. We had a Spanish-speaking and a Chinese-speaking secretary and an Indonesian-speaking foods director. Our custodian was Vietnamese, and our kitchen staff were Chinese speakers. At FACTS, all adults—including custodians, kitchen staff, and secretaries—were called "Teacher." We each decided to go by our first name or our last name, but the front part was always "Teacher." It didn't matter what languages we spoke or didn't speak. Of course, we also hired teachers who were bilingual as role models.

We made sure to translate all important documents into multiple languages, and we invested in telephonic interpretation for talking with parents during report card conferences and other conversations. We also invested in simultaneous interpretation equipment—we had the technical capacity for interpreters in four different languages for community meetings.

Schools without bilingual programs can also create spaces to honor language. At the beginning of the school year, I often did poetry writing with the entire staff. We each wrote poetry in whatever language we chose and then people translated the final products. We hung the poems on the walls for the kids when they first came back to school. So the kids saw that the poetry was in multiple languages and reflected multiple cultural experiences, and also saw that the teachers and support staff wrote poetry. All schools deliver important messages to children about the significance of language and the people who speak those languages. ☼

Deborah Wei has taught ESL and been an administrator in Philadelphia, New Delhi, India, and now serves as the director of the elementary school at the Crossroads School in Santa Monica, California. She has been a social justice activist most of her life.

Grace Cornell Gonzales is an editor for Rethinking Schools and has worked for nine years as a bilingual elementary school teacher in California and Guatemala City.

Putting Out the Linguistic Welcome Mat

BY LINDA CHRISTENSEN

MICHAEL DUFFY

My friend Karen works as a relatively new principal in a rural Oregon school where the sons and daughters of winery owners rub elbows with the sons and daughters of their field workers. Recently, she recounted a story about a typical day: "When I came into my office after lunch duty, three Latino students sat waiting for me. The students told me the substitute kicked them out for speaking Spanish in class. After verifying the story, I told the substitute her services would no longer be needed at our school."

Karen is a full-time warrior for students. She battles remarkable linguistic prejudice and historical inequities to make her school a safe community for her Latino students. Before she arrived on campus, for example, school policy excluded Spanish-speaking English language learners from taking Spanish classes. Latino students had to enroll in German classes to meet their world language requirement. At another urban school, in the Portland area, a group of teachers tallied the grammatical errors their administrator made during a faculty meeting. Their air of superiority and smugness made my teeth ache. This same smugness silences many students in our classrooms when we value how they speak more than what they say.

"Nonstandard" language speakers must negotiate this kind of language minefield whenever they enter the halls of power—schools, banks, government agencies, and employment offices. Language inequity still exists, whether it's getting kicked out of class for speaking in your home language or being found unfit for a job, a college, or a scholarship because of your lack of dexterity with Standard English.

As educators, we have the power to determine whether students feel included or excluded in our schools and classrooms. By bringing students' languages from their homes into the classroom, we validate their culture and their history as topics worthy of study.

A Curriculum on Language and Power

Author Toni Morrison (1981) writes about the power of language, and Black English in particular:

> It's the thing Black people love so much—the saying of words, holding them on the tongue, experimenting with them, playing with them. It's a love, a passion. Its function is like a preacher's: to make you stand up out of your seat, make you lose yourself and hear yourself. The worst of all possible things that could happen would be to lose that language. There are certain things I cannot say without recourse to my language.

These days, most of our schools and school boards fashion mission statements about "embracing diversity." Multilingual banners welcome students and visitors in Spanish, Russian, and Vietnamese in the hallways of school buildings. But in the classroom, the job of the teacher often appears to be whitewashing students of color or students who are linguistically diverse, especially when punctuation and grammar are double-weighted on the state writing test. If we hope to create positive communities in which students from diverse backgrounds can thrive academically, we need to examine how our approach to students' linguistic diversity either includes or pushes out our most vulnerable learners.

During 30 years as a language arts classroom teacher, I realized that if I wanted my students to open up in their writing, to take risks and engage in intellectually demanding work, I needed to challenge assumptions about the superiority of Standard English and the inferiority of the home language of many of my Black students: African American Vernacular English, Black English, or Ebonics. When students feel attacked by the red pen or the tongue for the way they write or speak, they either make themselves small—turning in short papers—or don't turn in papers at all. To build an engaging classroom where students from different backgrounds felt safe enough to dare to be big and bold in their writing, I had to build a curricular platform for them to stand on.

I started this work by intentionally inviting students to tell their stories in their home languages. I brought in August Wilson's plays, Lois-Ann Yamanaka's stories, and Jimmy Santiago Baca's poetry to validate the use of dialect and home language. But I learned that this wasn't enough. To challenge the old world order, I needed to explore why Standard English is the standard—how it came to power and how that power makes some people feel welcome and others feel like outsiders.

I finally realized that I needed to create a curriculum on language and power that examined the roots of language supremacy and analyzed how schools perpetuate the myths of the inferiority of some languages. I also discovered that students needed stories of hope: stories of people's resistance to the loss of their mother tongues and stories about the growing movement to save Indigenous languages from extinction.

Legitimizing the Study of Ebonics/Black English

Depending on how many pieces of the unit I include, this curriculum takes five to 10 weeks. Students watch films and read literature, nonfiction texts, and poetry. They write narratives, poetry, and a culminating essay about language. For their final exam, they create a take-it-to-the-people project that teaches an audience of their choice one aspect of our language study that they think people need to know in order to understand contemporary language issues. The curriculum includes any of the following five segments: Naming as a Practice of Power; Language and Colonization; Dialect and Power; Ebonics; and Language Restoration.

During this unit, we do discuss code-switching, or moving between home language and the language of power—Standard English—during our readings. As a teacher in a predominantly African American school where the majority of students exhibited some features of African American Vernacular English (AAVE, also called Ebonics or "Spoken Soul"), I needed to learn the rules and history of the language so I could help students move between the two language systems. In my experience, teaching Black students the grammar structure and history of AAVE evoked pride in their language, but also curiosity. All students—not just African Americans—benefited from learning that African American language has a highly structured grammar system.

Teaching about Ebonics has been a no-go zone for many teachers since the controversy over a 1996 Oakland Unified School District resolution that recognized Black English as a language of instruction. Stanford linguistics professor John Rickford noted in his book *Spoken Soul:*

> Ebonics was vilified as "disgusting Black street slang," "incorrect and substandard," "nothing more than ignorance," "lazy English," "bastardized English," "the language of illiteracy," and this "utmost ridiculous made-up language."

As Rickford pointed out, the reactions of linguists were much more positive than those of most of the media and the general public. Although they disagree about its origins, "linguists from virtually all points of view agree on the systematicity of Ebonics, and on the potential value of taking it into account in teaching Ebonics speakers to read and write" (Rickford, 1997).

In an African American literature class I taught at Grant High School in Portland, Ore., I introduced the Ebonics part of the language curriculum by giving the 31 students (28 of whom were Black) a concept chart and asking them to fill in a definition of Ebonics, write a few examples, and note where it originated. All but one student wrote that Ebonics is slang. Most wrote that Ebonics came out of Oakland or the West Coast or the "ghetto." It was clear that their impressions were negative.

None of the Black students in the group used Ebonics/AAVE exclusively. But many of them used aspects of Ebonics in both their speech and their writing. One of my goals was for students to recognize the difference between slang and Ebonics/Black English when they hear it in their school, churches, and homes—and to be able to distinguish it when they are using it. The term "Ebonics" (from ebony and phonics) was coined by Professor Robert Williams in 1973, during a conference on the language development of Black children (Rickford, 2000). In her essay "Black English/Ebonics: What it be like?" renowned scholar and linguist Geneva Smitherman writes that Ebonics "is rooted in the Black American Oral Tradition and represents a synthesis of African (primarily West African) and European (primarily English) linguistic-cultural traditions" (Smitherman, 1998).

In the class, we read Rickford's essay "Suite for Ebony and Phonics" aloud together paragraph by paragraph, stopping to discuss each part. Is Ebonics just "slang," as so many people have characterized it? No, because slang refers just to the vocabulary of a language or dialect, and even so, just to the small set of new and (usually) short-lived words like chillin ("relaxing") or homey ("close friend") that are used primarily by young people in informal contexts. Ebonics includes nonslang words like ashy (referring to the appearance of dry skin, especially in winter), which have been around for a while, and are used by people of all age groups.

Ebonics also includes distinctive patterns of pronunciation and grammar, the elements of language on which linguists tend to concentrate because they are more systematic and deep-rooted (Rickford, 1997).

We also read "From Africa to the New World and into the Space Age: An Introduction and History of Black English Structure," a chapter from Geneva Smitherman's 1977 book *Talkin and Testifyin: The Language of Black America*. Her discussion of the grammar structure of Ebonics led to a wonderful day of conjugating verbs. For example, we discussed the absence of a third person singular present tense in Ebonics (example: I draw, he draw, we draw, they draw); students then conjugate verbs using this grammar rule. The zero copula rule—the absence of *is* or *are* in a sentence—provided another model for students to practice. Smitherman gives as an example the sentence "People crazy! People are stone crazy!" The emphasis on *are* in the second sentence, she points out, intensifies the feeling. I asked students to write zero copula sentences and we shared them in class.

Empowered by Linguistic Knowledge

After I started teaching my students about Ebonics, many of them began to understand how assumptions about the supremacy of Standard English had created difficulties in their education. One student, Kaanan, wrote:

> When I went to school, teachers didn't really teach me how to spell

or put sentences together right. They just said sound it out, so I would spell it the way I heard it at home. Everybody around me at home spoke Ebonics, so when I sounded it out, it sounded like home and it got marked wrong. When I wrote something like "My brother he got in trouble last night," I was marked wrong. Instead of showing me how speakers of Ebonics sometimes use both a name and a pronoun but in "Standard English" only one is used, I got marked wrong.

Another student, Sherrell, said:

I grew up thinking Ebonics was wrong. My teachers would say, "If you ever want to get anywhere you have to learn how to talk right." . . . At home, after school, break time, lunch time, we all talked our native language which was Ebonics. Our teachers were wrong for saying our language wasn't right. All I heard was Spanish and Ebonics in my neighborhood. They brainwashed me at school to be ashamed of my language and that almost took away one of the few things that African Americans had of our past life and history.

Throughout the Ebonics unit, I asked students to listen and take notes and see if they could spot the rules of Ebonics at work in the school halls, at home, or at the mall. To celebrate and acknowledge a language that so many of my students spoke without awareness, I pointed out Ebonics in class as students spoke. Often, they didn't hear it or recognize it until we held it up like a diamond for them to examine.

One day my student Ryan handed me an unexpected gift when he asked if I'd ever heard the rapper Big L's song "Ebonics." I confessed my ignorance, but I looked it up on the web and downloaded the music and lyrics. The song is clever, but because the performer misunderstands Ebonics as slang, he provided a great audience for my students to rehearse their arguments about Ebonics. In one essay, for example, Jerrell wrote:

"Ebonics is slang shit," rapper Big L said in his song titled "Ebonics." In this song he tells a lot about the slang that young African Americans use, but this is the problem. He is talking about slang; there is no Ebonics in his lyrics. The misconception people have is that slang and Ebonics are the same thing. The problem is that slang is just a different way of saying things. For example, in his slang you say money, you can also say bread, cheese, cheddar, cash, dough, green, duckets, Washingtons, chips, guap, and many more. However, when you use Ebonics, there is a sentence structure that you have to use. Don't get me wrong, slang and Ebonics go together like mashed potatoes and gravy, but there is a difference between the two. As my classmate said, "Slang is what I talk; Ebonics is how I speak it.

In his end-of-unit reflection, Jayme wrote that he appreciated "the knowledge that was given to us about the language that we speak and how it related to our roots in Africa." Hannah wrote, "Kids who have been taught that the way they speak is wrong their entire lives can now be confident." And I love the sassiness of Ryan's conclusion: "Ebonics is here to stay and shows no sign of fading away in either the Black or white communities. In the words of Ebonics: 'It's BIN here and it's 'bout to stay.'"

Inclusive School Communities

When I took students to local universities to share their knowledge about language during our take-it-to-the-people project, Jacoa told aspiring teachers at Portland State University, "On my college application, I'm going to write that I'm fluent in three languages: English, Spanish, and Ebonics. Call me if you need more information."

As educators, when we talk about building inclusive communities in which all students can learn, we must also examine how our policies and practices continue to shame and exclude students in ways that may not be readily apparent. We signal students from the moment they step into school, whether they belong or whether we see them as trespassers. Everything in school—from the posters on the wall, to the music played at assemblies, to the books in the library—embraces students or pushes them away. Approaching students' home languages with respect is one of the most important curricular choices teachers can make. ☼

Linda Christensen is the director of the Oregon Writing Project at Lewis & Clark College in Portland, Ore., and a Rethinking Schools editor. Previously, she taught language arts in Portland Public Schools for 30 years. She is the author of Reading, Writing, and Rising Up: Teaching About Social Justice and the Power of the Written Word *and* Teaching for Joy and Justice.

This article first appeared in the September 2008 issue of *Educational Leadership*. Reprinted with permission. Learn more about ASCD at ascd.org.

Note from the author: In my *Rethinking Schools* article "The Politics of Correction" (Fall 2003), I discuss more fully how I address moving students between their home language and the language of power, Standard English.

References
LeClair, Thomas. 1981. "'The Language Must Not Sweat': A Conversation with Toni Morrison." *New Republic*. March 21.

Rickford, John R., and Russell J. Rickford. 2000. *Spoken Soul: The Story of Black English*. John Wiley & Sons.

Rickford, John. R. 2008. "Suite for Ebony and Phonics." stanford.edu/~rickford/papers/SuiteForEbonyAndPhonics.html.

Smitherman, Geneva. 1977. *Talkin and Testifyin: The Language of Black America*. Houghton Mifflin.

Smitherman, Geneva. 1998. "Black English/Ebonics: What it be like?" *The Real Ebonics Debate*. Rethinking Schools.

Ebonics and Culturally Responsive Instruction

What should teachers do?

BY LISA DELPIT

BARBARA MINER

T he "Ebonics Debate" has created much more heat than light for most of the country. For teachers trying to determine what implications there might be for classroom practice, enlightenment has been a completely nonexistent commodity. I have been asked often enough recently, "What do you think about Ebonics? Are you for it or against it?" My answer must be neither. I can be neither for Ebonics or against Ebonics any more than I can be for or against air. It exists. It is the language spoken by many of our African American children. It is the language they heard as their mothers nursed them and changed their diapers and played peekaboo with them. It is the language through which they first encountered love, nurturance, and joy.

On the other hand, most teachers of those African American children who have been least well served by educational systems believe that their students' life chances will be further hampered if they do not learn Standard English. In the stratified society in which we live, they are absolutely correct. While having access to the politically mandated language form will not, by any means, guarantee economic success (witness the growing numbers of unemployed African Americans holding doctorates), not having access will almost certainly guarantee failure.

So what must teachers do? Should they spend their time relentlessly "correcting" their Ebonics-speaking children's language so that it might conform to what we have learned to refer to as Standard English? Despite good intentions, constant correction seldom has the desired effect. Such correction increases cognitive monitoring of speech, thereby making talking difficult. To illustrate, I have frequently taught a relatively simple new "dialect" to classes of preservice teachers. In this dialect, the phonetic element "iz" is added after the first consonant or consonant cluster in each syllable of a word. (Maybe becomes miz-ay-biz-ee.) After a bit of drill and practice, the students are asked to tell a partner in "iz" language why they decided to become teachers. Most only haltingly attempt a few words before lapsing into either silence or into Standard English. During a follow-up discussion, all students invariably speak of the impossibility of attempting to apply rules while trying to formulate and express a thought. Forcing speakers to monitor their language typically produces silence.

Correction may also affect students' attitudes toward their teachers. In a recent research project, middle school, inner-city students were interviewed about their attitudes toward their teachers and school. One young woman complained bitterly, "Mrs. ___ always be interrupting to make you 'talk correct' and stuff. She be butting into your conversations when you not even talking to her! She need to mind her own business." Clearly this student will be unlikely to either follow the teacher's directives or to want to imitate her speech style.

Group Identity

Issues of group identity may also affect students' oral production of a different dialect. Researcher Sharon Nelson-Barber, in a study of phonologic aspects of Pima Indian language, found that, in grades 1 through 3, the children's English most approximated the standard dialect of their teachers. But surprisingly, by 4th grade, when one might assume growing competence in standard forms, their language moved significantly toward the local dialect. These 4th graders had the *competence* to express themselves in a more standard form, but chose, consciously or unconsciously, to use the language of those in their local environments. The researcher believes that, by ages 8 or 9, these children became aware of their group membership and its importance to their well-being, and this realization was reflected in their language.[1] They may also have become increasingly aware of the schools' negative attitude toward their community and found it necessary—through choice of linguistic form—to decide with which camp to identify.

What should teachers do about helping students acquire an additional oral form? First, they should recognize that the linguistic form a student brings to school is intimately connected with loved ones, community, and personal identity. To suggest that this form is "wrong" or, even worse, ignorant, is to suggest that something is wrong with the student and his or her family. To denigrate your language is, then, in African

American terms, to "talk about your mama." Anyone who knows anything about African American culture knows the consequences of that speech act!

On the other hand, it is equally important to understand that students who do not have access to the politically popular dialect form in this country are less likely to succeed economically than their peers who do. How can both realities be embraced in classroom instruction?

It is possible and desirable to make the actual study of language diversity a part of the curriculum for all students. For younger children, discussions about the differences in the ways television characters from different cultural groups speak can provide a starting point. A collection of the many children's books written in the dialects of various cultural groups can also provide a wonderful basis for learning about linguistic diversity,[2] as can audiotaped stories narrated by individuals from different cultures, including taping books read by members of the children's home communities. Mrs. Pat, a teacher chronicled by Stanford University researcher Shirley Brice Heath, had her students become language "detectives," interviewing a variety of individuals and listening to the radio and television to discover the differences and similarities in the ways people talked.[3] Children can learn that there are many ways of saying the same thing, and that certain contexts suggest particular kinds of linguistic performances.

Some teachers have groups of students create bilingual dictionaries of their own language form and Standard English. Both the students and the teacher become engaged in identifying terms and deciding upon the best translations. This can be done as generational dictionaries, too, given the proliferation of "youth culture" terms growing out of the Ebonics-influenced tendency for the continual regeneration of vocabulary. Contrastive grammatical structures can be studied similarly, but, of course, as the Oakland policy suggests, teachers must be aware of the grammatical structure of Ebonics before they can launch into this complex study.

Other teachers have had students become involved with standard forms through various kinds of role play. For example, memorizing parts for drama productions will allow students to practice and "get the feel" of speaking Standard English while not under the threat of correction. A master teacher of African American children in Oakland, Carrie Secret, uses this technique and extends it so that students video their practice performances and self-critique them as to the appropriate use of Standard English. (But I must add that Carrie's use of drama and oration goes much beyond acquiring Standard English. She inspires pride and community connections that are truly wondrous to behold.) The use of self-critique of recorded forms may prove even more useful than I initially realized. California State University-Hayward professor Etta Hollins has reported that just by leaving a tape recorder on during an informal class period and playing it back with no comment, students began to code-switch—mov-

Should teachers spend their time relentlessly "correcting" their Ebonics-speaking children's language so that it might conform to what we have learned to refer to as Standard English?

ing between Standard English and Ebonics—more effectively. It appears that they may have not realized which language form they were using until they heard themselves speak on tape.

Young students can create puppet shows or role-play cartoon characters—many "superheroes" speak almost hypercorrect Standard English! Playing a role eliminates the possibility of implying that the child's language is inadequate and suggests, instead, that different language forms are appropriate in different contexts. Some other teachers in New York City have had their students produce a news show every day for the rest of the school. The students take on the personae of famous newscasters, keeping in character as they develop and read their news reports. Discussions ensue about whether Tom Brokaw would have said it that way, again taking the focus off the child's speech.

Although most educators think of Black language as primarily differing in grammar and syntax, there are other differences in oral language of which teachers should be aware in a multicultural context, particularly in discourse style and language use. Harvard University researcher Sarah Michaels and other researchers identified differences in children's narratives at "sharing time."[4] They found that there was a tendency among young white children to tell "topic-centered" narratives—stories focused on one event—and a tendency among Black youngsters, especially girls, to tell "episodic" narratives—stories that include shifting scenes and are typically longer. While these differences are interesting in themselves, what is of greater significance is adults' responses to the differences. Courtney B. Cazden reports on a subsequent project in which a white adult was taped reading the oral narratives of Black and white 1st graders, with all syntax dialectal markers removed.[5] Adults were asked to listen to the stories and comment about the children's likelihood of success in school. The researchers were surprised by the differential responses given by Black and white adults.

Varying Reactions

In responding to the retelling of a Black child's story, the white adults were uniformly negative, making such comments as "terrible story, incoherent" and "[n]ot a story at all in the sense of describing something that happened." Asked to judge this child's academic competence, all of the white adults rated her below the children who told "topic-centered" stories. Most of these adults also predicted difficulties for this child's future school career, such as "This child might have trouble reading," that she exhibited "language problems that affect school achievement," and that "family problems" or "emotional problems" might hamper her academic progress.

The Black adults had very different reactions. They found this child's story "well formed, easy to understand, and interesting, with lots of detail and description." Even though all five of these adults mentioned the "shifts" and "associations" or "non-linear" quality of the story, they did not find these features distracting. Three of the Black adults selected the story as the best of the five they had heard, and all but one judged the child as exceptionally bright, highly verbal, and successful in school.[6]

This is not a story about racism, but one about cultural familiarity. However, when differences in narrative style produce differences in interpretation of competence, the pedagogical implications are evident. If children who produce stories based in differing discourse styles are expected to have trouble reading, and viewed as having language, family, or emotional problems, as was the case with the informants quoted by Cazden, they are unlikely to be viewed as ready for the same challenging instruction awarded students whose language patterns more closely parallel the teacher's.

Most teachers are particularly concerned about how speaking Ebonics might affect learning to read. There is little evidence that speaking another mutually intelligible language form, per se, negatively affects one's ability to learn to read.[7] For commonsensical proof, one need only reflect on non-Standard English-speaking Africans who, though enslaved, not only taught themselves to read English, but did so under threat of severe punishment or death. But children who speak Ebonics do have a more difficult time becoming proficient readers. Why? In part, appropriate instructional methodologies are frequently not adopted. There is ample evidence that children who do not come to school with knowledge about letters, sounds, and symbols need to experience some explicit instruction in these areas in order to become independent readers. Another explanation is that, where teachers' assessments of competence are influenced by the language

The linguistic form a student brings to school is intimately connected with loved ones, community, and personal identity.

children speak, teachers may develop low expectations for certain students and subsequently teach them less.[8] A third explanation rests in teachers' confusing the teaching of reading with the teaching of a new language form.

Reading researcher Patricia Cunningham found that teachers across the United States were more likely to correct reading miscues that were "dialect" related ("Here go a table" for "Here is a table") than those that were "nondialect" related ("Here is a dog" for "There is a dog").[9] Seventy-eight percent of the former types of miscues were corrected, compared with only 27 percent of the latter. She concludes that the teachers were acting out of ignorance, not realizing that "here go" and "here is" represent the same meaning in some Black children's language.

In my observations of many classrooms, however, I have come to conclude that even when teachers recognize the similarity of meaning, they are likely to correct Ebonics-related miscues. Consider a typical example:

> Text: Yesterday I washed my brother's clothes.
> Student's Rendition: Yesterday I wash my bruvver close.

The subsequent exchange between student and teacher sounds something like this:

> {"washed."} S: Wash.
> T: No. Look at it again. What letters do you see at the end? You see
> "e-d." Do you remember what we say when we see those letters on

the end of the word?

S: "ed"

T: OK, but in this case we say washed. Can you say that?

S: Washed.

T: Good. Now read it again.

S: Yesterday I washed my bruvver.

T: Wait a minute, what's that word again? {Points to "brother."}

S: Bruvver.

T: No. Look at these letters in the middle. {Points to "brother."} Remember to read what you see. Do you remember how we say that sound? Put your tongue between your teeth and say "th."

The lesson continues in such a fashion, the teacher proceeding to correct the student's Ebonics-influenced pronunciations and grammar while ignoring that fact that the student had to have comprehended the sentence in order to translate it into her own language. Such instruction occurs daily and blocks reading development in a number of ways. First, because children become better readers by having the opportunity to read, the overcorrection exhibited in this lesson means that this child will be less likely to become a fluent reader than other children that are not interrupted so consistently. Second, a complete focus on code and pronunciation blocks children's understanding that reading is essentially a meaning-making process. This child, who understands the text, is led to believe that she is doing something wrong. She is encouraged to think of reading not as something you do to get a message, but something you pronounce. Third, constant corrections by the teacher are likely to cause this student and others like her to resist reading and to resent the teacher.

Language researcher Robert Berdan reports that, after observing the kind of teaching routine described above in a number of settings, he incorporated the teacher behaviors into a reading instruction exercise that he used with students in a college class.[10] He put together sundry rules from a number of American social and regional dialects to create what he called the "language of Atlantis." Students were then called upon to read aloud in this dialect they did not know. When they made errors he interrupted them, using some of the same statements/comments he had heard elementary school teachers routinely make to their students. He concludes:

> The results were rather shocking. By the time these PhD candidates in English or linguistics had read 10–20 words, I could make them sound totally illiterate. . . . The first thing that goes is sentence intonation: They sound like they are reading a list from the telephone book. Comment on their pronunciation a bit more, and they begin to subvocalize, rehearsing pronunciations for themselves before they dare to say them out loud. They begin to guess at pronunciations. . . . They switch letters around for no reason. They stumble; they repeat. In short, when I attack them for their failure to conform to my demands for Atlantis English pronunciations, they

sound very much like the worst of the 2nd graders in any of the classrooms I have observed.

> They also begin to fidget. They wad up their papers, bite their finger-nails, whisper, and some finally refuse to continue. They do all the things that children do while they are busily failing to learn to read.

The moral of this story is not to confuse learning a new language form with reading comprehension. To do so will only confuse the child, leading her away from those intuitive understandings about language that will promote reading development, and toward a school career of resistance and a lifetime of avoiding reading.

Unlike unplanned oral language or public reading, writing lends itself to editing. While conversational talk is spontaneous and must be responsive to an immediate context, writing is a mediated process that may be written and rewritten any number of times before being introduced to public scrutiny. Consequently, writing is more amenable to rule application—one may first write freely to get one's thoughts down, and then edit to hone the message and apply specific spelling, syntactical, or punctuation rules. My college students who had such difficulty talking in the "iz" dialect, found writing it, with the rules displayed before them, a relatively easy task.

To conclude, the teacher's job is to provide access to the national "standard" as well as to understand the language the children speak sufficiently to celebrate its beauty. The verbal adroitness, the cogent and quick wit, the brilliant use of metaphor, the facility in rhythm and rhyme, evident in the language of Jesse Jackson, Whoopi Goldberg, Toni Morrison, Henry Louis Gates, Tupac Shakur, and Maya Angelou, as well as in that of many inner-city Black students, may all be drawn upon to facilitate school learning. The teacher must know how to effectively teach reading and writing to students whose culture and language differ from that of the school, and must understand how and why students decide to add another language form to their repertoire. All we can do is provide students with access to additional language forms. Inevitably, each speaker will make his or her own decision about what to say in any context.

But I must end with a caveat that we keep in mind a simple truth: Despite our necessary efforts to provide access to Standard English, such access will not make any of our students more intelligent. It will not teach them math or science or geography—or, for that matter, compassion, courage, or responsibility. Let us not become so overly concerned with the language *form* that we ignore academic and moral *content*. Access to the standard language may be necessary, but it is definitely not sufficient to produce intelligent, competent caretakers of the future. ✻

Lisa Delpit is the Felton G. Clark Distinguished Professor of Education at Southern University and A&M College in Baton Rouge, Louisiana, where she helps prepare teachers and principals to excel in urban settings.

Note from the editors: "Ebonics and Culturally Responsive Instruction" appeared in the 1997 *Rethinking Schools* special edition on Ebonics.

Endnotes

1. Nelson-Barber, Sharon. 1982. "Phonological Variations of Pima English." *Language Renewal Among American Indian Tribes: Issues, Problems and Prospects* (R. St. Clair and W. Leap, eds.). National Clearinghouse for Bilingual Education.

2. Some of these books include Clifton, Lucille. 1973. *All Us Come Cross the Water.* Holt, Rinehart, and Winston; Green, Paul (aided by Abbe Abbott). 1959. *I Am Eskimo: Aknik My Name.* Alaska Northwest Publishing; Jacobs, Howard, and Jim Rice. 1983. *Once upon a Bayou.* Phideaux Publications; Edler, Tim. 1981. *Santa's Cajun Christmas Adventure.* Little Cajun Books; and a series of biographies produced by Yukon-Koyukuk School District of Alaska and published by Hancock House Publishers.

3. Brice Heath, Shirley. 1983. *Ways with Words.* Cambridge University Press.

4. Michaels, Sarah, and Courtney B. Cazden. 1986. "Teacher/Child Collaboration as Oral Preparation for Literacy." *Acquisition of Literacy: Ethnographic Perspectives* (B. Schieffelin and P. Gilmore, eds.). Ablex.

5. Cazden, Courtney B. 1988. *Classroom Discourse.* Heinemann.

6. Ibid. *The teacher must know how to effectively teach reading and writing to students whose culture and language differ from that of the school, and must understand how and why students decide to add another language form to their repertoire.*

7. Sims, Rudine. 1982. "Dialect and Reading: Toward Redefining the Issues." *Reader Meets Author/Bridging the Gap* (J. Langer and M. T. Smith-Burke, eds.). International Reading Association.

8. Ibid.

9. Cunningham, Patricia M. 1976. "Teachers' Correction Responses to Black-Dialect Miscues Which Are Nonmeaning-Changing." *Reading Research Quarterly* 12.

10. Berdan, Robert. 1980. "Knowledge into Practice: Delivering Research to Teachers." *Reactions to Ann Arbor: Vernacular Black English and Education* (M. F. Whiteman, ed.). Center for Applied Linguistics.

Mi Love di Way Mi Chat

Patwa and bilingual education in Jamaica

BY JACQUI STANFORD

JAKE BREWER/FLICKR CREATIVE COMMONS

ome with me on a walk through the Jamaican school where I taught English to high schoolers. The setting is idyllic: blue skies, green foliage, yellow sunshine, silver zephyrs—and everywhere, the distinctive sounds of Jamaica. As students move around the campus, they share news and tell stories in Patwa. Shouts from the playground are in Patwa. Punch lines to lunchtime jokes are delivered in the logic and rhythm of Patwa. When the bell rings and classes are in session, you walk down corridors to the same rich Jamaican accent; however, you no longer hear Patwa. Classes are in English.

English is the official language of Jamaica and the language of instruction in schools. Yet many Jamaicans are not fluent in English. Most Jamaicans, however, fluently communicate in their native language, Patwa. Patwa emerged when English and African groups started to coexist during slavery and is now firmly established as the primary means of communication in Jamaica. It is the mother and emotional tongue preferred by many.

Jamaicans have had the means to read and write in Patwa for some time. In fact, the New Testament of the Bible was recently published in Patwa, using the Patwa writing system linguist Frederic Cassidy developed in the 1960s. But Patwa literacy is not taught in schools. There is also no widely accepted standard way to write Patwa, making it difficult for Jamaicans to read and write proficiently in their native language.

This situation perhaps persists because Patwa has been slighted, snubbed, and ranked as subordinate to English. The controversy that accompanied the publication of the Patwa Bible, for example, highlighted many of the struggles faced by Patwa advocates. Although there was some support and pride, there was also staunch refusal to accept Patwa as a language. Some argued that even if Patwa is a language, there is questionable value in advancing its status and literacy. There is resistance to Patwa because of its association with slavery and Black culture. Resistance to Black diaspora languages runs deep.

Yet Jamaican students are bilingual—although they are generally not recognized as such—and they deserve the opportunity to develop both of their languages during their school careers. Just as is the case with Ebonics in the U.S. context, difficulties and resistance remain with respect to including Patwa in mainstream curricula in Jamaica, even when there is evidence of how that would improve teaching and learn-

There is resistance to Patwa because of its association with slavery and Black culture.

ing. Excluding Patwa from schools fails to credit students' abilities and can even cause them harm—by denying them the means to express themselves in their home language and humiliating them for using their native tongue.

Growing Up Bilingual in Jamaica

I came from a Patwa-speaking home and community and arrived at primary school as a Patwa-speaking Jamaican child. My primary school did a great job of teaching English; by the time I reached high school, I was a fluent and confident English speaker. By then, I had grown accustomed to being taught in English. I can't remember questioning the prevailing idea that Patwa was inferior to English, that it was a language that sophisticated, educated people shunned.

In high school, things changed. I attended a school that primarily educated children of wealthy families. Here language was a marker of status. Suddenly, those inevitable moments when someone unintentionally spoke Patwa in the middle of speaking English were significant.

One day in class, I made the mistake of saying, "I had drugs in my hot cocoa." Jamaicans know what this means: that there was residue or sediment in the drink. *Drugs* is the commonly used Patwa word for the English word *dregs*. One of my classmates corrected me with disdain. I felt humiliated. As the classmate guessed, I had used a Patwa word in an English sentence because I didn't know it was a Patwa word.

The teacher did not intervene. I was simply left to feel ashamed.

Patwa was not celebrated in my high school. In literature classes, we studied a few books by Caribbean—including Jamaican—authors. But these books were in English, with Patwa sporadically appearing as dialogue. Patwa itself remained absent from the formal curriculum, except for a fleeting sojourn into Miss Lou's poetry.

Dr. Louise Bennett-Coverley, affectionately known as Miss Lou, is to Jamaica what Dr. Maya Angelou and Zora Neale Hurston are to the United States, particularly Black America. More than 50 years after her appearance on the international stage, and a decade after her death, Miss Lou remains the unchallenged mother of Jamaican poetry. She is celebrated for her masterful use of Patwa. At a time when colonial rule reinforced the status of English, Miss Lou broke new ground chronicling and performing the Jamaican experience in Jamaican Patwa—locally and internationally. Her skillful use of Patwa effectively revealed the facility, logic, and meaning-making inherent in the way Jamaicans speak.

I was introduced to Miss Lou's work as something of a novelty. The message from the teacher seemed to be "Take a look at this. Now let's get back to business." Even though we spent just one or two classes on Miss Lou's poetry, I enjoyed the novelty immensely. I jumped at the opportunity to read her poem "Colonization in Reverse" (see p. 134) in class.

Years later, I still relive that moment, recognizing that it influenced the rest of my life. That moment—standing in front of the class, reading a Patwa poem in English class—was imbued with identity, history, politics, and pure pleasure.

Bringing Patwa into My Own Classroom

When I became a high school English teacher in a rural, all boys' school, my own experiences informed my pedagogy. The system remained the same: All classroom instruction was in English. I had a curriculum to teach. There were some opportunities to engage with Caribbean writers, but the curriculum did not directly address Patwa.

At the start of the school year, I established that I enjoyed speaking and valued Patwa. I shared that it is my primary language, which I speak every day and use in my creative work. I was also careful to clarify that my classes were intended to help students get good at English. We would discuss why this was important—for example, to progress to university and find employment. When I felt we understood that English was necessary—as opposed to better than Patwa—I invited students to take up the challenge to get as fluent in English as they were in Patwa, so that they could be good at both.

This introduction was well received by students. For the majority, English was being acquired as an additional language, and the recognition and validation of Patwa reduced the fear of making mistakes and being embarrassed when participating in class speaking English. This was of further importance in a school with students who came from rural communities, where it was very likely that Patwa was dominant.

I also knew that, as Patwa-speaking Jamaican children, my students arrived in the classroom steeped in the use of figurative language. From an early age, they were encouraged to develop a taste for play on words, pithy proverbs, snappy analyses, word economy, and dry, wry, even disinterested deliveries. My job was to get my students to tap into these rich resources in both their languages, and to be proud of the expertise they already had.

Teaching Shakespeare in Jamaica

Rather than using Jamaican culture and language as an add-on or fleeting novelty, students should consistently have the opportunity to see and use Patwa as a language of academic expression. This can be done very effectively, for example, when teaching Shakespeare.

To introduce students to Shakespeare, I would walk into the class dressed as a religious Rastafarian woman, with my head wrapped and my body robed in white. I would start with "Friends, Romans, countrymen, lend me your ears. This week we learn about Shakespeare." I would then read the rest of the monologue from Julius Caesar:

> Friends, Romans, countrymen, lend me your ears;
> I come to bury Caesar, not to praise him;
> The evil that men do lives after them,
> The good is oft interred with their bones,
> So let it be with Caesar . . . The noble Brutus
> Hath told you Caesar was ambitious:
> If it were so, it was a grievous fault,
> And grievously hath Caesar answered it . . .
> Here, under leave of Brutus and the rest,
> (For Brutus is an honorable man;
> So are they all; all honorable men)
> Come I to speak in Caesar's funeral . . .

I would expect students to recognize many of the words and understand the gist of the speech. I would also expect them to react to how strange and different Shakespeare's language sounds from Modern Standard English

I might open the class discussion by asking "What is Mark Antony talking about?" I would anticipate, even encourage, the resident joker's inevitable response: "Only God knows!" The laughter that followed was a gift that I could use to increase interest in discussing Shakespeare's language.

"What do you think about the language?" I might ask. "Would it be better to read Shakespeare in Modern English? Why?"

I would expect students to respond with opinions like "It sounds old-fashioned," or "It would be much easier to understand in Modern English."

I might then ask "What if Mark Antony's speech was in Patwa? What difference would that make?"

"Well, it would sound Jamaican. . . ," a student might respond.

My goal would be for students to see that, despite the differences in the style and the perceived strangeness of the language, they could understand and interpret Shakespeare's words. I would ask some questions to demonstrate how much they did in fact understand: "OK, so who is Mark Antony talking about? What's the occasion?"

After students recognized that the speech was Mark Antony's funeral oration for Caesar, I would push through to higher-order thinking: "Who do you think the speech favors? Brutus or Caesar? How do we know?" I would then guide students to puzzle over the apparent contradiction between Mark Antony's words and his intention—how he praises Brutus by repeating that he is honorable but subtly undermines him by raising doubts about Caesar's supposed ambition.

Once students recognized that they had captured the meaning of the speech, I would circle back to Patwa. I would tell students that they now had opportunity to tap into their learning and show what they understood by translating Shakespeare's words into Patwa. This would also give them the opportunity to be creative. I might set the stage with my own interpretation—something like this:

> Year 10, ear dis now. Caesar dead and gaan. Wheh fi do? Who have nuh time fi nuh nine night? Guh mek nuh whole heap a naise bout how him did do dis or how him did do dat or ray-ray? Ongle ting people might memba is wickedniss. A suh life guh.

> Di Bass Man Brutus seh Caesar did have a big head. An if dat was true, well dat was an abomination, and right now him more dan pay fi it.

> (Still, Brutus gi I a blye fi seh a few words. Fah Brutus is a desant-desant man. Di whole a dem man deh desant.)

With this scaffolding, students would then work in groups to rewrite and perform the whole speech as if Mark Antony was a Jamaican dancehall DJ performing at a stage show. Invariably, "Friends, Romans, countrymen, lend me your ears," would yield to versions of "People! Listen up!" "Massive! Hear me now!" "Follow me, massive and crew!" This, along with guaranteed bursts of laughter, would encourage students to engage with, and even look forward to, Shakespeare. Interpreting Shakespeare into Patwa would also give them the opportunity to experience Patwa working as a language of academic expression.

The Possibility of Bilingual Education

In recent years, more people have started advocating for bilingual education in Jamaica. In fact, there have been attempts to create bilingual programs in Patwa and Standard English.

About a decade ago, the Bilingual Education Project of the Jamaica Language Unit, based at the University of the West Indies at Mona, created and piloted a bilingual program as a radical intervention study in three schools. They used the Cassidy system to translate mathematics, social studies, and language arts texts into Patwa; developed curricula; and trained and supported teachers. The teachers taught in Patwa and English, with the goal of biliteracy for students. The program was monitored and evaluated with favorable results after four years.

Although the program was deemed successful, the Ministry of Education, Youth, and Culture (MoEYC), which had approved the pilot, would not scale it. The MoEYC maintained that their primary concern was to improve the country's poor performance in English literacy, not to foster biliteracy or cultivate Patwa as a language of academic expression. Essentially, the MoEYC defended monoliterate bilingualism—in favor of English. They argued that there was no convention for an orthographic system for Patwa, and that they had to contend with legitimate financial concerns and prevailing negative attitudes toward Patwa as a language of instruction.

What a shame that these experiments with biliteracy and bilingual instruction have not yet gained traction. Valuing the languages and cultures our students bring to school nurtures their confidence and development. When Patwa is brought into the school space, students feel it is safer to cultivate their authentic voices; it enables them to access and express parts of themselves that may not be accessible when speaking a language that isn't their first tongue.

Developing and Cementing Patwa Literacy

Despite its long absence from schools and official spaces, many Jamaicans feel deeply connected with and are passionate about Patwa. Nowhere was this more evident than on Twitter during the summer 2016 Rio Olympic Games. In a phrase, JamaicaTwitta blew up. An "analysis show" emerged, with Jamaicans reveling in the exploits of #TeamJamaica in, as Jamaicans would say, raw-bawn (unadulterated) Patwa. Importantly, Jamaicans—seemingly from a cross section of ages, gender, and backgrounds, located in Jamaica and internationally in its diaspora—were talking to each other by *writing* in Patwa. And the end product was both immensely entertaining and also made for compelling intellectual reading. It was fascinating to watch the spelling of words being negotiated dynamically and democratically, and to see the spellings that won out becoming stabilized in use.

> **"What if Mark Antony's speech was in Patwa? What difference would that make?"**

Schools could be part of this exciting process of developing and cementing Patwa literacy. Jamaican students deserve to have both of their languages developed during their school careers. This may be a less daunting task if Patwa literacy is not conceived of as the translation of all English texts into Patwa texts. Perhaps progress can be made by beginning with a study of existing material already written in Patwa. A full curriculum could be developed around Miss Lou's works, providing coordinated instruction from primary to tertiary levels, including the training of teachers in Patwa pedagogy.

At the very least, and with some urgency, Jamaican students deserve to have their first language officially recognized and protected in schools. They deserve formal recognition as bilingual speakers. Their linguistic abilities and achievements ought to be acknowledged and celebrated. They also deserve to have their native language developed, honored, and included in school spaces alongside appropriate support and scaffolding, as they develop their Standard English language skills and literacy. They are learners acquiring an additional language while being taught in an immersion bilingual program, and they deserve support like any other bilingual learner.

> **Jamaicans—seemingly from a cross section of ages, gender, and backgrounds—were talking to each other by *writing* in Patwa.**

No Jamaican child should feel shame for saying a Patwa word in any class in Jamaica. Every student in Jamaica should feel the pride that I felt when reading Miss Lou's "Colonization in Reverse" in front of my class—the pride that comes from an unbroken connection with your culture and your native tongue. ☼

Jacqui Stanford, PhD, has been an educator for more than 20 years, working internationally on school improvement and culture at the government policy and university levels in the United States and United Kingdom, and in Jamaica where she taught high school English. Her spoken word poetry in Patwa is available at soundcloud.com/jacquistanford.

Note from the author: Many thanks to Desrine Bogle for reading a first draft of this article.

References

Bennett-Coverley, Louise. 1966. "Colonization in Reverse." *Jamaica Labrish: Jamaica Dialect Poems.* Sangster Press.

Cassidy, Frederic G. 1971. *Jamaica Talk: Three Hundred Years of the English Language in Jamaica.* Macmillan Education Ltd.

Cassidy, Frederic G., and Robert B. Le Page. 1980. *Dictionary of Jamaican English.* Cambridge University Press.

Devonish, Hubert. 2012. "From a Semi-Lingual to a Bilingual Jamaica." *Talking Tongues Blog.* August 24. icclr.wordpress.com/2012/08/24/from-a-semi-lingual-to-a-bilingual-jamaica/.

Jamaica Language Unit. 2014. "Bilingual Education Project." Department of Language, Linguistics, and Philosophy, University of the West Indies at Mona. mona.uwi.edu/Dllp/jlu/projects/index.htm.

UWI Notebook. 2010. "Researchers: Bilingual Education Yields Better Results." *The Gleaner.* June 27. jamaica-gleaner.com/gleaner/20100627/arts/arts3.html#disqus_thread.

Colonization in Reverse

Louise Bennett-Coverley

Miss Lou
1919 - 2006

JAMAICAN POET FOLKLORIST WRITER EDUCATOR
PRESERVED THE PRACTICE OF PERFORMING POETRY AND FOLK SONGS AND STORIES IN PATOIS

MARIA PAPAEFSTATHIOU

Wat a joyful news, miss Mattie,
I feel like me heart gwine burs
Jamaica people colonizin
Englan in Reverse

By de hundred, by de tousan,
From country and from town,
By de ship-load, by de plane load
Jamaica is Englan boun.

Dem a pour out a Jamaica,
Everybody future plan
Is fe get a big-time job
An settle in de mother lan.

What an islan! What a people!
Man an woman, old an young
Jus a pack dem bag an baggage
An turn history upside dung!

Some people doan like travel,
But fe show dem loyalty
Dem all a open up cheap-fare-
To-England agency.

An week by week dem shipping off
Dem countryman like fire,
Fe immigrate an populate
De seat a de Empire.

Oonoo see how life is funny,
Oonoo see da turnabout?
jamaica live fe box bread
Out a English people mout'.

For wen dem ketch a Englan,
An start play dem different role,
Some will settle down to work
An some will settle fe de dole.

Jane says de dole is not too bad
Because dey payin she
Two pounds a week fe seek a job
dat suit her dignity.

me say Jane will never fine work
At de rate how she dah look,
For all day she stay popn Aunt Fan couch
An read love-story book.

Wat a devilment a Englan!
Dem face war an brave de worse,
But me wondering how dem gwine stan
Colonizin in reverse.

Building Bridges

A dual-language experience for high school students

APRIL S. SALERNO AND AMANDA K. KIBLER

FAVIANNA RODRIGUEZ

High school students sat on beanbags, reading their picture books aloud to 1st graders. Some read from hard copies, some from iPads. Some read in Spanish, some in English. All around there were smiles, as the teens read the stories they had written, and the children pointed to the illustrations they had drawn. Alex, a 16-year-old Latino student, finished reading one storybook and asked his young partner, Luis, which book he'd like next. Luis picked another student-published book about dinosaurs.

Alex pointed to the words on the page, written in both English and Spanish. He asked Luis, "You want to read the Spanish?" Luis smiled big but said quietly that he didn't know how.

Alex gave a disapproving but encouraging look and told him, "You got to know the Spanish."

Luis hung his head. "I know some of the words, but . . ." The "but" hung heavy in the air. Alex seemed to understand without Luis saying more.

"You want me to read the Spanish?"

"Yeah," Luis answered, relieved.

The reading day was a culminating activity of Languages Across Borders (LAB), a yearlong dual-language extracurricular program designed to develop high school students' biliteracy and disrupt linguistic segregation at Hamilton High School, a Virginia public school where about 4 percent of the 1,100 students were designated English learners. At Hamilton, English learners were often in tracked courses separated from other students, especially students taking advanced classes. English learners, like Alex, were often viewed based on what others thought they needed—math credits, passing test scores, and grades good enough to keep playing soccer. English-dominant students, on the other hand, were often viewed on what they offered—participation in the high school choir, the annual school musical, the golf team.

Hamilton students whose home language was Spanish had limited opportunities in traditional foreign-language Spanish courses to develop their Spanish oral or literacy skills; Spanish courses were designed for students without previous experiences with the language. And Spanish learners had few opportunities for authentic Spanish conversations with peers proficient in Spanish. As we observed this pattern in this and other schools, we wondered: Why do students share school facilities but not access to the same people, curricula, or opportunities? How could we design a program to provide opportunities for English learners and Spanish learners to collaborate in authentic ways as partners and equals, at least on an interpersonal level, even if we were unable to address the larger inequities of access resulting from systematic tracking?

Organizing Languages Across Borders

Having both worked as English and ESL teachers, and now working as researchers at a nearby university, we partnered with three Spanish teachers and two ESL teachers at Hamilton to facilitate the program. With administrator approval, ESL/English and Spanish department chairs connected Amanda with potentially interested teachers. Amanda met with teachers individually, sharing ideas for activities and curriculum development, as well as discussing teachers' responsibilities in facilitating the program sessions and giving feedback on the curriculum.

Teachers recruited students for LAB from ESL and advanced Spanish classes at Hamilton. We hoped that the program would offer benefits for all students, regardless of language background. Students said they joined for many reasons: because they wanted to meet people, wanted to improve their Spanish or English or both, or thought bilingual experiences looked good on résumés. Because LAB was voluntary and extracurricular, we wanted the program schedule to be responsive to students' availability. Challenged with students' transportation issues and after-school conflicts, we eventually decided to hold three LAB meetings a week: two meetings during half-hour tutoring sessions before school and one after school for 45 minutes.

In all aspects of the program, we wanted students to take ownership of LAB. Attendance was never mandatory. We structured activities so students could attend when they wanted to and were able.

Building Community and Autonomy

We began our first LAB sessions with community-building conversations. Students worked in cross-language pairs to answer questions—rotating in Spanish and English—on high-interest topics (e.g., What would you do if you want to get a job so you can buy a car, but your family wants you to focus on school?). We followed up with project-based activities, which students could choose to do or skip at various "stations." One popular project-based activity was working with cross-language partners to make bilingual movies using online tools.

At the end of each session, students recorded what they had done that day in individual folders. The next time they attended, they could choose either to pick up where they and their partner had left off or begin a new task with a new partner.

Why do students share school facilities but not access to the same people, curricula, or opportunities?

As the year went on, we encouraged students to initiate their own project ideas. Generally, we tried to let students lead; we wanted to give them opportunities to practice language through authentic tasks, such as facilitating meetings. We stepped in and prompted students, however, if we saw they were overlooking necessary details.

In October, a group of mostly English learners introduced the idea of planning a Day of the Dead event to showcase various cultural traditions associated with the holiday. Interested students held meetings during LAB sessions to plan activities. During these meetings, students who were familiar with the holiday explained traditions to those who were less familiar. Students created and posted fliers to invite others at the school, brought in food on the holiday, and led a meeting where LAB members and others from the school could remember and tell about (in Spanish or English) friends and relatives who had passed away.

With that success under their belts, LAB members had more confidence planning activities and leading LAB initiatives. Many students said they wanted the program to somehow involve community service but were unsure how to get started. In December, we invited a bilingual employee from a local nonprofit to tell students about her volunteer work as an English-Spanish interpreter at a local hospital. Afterward, students generated various ideas for a bilingual service project. Students discussed options and ultimately decided to write bilingual storybooks for bilingual 1st-grade students at a feeder elementary school, which enrolled about 625 students, about 30 percent of whom were classified as English learners.

Organizing the Book Project

Up until the book project, LAB activities had generally involved flexible grouping, with students entering and exiting groups as they wished or needed, according to interests in individual activities or projects. Because all students wanted to take part in the book project, we established ongoing cross-language groups, which lasted several sessions. We allowed LAB members to give us input about who they thought they would work well with. Using this information, we assigned LAB members to work in groups of four to six to write books.

We wanted students to have opportunities to negotiate language and content with each other, without necessarily having to involve a teacher. Materials—including activity guides and example children's books—guided students through reviewing features of bilingual children's books, selecting topics and characters, planning plot outlines, storyboarding scenes, soliciting illustrations from the 1st-grade students, and ultimately designing books using an online book-writing program. We designed the activity guides in both languages so that students could choose which language(s) to use while they self-facilitated their groups. The structured bilingual materials also allowed students to work through activities at their own pace, regardless of attendance. Groups kept track of their work in a folder, and book-writing materials stayed in the classroom to prevent an absent student from having taken home materials others needed in order to make progress.

Creating Bilingual Books

During one typical session, students meandered into the Spanish classroom alone or in clusters, some bringing breakfast trays from the cafeteria. Others grabbed an orange and juice box from the snack table we set up at the back of the room. Ms. Mason, one of the Spanish teachers facilitating the day's session, called for students' attention: "OK, *muchachos*!" She provided instructions in Spanish on how students should continue planning their storybooks. Ms. Terrance, another Spanish teacher, then repeated instructions in English. In LAB, teachers gave instructions in both languages, though an alternative might involve students translating or explaining directions to each other.

One group—Alex, Emily, Javier, and Madison—watched a video podcast from the 1st graders. We had asked the 1st-grade teacher to create the videos, explaining the children's reading interests. The children on the screen giggle and, in Spanish, introduce themselves and explain that they like books about dinosaurs, superheroes, princesses, and animals. "*Hola, mi nombre es Valentina*" (Hi, my name is Valentina), one little girl says, laughing. "*Me gustan animales y princesas. Gracias.*" (I like animals and princesses. Thank you.)

Emily looked up from the video and commented, "I want to make them the coolest book ever!" Emily and Madison then tried to decipher the 1st graders' Spanish in English. Alex and Javier watched Emily and Madison talk, letting them puzzle through the Spanish from the video without offering translations.

Eventually, Emily—who was assigned to be the group's facilitator for the day—asked, "How do you say princesses in Spanish?"

Javier responded, "*Princesas.* They also like *superhéroes* like Spiderman, Superman."

Emily asked, "How do you spell that?" Javier helped her with the spelling while she wrote on the group's paper, which at this point asked students to plan their topics, characters, and setting.

After reading the paper, Emily turned to Alex, "What would you like our story to be about?"

"Superman, Spiderman," he said.

Emily suggested a compromise, "Can we incorporate superheroes and animals?"

Madison answered, "They can be saving animals."

"On the farm," Emily added. "*Cómo se dice* farm?" (How do you say farm?)

"Farm. *Granja,*" Javier responded.

Emily wrote that on the paper, and then veered off topic saying excitedly in English that she had heard a weather report that today would be an unusually warm early spring day. Still using English, she turned to Javier and asked him about soccer; he answered that there were tryouts after school. They discussed soccer for a while before turning back to their writing. In LAB, groups weren't always discussing work, but we did not admonish students for being off-task. We gave students a great deal of freedom to work—or not—as they wished. We viewed such interactions as positive signs that students were building friendships.

Ultimately, these students wrote about a piglet kidnapped by a snake and saved by a group of superhero animals; in the end, the snake repents and becomes friends with all the animals.

Looking Back

In many ways, LAB was imperfect. Though students had choices about languages they used, conversations like the one above often occurred in English. This speaks to the strong pressures to use English in the school and larger dominant culture. Cross-language groups often talked socially in English, and English-dominant students often initiated group work, beginning and often continuing in English.

Above, for example, Emily was initiating and facilitating small-group work. This was only partly because she was assigned that day to be group leader. In fact, we began assigning this role on a rotating basis after we noticed that several English-dominant students, including Emily, were assuming leadership. We hoped that by assigning roles, we would help students share responsibilities and possibly shift toward more use of Spanish. Though we did see some changes, we can't say our efforts were even nearly powerful enough to change the institutional norms that encouraged English-dominant students to take on leadership roles.

Looking back, we realize that all students might have benefited from more explicit training in how to facilitate a group (or to support others in doing so). We might also have pressed harder to encourage Spanish learners to facilitate discussions in Spanish. Or we could have alternated language by day or task. By doing so, we might have more closely approached a language balance and disrupted traditional norms that placed English-dominant students in comfortable language and facilitation roles. We recognize, too, that factors affecting students' interactions and language choices are complex. It is possible that our "pressing" for more Spanish or assigning days might not have been powerful enough to disrupt larger social structures and sociolinguistic positioning.

Still, despite not offering this training or explicit language structure, students talked about being able to contribute to the book project on two levels: to peers who sometimes needed language help and to the children for whom they were writing books.

"I was one of the guys who was giving ideas for what to write on the paper for the book," Javier stated proudly. "We were four people in our group, and we were all working together, all giving ideas."

Dual-language programs generally stop at the end of elementary school, and very rarely continue past middle school. Yet dual-language experiences between high school English learners and Spanish learners offer a promising way to promote bilingualism and biliteracy. They also can facilitate friendships that modestly reduce school-based linguistic segregation. This program was indeed a small effort, taking up 30 or 45 minutes of students' day a few times a week, occurring during voluntary time, not during the regular school day. Yet despite institutional barriers—tracking, tight schedules, teachers' heavy workloads, pressures to spend academic time on test preparation—we found that it is possible to create a "dual-language like" experience for high school students. As Javier put it: "Other people are wanting to learn a different language. So it makes sense because you can communicate with them in Spanish, and they can communicate with you in English, which helps both of us at the same time."

> **We began assigning the group leader role on a rotating basis after we noticed that several English-dominant students were assuming leadership.**

Even without a program like LAB, educators can take steps to reduce language-based segregation. We can advocate for changes to schools' tracking policies so that students from different linguistic backgrounds have opportunities to collaborate with each other. We can look inside our own classrooms and consider whether English learners have opportunities to interact meaningfully with skilled English-dominant peers by acting as language or content experts.

Our program certainly did not address the larger institutional system of tracking or the ways that students experienced inequity in their regular daily school lives. It is, in fact, difficult at times to work out when tracking leads to isolation of English learners and when it also offers them separate, "safe" spaces to learn. There remains much work to be done in addressing systemic equity issues for English learners. But alongside advocacy for systemic change, we also believe there is merit to smaller changes made at the classroom level. If we want our schools to be places where young people truly learn to value each other—rather than just share the school roof for a set period of time each day—we must explore how we can encourage them to work together in ways that value all students' contributions. ✿

April S. Salerno (ass3jw@virginia.edu) taught English language arts in New Mexico and English as a foreign language in the Republic of Moldova. She is now a postdoctoral research associate at the University of Virginia. Amanda K. Kibler (akk2v@virginia. edu) is a former secondary English and ESL teacher. She is now an associate professor of education at the University of Virginia, and her research focuses on multilingual adolescents' language and literacy development. Student, teacher, and school names have been changed.

Note from the authors: We would like to thank Christine Hardigree and Ashley Simpson Baird for their work as research team members. The project was funded by Youth-Nex, the University of Virginia Center to Promote Effective Youth Development.

Ganas Means Desire

An after-school program links Latina/o university students with middle schoolers

BY ROSCOE CARON

FAVIANNA RODRIGUEZ

Colorful posters, many of them student-made, celebrate Latina/o cultural icons and historic events. Twenty-five Latina/o middle school students chat at desks that ring the perimeter of the room.

"*¡Dame mi lápiz pa'tras!*" Rosa calls out to Ricardo.

"I need your pencil to help me get good grades!" Ricardo smilingly teases before handing Rosa's pencil back.

The chatter suddenly stops as seven Latina/o college students from the University of Oregon begin clapping their hands in unison in the United Farm Worker "Unity Clap," developed in the fields of California during the organizing drives of the 1960s as a form of communication and solidarity. The middle schoolers join in the slow rhythmic clap, picking up speed until it sounds like applause. Then it stops and the room is silent. Today's session of Ganas, a program that links Latina/o middle schoolers with members of the University of Oregon MEChA chapter, is beginning.

A Ganas Meeting

Leah, a college sophomore and one of two Ganas coordinators, stands in the middle of the room. "Today, after we work on our homework, we will have a special guest, Guadalupe Quinn. Guadalupe has been working on immigration issues for more than 20 years. She knows all about what is happening with laws in Oregon and in Washington, D.C., and you can ask her your questions. But right now, let's get to work on our school stuff."

As students start on their homework, Spanish and English flow naturally around the room. The college and middle school students communicate in whatever ways are comfortable and practical. Some of the Latina/o middle school students speak little English and some speak little Spanish. For the vast majority, Spanish is the home language.

Books open, papers rustle, and the college students circulate to check in with Ganas students. Ricardo, a senior majoring in ethnic studies, asks Sofia and Isabela what they are working on. Sofia responds: "We have to do a project on elements for our science class. I'm doing mine on Argon and Isabela's doing Krypton."

Andrea, a sophomore Spanish major, is talking with Emilio and Rafael. The 8th graders want to know how she decided to go to the University of Oregon. She pulls up a chair and replies, "*¡Buena pregunta!* My cousin went to U of O and had a great time. And my parents wanted me to go to a school not too far away from home."

Ganas meetings are a space for formal and informal relationship building, and academic, cultural, and organizing activities. Some students are working on algebra problems at the whiteboard with one of the Mechistas. Some work on projects on laptops. After 45 minutes of academics, the Ganas students are ready to go to the cafeteria for their snack, provided by the school district's after-school program.

When they return, Guadalupe is waiting for them. They form a large circle with their chairs. Guadalupe talks about the proposed driver's card legislation in the Oregon legislature and the Obama administration's Deferred Action for Childhood Arrivals program that a number of the students' siblings have applied for.

Elena, a 6th grader asks, "Everybody says that *la migra* hangs out at Walmart looking for people to arrest. Is that true?" Other students ask about a hostile motor vehicle department office, about the inside of the Lane County jail, and about green cards. When Guadalupe has finished, Leah makes a couple of announcements about upcoming events before the students head home.

Ganas Beginnings

Within a short time after I began work as a 7th-grade teacher at a new middle school in 1996, I knew that things were not right. The school had the district's second-largest Latina/o population, yet seemed to be living in the monocultural past.

On a regular basis, messages would be hand-delivered to my classroom, requesting that one of the Latina/o students be sent to the vice principal's office. The class would quiet as I called the student up to get the hall pass to the office. The Latina/o students, 14 percent of the school's population, knew they did not belong in their school. Their languages and their cultures were invisible. Some of them fought back and were called to task in the office. Others seemed to carry their sadness with them all day long, the weight of the load lowering their heads and their vision.

I wondered how to address the situation. The answer came through discussions with my friend, Jim. Jim is Mexican American and worked as an academic advisor to students of color at the University of Oregon. He was also an advisor to the university's MEChA chapter.

MEChA, the nation's largest Latina/o student union, stands for Movimiento Estudiantil Chicano de Aztlán (Chicano Student Movement of Aztlán). Formed in the late 1960s, MEChA's founding document (*El Plan de Aztlán*) made clear the imperative of honoring and maintaining connection with those who had come before, those whose sacrifices and labors had made enrollment in college possible.

Jim and I developed a rough plan: He would bring MEChA students to the school to support Latina/o kids. I would do the logistical work: school communications, parent forms, scheduling. The name of the program would be Ganas, which means "desire." The goal: to develop bicultural leaders.

Jim and I pitched the idea to the MEChA students, who were enthusiastic. The middle school's principal was cautiously supportive. With no template and no funding, we set off.

I went through the school's demographic records to identify all Latina/o students and invited them to a pizza lunch discussion to learn about the new program. The Mechistas selected a Ganas coordinator from their ranks. We started meeting twice a week, on days that worked out best for the college students. Jim and I provided money for simple snacks. We began fashioning a program that combined academic tutoring, cultural learning and support, Spanish language affirmation, and leadership training.

> **On a regular basis, messages would be hand-delivered to my classroom, requesting that one of the Latina/o students be sent to the vice principal's office.**

The Ganas Leaders

We wanted students to have an authentic role in building the organization. The MEChA students nominated four middle school students to be part of a leadership team. They became my co-workers as we adopted a community-organizing model to getting everything done—from making copies, to distributing reminder notices, to making phone calls, to writing press releases announcing upcoming Ganas events, to doing logistical planning with the Mechistas via email. These student leaders conducted surveys of fellow Ganas students and intervened with students who were not performing to the academic or behavioral standards of Ganas. They led discussions, arranged for guest speakers, and collected field trip permission forms.

Not only was having this group consistent with the goal of leadership skill development, the student leaders were essential for generating interest in Ganas. A homework club is simply not enough to keep middle school kids staying after school twice a week. It's the constant variety of activities that made Ganas exciting and dynamic. Ganas was like a perpetual motion machine—in much the same way that middle schoolers are. As soon as we had completed a field trip or a public presentation, we were already planning and talking about the next event that we would engage in together.

Culture, Language, Mentorship

Over the years, Ganas has grown into a comprehensive yearlong program. The various Ganas components and activities evolved organically, based on the ideas of the middle school students, the Mechistas, staff coordinators, and community members.

Throughout the year, the Mechistas teach lessons about social justice and history, both to the whole group and in their elbow-to-elbow homework help. Driving back to campus, the Mechistas discuss what they think the middle schoolers need to learn about. This might lead to a presentation, a video, or one-on-one discussions about the Bracero Program, the United Farm Workers, the Zoot Suit Riots, or the Chicano Movement.

The Mechistas also help the middle school students explore issues of race and bias through group and one-on-one discussions. They help the middle school students analyze selections in social studies textbooks and explore how to bring different perspectives into classrooms. Sometimes the problems are tough for middle schoolers to tackle: What if your teacher makes you feel invisible in class? What if you've been turned automatically into the class translator for new students?

The Mechistas bring in guest speakers from the community and take turns sharing their life stories. They talk about their families, their struggles in school, and their journeys to become university students. They talk about pain, alienation, and resilience. They talk about the strength that comes from language, culture, community, and dreams. Their personal narratives make college feel like a real possibility. The message from the Mechistas is "I have done this and I believe that you can, too. *Sí, se puede.*"

Toward the end of the school year, the Ganas students put on a cultural showcase assembly for the school and community. Through discussions, the group decides what to incorporate into this year's event: dance, live music, fashion, art, video, speakers, etc. These assemblies have become impressive productions with themes such as "Viva la mujer," which featured Dolores Huerta as a keynote speaker; and "In the Spirit of Cesar and Dolores," which featured the president of Oregon's farmworker union, PCUN (*Pineros y Campesinos Unidos del Noroeste*).

Language is an essential component of Ganas as well. As 7th grader Maria said: "I can speak Spanish and feel comfortable and safe. People understand my culture and what I'm saying." Former Ganas student Alondra commented: "When we spoke Spanish to each other it was like saying, 'We know what our roots are and we are proud of them.'"

Relationships are also built through day-to-day activities. Midterm grades present the opportunity for MEChA students to look at each student's grades, elbow-to-elbow, and to congratulate, challenge, and problem-solve with the students. MEChA students also sit in on parent-teacher conferences in order to connect with parents and to gain insights into family and classroom dynamics.

Throughout the year, the middle school students take part in a number of ME-ChA activities that link them to the university and give them a vision for future academics. They attend a number of MEChA meetings on campus, where college students discuss political issues and plan activities and events. They shadow MEChA students for a day, accompanying them to all of their classes. Ganas students also spend a day at Lane Community College, meeting with administrators, attending Chicano Studies classes, and touring campus.

The Impact of Ganas

From the beginning of Ganas, student grades improved markedly and discipline referrals plummeted. Latina/o students began to gain leadership visibility at the school.

For some of the MEChA college students, far away from their families, Ganas becomes an emotional anchor, and Ganas students become surrogate brothers and sisters. And many MEChA students come face-to-face with their own middle school experiences—the pain, the denial, and the shame of not having their home language or culture recognized at school. Sarita, current bilingual educator and assistant principal, reflected: "I will never forget a Ganas bonding session with two middle school Chicanitas who expressed their need to be seen, to be heard, to be important, to be understood. It was at that moment that I realized that I had felt the exact same way throughout my K–12 education."

> "We know what our roots are and we are proud of them."
> —Alondra, former Ganas student

Seeing the power of embracing language, identity, and culture within a school setting, many MEChA students come to reconsider their course of study. Students who were majoring in business, sociology, and ethnic studies now want their future jobs to provide support for Latina/o students. The love, joy, and sense of accomplishment they experienced working with the middle school students has led dozens of MEChA students to careers in teaching, counseling, college transition programs, and other forms of Latina/o student and parent advocacy.

Over the years, Ganas leadership and activism have extended to the larger community. Ganas students organized the local Latina/o community during a campaign to name a new elementary school after Cesar Chavez. An initial vote by the school board indicated little support for the name, with only one out of seven members in favor. The middle schoolers asked the Mechistas to help mount a campaign. Together they organized a candlelight march and mass gatherings at school board meetings. They worked to write and deliver impassioned testimony. The campaign ultimately succeeded by a 4-to-3 vote.

After 19 years—and three different homes in the Eugene district—Ganas is still going strong. Although Eugene teachers and administrators have not universally supported Ganas, MEChA students have forged a program that has made a significant difference in the lives of hundreds of Latina/o middle school and college students.

Many school volunteer programs have a short shelf life. As Ganas celebrates its 20-year anniversary, its continued existence is a testament to passionately devoted MEChA students, staff members, parents, community members, and students who have lived the meaning of Ganas: Desire. ✿

Ganas co-founder Roscoe Caron taught middle school for almost 25 years and currently teaches at the University of Oregon College of Education. He is a former forestry worker with Hoedads Coop Inc.

Chapter 4

EQUITY AT THE CENTER

RICARDO LEVINS MORALES

Introduction

Since its founding, dual-language school La Escuela Fratney has consciously striven to create equality between Spanish and English, with a commitment to teaching multicultural, anti-racist curriculum. Yet Bob Peterson tells the story of how one day, Ahmed Mbalia, a professor of Africology, asked him to take a look inside one of the classrooms. Mbalia pointed to the walls: "Don't get me wrong Bob, kids need to know the presidents, but to have Washington—a big-time slave owner—and Lincoln as the only posters in a room in a school that prides itself on being multicultural? Come on."

This vignette—and the other articles in this chapter—remind us that equity does not happen automatically when we set out to teach in two languages. Sometimes in our diverse groups of students, not everyone's voices are heard and not every child sees their culture as equally validated. This same dynamic can also play out between languages. Despite teaching in two languages, English is often the default schoolwide mode of communication—with announcements, assemblies, and staff meetings conducted in English. The lack of quality resources in other languages, from instructional materials to well-stocked bilingual libraries, contributes to English dominance. In such contexts, it is not surprising to notice students favoring English at the expense of their home languages.

We can identify and tackle issues of equity by exploring challenging questions. The teachers in this chapter ask themselves how they can create classrooms inclusive of students who speak a third or fourth language at home. They consider how they can meet students' language needs alongside their special education needs. They challenge the hegemony of English in their classrooms and urge their students to do the same. And it's not only classroom teachers that want and need to do this; César Chávez Elementary School in San Francisco and La Escuela Fratney in Milwaukee offer examples on a schoolwide level.

This work is based in continuous critical reflection. It is about being open to the observations of community members, students, teachers, administrators, and parents. Our classrooms and schools must be safe spaces where we can question details—and work to keep equity at the center.

La Escuela Fratney

Creating a bilingual school as a greenhouse of democracy

BY BOB PETERSON

BARBARA MINER

O
n New Year's Day in 1988, a small group of teachers and parents issued a public call for the Milwaukee school board to allow them to establish an "anti-racist, whole language, two-way bilingual, site-based managed, integrated, neighborhood, specialty school." We organizers called it La Escuela Fratney for short.

As community and teacher activists in the era of Reagan, we weren't accustomed to winning many organizing campaigns. We were surprised when, despite the superintendent's strong opposition, we convinced the school board to allow us to create a new school. We had only a few months lead time before the school was to start.

As the first two-way bilingual school in Wisconsin, and one of few explicitly anti-racist, social justice public schools in the country, Fratney broke new ground in numerous ways. My work at Fratney for two and half decades (the first few years as program implementer and the rest as a 5th-grade teacher) taught me a lot about the challenges of starting and sustaining an innovative public school. It also led me to the idea that schools should be reimagined as greenhouses of democracy and social justice—centers of renaissance and resistance in our communities.

The "old" Fratney Street School was a public school in the Riverwest neighborhood where I lived, one of the Milwaukee's few racially integrated, working-class neighborhoods. The school was built in 1903, the same year as the Wright Brothers' Kitty Hawk flight and 10 years before Harriet Tubman died.

For decades, the old Fratney school operated as a traditional, monolingual school. In the early 1980s, the school board decided to build a large new school six blocks away from Fratney on the site of another school that had served severely disabled students for many years. The entire Fratney student body would ultimately be transferred to the new state-of-the-art building designed to educate disabled and non-disabled students together. District officials originally considered razing the Fratney building, but later proposed to use it to create a school that would train struggling teachers.

At the time, I was working at a school with a developmental bilingual program on the other side of the city. It was a strong bilingual program, but the curriculum was textbook based and teacher-centric. When I realized that the Fratney building was to be vacated, a few colleagues and I hastily organized bilingual teachers, parents, and neighborhood members into Neighbors for a New Fratney. Some of the folks were affiliated with Rethinking Schools, which has its office in the same neighborhood. After a few discussions, we issued our New Year's Day press release, launched a petition drive, and circulated our 12-page vision statement that called for a two-way bilingual, democratically governed school that would encourage staff, students, parents, and community members to discuss problems that confront our community and world.

We collected signatures, held community rallies, organized support among community leaders, and went en masse to school board meetings. Within two months, we won the right to create our own public school.

Working to Find the Right Program Model

From the start, we were committed to a two-way bilingual program in which native Spanish and English speakers would be in the same classrooms, receiving their instruction in both English and Spanish. Our underlying belief was that all children have a basic human right to learn and develop two languages, including their native tongues. Moreover, by having a mix of Spanish-dominant and English-dominant students in each classroom, we maximized the possibility of having racially integrated classrooms.

By consciously striving to create equality between Spanish and English, we modeled a broad concept of equality to our students. We believed that, when there is intentional effort to nurture the intimate link between culture and language, bilingual instruction also promotes multicultural understanding. And a two-way bilingual approach enhances students' self-esteem, because students learn that—no matter what social class they come from—they bring something of value to the classroom: their languages.

Two-way bilingual programs in the United States, however, face numerous challenges. Because English is so clearly the language of power and cultural dominance within the United States, there is tremendous peer and societal pressure on students to abandon their home languages. At Fratney we learned that successful bilingual learning requires a determined commitment to privilege the nondominant language at the school level and in classrooms. For us, this meant a strict separation of the two languages and learning environments, so children were required to use their second language and teachers stayed in the target language. We found that when classes were conducted bilingually (i.e., a teacher explains the material first in one language and then in the other), students tended to rely on their native tongue.

By the end of our second year, we realized that English was still too dominant in our school. We critically examined our practices and tried to learn from the experience of two-way bilingual schools in other states. Staff held discussions, and parents and teachers on the site-based council explored alternatives. We especially focused on the distinctive instructional approach being used in our two kindergarten classes. At the beginning of our third year, we adopted the instructional method used in these kindergartens for the whole school: Two teachers of the same grade team-taught between 54 and 60 children in two groups of 27 to 30 children per class. One day, students would go to the Spanish room and receive instruction in Spanish; the next day, they would go to the English room and receive instruction in English. The teachers were both bilingual, but one would teach in English and the other in Spanish.

Within two months we won the right to create our own public school.

This approach increased the use of Spanish because the language-specific classrooms clearly signaled to students what language they were to use. It also encouraged team teaching. At the same time, it complicated other matters such as assessment, report cards, and parent-teacher conferences.

A few years later, the 4th- and 5th-grade teachers decided to alternate classes every two weeks instead of every other day. For example, in 5th grade, which I taught for many years, we had 50 to 60 students. We divided the students in two groups— the red group and blue group—and for two weeks I would teach the red group in English and the other teacher would teach the blue group in Spanish, her native language. After two weeks, the students would change classrooms and each teacher would teach the other group. Working with the same group of students for two weeks at a time allowed us to build on instruction from one day to the next. This was particularly important for major projects and for our reading program: Students working in literature circles were able to complete a new chapter book during each two-week session.

In the earlier grades, we continued to experiment with different models to ensure that students received sufficient instructional time in Spanish. These models were influenced by many factors—including the levels of funding that determined class size and the specific language strengths of our teachers. We decided to substantially increase Spanish language instruction to 80 to 90 percent in the earlier grades, progressively adding more English until there was a 50/50 balance in the 4th and 5th grades. This required that teachers carefully plan the amount of time spent in Spanish and determine which subjects would be taught in which languages.

Multicultural, Anti-Racist Curricula

Fratney was developed around a commitment to multiculturalism. In "A Proposal for a Basic Curriculum for Fratney Street School," developed by five teachers in the summer before the school opened, and adopted as our working curriculum for the first years, we stated:

> Multicultural, anti-racist education is more than just familiarizing our students with a few facts, faces, and foods of various nationalities who live in our country. Children should develop "ethnic literacy" to understand, analyze, and respect their own cultural roots, an understanding of the historical nature of racial oppression, and the advantage of a multicultural, multilingual society. The school will have an "anti-racist teaching policy" to help children develop anti-racist attitudes, make them aware of how racist oppression has hurt all American citizens for centuries, and the need to fight against it.

Such a goal is much easier to write than implement. Most educators at Fratney had little experience with anti-racist education—schools of education and the Milwaukee school district neglected professional development in this area. Although we had materials from the Council on Interracial Books for Children and a few books and other resources on multicultural education, our library was just starting up. Materials in Spanish were particularly sparse in the early 1990s.

There were other problems as well. Our curriculum, despite—or maybe because of—its progressive values and methods, wasn't explicit enough to guide teachers who were unfamiliar with our activity-based, child-centered approaches. For many subject areas, there was no clear scope and sequence. A few teachers didn't put in the essential extra effort needed to create their own curriculum, and their classrooms were often rudderless. We put too much confidence in individual teacher skills and had limited capacity to help those teachers who floundered.

Even some of the teachers who were more experienced in classroom management and basic curriculum had blind spots regarding race. This was brought home to me the first year as I worked with Ahmed Mbalia, a professor of Africology at the University of Wisconsin-Milwaukee.

"Come with me, Bob," he said one day when he came into the parent resource room where I was working. "I have to show you something to make my point."

Ahmed was a member of the parent/staff curriculum committee and played a positive role in supporting our efforts to deepen our understanding of multiculturalism. He often wore an African dashiki over his large frame and his deep voice commanded respect, no matter where he was. I followed him up three flights of stairs and across the hallway into his son's 2nd-grade classroom. Mary, a white teacher, seemed to have good classroom control and an engaging curriculum. As we approached the room, Ahmed said, "Bob, just go into the classroom and look around. Tell me what you see." We entered, pardoned our presence, and circulated among groups of students who were busily writing, some in pairs, others individually. I felt pleased that the kids were engaged and I focused my attention on them. After a while, Ahmed and I left. In the hallway, Ahmed turned to me.

"Well?"

I felt like a kid being tested. "I think the kids were pretty engaged. They weren't writing about a social issue but they were writing."

"Anything else?"

"What are you getting at? I am obviously missing something."

"Stick your head back in and look at the walls."

I went over to the door and, as discreetly as possible, looked in and saw only two posters on the walls. My heart sank.

I turned back to Ahmed. "Yeah, I see, lots of work to do."

"Don't get me wrong, Bob. Kids need to know the presidents, but to have Washington—a big-time slave owner—and Lincoln as the only posters in a room in a school that prides itself on being multicultural? Come on."

I talked to Mary about the posters. She acknowledged that she hadn't considered the unspoken message inherent in her choice of posters. She agreed to change her poster selection and invited Ahmed into her classroom to teach some lessons. He talked to the kids about African history, including the university at Timbuktu and European colonialism.

At times, some of the white, middle-class parents resisted. They had enrolled their children to learn Spanish, but didn't necessarily embrace our approach to anti-racism and social justice. A few raised concerns that we were teaching only "minority" history and shortchanging students of European heritage. Others complained that their kids weren't learning the national anthem and the Pledge of Allegiance. Some teachers felt that such criticism, if left unchecked, would push Fratney back into the mainstream, where curricular content might mention democracy but violate one of the fundamental building blocks of democracy—the equality of all people—by privileging Eurocentric points of view.

We realized that a school that wants to foster a healthy democratic atmosphere should be committed to ongoing conversations about controversial topics, inviting all perspectives in. We also knew it was not enough just to agree that our school be anti-racist—a few pages outlining such a curricular approach and some decent resources would not magically transform our teaching. We needed to develop a school commitment to multicultural/anti-racist education that included more than just the handful of our school's founders.

We borrowed an idea from All London Teachers Against Fascism. In the 1970s there had been an explosion of racist attacks against immigrants in England, committed by white youth called skinheads. At the same time, left-wing activists swept municipal elections in London. They were in charge of public schools and wanted to launch an anti-racist, multicultural campaign. Some people in leadership proposed that they write up policies and demand that all schools implement them. Others countered that a better strategy would be to require each school to develop its own anti-racist, multicultural statement through joint meetings of parents, students, educators, and community members. This approach was adopted, and it generated a great deal of education on racial inequality; a flood of creative ideas; and a widening circle of teachers, parents, and other community members committed to implementing something that they had a role in developing. We decided to follow this example.

We knew it was not enough just to agree that our school be anti-racist—a few pages outlining such a curricular approach and some decent resources would not magically transform our teaching.

Working through the parent curriculum committee, the site-based management council, and staff meetings, parents and staff went through five drafts to come up with a joint statement that outlined the philosophy and implementation of multicultural, anti-racist education at La Escuela Fratney.

The statement was grounded in respect for all people, regardless of sex, religion, physical or mental abilities, sexual orientation, or class background. It addressed key concepts: Multiculturalism/anti-racism takes many forms and should be included in all curricular areas; bilingualism should foster multiculturalism; students and their families are also teachers; and we must bring the world into our school and construct cooperative, anti-biased learning environments.

We also found it useful to view multicultural, anti-racist education as a continuum, as described by James Banks and Enid Lee. The continuum begins with teachers talking about the contributions of people of color, then adding material to the existing curriculum, then integrating instruction on non-European cultures into many subject areas. It then develops into a more transformative stage in which students and teachers critique the messages they get from television, children's books, and textbooks. The ultimate goal is that students and teachers not only understand the world, but engage in social action to change it—to make it more fair and equal.

In subsequent years we revisited the statement and used our themes and other curricular guidelines to strengthen our work. For example, we recognized that without a schoolwide scope and sequence, a student might go from kindergarten through 5th grade and study little Asian American history; they might have stories about Harriet Tubman and Martin Luther King repeated, but not learn about Black history in depth. New staff needed to know specifics of what each grade level should cover.

Unifying Themes and Integrated Curriculum

While children need specific instruction in math and reading, they benefit immensely from an integrated, project approach to learning. To foster this, we developed four schoolwide themes, one for each quarter. The themes (see p. 160) stress social responsibility, activism, and respect for our students' lives and heritage. These themes and subthemes help new teachers understand our underlying philosophy and encourage students, staff, and parents to work together on projects, celebrating them in schoolwide theme events held four times per year.

Deepening a school's commitment to student-centered, critical, and socially relevant education is a never-ending process. One way we institutionalized this in 5th grade was through student-led parent-teacher conferences in which students reflected on their learning, showed projects to parents, and set goals for their future learning. This culminated in an end-of-year student exhibition—students displayed major projects that they'd worked on in 5th grade and in earlier grades as well. Staff, parents, younger students, and community members attended the exhibition, which gave purpose to students' work and encouraged teachers to be deliberate about the assignments they gave to children. It also motivated younger students to look forward to the creative projects in store for them when they got to upper grades.

When I taught 5th grade, student projects included five booklets: an English-language autobiography, a Spanish-language report on an animal in danger of extinction, a bilingual poetry book, a bilingual biography of a famous person who worked for social justice, and a bilingual "Journey Through Elementary School" booklet that included drawings and reflections on their school experience.

Active learning has been a hallmark of Fratney curriculum as well. In 5th grade, my students did role plays—putting Columbus on trial for genocide and conducting a mock U.S. constitutional convention that included women, enslaved and free Africans, Iroquois, and indentured servants, as well as the businessmen and slave owners who attended the actual convention.

Fratney staff developed a strong relationship with the Urban Ecology Center. With financial support from a local business partner, Fratney students visit the center a couple times a year to explore varied environmental issues. Fourth and 5th graders go on a three-day, two-night camping trip at an environmental camp on the banks of the Wisconsin River.

Whether teaching about environmental or social issues, Fratney teachers are disposed to the notion that education should be transformative. We aren't just teaching students to read words, but also to read the world, and when possible, change it. Many Fratney teachers apply that to their own lives as well. By modeling activism and highlighting stories of children and young people who in the past and present have worked to improve their communities and the world, we nurture a sense of social responsibility and empathy for others.

Over the years, this has led Fratney to be the focal point for various organizing efforts that were launched into the broader community—from resistance to standardized testing, to the birth of the Milwaukee-based Educators' Network for Social

Themes for La Escuela Fratney

Theme I: We respect ourselves and our world.

- Every living thing has needs.
- I am somebody important.
- We all have a cultural heritage.
- We need to live in peace.
- TV can be dangerous to our health.

Theme II: We are proud to be bilingual, multicultural learners.

- Diversity is a strength in our society.
- There are many benefits to being bilingual.
- We communicate in many languages and in many ways.
- We learn from and teach each other in our Fratney community.
- We recognize and respect our multiple languages, cultures, and experiences.
- We learn to counteract the stereotypes contained in cartoons, books, magazines, and the media.

Theme III: We can make a difference on planet Earth.

- We have been shaped by the past, we shape the future.
- African American people have contributed greatly to our nation.
- We celebrate the contributions of women.
- People of all nationalities have worked for justice and equality.
- We need to overcome prejudice and racism.

Theme IV: We share stories of the world.

- My family's story is important.
- We learn about other people through their stories.
- We can all be storytellers and actors.

Justice, to substantive parent and staff organizing against Gov. Scott Walker's attack on public schools and teachers.

This commitment to social justice also includes the involvement of students. For example, students have organized to preserve a neighborhood swimming pool, get additional funding for a new tot lot, oppose child labor, save our librarian from budget cuts, and participate with their parents and teachers in protests against the Iraq War and in "Day Without Latinos" marches in favor of immigrant rights.

Asking the Right Questions

The new Fratney contrasted with the many charter schools that came after Fratney started. We pursued our vision as a regular public school, and were not granted the extra resources or the latitude to screen out children with special learning needs that some charters have taken advantage of. Visitors to our school would often inquire, "Are you a charter school? You doing such creative things." I would proudly respond, "No, we are a public school and believe all public schools should be innovative."

When we saw a need to change or add to district policies, we did so in collaboration with other schools—in hopes that change would be made across the district. One example early on was when we advocated for site-based hiring. We needed teachers who were committed to our school's mission and not assigned solely on the basis of district seniority. We eventually convinced the union and the administration to agree to a memorandum of understanding that would allow us (and a handful of other schools) to have school-based committees of teachers, parents, and principals interview and hire teachers. This practice proved so popular that a few years later the union and the administration made it district policy.

> **"We are a public school and believe all public schools should be innovative."**

At Fratney, we know we don't have all the answers, but we try to ask the right questions. Some of these include: How can we provide adequate educational and social services to students from economically oppressed neighborhoods in the midst of massive cutbacks to education and the social safety net? How can we serve the needs of emerging bilingual students in a society increasingly hostile to immigrants and languages other than English? How can we construct a bilingual curriculum that meets the academic and linguistic needs of all students? How do we refresh our commitment to anti-racist, social justice education as new staff, parents, and leadership emerge at the school? How can we balance putting energy into the needs of one's own classroom and school, with the need to address broader educational and social struggles that directly affect our students and school? How can we sustain significant parent involvement from all sectors of the school community and integrate the perspectives of both parents and staff? How can we maintain the integrity of our child-centered, social justice curriculum in the midst of test-and-punish pressures?

There are no simple answers to these questions—the important thing is that they are addressed on a regular basis. As we wrestle with these questions, we are sustained by a shared commitment to our mission and pedagogical approach, deep collaboration between our principal and teachers and other staff, a long tradition of significant parent/community involvement, and an understanding that our success at school is connected to social justice in our community.

La Escuela Fratney, like democracy itself, is a work in progress. ☼

Bob Peterson (bob.e.peterson@gmail.com) is a founding editor of Rethinking Schools and a founder of La Escuela Fratney. He taught 5th grade for 30 years in the Milwaukee Public Schools and served four years as president of the Milwaukee Teachers' Education Association.

References

Banks, James. 1991. *Teaching Strategies for Ethnic Studies*. Allyn & Bacon.

Christensen, Linda, Mark Hansen, Bob Peterson, Elizabeth Schlessman, and Dyan Watson. 2014. *Rethinking Elementary Education*. Rethinking Schools.

Miner, Barbara. 1981. "Taking Multicultural/Anti-Racist Education Seriously: An Interview with Enid Lee." *Rethinking Schools* 6.1:6.

Peterson, Bob. 2007. "La Escuela Fratney: A Journey Toward Democracy." *Democratic Schools: Lessons in Powerful Education*, 2nd Edition. Heinemann.

Building Bilingual Communities at César Chávez Elementary

An interview with Pilar Mejía

BY ELIZABETH BARBIAN AND GRACE CORNELL GONZALES

*César Chávez
Elementary School*

During Pilar Mejía's time as principal of César Chávez Elementary School in San Francisco, the school housed four side-by-side bilingual programs, through which students learned in Spanish, Cantonese, Ebonics, and American Sign Language (ASL). We spoke with Pilar about the path that led her to become a bilingual teacher and administrator, how she fostered the development of Chávez's multiple bilingual programs, and how she facilitated autonomy within programs while building solidarity between the diverse teachers and students at the school.

Rethinking Bilingual Education: How did your experiences learning English as a child shape you as an educator?

Pilar Mejía: My parents immigrated to Los Angeles from Ecuador in 1951 when I was almost 6. When I entered 1st grade, I remember being bewildered because

I didn't understand anything. As the first child, I was outgoing and loved to sing, dance, and recite poetry. But when we came to the United States, I shut down and felt empty because I could not share who I was. I lost my public voice the first day of school and did not regain it until I was a grown woman.

But it was not just my voice that I lost. I experienced a daily rejection of who I was. When my family moved from our Latinx (primarily Mexican) barrio in Los Angeles to the suburbs in Orange County, I started 6th grade a few weeks late. When I was taken into the classroom, the teacher smiled and found a seat for me among the white children—because I am a white Latina. I saw the Mexican students in a corner and knew that I belonged there with them. On the playground, I longed to play with the other Latinx children and speak Spanish, my mother tongue. But I was afraid of challenging my teacher or disrupting the way things were.

When I was placed with the white children, I was treated like I was smart. I was in the high reading group for the first time. As an adult, I can literally "feel" white skin privilege and remember that, as a child, it put me in with the kids who were participating fully—that it gave me advantages but also made me feel lost.

I see myself in every child that enters school without understanding English, and this has influenced my commitment to being an educator, a social justice activist, and an advocate for bilingual education. But more, I understand white supremacy at a "gut" level because I have often benefited from it, sometimes at the price of my identity.

As an older, retired educator, I am sometimes surprised at the pent-up rage that still lives in me from those many years of living without a voice. Even in high school, when I was proficient in English and had no accent, I could not speak in class without getting bright red as I stammered through my response to the teacher's question. The only class in which I felt comfortable was a high school Spanish class where the teacher was Mexican.

RBE: How did you become involved in bilingual education?

PM: I moved to San Francisco in 1967 when I was pregnant with my first son. When he started preschool, I became a school bus driver. A couple of years later, I started work as a teacher's aide in a bilingual classroom in the Mission District, the Latinx barrio where I lived. The expectation of the bilingual program was that children would have access to their native language as they learned English, yet often the teachers in these classrooms were not fluent Spanish speakers themselves. I saw how little the teacher I worked with (who was not bilingual) included of the children's cultures, languages, and experiences. That was in the late '70s when schools often celebrated the "heroes and holidays" of multicultural education, but were often ignoring the languages and cultures of children in their classrooms. When students' home languages were used, it was mostly as a tool to transition students into English. I knew I could do a better job. I had two children and worked hard to get a degree and my teacher's credential. When I finally became a teacher, I made sure my classroom was focused on bilingualism and biliteracy.

I loved teaching, but often felt blocked by administrators who did not know how to include the Latinx community. One time, a non-bilingual teacher's aide was assigned to my K–1 classroom. When I asked about this, I was told that no one else had applied. I quickly wrote a letter in Spanish to the parents and we got several applicants. I realized that more proactive administrators were needed, so eventually I decided to go back to school to become an administrator.

I had done summer school, Saturday school, and other typical short-term administrative experiences when I got a call from a friend at Hawthorne Elementary School, one of the largest schools in the Mission District. Their principal had left, and because several of the teachers knew me, they asked me to fill in until they had interviews at the end of the school year. It was a perfect fit for me, especially because there was a strong Spanish bilingual program and a solid Chinese (Cantonese) bilingual program. I was interviewed and hired as principal, and a few years later we changed the name of the school to César Chávez.

Building Bilingual Programs in Multiple Languages

RBE: César Chávez had bilingual programs in Cantonese, Spanish, ASL, and Ebonics. How did the four bilingual programs evolve during your time there?

PM: When I arrived at the K–5 school, there was one Spanish bilingual classroom at each grade level. There was also a Chinese bilingual strand that was transitional, with very little high-quality home language instruction at the upper grades and minimal focus on Chinese literacy. There were two Deaf education classrooms, one with students in pre-K and kindergarten and the other with students in 1st and 2nd grade (the Deaf students were transferred to another school for grades 3–5). The rest of the classrooms were English only.

When I began as principal, I made it very clear that instruction in the bilingual programs would be bilingual, and that biliteracy would be a focus. The school already had a reputation for having a strong Spanish bilingual program; most of those teachers were Latinas from the neighborhood. As we shifted focus to improving our bilingual programs, those teachers were an inspiration to the Chinese bilingual teachers. The Chinese programs in our district had tended to be transitional, but ours became a strong maintenance program within a couple of years. We hired qualified Cantonese-speaking educators for the upper grades and established a clear focus on developing literacy skills in Chinese. As the Deaf education teachers saw the other bilingual programs expand and strengthen, they decided that they wanted to define themselves as bilingual as well—acknowledging and reinforcing their native language, ASL, while also teaching English literacy. A few years later, the African American teachers and parents developed the African-Centered program, open to all students, which focused on strengthening students' pride in their heritage and ancestral roots as well as valuing Ebonics and learning Standard English. There was also a program where students learned only in Standard English, which parents and teachers had chosen to call the Multicultural program.

With the leadership of the African-Centered program, we developed a school vision that included the right to self-determination. This meant that each program made decisions about how best to educate children. For example, the Spanish bilingual team decided to change their classes into K–2 and 3–5 multi-age classrooms because they wanted to give children the opportunity to learn from each other and work at their own pace. Eventually, many of the classrooms in other strands became multi-aged as well. Each program made its own decisions based on their students' needs.

I saw my role as facilitator and co-leader. When I arrived, I could see that the staff was already pushing for change. The changes that followed didn't come from me, but I saw what was happening and put my weight behind them. It was truly an amazing and humbling experience to work with such energetic and committed people who were so ready to engage in deep and principled struggle about how to best educate our children. I went home every day with my body tired but my spirit energized.

RBE: What were some challenges you faced as the administrator of a school with programs that incorporated so many languages?

PM: At the beginning, one of the biggest challenges was staying calm and pretending to be "neutral" in the face of the status quo practices. For example, early on a veteran teacher from the English multicultural program was taking her young students on a tour of the school and asked me to say hello to the students. When I said "*Buenos días*," she told me (in front of the students) "Speak English!" Her reasoning was that I shouldn't speak Spanish because not all of the students were Latinx. But I continued saying good morning in Cantonese, Tagalog, ASL, and a few other languages, and worked to make sure that this was an accepted practice at the school. During schoolwide morning circle, I invited students to say good morning in their home languages.

Although I was able to learn some ASL, it was certainly challenging to attempt to learn Cantonese. In a school with multiple bilingual programs, it is likely that the principal won't be able to speak each language or have the same degree of familiarity with every community the school represents.

Another challenge was integrating the programs. I knew we wanted the four programs to work together instead of separately. I also wanted to respect each person's and program's expertise. With families and teachers coming from so many different linguistic and cultural backgrounds, I knew we would need to focus on integration and unity. I made sure that we made decisions by consensus and that all the school's communities were represented on the staff leadership team.

RBE: How were you able to involve parents across such a variety of languages and cultural backgrounds?

PM: The School Site Council (SSC)—which had representatives from all the programs and a majority of parents—was the highest decision-making body in the school. At our SSC meetings, we always had Spanish and Chinese translation. At the beginning of the meeting, we would ask how many people spoke each language and then conduct the meeting in the majority language, which was frequently Spanish. By the end of my time at Chávez, we had headsets for the whole SSC and experimented with simultaneous translation in all three spoken languages. Participants would contribute in their dominant language and translation would be provided through the headsets.

It seemed like there were always parents in the school. Whenever there was a community event (spring show, graduation, fall festival, etc.), we sent buses—one to the Western Addition (the community where many of our African American students lived) and another to China-town—to bring parents to the school. During the week of parent-teacher conferences, the Chinese teachers conducted evening parent-teacher conferences at a school in Chinatown, which was more central to where many of the families in their program lived. We also had a family center at

> **I understand white supremacy at a "gut" level because I have often benefited from it, sometimes at the price of my identity.**

Chávez, which was a room where parents and families could drop in and spend time. I really encouraged parents to visit classrooms, and teachers welcomed them.

Another way we involved diverse groups of parents was through a grant called Families Building Literacy, which created family literacy projects. The Families Building Literacy grant funded three parent liaison positions: A Spanish-speaking parent, a Cantonese-speaking parent, and an African American parent were paid to organize parents for about five hours a day. The parent liaisons had their offices in the family center and organized all the different parent activities—making sure there were room parents, maintaining a phone tree, keeping the family center comfortable and inviting for parents, and helping get volunteers into the classroom.

Fostering Solidarity and Self-Determination

RBE: How did you promote unity among teachers in different programs?

PM: The programs had a great deal of autonomy, but we also wanted to learn from each other, so teachers met in "collegial teams." These teams included representatives from each program who shared grade levels; for example, the 3rd-grade team included 3rd-grade teachers from the Chinese, Spanish, African-Centered, Multicultural, and Deaf education programs. One of the goals was to integrate students across programs through collaborative activities. The teams met once a month; they worked independently and evolved based on their own goals, reflection, and evaluation. The teaching staff took weekend retreats a few times, including Tribes, a cooperative learning and community-building training, which teachers could also use with children.

We tried to share the various talents of staff and parents whenever we could. Teachers took an active role in planning and leading staff meetings. Everyone signed up on a list, which included a facilitator, minute taker, turn recorder, and joke teller (since the staff decided to make staff meetings two hours long, we needed a break).

We made decisions by consensus—sometimes a very messy process, but well worth it. We used a "hand to fist" method. One teacher made a chart that showed an outstretched hand (full agreement), four fingers held up (almost full agreement), three fingers (in the middle), two fingers (still not sure), one finger (no, and I'm willing to make a suggestion), fist (absolutely not and I have another idea to share). It was amazing how often this process helped us reach a consensus. We used the "hand to fist" method to decide things like what committees to have, which topics to explore during professional development days, which consultants to hire, and who would write grants.

At one point, we were able to get the district to fund a vice principal position. Of course, we wanted one of the teachers from our school to fill the role. Our interview process came down to two very qualified teachers—a Latina teacher from the Spanish program and a teacher from the Chinese program who was the computer lab coordinator. We struggled to reach consensus with the hiring decision since both teachers brought different and important skills to the role. As we discussed the problem using our consensus process, we realized that the two teachers could share both the vice principal position and the computer lab coordinator position. If we had voted, there would have been winners and losers, but when consensus is used, eventually an answer emerges.

RBE: How did you help students build meaningful relationships with each other across the different programs?

PM: Because our staff was mostly composed of people of color, we were acutely aware of the need for integration. We noticed that, in the yard, students mostly played with kids in their own classroom or program. So we came up with "family time," which integrated students from the various programs, but in similar grade levels, for several blocks each week. Each collegial team decided how they would integrate their students. For one unit, the 3rd-grade team decided to focus on math. Each teacher developed a weeklong series of hands-on math activities that included cooperative learning strategies; mixed groups of students rotated through each class and later reflected on how they felt working together.

Another family time unit—one of my favorites—was a study of bread in various cultures. Students and their families investigated and wrote about breads that were important to their families and cultures, such as tortillas, naan, chapati, pupusas, and bagels. The teachers invited students' relatives to bake bread with the children. Mouths were watering when the smell of baking bread drifted through the hallways.

RBE: Some common challenges faced by bilingual program administrators and teachers include finding relevant professional development and quality classroom materials in non-English languages. What was your approach to providing these for the different bilingual programs?

PM: Following our philosophy of self-determination, teachers were the ones who decided what professional development (PD) to take. For example, the African-Centered team could decide that they wanted to take a PD with Asa Hilliard about Ebonics at San Francisco State University. But a teacher could also individually choose to take a PD that addressed a skill she felt she needed to develop. At the time, there was adequate funding for professional development, both through the district and because we wrote grants.

We also incorporated peer coaching: teachers assisting each other, engaging in dialogue, and collectively reflecting. I promoted this because I felt so adamant about not being the "boss" who "made" teachers do this or that. I wanted classroom educators—including paraprofessionals—to be the ones holding each other accountable and supporting each other.

The teachers decided what materials to purchase for their programs. At that time, the district leadership was very supportive of bilingual education and even sent teachers to China, Mexico, and other Latin American countries to purchase books and materials. We also tried to create curriculum generated by students' experiences and questions. We contracted community artists, writers, and poets whenever possible, so students and often teachers wrote stories. We had binding equipment to turn our writing into books that we could keep in the library.

RBE: How do you advocate for bilingual education now?

PM: I feel fortunate to have taught during a time when civil rights and other social justice struggles made it possible to honor and reinforce students' languages and cultures. Today, so much money is being spent on high-stakes testing that little is left to support the kinds of goals we reached for at César Chávez School. Support for linguistic and cultural diversity is being diminished in the name of standardization.

Still, I continue to work with the Latin American Teachers Association (LATA) and with the California Association for Bilingual Education (CABE). I go to marches supporting Black Lives Matter and in solidarity with struggles in Latin America. Gathering and organizing with others who speak out and stand up keeps me hopeful that our schools will change—and that more people are understanding the importance of advocating for children's languages and cultures as a human right. ☼

Pilar Mejía is a retired bilingual educator who worked for more than 40 years in San Francisco, where she is still a social justice activist.

Elizabeth Barbian (formerly Schlessman) has taught bilingual students and worked with teachers in the United States, Bolivia, Tanzania, and South Africa. She currently lives in the Denver area. Grace Cornell Gonzales is an editor for Rethinking Schools and has worked for nine years as a bilingual elementary teacher in California and Guatemala City.

Why Are We Speaking So Much English?

Promoting equity in dual-language classrooms

BY DEBORAH PALMER

DAVID BACON

n a 1st-grade two-way dual-language classroom that I was visiting, the teacher held up a book and asked the class, "*¿Ya conocen este libro, verdad?*" (You already know this book, right?) Many of the students nodded or called out "yes," or "*sí.*" Then one student asked, "Can we read it in English?" The teacher replied, "*Hoy vamos a leerlo en español*" (Today we are going to read it in Spanish) and was met with general groans from the class. Without missing a beat, she added, "*Quizás mañana podamos leerlo en inglés.*" (Maybe tomorrow we can read it in English.) The students cheered.

The students' desire to move into English brought me back to my own 4th-grade dual-language classroom, about 15 years ago in Redwood City, California. I too struggled to get students to use their Spanish during Spanish instruction, even those who were Spanish-dominant and from Spanish-speaking homes. I tried many things—from incentive programs, to inviting Spanish-speaking adults to come speak to the class, to heart-to-heart conversations about our mutual goal of being bilingual. My school was committed to raising the status of Spanish; we had a 90/10 program with rigid adherence to a language policy that favored Spanish-medium materials and Spanish-language instruction during "Spanish times." Yet, my 9- and 10-year-old students—all of whom had been in the program at least four years—would still revert to English with one another. Increasingly, I started to wonder if it wasn't just the English language that was being favored. I began to recognize that students from more privileged backgrounds who spoke English at home were overrepresented when it came to class participation, in both Spanish and English.

Two-way dual language seemed to me, as it does to many, to be a "win-win," providing integrated, additive, and academically enriching classrooms for too-often-marginalized Spanish-dominant students—as well as a phenomenal opportunity for second language learning and cross-cultural experiences for English-dominant students. The model seemed to solve the decades-old tension between ensuring equitable opportunities for kids of color through integrated learning contexts, and ensuring equitable access to curriculum for ELL students through providing home language support. And, because two-way programs include English-dominant kids, they are often able to garner support from a much broader base than transitional or developmental bilingual programs.

However, it's important to ask: Who benefits most from two-way dual language? Who are these programs actually serving? In Massachusetts, for instance, the Unz law that passed in 2002 as "Question 2" forbade the use of students' primary languages in the classroom before they were fluent in English. But there was an explicit exception made for two-way dual-language programs. Why? Because without this exception, English-dominant children would have been denied access to bilingual programs. This is a textbook example of what critical race theorists would call "interest convergence": Spanish-dominant Latina/o students are allowed access to a bilingual, bicultural education only insofar as it serves the needs of the English-dominant, mainly white population.

Actually, I believe it goes further than that: The Spanish-dominant students in those two-way-immersion classrooms serve as language models for Spanish; in a very real sense, they are the "tools" that make the programs strong. Advocates of two-way dual language argue that Spanish-dominant Latina/o students benefit from being positioned in leadership roles, and that they also benefit from their English-dominant classmates' language modeling. This is the ideal, but only when we are actively working to ensure equitable learning spaces in our schools. The hegemony of English and whiteness in our society is also present in our two-way dual-language classrooms. If we are not vigilant and intentional, our classrooms risk reifying the very power structures we're setting out to disrupt—sending an inadvertent message to native speakers of languages other than English that they are second-class citizens, there to serve the needs of the white, English-dominant students.

How Does This Happen?

We live in an English-dominant society. It is undeniable that the power structures in the United States expect everyone to speak, read, write, and understand English. Other languages are a bonus, a luxury, an extra. English is a must. Speakers of languages other than English, especially those who are not white and middle class, have long suffered racism and oppression in the United States.

If you are English speaking, it is a wonderful—and high-status—choice for you to add on another language. However, if you are a member of a language minority community in the United States, your home language will likely not be valued, and there is tremendous pressure for you to acquire English as quickly and well as possible. In fact, speakers of other languages who enter English-only school programs at age 5 or 6 are at risk to lose their primary language by the time they enter middle school.

These dynamics mattered in my classroom. There was an intrinsic difference between the experiences of Spanish-dominant and English-dominant members of my class in terms of urgency and drive to learn the second language. Ultimately, there were much higher consequences for the failure to acquire English than for the failure to acquire Spanish. Students had access to more opportunities outside the classroom in English than in Spanish. All of the standardized tests my students had to take were in English. What's more, I noticed that classroom visitors, the press, and even people we encountered on field trips tended to celebrate my English-dominant students' smallest utterances in Spanish, while dismissing Spanish-dominant students' astounding English acquisition as a matter of course.

There was also a wide socioeconomic gap between the families of Spanish-dominant students (primarily working-class immigrants) and English-dominant students (primarily middle-class and white). The middle-class white children often came in with more practice in the kinds of discourses valued in schools in the United States; their parents knew how to navigate the education system and had no qualms about advocating on their behalf. On the other hand, many of the working-class immigrant parents, schooled in other countries and often with far less experience in formal schooling systems, sometimes hesitated to assert their children's needs. In addition, Spanish-dominant students' everyday language practices—their ways of talking and knowing—were in many ways silenced in the classroom because they did not fit as well with mainstream school expectations.

With all of these imbalances, my Latina/o students often took a back seat in class discussions. I was often at a loss to know how to ensure that students all got to shine as "knowers" in my classroom.

What Can We Do?

The first and most important thing we can do is learn to notice. As with any structural inequity, we cannot counter what we cannot see.

I've had the privilege of watching several excellent and dedicated bilingual teachers try their best to create an equitable classroom environment. Between their experiences and my own, I have developed this list of suggestions for bringing equity, both between students and between languages, to the center of our classrooms.

Value students' language practices. The children we teach come from all over the Spanish-speaking world, including our own local communities. Their everyday language practices will naturally mix English with Spanish, both in their structure and word choice; these practices are not wrong, they may just be different from what's expected in school. Although students depend on school to help them develop standard registers of language that will give them access to the halls of power, it needs to be an additive process. Do not be afraid to let your students explore language mixing or non-standard dialectical practices; do not correct them when they refer to their "Papi's troque" or playing in their "yarda." On the contrary, embrace these as the semiotic tools, the windows into their unique identities, and the beautiful means of expression that they are.

De-center majoritarian stories in your curriculum. Make sure that the stories you share, the history you teach, even the objects and examples sprinkled through the math problems that your students tackle, reflect and represent all the students in your class. The "standard" curriculum provided in my school district did not reflect my Latina/o working-class students' lives. The more successful bilingual classrooms I see center reading instruction around culturally relevant literature, teach history from multiple perspectives, and ensure children have diverse choices of role models (see Chapter 2 for examples).

Scaffold, scaffold, scaffold—but do not simplify. Do not water down instruction in order to ensure comprehension. This can be hard to resist, especially given the reality of the pressure to get kids to perform on high-stakes tests. For authentic learning, it is OK for children to miss a few details (or even a lot of details) in a content lesson in their second language. On the other hand, it is not OK for children to hear simplified, basic concepts repeated and repeated in their primary language in order to accommodate second language learners; this will not accomplish anyone's goals. Speak to your students about complex, rich, and important ideas as if they will understand you, even if you believe they do not.

Do not be afraid to intervene to correct imbalances and ensure equity in the moment. I once witnessed a 2nd-grade teacher put up her hand to stop an English-dominant boy from answering her question during guided reading, saying, "*no interrumpas*" (don't interrupt), giving the floor back to the Spanish-dominant child who had not yet offered his response. I realized how often I had failed to make this same clear statement to my own students. As this teacher told me, for the most part her white middle-class children "need to learn humility, and learn how you can learn from someone else," while many of her Latina/o children need to see themselves in the center of the classroom and curriculum. Direct intervention can support this.

Notice the way children are being positioned (Davies & Harré, 1990). Positioning happens constantly in interaction. When I said to a 4th grader seeking my help, "Go ask Luisa, she can help you spell that," I was positioning Luisa as an expert speller. When I quietly commented to Ramón, "If this math is too difficult for you, we can find you an easier set of problems," I was positioning Ramón as having difficulties with mathematics. Children also position one another constantly, as experts or novices in sports, academics, languages, and as friends or adversaries in their social worlds. As teachers, we can intentionally organize a situation that positions certain children as experts in new ways; we can help children "try on" new identities.

Establish routines that encourage equity. A master 2nd-grade teacher asserted, "Structure promotes equity." It can be easy to get carried away when teaching and forget to take concrete steps to foster equitable participation. Because of this, we need to set up systems that consistently promote equity in our classrooms.

- Develop routine turn-taking patterns that allow all voices to be heard in class discussions. I had a "talking stick" that we passed around during circle time, and students knew that when they got the stick they had the class's attention.
- Create opportunities in the midst of whole-class instruction, such as turn-and-talk or Think/Pair/Share, for students to rehearse and talk through their ideas with a partner before sharing in front of the class. I love that buzz in the classroom when everyone is working out their ideas; as we know, the more talking, the more learning.
- Structure complex pair or group work that requires all participants to take responsibility for the group's success, and that positions each group member with valuable capital to contribute. This requires planning: Children need assigned roles with clear responsibilities, preparation and practice to take on those roles, and a clear system of accountability for both individual and group success. A teacher who I know hands children two different colored pencils during collaborative writing activities. The kids write together in the same journal, talking through their messages and helping each other compose and decode. When they share their final product together with the class, the teacher can identify the contributions of each child.
- Match children carefully and regroup frequently to avoid having dynamics of imbalance and inequity repeat themselves at the partner level. Ensure there is not too broad of a gap in skills between children who are partnered for academic work, and/or that their strengths and needs are complementary, so that their interactions will be collaborative and mutually beneficial. Spread strong English-dominant students out so they do not dominate conversations at certain tables.

These are, of course, all suggestions that support "good teaching" in general. Making discourse patterns explicit and expecting every member of your class to adhere to participation rules promotes active participation from all students.

Teach students to recognize linguistic imbalance. Students of all ages can engage in conversations about which languages they see being used where, and why. By 3rd or 4th grade, children should understand why they see English everywhere and what forces are pushing them away from deepening their Spanish. They should be able to talk about linguistic equity themselves and explain the ways that English dominates in our society and in their own worlds. We can build these lessons into curriculum by sharing stories like *Pepita habla dos veces/Pepita Talks Twice* by Ofelia Dumas Lachtman and *La mariposa* by Francisco Jiménez, which address issues of English dominance and the power of bilingualism. We can also encourage students to share their personal experiences and feelings about the different languages they speak in school and at home.

What Does Linguistic Imbalance Look Like in Schools?

Here are some examples from schools I've visited (including my own), of ways in which the status differences between English and Spanish may be observed. Most of these examples can be applied to other languages; I am merely drawing on my own experiences in Spanish/English bilingual contexts:

- School (and public) libraries usually contain more English than Spanish titles. When they're there, Spanish titles are more frequently at low reading levels, with very few longer, more complex texts available in Spanish. Sometimes Spanish texts are classified as "foreign language" books. And often, they are hiding in a corner someplace, while their English counterparts are prominently and attractively displayed.

- Labeling of children often normalizes English. In my school district, the district labeled English-dominant children "monolinguals" or "English onlys," even when they had some Spanish; Spanish-dominant children were referred to as "English language learners." Both labels referenced only the children's English competence, paying no attention to other languages.

- Important signage throughout schools is often in English only; if signage is available in Spanish, the lettering is sometimes smaller, handwritten, or appears below the English.

- Intercom messages in many schools come through in English only. Sometimes a school will make an effort to make announcements bilingually on designated "Spanish" days. It is rare (and risky) for a school in a U.S. context to make an important announcement in Spanish only.

- Office staff in many schools approach visitors in English first, even if they are known to be bilingual or Spanish-dominant.

- Even in bilingual programs where teachers use mostly or all Spanish with their students in class, teachers usually talk amongst themselves in English.

- Schoolwide meetings are often presented in English only. Translation into Spanish may be provided to individuals (usually parents) who need it, thus framing non-English speakers as lacking the skills to participate equally in the meeting. Spanish is not often used as the public language, which might require English monolinguals to seek translation.

- Principals are often English dominant—in fact in most districts there is no requirement that principals at bilingual schools be bilingual—thus rendering them incapable of engaging directly with a significant percentage of the families in their schools. They also may not understand a lot of the instruction happening in their own bilingual classrooms.

Students as Advocates

Teachers aren't the only ones who can advocate for equity. Students can also be given the tools to address linguistic imbalance. We can ask students to be vigilant in their own classrooms and schools. Do they speak up when signs are posted or notices go home in English only? Do they ask the librarian or the principal why there aren't more books in Spanish in the library?

When Proposition 227 passed in California in 1998, my 4th graders were outraged that it seemed like a law was threatening to take apart their bilingual community. The morning after the election, we spent our circle time discussing the implications of the new law and then wrote in our journals about our feelings and concerns. Later in the day we returned to the issue, brainstorming things students could do to speak out against the proposition. We discussed who they could speak to who had the power to influence the policies in our school; one student suggested the school district's board of trustees. After that, they wrote impassioned essays to our school board. They implored the board to please not let this "dumb law" stop them from being bilingual at school, vehemently describing their visions for a bilingual, multicultural future. Together, we revised, translated, edited, and practiced their essays, and, as a group, five of the students and their parents came to the public comments period at the next board meeting. All of their essays were written in both English and Spanish, but the students organized themselves so that originally English-dominant children began with their Spanish essays, reading the English second, while originally Spanish-dominant students began in English. The board—and the audience—were touched by their proud bilingual voices.

In the 18 years since my 4th graders spoke out against Proposition 227, fewer and fewer Latina/o Spanish-dominant children have had access to rich, critical bilingual education at school. Meanwhile—in large part because of their attraction for mainstream English-dominant families—two-way dual-language programs have expanded exponentially throughout the United States. There is so much possibility in bringing together children from diverse race, class, and language backgrounds and helping them learn from each other. But we must take responsibility to ensure that two-way dual-language programs are equitable spaces for all learners—it's the only way to ensure that all students are empowered to realize their potential. ☼

Deborah Palmer was a two-way dual-language 4th- and 5th-grade teacher in California in the late 1990s. Now she is an associate professor of bilingual education at the University of Colorado Boulder.

References

Davies, Bronwyn, and Rom Harré. 1990. "Positioning: The Discursive Production of Selves." *Journal for the Theory of Social Behaviour* 20.1:43–63.

Lachtman, Ofelia Dumas. 1995. *Pepita habla dos veces/Pepita Talks Twice*. Arte Público Press.

Jiménez, Francisco. 2000. *La mariposa*. HMH Books for Young Readers.

The Intersection of Language Needs and Disability

BY ROBERTO FIGUEROA

FAVIANNA RODRIGUEZ

The first time I met Banoy, we talked about the Seahawks. The second time I met Banoy, I watched as he tore the school apart.

The first meeting was on one of those perpetually gray Puget Sound days during a fire drill. Banoy, a 5th grader, was walking outside with his resource room teacher. He wore shorts and a Seahawks hoodie.

"So you're a football fan, huh?"

Banoy looked at me for a few seconds before answering. "Yeah."

"Oh man, me too. Who's your favorite player?"

Again, a few seconds pause, this time with a small smile around his eyes. "Marshawn Lynch."

"Me too. What do you like about him?"

This time I didn't get an answer. Banoy kept smiling and shrugged. I laughed and remarked on Marshawn Lynch's incredible ability to stay on his feet and push through the pile, then high-fived Banoy to thank him for taking time out of his day to talk to me.

The second time, I met Banoy in the self-contained behavior class he had recently been moved to. He didn't want to do his math. With 20 minutes left in the period, the classroom teacher told Banoy he needed to do his math or he'd get a 1 out of 5 for the period. For the next three hours, Banoy was in a state of destruction. Any attempt to talk to him was met with a high-pitched "Nooooo" accompanied by the sound of ripping, breaking, or kicking. Teachers and paraprofessionals kept trying to talk to him, and when that failed, they would attempt to cut off his space by holding their arms out and slowly encircling him, telling him, sometimes all at once, that he needed to calm down. I asked the staff to stop talking to him and let me follow him to ensure his safety.

When I first walked into Banoy's classroom, I had asked about his visual schedule. The classroom didn't have one. Banoy had a severe communication disorder, but I didn't see any language supports. In all my conversations with the staff about Banoy, no one spoke about his home language, Tagalog.

In the space of three months, Banoy had gone from kicking at the legs of his desk to tearing down student work in the hallways. I kept hearing the team talk about Banoy's disability, Emotional Behavior Disorder (EBD), but nothing about his language needs. At one meeting, I pointed out that Banoy went home to a non-English household, and that his mother had shared that he could barely speak in Tagalog. The school staff had missed this as evidence that Banoy was not just having difficulty learning a second language, but had a severe receptive and expressive language disorder. His language needs, up until then, had not been considered part of the necessary programming to stop his outbursts and destructive behavior. Banoy needed short and consistent phrases during periods of escalation. Too much talking at him was actually driving him to be more violent and out of control.

Language needs were an afterthought, with no real analysis of the intersection between language needs and disability.

As a special education teacher, I worked with numerous students with IEPs who spoke a language other than English at home. Yet I was frustrated by a shortage of school psychologists with the ability and training to give assessments in different languages. Language issues were not explored on the evaluations of emerging bilingual students, leading to both under- and overdiagnosis of disabilities. Language needs were an afterthought, with no real analysis of the intersection between language needs and disability.

I now work as a special education specialist in a district with more than 140 student home languages. This cultural and linguistic diversity represents the new normal in many special education programs and districts around the country, yet special education teachers receive very little training and guidance around identifying students' language strengths and needs. How might Banoy's educational experiences have changed if his teachers designed instruction with his language needs in mind and celebrated his emerging bilingualism as an asset? My hope is that this article might provide general education and special education teachers some guidance on the intersection of a few specific disability categories and the language needs of emerging bilingual students.

Learning in a Second Language

When I studied at a university in Oaxaca, Mexico, I was shocked at the amount of time it took me to read texts. I'm a fast reader in English, able to tear through chapters in quick succession. But in Spanish I had to be deliberate. Even when I didn't have to translate in my head, I still had to run my eyes over the words slower and slower the deeper I got into a text.

It's the same for our students. There is an extra cognitive load that occurs when working in a second language. In fact, the additional time it takes to process another language can look very similar to a learning disability—though they are in fact quite different.

I didn't realize it then, but I really learned a lot from my time as an adult language learner. I got to experience the joys of being a part of a whole new community and world. I also got to experience the difficulty of trying to explain a clear picture in my head with a twisted tongue to a confused teacher.

As an adult, I was able to put my positive and negative experiences into context, push forward, and, even on my hardest days, know I was making progress. Our students don't always have that luxury. The increased length of time it takes them to work through content, along with feelings of frustration and embarrassment, can greatly affect the way emerging bilingual students learn. As teachers, we have the opportunity to help students experience and celebrate the joys and successes of language learning. We give our students with disabilities the best chances of experiencing those positives by scaffolding and programming for their language needs.

Over the years, I've gathered and developed a variety of strategies geared toward the intersection of some common disability categories and students' language needs. The following strategies are aimed at the middle grades, but can be adapted toward younger and older students. They are geared toward moderate intensity disabilities, but can also be adapted for milder or more severely impacted students. Of course, each disability listed could take up its own book; the goal here is to provide some concrete steps to lay a foundation for effective practices.

Emotional Behavior Disorder

Banoy's extreme behaviors had a purpose. Don't want to do work? I'm going to tear up all the papers and break every pencil I can find. Want attention from someone? I'm going to kick the legs of their chair until their eyes are pointed at me. For many of us, this seems illogical. Who likes being punished? But for Banoy, each behavior served a specific function.

Students under the EBD category are the students who need the most positive reinforcement and support for prosocial behaviors, yet they often experience the most punishments and negative interactions. They frequently have difficulty regulating their emotions and their behavior. As a result, their behavior becomes maladaptive.

Maladaptive behavior gets students what they want, but in an inappropriate way that has long-term negative implications. For example, students who are confused by an assignment often want to avoid showing their confusion to the teacher. A student with strong adaptive behavior may ask a trusted peer for help or go back over class notes. A student with maladaptive behavior might instead throw pencils, talk with peers, or crumple up the paper, ultimately getting kicked out of class. In both instances, the teacher does not discover that the student cannot complete the assignment independently.

As we work with emerging bilingual students who carry an EBD label, it is important that we view communication not just as language, but also as body movement and facial expressions. Every smile, scowl, toss of the hair, or eye roll from a student—or teacher—communicates something. A teacher's words can be positive, but, if delivered with a scowl, a student may see the facial expression and not hear the message. An added challenge when working with language learners is that they may not fully understand our words. This makes it even more essential to identify ways that we communicate nonverbally. Teaching students to understand this type of communication becomes a key piece of instruction.

Banoy's teachers may have thought their words were soothing and comforting, but the only thing Banoy saw was a group of adults talking rapidly; more often than not, the talking would set him off. It is important to be aware of the ways students interpret our words and actions. As a classroom teacher, I tried to be a patient person who never yelled, but it amazed me how many times, in restorative conversations with students, they felt I had yelled or been disrespectful. Students can have impressions of social interactions that wildly diverge from ours, and it is our responsibility as adults to take the time to teach meanings and clear up misconceptions that get in the way of forming positive relationships.

> **Every smile, scowl, toss of the hair, or eye roll from a student—or teacher—communicates something.**

One helpful strategy is collaborating with students to identify and discuss specific words, gestures, and actions that signify positives and negatives. Making the meanings explicit adds clarity to social interactions. Hearing a reprimand from a teacher may make some students think that the teacher is angry or does not like them personally. Directly explaining "When I tell you to stop, I'm not angry" can keep a student from interpreting neutral communication as negative. It is just as important to teach students the meaning of positive gestures. Discussing high-fives by saying "When I do this, it means you did something great" leaves less room for interpretation. Fist bumps, nods, or even light clapping with a smile can tell a student they're doing the right thing—if they've been explicitly taught that's what it means.

But it isn't enough to simply help students decode positive, neutral, and negative communication. It's also important to assure that you are actually giving enough positive reinforcement. To do this, you can take five Post-it notes, crumple them up, and put them in one pocket. For each positive statement or positive physical action (e.g., "Thank you for sitting down so quietly! High-five!"), take one of those balls and move it to the other pocket. Any time a negative statement or gesture is used ("Don't do that!" "Put that down!"), move all the paper balls back into the first pocket. If you aren't moving all five over consistently before moving them back, you are not providing enough positive reinforcement.

A longer-term strategy is to practice positive interactions with specific vocabulary and phrase scripts. In a way, the instruction will resemble a drama class, with the behavior to be improved as the focus. Just as a student who is learning math needs to practice math before a test, a student learning appropriate behavior needs to practice that behavior before trying it out in class—especially for those interactions that tend to lead to maladaptive behavior. I wonder how many escalations could have been avoided if Banoy had been given opportunities to practice using the phrases "I need space" or "I need a break."

Emerging bilingual students with emotional disturbances can be some of the most challenging students to work with, due to their added communication needs and the sometimes intense nature of the behaviors displayed. As teachers, we need to understand that the most effective way to change behavior is not through punitive measures, but by fostering positive relationships and providing explicit instruction about communication.

Specific Learning Disability

Students who have a Specific Learning Disability (SLD) struggle with retaining and acquiring new knowledge in any combination of math, reading, writing, and language. A breakdown of executive functioning systems is at the root of specific learning disabilities, as well as other disabilities like Attention-Deficit/Hyperactivity Disorder (ADHD). Executive functioning is the control center for higher-level thinking. It's handled by the frontal lobe of the brain, and "allows humans to comprehend and mentally represent their immediate environment, to retain information about their immediate past, to support the acquisition of new knowledge, to solve problems, and to formulate, relate, and act on current goals" (Baddeley, 1992).

I've seen the most crossover between specific learning disabilities and language needs, as they can resemble each other. A student with an SLD needs more targeted support for learning and more time, which can be very similar to a student learning English. But although both an emerging bilingual student and a student with a learning disability may need more time, the reason for that need is different. Emerging bilingual students are processing information through a second language, increasing their cognitive load. Students with learning disabilities are experiencing a processing block in the brain. It follows that an emerging bilingual student with a learning disability is experiencing both a processing block and an increased processing load.

No matter which subject is affected by the disability, emerging bilingual students will often greatly benefit from a weekly academic word wall that has two or three terms. Choosing a small number of words or phrases allows for reinforcement of each term over the course of the week. Academic instruction will still take place, and other vocabulary words or phrases may be introduced through that instruction, but the emphasis should be on mastering the word wall terms.

Soon after introducing the word wall, it is helpful to set a global accommodation by shortening practice assignments. Practice is important, but when we overload our students, we create frustration, confusion, and exhaustion. We want students to be able to interact with a subject, not be intimidated with the amount of work they need to do. This means chunking larger assignments into smaller pieces, so that students can do the amount of work that is appropriate for them. For example, in a math class, a practice sheet of 20 questions might be chunked into two groups of 10. If the student finishes the first set of 10, she can continue on to the second set of 10, but she won't be initially overwhelmed by seeing all 20 questions in front of her. It's also important to grade students on what they do, not on what they don't do; if a student completes 11 out of the 20 questions on a test, the percentage score she is given should be out of 11, not out of 20.

Finally, students learning English and struggling to process academic information need new and interactive ways to engage with content. Creating discussion groups in any subject—at any grade level—is a fantastic way of engaging students while not overloading them. Talking with peers helps move knowledge into working memory, encourages students to learn from each other, and allows them to practice expressing new ways of thinking about problems as they explain their solutions out loud to other students. To further support language learning, you can encourage the use of the target academic vocabulary during discussions. For example, a goal for the day could be to use one of the word wall words, like "photosynthesis," during a discussion. This could be a goal for a specific student, or for the whole class.

Attention-Deficit/Hyperactivity Disorder

A student with ADHD has a delay in executive functioning. The most visible aspect of ADHD is often hyperactivity, but hyperactivity isn't necessarily present in each case of ADHD. Instead, the real constant is inattention.

A colleague of mine once relayed an analogy about ADHD after we heard someone say for the millionth time, "They're in 8th grade! They should know how to pay attention by now, even with ADHD! They've gotten all sorts of accommodations and modifications for years, and they still can't pay attention. They just don't want to pay attention."

My colleague turned to me and said, "Hey, Roberto, how long have you been wearing glasses?

"Oh, since 7th grade."

"Great! Give them to me, since you don't need them anymore."

"What?"

"According to what we just heard, you've been wearing glasses for almost 20 years now. Your vision has been accommodated that whole time. Shouldn't your eyes just know how to see correctly by now?"

That was one of the strongest "ah-ha" moments I've ever had. It also led me to do more research on ADHD and the way it shows up in the brain. If you search online, there are many communities talking about how ADHD doesn't actually exist. Yet scientifically, we know it does. Brain scans, peer-reviewed studies, and the work of ADHD advocates demonstrate that the existence of ADHD should not be in question, although it remains important to watch for overdiagnosis. Students who have ADHD face extra challenges because the nature of their disability so closely resembles disinterest or low motivation.

Accommodating a disability like ADHD doesn't involve forcing change ("Pay attention!"). The same way no one goes up to a paraplegic and says, "You just don't want to walk," no one should be going up to a student with ADHD and saying, "You just don't want to pay attention." For a student with ADHD, accommodations—such as structured breaks or lessons designed to increase student engagement—don't teach a student how not to have a disability. Instead, they teach students how to use structures to better access the world around them. The same is true for emerging bilingual students and accommodations. Learning a language is not a skill acquired in a short time, even in an immersion setting. According to research, full mastery of another language can take up to five to seven years (Cummins, 1981). In that time, the use of accommodations does not hamper student progress; it allows students to better access learning.

> **"You've been wearing glasses and contacts for almost 20 years now. Shouldn't your eyes just know how to see correctly by now?"**

When planning accommodations for emerging bilingual students with ADHD, implementing appropriately timed breaks is essential. A break is not free time, nor is it unstructured. A teacher should learn to recognize signs that a specific student needs a break—in one student's case, for example, signs might include getting up out of his chair or drumming his pencil against the table. The teacher can then signal to that student that this is a good time to take a break, giving him two options for what to do with his time. The options might include sitting down to do a puzzle in another area or reading a book of his choice quietly. These break options are related to academics, but are less cognitively demanding than participating in regular instruction. Once the student has settled down and is ready to rejoin the class, he can come right back.

It's also important to think about how to structure instruction to help students maintain focus. Students learning English are not just processing the information, but also the manner in which the information is presented. All-verbal instruction can sap the cognitive stamina of an emerging bilingual student. Add in ADHD, and verbal instruction will likely result in the student not paying attention and possibly acting out. Research shows that it takes more effort for a student with ADHD to attend to tasks; for emerging bilingual students, that means more effort spent understanding the language of a lesson before they are able to process the content. Because of this, it's essential to use visuals, realia, and movement when teaching emerging bilingual students with ADHD.

With all of this in mind, workstations can be one of the best lesson structures to ensure student engagement. For example, a student might spend 10 minutes doing independent work, 10 minutes discussing content with peers, and 10 minutes working collaboratively on a poster; in just 30 minutes, they experience multiple modes of engagement. Switching between stations keeps students moving and actively engaged.

Language Advocates

However important these individual strategies may be, the key to effective scaffolding, programming, and planning for bilingual and multicultural students is a mind-set: Linguistic and cultural diversity strengthen society. The students we work with have limitless potential and a wealth of experiences from which to draw. From an individual standpoint, their emerging bilingualism confers a host of cognitive and social benefits. From a social standpoint, their growing ability to communicate in more than one language is a key resource for our society.

In addition to the strategies listed above, there are many language-centric strategies that demonstrate to students the value we have for their emerging bilingualism. Students know they are valued when, for example, their home language and culture are woven into the curriculum. We can recognize their linguistic expertise by asking them to teach us words or phrases in their home languages. These should be expressions that can be used in class or during transitions—"good morning," "goodbye," and "thank you" are obvious choices. It's best if this vocabulary is also visibly displayed on the wall so that it becomes part of the visual environment of the classroom. Curriculum units can and should weave in students' home cultures through read-alouds that represent students' backgrounds and by making students' lives part of the curriculum.

> **The key to effective scaffolding, programming, and planning for bilingual and multicultural students is a mind-set: Linguistic and cultural diversity strengthens society.**

It's not enough to try to bring in language and culture during instructional time; we must also make sure this focus is reflected in our interactions with individual students. As teachers we should always be asking ourselves, "How am I connecting with my students? Am I asking them about their lives? Am I sharing who I am and giving them a chance to show me who they are?" Often our one-on-one conversations are geared toward goals and academics, yet all students—especially emerging bilingual students with special needs—want and need to know that the adults at school recognize them and are there for them. Authentic conversations with students shouldn't just be about likes or dislikes, about favorite sports teams, foods, or music. We should embrace opportunities to talk to students about where we're from and ask them about their families and their cultures. By sharing about our own lives and discussing similarities and differences between our families' traditions, cultures, or values, we can show students that we honestly desire to know them and to create space for them to express who they are in school.

What would our schools look like if we explicitly valued students' home languages and disability needs? Assessment for special needs would consider students' language backgrounds, and teachers would be trained to structure their instruction to support special-needs students who are also learning in a new language. Special education and general education teachers would plan together, building on each other's strengths, to create lesson plans that contain programming for all the different students in their classrooms. Outside the classroom, parents would have access to translators and home language materials to help them advocate for their students' needs. Most importantly, we would not just advocate for students' learning; we would work with them as partners—learning about their preferences and abilities, viewing their bilingualism and biculturalism as true assets, and helping them to advocate for themselves. When you partner with someone, their opinions, needs, and strengths have value to you. And as a partner, there is a responsibility not just to give, but to receive as well. Our students have a lot to give and teach us. ☼

Roberto Figueroa has worked as a special education teacher, teacher coach, and multipurpose specialist. He is currently a behavior program specialist for a large district in Washington State.

References

Baddeley, Alan. 1992. "Working Memory." *Science* 255.5044:556-59.

Cummins, Jim. 1981. "Age on Arrival and Immigrant Second Language Learning in Canada: A Reassessment." *Applied Linguistics* 2.2:132-149.

Beyond Bilingual

Including multilingual students in dual-language classrooms

BY LEAH DURÁN, MICHIKO HIKIDA,
AND RAMÓN ANTONIO MARTÍNEZ

"They are *bilingüe*, but I am *trilingüe*," Malik told Ramón during a conversation about his classmates. Malik, a 6-year-old boy from a Sudanese family, was enrolled in a Spanish/English dual-language program. As he explained to Ramón, he was *trilingüe*—trilingual. He spoke English and Spanish at school with his friends and his teachers, and Arabic at home with his parents, who had emigrated from Sudan. By claiming his trilingualism, Malik rejected the way we had chosen to label him: a wake-up call for us.

As educators committed to recognizing the strengths that working-class students of color bring to the classroom, we've grown accustomed to viewing "bilingual" as a positive label—particularly compared to alternatives like "English language learner" or "limited English proficient." We used the term "bilingual" very deliberately in our teaching to disrupt descriptions that highlight what students presumably lack rather than their strengths, accomplishments, and potential. We've continued to use "bilingual" in our work as teacher educators and researchers. Yet students like Malik have taught us that when we rely too heavily on this label, we may be underestimating them and their capabilities. And we aren't the only ones. Multilingual students like Malik are often present but rarely accounted for in bilingual programs.

Home and heritage languages play an important role in students' lives, families, and identities. Malik was rightly proud of his growing proficiency in Arabic when he said, "My mom taught me about my real language." Kevin, a classmate, told us how he intentionally talked in Tagalog to his new baby sister, noticing that when he did, "She screams like she's happy."

Other students talked about speaking less and less of their home language over time. Alicia, a 2nd-grade Filipina, noted that she now spoke Spanish and English better than Tagalog, although she still knew important phrases like "Thank you," "You're welcome," and "Where is your mom?"

Even in the absence of institutional support for their heritage languages, many of these students worked to maintain their multilingualism. They taught each other (and us) some of the words and phrases they knew, and they were eager to learn from each other. What would it look like if all students were given opportunities to sustain and develop their heritage languages in addition to the target languages of bilingual programs?

Multilingual Students' Successes and Struggles

When Malik was a 1st-grade student in a K–1 dual-language classroom, he stood out as an engaged, confident, and curious language learner. He asked questions often—"What does this word mean?"—and tried out many of the new words he learned. During read-alouds, he often probed for meaning or clarification. While listening to his teacher read aloud from the poetry anthology *My Mexico/México mío*, Malik asked: "What's a *ramillete*?" His teacher turned this question back to his classmates and no one responded. Following the teacher's explanation—"It's a bunch of flowers, like a bouquet"—Malik was excited to note, "I know bouquet!" Corrections from his classmates didn't seem to faze him, and English-monolingual visitors

DAVID BACON

to the classroom sometimes asked him to translate a classmate's Spanish for them, which he did handily.

Malik was not the only multilingual student in his class. A number of his classmates were learning Spanish and English as third, or even fourth languages. One of Malik's multilingual classmates was Samantha, a student whose family came from the state of Oaxaca in Mexico. At home, she spoke mostly Zapoteco (the term she used to refer to her family's Indigenous language, which is from the Zapotec language family), and Spanish. With one uncle, she communicated with hand signs, which she described as "signing." According to Samantha, she liked Zapoteco best.

Samantha's teacher identified her as one of the students who was most successful in the dual-language program. At recess, she switched seamlessly between English and Spanish, depending on who joined her group to play. Her closest seatmate also had family roots in Oaxaca, and Samantha would occasionally pause while writing a story in English or Spanish to ask him a question in Zapoteco. She kept a notebook with her to write down new words, especially Zapoteco, which she was learning from her mother at home.

Although teachers recognized that Malik and Samantha were both thriving in a bilingual educational environment and actively maintaining their home languages, teachers sometimes perceived other multilingual students as being at a disadvantage. For example, Kevin, the Filipino student who spoke Tagalog at home, was sometimes described as struggling. His teachers and parents sometimes questioned whether he belonged in a Spanish/English classroom because of his perceived lack of proficiency in Spanish. When he was in 2nd grade, they decided to send him to the classroom next door for math instruction in English. One of Kevin's teachers expressed concerns about whether or not the dual-language model was meeting his needs. She wondered if the program was a poor fit for him and other students for whom Spanish was not the primary language.

> **Kevin told us how he intentionally talked in Tagalog to his new baby sister, noticing that when he did, "She screams like she's happy."**

When we visited his classroom, we noticed that Kevin was sometimes treated no differently from his peers in ways that might have limited his learning. When he asked what the word "lentil" meant, for example, his science teacher translated it to the Spanish equivalent—*lenteja*—for him. Although this translation was likely helpful to many of his classmates, Kevin remained confused.

In contrast, later in the lesson, when Kevin asked about the meaning of the word "inch," the teacher held up a ruler to demonstrate what an inch looked like, and he nodded, satisfied. This visual and interactive explanation of "inch" served to help Kevin learn a new concept, where a word-to-word translation of "lentil" into Spanish had failed.

Another day, a substitute teacher read Derek Munson's *Pastel para enemigos* (*Enemy Pie*) to the class. Kevin raised his hand to state that he didn't understand the story. As the discussion progressed, it became clear that he didn't know the word *enemigo* (enemy), and without understanding that word, the story had not made sense to him. When it was time to talk about the book and write a response at the end, he was stumped. Perhaps the book would have made more sense to Kevin if the teacher had begun the story with a preview and a group discussion of the important ideas: What is a friend? What is an enemy? How do you make friends and enemies?

By the time he reached 3rd grade, Kevin had transferred out of the Spanish/English strand in response to concerns that his parents and teachers had about his Spanish proficiency. Although there were times where his emergent Spanish proficiency created tension and confusion, we also saw many moments in which Kevin used Spanish quite adeptly. He made helpful edits to his friends' writing—for example, correcting *diverti* to *divertí* in a partner's composition by adding the necessary accent mark. He read Spanish books during independent reading; deciphered Spanish word problems; and followed directions, held conversations, and participated in classroom life in a language that he, his parents, and his teacher seemed to think he was struggling to understand.

Although the struggles he had were real, we think that he was capable of successfully learning in this Spanish-English classroom. In fact, there's evidence that dual-language programs are more beneficial than English-only classrooms for multilingual children's academic achievement, language learning, and sense of identity (Rolstad, 1997). However, teachers working with any student—especially those who are learning a second or third language in school—need to weave support for language learning into every moment of the day. Language practice and support—including realia, visuals, and context clues—are critically important for multilingual students. In Kevin's case, this kind of consistent language support might have made a difference.

Explicitly Valuing Students' Home Languages

Teachers need to go beyond providing support for target instructional languages to recognizing and valuing students' home languages. We've had the opportunity to visit classrooms where teachers noticed, encouraged, and supported students' home and heritage languages, inviting students to write and talk about them as central aspects of their identities and family life. For example, one teacher often modeled her own interest in and curiosity about language. During a small-group guided reading lesson, Malik and his classmates came across a new word, *rabipelado* (opossum). In her explanation of this new word, the teacher talked about her own enjoyment of knowing other words for opossum, including *zarigüeya* (from Guaraní) and her favorite, *tlacuache* (from the Nahuatl word). Despite not knowing the Arabic or Tagalog equivalents, she was able to convey an interest in and enthusiasm for languages.

Another teacher asked her students to write "I am" poems, describing important aspects of their identities. In conversation with her students about what to include in these identity poems, she noticed that they considered their family roots and home languages to be key parts of that identity. She adapted the assignment in response, and displayed the finished poems prominently in the classroom until the end of the year. Samantha's (excerpted here) read:

> **I am...**
> I am fun.
> I am cute.
> I am a reader.
> I am a writer.
> I am a girl.

I speak Zapoteco, Spanish, and English.
I was born in the USA, but I also have Oaxacan roots.

Samantha is also leading a language inquiry project at the school, investigating how many other Zapoteco speakers there are and how many different dialects of Zapoteco they speak. She and two other Zapoteco speakers worked with us to put together a survey, which they gave to approximately 100 high school students on their K–12 campus. They identified 10 students who had some exposure to Zapoteco at home, and they were able to interview five of these students to get their perspectives on speaking Zapoteco. Samantha made sure the question "Do you love the language?" was on the survey.

Ideally, the starting points for this kind of inquiry are students' own questions and curiosities about language. Teachers hoping to support their multilingual students need to start from a similar place of curiosity. We can ask ourselves: Who are my students? What languages and dialects do they know, and what do their families know? Who else in the community could serve as a resource? How might we incorporate these languages and dialects as resources for teaching and learning? How can we cultivate and communicate an appreciation for the languages, cultures, and perspectives our students bring?

Even when we don't speak our students' home languages, we can:

- Carve out time in the day for multilingual students to teach their peers words, phrases, songs, or poems in their home languages.
- Find picture books with writing in students' home languages to read and display in the classroom.
- Invite students and their families to create books that use their home languages through homework assignments or in-class activities.
- Make sure that students' home languages are celebrated and visible in print around the classroom and in the hallways.
- Invite multilingual community members (grandparents, parents, other students at the school, university volunteers) to be tutors, translators, or language teachers in our classrooms.
- Model being language learners ourselves: Ask students to teach us words and phrases, and use them. Let students see us play with language and take risks with language. Encourage the kind of curiosity about language and new words that many students already have.
- Guide students in using their home languages to help them develop their second or third languages, whether through multilingual journals, code-switching, or talking about similarities and differences across languages.
- Give class and homework assignments that invite and encourage students to respond in their home languages and that involve

parents.

- Support parents in their efforts to develop their child's home language.
- Assume multilingualism is valuable and normal, and that multilingual students can be successful in bilingual programs.

Many of these are familiar strategies within ESL or bilingual contexts, yet we may not always recognize how useful and important they can be to support multilingual students who speak a home or heritage language that is not one of the school's target languages.

What Can Schools Do?

Students like Malik, Samantha, and Kevin are often invisible in the policy discussions about bilingual education. Bilingual programs generally operate under the assumption that the students they serve are learning in *either* their first *or* their second language, and plan for instruction accordingly. In the case of dual-immersion bilingual education, teachers and administrators may also operate under the assumption that students are mostly *either* Latina/o and learning English *or* white, native English speakers learning Spanish. Yet bilingual classrooms are full of students who don't fall into these categories. In the hyper-diverse classrooms that are becoming more and more common in the United States today, bilingual programs serve many children who are beyond bilingual. Some of the approaches that schools have traditionally used to teach a second language to monolingual children will not meet these students' needs.

Who are my students? What languages and dialects do they know?

In the school that Malik, Samantha, and Kevin attended, the official policy left home language support for multilingual children up to parents and families. This absence of official policies about how to support multilingual students represents a blind spot in bilingual education more generally. Given that this kind of linguistic diversity is increasingly common, one of the most important issues facing bilingual programs is what to do to support all of their students, including those who are multilingual and multidialectal. Failure to provide this support can result in students like Kevin being pushed out of programs that could ultimately benefit them.

Providing support for multilingual students might mean that, instead of only allocating instructional time to the target languages, bilingual programs consider times when multilingual students might be invited to teach, use, or learn more in their home languages. It would also mean recruiting community members to help translate fliers, newsletters, and displays, and finding home language books and media for the library. This responsibility cannot lie with teachers alone; administrators and policy makers must give time, resources, and attention to supporting the home languages and cultural identity of all children.

Students like Malik, Kevin, and Samantha are multilingual role models for the rest of us. With intentional support, they can and do thrive in dual-language programs and beyond. ☼

Leah Durán is an assistant professor in Teaching, Learning & Sociocultural Studies at the University of Arizona. Michiko Hikida is an assistant professor in language, education, and society at Ohio State University. Ramón Antonio Martínez is an assistant professor in the Graduate School of Education and the Center for Comparative Studies in Race and Ethnicity at Stanford University. All three began their education careers as elementary school teachers. Student names have been changed.

Reference

Rolstad, Kellie. January 1997. "Effects of Two Way Immersion on the Ethnic Identification of Third Language Students: An Exploratory Study." *Bilingual Research Journal* 21:43–63.

Making Space for Spanish

BY ALEXANDRA BABINO AND CAROL WICKSTROM

MELANIE CERVANTES

Several students were talking to me at the same time, excitedly asking a question, relating a story, or sharing a new iPad app. María and Guadalupe began passing out binders to their fellow classmates. The remaining students took their seats, arranged in a semicircle. This was the daily routine in my 4th-grade, dual-language, gifted and talented class for each of the three times a week that I pulled this group for their hour and a half session.

"Today's Free Friday," Jacqui reminded the class.

"Yesss!" Roberto enthused. "I love free writing."

"Me too!" responded Dana and Kevin at the same time.

Once all students had their binders, I transitioned to our daily warm-up. "OK, since we completed our last project in English, for the next nine weeks we will work on our project in Spanish. That means today's free writing will be in Spanish."

"What?!" Gabriel protested. Two girls gave a deep sigh.

Jacqui stood up and asked solemnly, "Do we have to write in Spanish?" The class grew quiet, waiting for my reply.

I paused and asked, "Why don't you want to write in Spanish?"

I'd like to say that the question "Do we have to write in Spanish?" was a one-time event. Yet, in nearly a decade as a Spanish dual-language teacher, I have heard this question and similar sentiments expressed by students again and again. This question made me wonder: Why didn't our students—who had grown up in a 50/50 dual-language program, who spoke Spanish in their homes and communities—want to write in Spanish? What was happening in our dual-language school that caused students to prefer English? What was happening in my own classroom?

It Takes More than a Program

Of course, students' feelings about language aren't formed just in school. I started to read about why students may value English more and ran across the work of researchers such as Kim Potowski (2007) and Carmen Fought (2003), who explored reasons why Latina/o youth and dual-language students do and don't maintain their Spanish. One reason for preferring English over Spanish is that English can be perceived as the "cool" language. When I asked my students what their favorite TV shows and music were, none of them mentioned a Spanish-language show or musical group, even though all of them told me that they watched *novelas* and listened to Spanish-language music with their parents. Favorite shows and music were always mainstream English pieces.

English isn't just the language of novelty; it is also the language of power. It is the majority language in the United States, and so I wondered if my students sensed that English held more power in their interactions with their parents, teachers, and friends. Even when speaking with bilingual friends, students tended to speak in English. I wondered if they noticed which language was preferred in interactions between bilingual staff members. Did they see the successful bilinguals in their school community choosing to speak English most of the time?

In many ways, I was proud of our school and the ways it supported the development of students' Spanish. Our north Texas dual-language school followed a one-language, one-teacher model; students had a Spanish teacher for half of their instruction and an English teacher for the other half from kindergarten to 5th grade. In the regular classroom, my 4th-grade students switched teachers (and therefore languages) every week to allow for time to develop depth of curricular knowledge in one language before continuing in the other language. Since nearly 100 percent of the school's student population was native Spanish-speaking Latinas/os, the 970-student campus was considered a one-way dual-language program.

Approximately half of the 85-person faculty was bilingual, with the other half being monolingual ESL teachers. Two of the three campus principals were bilinguals of Mexican American heritage, as was one of the two campus counselors. Spanish and English could be heard over daily announcements, at school meetings, and during parent conferences. All home communications were written in both languages.

However, in my nine years at our school, I'd learned that it takes more than a schoolwide dual-language program to promote the continued use and value of two languages. If you looked closely, you'd find that most of the "fun" activities at school, like technology and physical education, were only offered in English. And although both languages were used during daily announcements and school events, English was usually presented first, followed by a truncated summary in Spanish. At school assemblies, even when a bilingual speaker was presenting, the presentation generally took place in English. In other words, English often became the higher or more valued language and Spanish, the lower, lesser-valued language. Even though English and Spanish were technically given equal time and attention in the classroom, the wider school and community contexts favored English.

> **What was happening in our dual-language school that caused students to prefer English? What was happening in my own classroom?**

My understanding was that, by choosing a 50/50 instead of a 90/10 model, the district's intention had been to allow students to access both languages from the beginning of school. But perhaps a more equitable dual-language design would have been a 90/10 model, where students begin school learning primarily in Spanish. Would changing program models mitigate the hegemony of English? I didn't know, but I decided to start by examining what I could control: what was happening within my own classroom.

Reflecting on My Teaching

I began to reflect on how I was privileging English in the classroom—in greater curriculum cycles, daily instruction, and moment-by-moment interactions with students. At the end of every unit and semester, I examined how much time—both formal and informal—was devoted to Spanish.

What percentage of Spanish and English work was shown in the classroom? What about instructional materials? What percentage of classroom conversation was conducted in Spanish—both formally and informally? What kind of comments did students share about each language?

More often than not, I found that English represented more than half of our speech, from instructional time to curriculum resources and informal interactions. Even though I had considered my use of English and Spanish to be fairly balanced, I realized it wasn't.

Sometimes I would use the English version instead of translating an article into Spanish, because the materials were only available in English and I was pressed for time. Other times, I thought it was easier to go with English because, even though I had the time to translate a science video, I didn't feel I had the energy. Still other times, I would conduct parts of class conversations in English because, even though I prepared the materials in Spanish, I felt like I didn't want to fight my students' Spanish pushback. That is, I didn't want to speak Spanish while students responded in English. I didn't want to have to continually (and politely) ask them to respond in

Spanish. Honestly, I was tired of the battle.

Yet, I still knew the battle was worth it. I knew I needed to consciously and systematically make space for Spanish.

Starting the "Spanish Conversation"

As with many situations in bilingual education, I didn't have a pat answer—no book, no teacher guide. Yet, I did know my values as a teacher. I valued Spanish and wanted to make space for Spanish, knowing that changing students' views wasn't something I could single-handedly do. I knew that this was a process.

Practically speaking, I decided to make space for Spanish through creating opportunities for dialogue about Spanish, providing strategic language scaffolds, and sharing my own story about language loss. I knew at a deeply personal level that English, as the language of power, would naturally overshadow Spanish if I didn't intentionally, strategically plan for these spaces and conversations.

I began to reflect on how I was privileging English in the classroom.

I wanted to know more about why my students didn't want to write in Spanish. So over the course of several months, my students and I took part in an extended dialogue on Spanish—in Spanish. How did they feel about it? Did they think it was important? And perhaps, most important to me as a writing teacher, why didn't they want to write in Spanish—their home language that they'd been instructed in since kindergarten?

On a Spanish-speaking class day, I asked what they thought about speaking Spanish: "*Entonces, ¿qué piensan sobre el español?*" (So, what do you think about Spanish?)

Kevin responded, "*A veces me confundo porque cuando hablo inglés se me olvidan las palabras en español y mezclo las palabras.*" (Sometimes I get confused, because when I speak English I forget Spanish words and I mix words.)

"*Pero ¿hablas español siempre o la mayor parte del tiempo en la casa?*" (But don't you speak Spanish all the time or most of the time at home?) I asked.

Roberto jumped in, eager to share his thoughts, "*Pues, sí. Es que es el único idioma que hablo con mis papás.*" (Well, yeah, it's the only language I speak with my parents.)

"*¿No hablas español con tus hermanos?*" (You don't speak Spanish with your siblings?)

Roberto responded: "*No mucho.*" (Not too much.)

Through these conversations, I learned about the role of Spanish in students' home lives. I also learned that sometimes they avoided Spanish at school because they were losing confidence in their ability to speak and write in Spanish in academic settings—as Kevin mentioned when he talked about forgetting and mixing words. I realized that, with native Spanish speakers in our bilingual program, we tended to scaffold English language instruction, but we didn't always strategically scaffold Spanish. And even though it was students' home language, they needed more support than we were giving them when it came to using Spanish academically.

We All Forget Sometimes

I continued the "Spanish conversation" with students as it came up. I not only provided opportunities to speak and write in Spanish but also opportunities to talk about speaking and writing in Spanish. We discussed different "kinds" of Spanish, including Spanish vocabulary and accents from countries other than my students' Mexico. We shared our thoughts and feelings of being confused in Spanish, why it seemed at times to be hard, and what we could do when it became hard.

"Sometimes I just forget the words," Guadalupe shared one day in class.

"Me, too," Gabriel agreed.

"That's OK," I responded, "I think all bilinguals feel that way sometimes. It's not that you don't know the word; it's just that you temporarily forgot it. That's why we have tools to help us."

We agreed to not make fun of each other for forgetting what many would call "common" words. I modeled forgetting words myself and asking for help. I believe my modeling, coupled with the explicit conversation about Spanish and bilingualism, set the stage for a classroom community that respectfully worked together. Any question could be asked by anyone, answered by anyone. As the teacher, I was both one of several sources for answers and an asker of questions. Many times you could hear some version of the following dialogue:

"Just use Google translator!"

"Wait! I think you call it *encanto*."

"Mrs. Babino, is it *encanto* or *joya*?"

Then I'd open up the discussion to the class. "*Entonces, ¿qué piensan? ¿Cuál palabra representa mejor la idea de* charm *de una pulsera?*" (So what do you think? Which word best represents the idea of a charm on a bracelet?) "*En este caso, ¿cuál tiene más sentido?*" (In this case, which makes more sense?)

The Hegemony of English at Home

Over the year, as I uncovered students' attitudes toward Spanish and English, we started discussing the power related to each language. Once, when I asked Yesenia if she thought Spanish was important, she responded: "Well, it's a little important."

Caught aback but intensely curious, I probed a little further: "Why is it a little important?"

"Well, I speak it with my grandma and my parents."

"Do they speak English, too?"

"They don't speak English," she responded.

We talked about how important it was to know Spanish so that we could communicate with people who weren't bilingual—Spanish-speaking family members, other members of the community, younger children at school. We discussed how continuing to develop our Spanish allowed us to widen and deepen our connections with all kinds of people and to value our full selves.

What other messages were students getting about Spanish being just a "little important" when compared to English? I continued, "Well, do your parents ever talk to you about English? What do they tell you?" Four students working on different projects piped in to join the conversation.

"*¡Échale ganas!*" (Work hard!) Kevin shared.

"*¡Aprende inglés!*" (Learn English!) added Jacqui.

"*Enséñame más inglés*" (Teach me more English), Daniela responded, with more students nodding their heads yes.

"So, they want you to study English," I paraphrased.

"Yes," Yesenia replied enthusiastically.

Listening to my students eagerly share how much importance their parents placed on learning English, I realized the hegemony of English occurred at home, too.

Supporting Spanish with Strategic Scaffolds

In addition to making space for Spanish through classroom dialogue, I also began to explore how I supported students' Spanish development in everyday instruction. I had noticed that students would often respond, "*¡Es difícil!*" (It's hard!) or "*Se me olvida*" (I forget) when we discussed how it felt for them to do academic work in Spanish. My response was to provide whatever academic supports I could. Just as I had used linguistic scaffolds with my students learning English, I used linguistic scaffolds for academic Spanish.

We previewed vocabulary and made word walls with pertinent words. We made cognate lists and spelling lists for Spanish words, just as we would for English words. We created word banks of synonyms for everyday words to increase our Spanish vocabulary.

In addition, I provided space for metalinguistic awareness, explaining how a language structure was similar and different in each language. For example, in clarifying the concept of contractions in English, I would say, "Contractions are a way we combine two words together. You'll notice that contractions have an apostrophe in English. Do we have apostrophes in Spanish?" Then I'd give students time to look through their Spanish chapter books to explore and answer the question. By the end, we'd draw the conclusion as a class that in Spanish, there are two contractions, *del* and *al* (which do not use apostrophes), but in English there are many contractions.

Sharing My Own Story

As rich and empowering as these conversations were, I didn't feel like they were enough. I hadn't yet fully given myself. Despite my intense insecurity, I decided to share my own bilingual story with my students and their parents—not just once, but again and again as it came up.

I shared how I grew up bilingual in an English-speaking town, with my mother, whose family was from Mexico, and my father, whose family was from the United States. I shared how one day at school a boy made fun of me for speaking Spanish, so I decided not to speak it again. Sure, I spoke it with my *abuelita*, my *primos*, and other members of my mom's family, but we only saw them once a month and visited Mexico once a year.

Over the course of five years, I forgot my Spanish and wrestled with my Mexican American identity. How could I be Mexican and not speak Spanish? How could I "look American" but feel Mexican in my heart? I didn't fit, but I earnestly wanted to feel Mexican and American at the same time. I wanted to connect with my family and our history. I wanted to connect with the students and families I worked with. And I wanted to connect with the vibrant Spanish-speaking world beyond our classroom and community. So I started the long and arduous 10-year journey of relearning Spanish.

After sharing my story I asked, "Would you want to forget Spanish and have to learn it all over again?" Students' eyes were wide as they stared at me.

"Ten years?"

"Yes," I'd soberly reply. "Ten years to get it back. That's why sometimes, now that I'm older, I speak Spanish like a native Spanish speaker and other times I don't. I'm both a native speaker and a Spanish learner." And in many ways, so are they.

"Spanish Conversations" Beyond the Classroom

My conversations with students helped me to realize that I need to advocate for space for Spanish outside my classroom as well. As a result, I've begun sharing the scaffolds and strategies I use with other teachers. I also started "Spanish conversations" with teacher colleagues and campus and district administrators, to advocate for more Spanish in our school and program. Our school now implements a 90/10 dual-language model.

Because these students are in 5th grade, this year will be my last with them before they move on to middle school. I plan to include a unit about bilingualism and bicultural identity in Spanish. More importantly, I will carry the lessons my students taught me about supporting and making space for Spanish into my future work as an educator. And instead of seeing the question "Do we have to write in Spanish?" as a protest, I will know that it is really an opportunity for thoughtful conversation and growth. ☼

Alexandra (Ale) Babino, PhD, has served as an English and Spanish language educator for the past 11 years. She also enjoys teaching bilingual education classes for several Dallas universities. Carol Wickstrom (carol.wickstrom@unt.edu) is a professor of language and literacy at the University of North Texas. She teaches courses to EC–6 preservice teachers. Student names have been changed.

References

Fought, Carmen. 2003. *Chicano English in Context.* Palgrave Macmillan.

Potowski, Kim. 2007. *Language and Identity in a Dual Immersion School.* Multilingual Matters.

El corazón de la escuela / The Heart of the School

The importance of bilingual school libraries

BY RACHEL CLOUES

A 30-foot-long gray whale skeleton visited my school library for a week in the spring. The whale arrived in many parts—giant vertebrae piled up in bins and boxes; long, curved ribs carefully carried up the stairs and down the hallway; the enormous and beautiful white skull pushed slowly on a wheeled cart from Mission Science Workshop, based in the neighborhood a few blocks away. As the teacher-librarian at a bilingual elementary school in San Francisco, I worked on coordinating Whale Week for more than a year. Now it was upon us, and I was grinning from ear to ear as I watched the children's mouths drop open at the sight of the huge collection of bones moving into our library.

Our students spent a month studying gray whales, which migrate each year along the California coast between Alaska and Mexico. It was an engaging schoolwide topic, especially because most of the children's families themselves migrated from Mexico and Central America. During Whale Week, each class spent an hour in our school library learning from the Mission Science Workshop staff, in English and Spanish, about whales. Each class worked together to assemble (and then disassemble) the gray whale skeleton, piece by piece, nestling numbered vertebrae together like a giant puzzle and tying ribs taller than 5th graders to a specially constructed wooden frame. Flippers—with finger bones clearly visible—fanned out from the whale's giant shoulder blades. The fully assembled skeleton spanned the entire length of our library.

Throughout the week, parents and community members stopped in to help with the bones and marvel. Several classes of 6th, 7th, and 8th graders from the middle school next door also visited. They helped our preschool and kinder students lift and place pieces of the skeleton. On display around the library were myriad books about whales and other ocean animals. The whale website I created with photos and digital

SIMONE SHIN

resources was up on the computer screens. Recordings of whale sounds emanated from computer speakers while the children worked to match together almost 200 sun-bleached bones.

This powerful, bilingual, integrated learning experience in our school library was a collaboration between many players: a community organization dedicated to bringing hands-on science to low-income Spanish-speaking youth in the Mission District, our school's science resource teacher, our gardening intern, classroom teachers, and me— the teacher-librarian. Funded through a modest library budget, our school's Whale Week is an example of the kind of creative, literacy-rich, and intercurricular learning opportunities possible with a robust school library program. It is one of many reasons we need our school libraries and teacher-librarian positions to be adequately funded.

In recent years and across the nation, school library programming has gone the way of art, music, PE, and other "supplemental" or "special" programs in public schools. Nowhere has this reduced funding for libraries had a more devastating impact than in California, where we currently have one credentialed school librarian for every 7,187 students, according to the state's department of education (2016). The California School Librarian Association (CSLA) drives home this shameful fact by pointing out that Texas—the state with the next largest population of students—has approximately one teacher-librarian for every 1,080 students; Mississippi can boast roughly a 1:575 ratio. California is at the very bottom of this absurd range of statistics. Each time I attend the annual CSLA conference, it is noticeably and sadly under-attended.

The non-prioritization of school libraries and librarians has a great impact on all students and teachers, of course, but bilingual schools are disproportionately affected. Many public school children, like those I teach, come from low-income communities and/or homes where English is not the primary language. Often there are not many books at home.

Stephen Krashen, the linguist, educational researcher, and longtime advocate for both bilingual education and school libraries, has repeatedly written about the strong correlation between children's access to books and their reading ability. "Bilingual education has done well," Krashen writes, "but it can do much better. The biggest problem, in my view, is the absence of books, in both the first and second language, in the lives of students in these programs." Bilingual schools need top-notch school libraries and credentialed teacher-librarians. When these programs are lacking or severely underfunded, the enormous potential schools have to contribute to building a peaceful, functional multilingual society is curtailed.

More than a Room Full of Books

There are many reasons why funding for school libraries plays such a pivotal role in the creation of strong bilingual programs, other than simply ensuring access to more books. A full-time teacher-librarian on staff who manages the library and teaches is a key player in the school faculty, especially if they are bilingual. We provide specialized, expert literacy support to classroom teachers and their students, along with an intimate knowledge of a far greater quantity and variety of up-to-date print and digital resources than any single classroom can support. A teacher-librarian may be one of the best-positioned people to connect content areas across the curriculum and grade levels, cultivating an interdisciplinary environment that can also nurture individual interests. Libraries provide safe spaces in schools, both physically and emotionally, for children to grow and learn. Students regularly tell me how much they love being in the library and, for many, the library space is preferred over the schoolyard during recess. For students who don't feel safe on the playground, the library is a critical refuge.

My teacher-librarian colleagues and I teach information literacy in a more in-depth way than most classroom teachers have the time to do. This includes working with students to practice research skills, learn source evaluation, locate and cite credible information, use an anti-bias lens, and try different presentation formats—all using multiple print and digital sources. These are skills all students need in a world so heavily impacted by the internet, but especially the children who may not have access to computers at home or families who can help them navigate an online environment with a critical eye. Digital citizenship, or how to use online tools appropriately, is another field in which teacher-librarians usually have a lot of training.

Library Closed for Testing

Like our bilingual classroom teacher counterparts, teacher-librarians in bilingual libraries face some extra challenges. It is not easy to purchase library books or subscribe to databases in languages other than English, as the selection is much more limited. Frequently only paperbacks are available instead of library-bound hardback books and, too often, publishers and library vendors run out of stock. Bilingual library collections require a larger budget for purchasing new books in both languages.

But the most painful challenge facing many teacher-librarians these days—bilingual or not—is the impact of high-stakes standardized testing on library programs and schedules. Computer-based testing requires many computers. Until school technology budgets catch up with the testing mandates (or the "stop high-stakes testing" movement wins the day) libraries are where the computers are, at least in underfunded, urban school districts like mine. Our library is also used for practice tests and to test groups of students with special needs.

This use of the library for testing is especially problematic in bilingual schools where children may take tests in two languages—the testing takes twice as long, while the library is closed to all other students and teachers. This happened the first spring my school shifted to computer-based testing—at the exact same time as a schoolwide research project. Classes had no access to library books or digital resources for an entire month, since every computer was used for testing.

With a set of new laptops and some creative scheduling, my school managed to get through testing a year later without closing the library. But many other school libraries in our district, especially at the elementary level, were not so fortunate. Teacher-librarian colleagues were asked to push books around to classrooms on a cart, or to spend most of their time proctoring exams in the library or computer lab. One colleague's library was closed for six weeks of testing. Although I understand the need for compromise in certain situations, I am deeply concerned about the message we're sending students regarding the importance of their library program. Our district mandates standardized testing during the same window of time in which the entire district, K–12, is engaged in a Common Core research theme. Libraries should not only be open during a focus on research, they should be central to it.

The Library as a Learning Commons

Despite the reputation of libraries in the past, today's model school libraries are not places where students must be silent. Instead, children are encouraged to speak up, work together, and share ideas and opinions while they develop their oral language abilities and critical thinking skills. Hosting the build-it-yourself whale skeleton in our library provided just such an opportunity for students to collaborate physically and verbally. Throughout the year, I strive to plan with classroom and specialist teachers as much as possible to co-teach lessons, provide curricular support, and share the responsibility of covering content standards.

Of course, like all librarians, I try to generate a love of reading for pleasure, too. The library, which I think of as the heart of the school, should be filled with exciting, diverse, recently published, award-winning literature that motivates students to learn to read, to read for pleasure and interest, and to develop reading skills in a new language.

A bilingual library reflects and validates students' home languages and cultures, and should be welcoming to all families. I have organized bilingual family library nights, poetry "coffeehouses" and other family-oriented events with the express purpose of inviting students' families into the library. In other school libraries I have visited, teacher-librarians are setting up "maker spaces" for creative projects, hosting book clubs for parents and children, facilitating bookmaking, and offering adult education classes. Opportunities for turning the library into a dynamic, inclusive learning commons are endless.

Bilingual schools need top-notch school libraries and credentialed teacher-librarians.

For many children, the school library provides their first experience of a lending library, and paves the way for them to become lifelong library users. The library stands as one of the few truly public spaces, a participatory commons that offers every person in the community the opportunity to grow and benefit. Our public library system in the United States is a physical expression of our First Amendment rights. And teacher-librarians serve as a solid bridge between schools and public libraries for students and families, especially those who are new to this country.

As Carl Sagan, the astronomer and author, eloquently said, "The health of our civilization, the depth of our awareness about the underpinnings of our culture, and our concern for the future can all be tested by how well we support our libraries." ☼

Rachel Cloues currently works as a public middle school teacher-librarian in San Francisco.

Note from the author: For more research on the relevance of school libraries visit the American Association of School Librarians website, ala.org/aasl/research.

*A Spanish translation of this article is available on the Rethinking Schools website at rethinkingschools.org/articles/el-corazon-de-la-escuela-la-importancia-de-las-bibliotecas-bilingues-en-las-escuelas.

References

Krashen, Stephen. 1995. "School Libraries, Public Libraries, and the NAEP Reading Scores." ala.org/aasl/sites/ala.org.aasl/files/content/aaslpubsandjournals/slr/edchoice/SLMQ_ SchoolLibraries_InfoPower.pdf.

Krashen, Stephen. 2000. "Bilingual Education, the Acquisition of English, and the Retention and Loss of Spanish." languagepolicy.net/archives/Krashen7.htm.

Sagan, Carl. 1980. *Cosmos: A Personal Voyage.* Random House.

Chapter 5

FAMILIES AND COMMUNITIES

RICARDO LEVINS MORALES

Introduction

razilian educator Paolo Freire, in his book *Teachers as Cultural Workers*, reminds us that it's not enough to simply get to know our students in the context of the classroom:

> Educators need to know what happens in the world of the children with whom they work. They need to know the universe of their dreams, the language with which they skillfully defend themselves from the aggressiveness of their world, what they know independently of the school, and how they know it.

Emergent bilingual students come to school with a wealth of knowledge and resources they have gained outside of school. Yet once we create a bilingual curriculum or label students as Spanish, English, or Hawaiian speakers, it is tempting to stop seeking to understand the nuances of students' lives, homes, and communities. In this chapter, educators offer a glimpse of how they work to connect school spaces with home and community spaces—and how they seek to know and integrate the worlds of students, families, and communities into their classrooms.

The articles that follow offer a mosaic of what this can look like in practice. For teachers working under the English-only laws in Arizona, it means creating after-school spaces where students and their families write together in Spanish. At a diverse dual-language program in San Francisco, it entails finding ways to involve all parents equitably across differences of language, race, and class. At Bruce-Monroe school in Washington, D.C., it takes the form of Latina/o and Black parents coming together to advocate for multicultural solidarity, better building conditions, and a dual-language program.

Effective involvement means wholeheartedly inviting families and communities into our classrooms and schools. But it goes beyond that. We must step out of our comfort zones as educators and explore the worlds of our students and our families. We must make their knowledge and experiences a fundamental part of our curriculum. And we must think about how our language goals for students transcend the classroom. How do students use their languages out in their worlds? How can school language nurture home language, and home language inform school language?

As he discusses the ways bilingual education is critical to Hawaiian language revitalization, Kekoa Harman points out that an integral goal of bilingual programs is to develop languages that students will use beyond the classroom:

> If we can't take the language back into the home, the language cannot live. That's at the core of this type of schooling. The hope is that our children are going to use the language within their own households one day. ☀

Cuentos del corazón / Stories from the Heart

An after-school writing project for bilingual students and their families

BY TRACEY FLORES AND JESSICA SINGER EARLY

FAVIANNA RODRIGUEZ

Parents and their children sat side by side in a tight circle with journals in hand. Gabriela's voice filled the room. She read from her narrative, describing advice she had received from her friend, Jeanni, who she met on her arrival to the United States from Mexico: *"Jeanni me ayudó a fortalecer mi interior a creer que el futuro de mis hijas se construye día a día, trabajando en equipo con [mi esposo] Julián y buscando los recursos disponibles para lograrlo."* (Jeanni helped me strengthen my inner self to believe that my daughters' future is forged day by day as I work as a team with [my husband] Julian and seek the resources to achieve it.) The opportunity to write and share this memory of support and friendship brought Gabriela, and many of the other writers sitting around her, to tears.

Gabriela was one of the parents in a bilingual after-school family writing project in Tracey's 2nd-grade classroom in central Phoenix. More than 80 percent of the student population at the K–8 school identified as Latina/o or Hispanic and almost 90 percent qualified for free/reduced lunch. Students had been sorted into an English Language Development (ELD) classroom because tests labeled them as not yet "proficient" in English. Since Arizona law mandates English-only as the language of instruction, the many students who speak Spanish or another language at home have little or no access to instruction in their native languages.

Signed into law in 2006, Arizona's HB 2064 called for a task force to create a "research-based" and prescriptive classroom model of instruction for language learners that would lead to English proficiency within one year. Under the direction of this task force, the state mandates language ability grouping and four hours a day of Structured English Immersion. This model perpetuates the segregation of English language learners (ELLs) based on language proficiency.

Opposed to this approach to emergent bilingual students and concerned about its impact on Tracey's 2nd graders, we decided to design and implement an after-school writing project.

We wanted Tracey's students to feel honored for their language abilities and to use their native languages in the writing and reading process. Tracey envisioned extending her classroom space to include parents, siblings, and cousins writing alongside one another as a community of writers who not only wrote and shared stories, but also supported one another in different facets of their lives. We hoped to build community, invite families' home languages into the classroom, value language learning and risk taking, and challenge the privilege of English in the school setting.

Our workshop sessions became one way to counter anti-immigration politics, press, and sentiment.

Tracey was the lead teacher for the project and the main contact for students and parents. Jessica co-taught the workshops with Tracey, co-developed the curriculum, purchased supplies and snacks, and designed and implemented a research study to examine and share this work.

It wasn't one of our original goals, but the project also became a source of support for families dealing with the impact of anti-immigration legislation in our state. During the semester of the family writing project, Gov. Jan Brewer's controversial Arizona SB 1070 passed, requiring police to question a person's citizenship if they had reason to doubt an individual was in the country legally. This resulted in immigration sweeps by federal and county law enforcement and regular police surveillance of predominantly Latina/o communities, including the neighborhoods surrounding the school. (The U.S. Supreme Court has since struck down some, but not all, of SB 1070.) Our workshop sessions became one way to counter anti-immigration politics, press, and sentiment.

The hostile political climate surfaced in parents' writing and conversations because everyone had to cope with it in their daily lives. For example, during the first weeks of the project, the undocumented father of one of the students was arrested. His wife frantically dropped off their daughter at the family writing project and explained to the group her need to leave early to go gather money to pay for his release.

It was a scary moment for all the families in the project and for us, too. Later in the semester, another mom told us that when her son was feeling upset, she encouraged him to sit down with her and write in order to make sense of his emotions. Through sharing stories and writing experiences, the family writing project became a sanctuary and source of support for families dealing with the immediate impact of the law.

¡Bienvenidos!

At the beginning of spring semester, Tracey recruited families for the family writing project during parent-teacher conferences. We also sent bilingual invitations home with the students in Tracey's class. We tried to select a start time that would work well for the students and their families. Many children walked to and from school with parents, grandparents, or caregivers. Once families were on campus to pick up their children, they often stayed for meetings and sports events. So the 3:30 start time worked well for us.

Within a few weeks, nine of Tracey's students, 10 of their parents, and assorted siblings were gathering each Tuesday afternoon from 3:30–5:00 p.m. to write, draw, revise, share, and discuss writing. Each session started with a mini-lesson in which we analyzed a particular aspect of a "text"—artwork, poetry, our own writing samples, bilingual picture books—and a particular writing strategy. After we modeled the writing strategy, the group practiced using the new skill together. This was followed by family and/or individual write time. Toward the end of the session, authors shared their writing. We generally finished with a written reflection.

The first weeks were designed to build community and confidence. As participants grew more comfortable with the writing strategies, we gave them opportunities to take a piece of writing from the beginning of the process through revision to publication.

With the support of the school secretary and Tracey's family, we translated all written communications and workshop materials into Spanish and English. Mini-lessons, instruction, and discussion were facilitated in both languages—often with the help of parents and students. Tracey is conversationally fluent in Spanish and Jessica speaks some Spanish, but less comfortably. As families and students watched us take risks in Spanish, they found ways to jump in to help translate, answer questions, or offer encouragement. We all collaborated to communicate as writers, readers, and learners in Spanish and English.

For the first time, many students wrote in their home language. Having spent their first years of schooling sorted into ELD classrooms, they had grown accustomed to reading and writing in "English only." As we spent time writing, sharing, and speaking in English and Spanish in the after-school setting, many students became more comfortable drawing on their home language.

Jessica recorded this example in her teaching journal after Week 2:

> Marco asked me how he should share his writing with his mom. "What if my mom is writing in Spanish and I am writing in English? I don't know Spanish."

Jessica encouraged Marco to share his writing in any language he preferred. So Marco read his work to his mom in English and then talked to her about the piece in English and Spanish. By the third week, he had started writing in Spanish. He shared his first attempt (in inventive spelling):

> *Cuando hue me cumple años you pose me cara en el pastel y tambien me ermano Pero me ermana no porke no hue so cumple años. So yo me la pase vien agosto con me familia y tube muchos regalos recuerdo qea me ermana yorava mucho.* (When it was my birthday I put my face in the cake and so did my brother, but my sister did not because it was not her birthday. So I had a good time with my family and had many presents. I remember that my sister cried a lot.)

Jessica asked him why he decided to try writing in Spanish and he said, "Because my mom doesn't know English and I want to learn to write and speak in Spanish better." Rather than having a teacher or a parent tell him which language to use, the family writing project gave him the space and support to negotiate his own language learning.

Drawing a Map of Stories

For the first session, we wanted to make it easy to brainstorm and shape ideas prior to writing. So we set out fresh boxes of crayons, markers, and blank paper as children and their families filtered into the classroom. In the front of the room, we placed an easel with a flip chart. We urged everyone to take a snack and then sit together at tables and desks around the room.

"Mis manos son famosas porque con ellas escribo." **(My hands are famous because I use them to write.) —Maria, a parent/writer**

Grabbing a marker, Tracey began to sketch a house on the flip chart. As she drew, she explained: "Sometimes when I want to write a story, I choose a particular place and begin drawing a map to help me remember the details of the stories that happened there. I'm going to draw a map of the neighborhood where I grew up until I was 8 years old. I'm thinking about and sketching special places from my neighborhood and points of interest. I want to be sure to add vivid details. I am going to think about the people from my neighborhood, too." Tracey continued sketching and talking aloud about the buildings, houses, parks, streets, and people who were part of her memories about her first neighborhood. She said she would use her map to help choose a story to write.

Then Tracey invited parents and students to practice the prewriting strategy. "Think about where you live and the people and places in your neighborhood. It could be where you live now, or where you lived before, or a neighborhood where you spend a lot of time, like your Nana and Tata's neighborhood. Sketch the special places and special points of interest. Let the drawing tell the story of a special memory that took place in the neighborhood."

The 2nd graders and their families eagerly opened the boxes of crayons and began sketching their own neighborhood maps. Isabel, Alicia's mom, drew the pueblo in México where she was raised and attended elementary school, and the nearby rancho that held many of her childhood memories. She titled her map "*Dónde en mi pueblo era un rancho solo.*" (In my town where there was only one farm.) Alicia drew a map of her neighborhood. She included a tree, her house, a tall yucca plant, her older sister, and a big green shrub. She wrote: "This is when I lived in my house with my family. I was 4 years old. My big sister was 6. And my little sister was 7 months. And I went to school over there, too."

> **We started to notice exciting links between the writing in the family writing project and the writing happening in Tracey's classroom.**

Drawing is a low-risk and enjoyable point of entry for many writers. In our project, it helped build safety and trust by placing the students' and parents' experiences, memories, and ideas at the center of the curriculum, making them the experts. The mapping activity modeled one way writers work through story ideas visually before drafting, and provided scaffolding for language learners at all levels.

In a reflection, 2nd grader Yajaira wrote: "When I draw first it helps me to explain about my drawing." Her classmate Cristina wrote: "I learned how to describe your writing and the special memories in your head or brain."

In later workshops, Isabel used this strategy to encourage Alicia and her sisters to begin a piece or to continue writing when they were stuck. She referred back to her daughters' maps and asked questions about details that weren't in their written stories. As she explained in a reflection, it was her own writing process that enabled her to help her children: "*Aprendí a agregar más detalles viendo el dibujo. . . . Ahora que lo vi y estaba escribiendo, recordé más cosas.*" (I learned to add more details by looking at the drawing. Now that I saw the drawing and was writing, I remembered more details.)

Honoring Our Daily Lives

The next Tuesday, families walked in to find chairs and tables arranged in a semicircle facing the easel and whiteboard. On each desk was a copy of Naomi Shihab Nye's poem "Famous," the model text for our second workshop (see p. 218). This poem was written in English; we translated it into Spanish so families could access the text in both languages. Families settled into their seats with writing notebooks, pencils, and snacks in hand.

Jessica began the workshop by asking the group, "What does it mean to you to be famous?"

A mother responded, "*Que todo el mundo sabe tu nombre.*" (That everyone knows your name.)

A student, Brisa, said, "Being famous means you're on TV and sing in concerts."

"It means you do good things," another student suggested.

"Have you ever thought about how you might be famous or how items in our everyday lives are famous to one another?" Jessica asked. "The poem on your desk is one way a writer thought about her world. Through her words, she illustrates the value of everyday objects, actions, and people have to one another. As we read the poem in English and then in Spanish, listen carefully. Underline 'golden lines'—words and phrases that speak to you, parts you like, parts you want to think about more, lines that stand out for any reason."

After Karina finished reading the poem in Spanish, Jessica said, "Now turn and talk to your family about what you underlined and why."

After families shared their golden lines, we discussed the poem's message and how it provides an alternative definition of what it means to be famous. Instead of defining fame as glamour, beauty, or notoriety, Nye suggests that fame can be the way we touch the lives of others.

As we shared golden lines and discussed the poem, Tracey wrote several of the families' responses to the poem on an anchor chart (Harvey and Goudvis). The anchor chart had two columns: golden lines in one column and the poetic strategy in the other. For example, one student, Janet, pointed out that she liked the place in the poem where Nye switches from describing how objects are famous to each other and begins to share how she wants to be famous. Tracey wrote the line "I want to be famous to shuffling men" on one side of the anchor chart to represent where the poet makes this change. Then, in the strategy column, Tracey wrote "shift from third person to first person" and "shift in poetic voice."

All of us realized (yet again) the power of putting our stories to paper.

Throughout the workshop, we used model texts like Nye's poem as examples of different writing genres, styles, and strategies, and also as a way for families to practice reading like writers. The anchor chart demystified Nye's craft so students and their parents could emulate her moves or create their own.

Next, we invited families to write about the ways they felt famous or hoped to be famous in the future.

Daniel, a father, wrote: "I want to be famous like my grandfather because he was a person who fought for Hispanic people's rights with Cesar Chavez."

Elizabeth, one of Tracey's 2nd graders, wrote: "I want to be famous like my parents, to show love and kindness and hard work for all people who need help."

Maria, one of the mothers, wrote: "*Mis manos son famosas porque con ellas escribo.*" (My hands are famous because I use them to write.) Second-grader Cindy wrote:

> The clouds are famous to the rain.
> The dark is famous to kids at night.
> The birds are famous to flying.
> The floors are famous to boots.

The desert is famous to hot.
The pens are famous to writers.
I want to be famous
like my mom and dad
because they are always
nice to me.

After we shared our poems, Jessica invited each family member to write a quick reflection about what they learned during the session. One student, Estefania, wrote that she enjoyed writing this piece because "I learned what is famous to my heart." One of the fathers wrote: "I learned more about writing poetry today. I also began to experience something new with my child today."

As the weeks went by, the group began to feel more comfortable. We started to notice exciting links between the writing in the family writing project and the writing happening in Tracey's classroom. For example, Marco wrote Tracey a letter during regular class time extending his ideas about famous things and people, including a compliment about the work that his mom was doing as an illustrator and writer.

> **We created an intentional bilingual learning space in a school that was forbidden to be bilingual.**

On the evening of our culminating author celebration, family members, neighbors, friends, spouses, siblings, and students gathered around the room to enjoy writing, food, and companionship. The counter by the door was filled with traditional dishes, salads, fast-food delights, and a special cake. One by one, the writers took their places in the author's chair and proudly shared their final narratives about positive change makers and everyday heroes in the language of their choice.

The Power of Story

For 12 weeks, families gathered to share writing. Tracey's students' younger siblings shared inventive drawings and strings of letters, and whispered stories into their big brothers' and sisters' ears. Parents shared stories with their children of special moments, memorable people, and family traditions. Students wrote stories about holidays and unforgettable childhood events. All of us realized (yet again) the power of putting our stories to paper.

Giving families time to write together was the heart of this project. In a final reflection, Karina wrote: "I learned that good moments with your family will always stay with you to remember when you want. You can draw them or write them."

Martha, another mother, wrote about the importance of writing with her daughter. "*Aprendí a recordar los tiempos en que [era] niña y los momentos que pasé con mi familia y a compartir parte de mi tiempo con mi hija.*" (I learned to remember the times from when I was a child and the moments that I spent with family, and to share some of my time with my daughter.)

Together with parents and students, we created a safe space and sense of community to empower families to share their stories and cultivate their voices. We created an intentional bilingual learning space in a school that was forbidden to be bilingual. When English-only instruction is mandated, it is possible to create biliterate learning spaces so parents can work alongside their children and in partnership with teachers to help our students succeed as writers. ☼

Tracey Flores is a former elementary and middle school teacher. She is currently a PhD candidate in English Education at Arizona State University. Jessica Singer Early is an associate professor of English and the director of English Education and the Central Arizona Writing Project at Arizona State University. All names have been changed.

Note from the authors: Our conception for the after-school family writing project built on work done by other sites of the National Writing Project, especially the Sabal Palms Writing Project in Texas and JoBeth Allen's Red Clay Writing Project at the University of Georgia. The neighborhood map workshop was originally developed by Lorraine Nelson at the South Coast Writing Project at the University of California. The lesson using Naomi Shihab Nye's poem "Famous" originated with William Stafford and was passed down to Jessica through his son, Kim Stafford, at the Northwest Writing Institute and the Oregon Writing Project at Lewis & Clark College.

*A Spanish translation of this article is available at on the Rethinking Schools website at rethinkingschools.org/articles/cuentos-del-corazon.

References

Allen, JoBeth. 2010. *Literacy in the Welcoming Classroom: Creating Family-School Partnerships that Support Student Learning.* Teachers College Press.

Early, Jessica Singer. 2010. "'Mi hija, you should be a writer': The Role of Parental Support and Learning to Write." *Bilingual Research Journal* 33.3:277–91.

Frank, Carolyn. 2003. "Mapping Our Stories: Teachers' Reflections on Themselves as Writers." *Language Arts* 80.3:185–95.

Harvey, Stephanie, and Anne Goudvis. 2007. *Strategies that Work: Teaching Comprehension for Understanding and Engagement.* Stenhouse.

Stafford, Kim. 2012. *The Muses Among Us: Eloquent Listening and Other Pleasures of the Writer's Craft.* University of Georgia Press.

Family Writing Project Resources

Alarcón, Francisco X. 2005. *Poems to Dream Together/Poemas para soñar juntos.* Lee & Low Books.

Carlson, Lori Marie, ed. 2013. *Cool Salsa: Bilingual Poems on Growing Up Latino in the United States.* Square Fish.

Cisneros, Sandra. 1994. *Hairs/Pelitos: A Story in English and Spanish from The House on Mango Street.* Dragonfly Books.

Cisneros, Sandra. 1994. *La casa en Mango Street.* Vintage Books.

Cisneros, Sandra. 1991. *The House on Mango Street.* Vintage Books.

Early, Jessica Singer. 2006. *Stirring Up Justice: Writing and Reading to Change the World.* Heinemann.

Espada, Martín, ed. 1994. *Poetry Like Bread: Poets of the Political Imagination from Curbstone Press.* Curbstone Press.

Fanelli, Sara. 1995. *My Map Book.* HarperCollins.

Garza, Carmen Lomas. 2005. *Family Pictures/Cuadros de familia.* Children's Book Press.

Garza, Carmen Lomas. 1996. *In My Family/En mi familia*. Children's Book Press.

Giovanni, Nikki. 1994. *Knoxville, Tennessee*. Scholastic.

González, Lucía. 2008. *The Storyteller's Candle/La velita de los cuentos*. Children's Book Press.

Herrera, Juan Felipe. 1998. *Laughing Out Loud, I Fly: Poems in English and Spanish*. HarperCollins.

Herrera, Juan Felipe. 2006. *The Upside Down Boy/El niño de cabeza*. Children's Book Press.

Lyon, George Ella. 1999. *Where I'm From: Where Poems Come From*. Absey & Co.

Medina, Jane. 2004. *The Dream on Blanca's Wall: Poems in English and Spanish/El sueño pegado en la pared de Blanca: Poemas en inglés y español*. Wordsong/Boyds Mills Press.

Meyer, Carolyn. 1994. *Rio Grande Stories*. Harcourt.

Nye, Naomi Shihab. 1995. *Words Under the Words*. Eighth Mountain Press.

Soto, Gary. 2005. *Neighborhood Odes*. Harcourt.

Winter, Jeannette. 2005. *The Librarian of Basra: A True Story from Iraq*. Harcourt.

Famous

Naomi Shihab Nye

The river is famous to the fish.

The loud voice is famous to silence,
which knew it would inherit the earth
before anybody said so.

The cat sleeping on the fence is famous to the birds
watching him from the birdhouse.

The tear is famous, briefly, to the cheek.

The idea you carry close to your bosom
is famous to your bosom.

The boot is famous to the earth,
more famous than the dress shoe,
which is famous only to floors.

The bent photograph is famous to the one who carries it
and not at all famous to the one who is pictured.

I want to be famous to shuffling men
who smile while crossing streets,
sticky children in grocery lines,
famous as the one who smiled back.

I want to be famous in the way a pulley is famous,
or a buttonhole, not because it did anything spectacular,
but because it never forgot what it could do.

Famoso
Naomi Shihab Nye

El río es famoso para el pez.

La voz fuerte es famosa para el silencio
que sabía que heredaría el planeta
antes de que alguien se lo dijera.

El gato durmiendo en el cerco es famoso para los pájaros
mirándolo desde el pajarero.

La lágrima es famosa, brevemente, para la mejilla.

La idea que llevas cerca de tu pecho
es famosa para tu pecho.

La bota es famosa para la tierra,
más famosa que el zapato de vestir,
que solo es famoso para los pisos.

La fotografía doblada es famosa para quien la carga
y nada famosa para quien está retratado.

Yo quiero ser famosa para los hombres que arrastran los pies
sonriendo mientras cruzan las calles, niños pegajosos en las filas de las tiendas,
famosa como el que me regresó la sonrisa.

Yo quiero ser famosa en la forma en que una polea es famosa,
o el agujero de un botón, no porque hizo algo espectacular,
sino porque nunca olvidó lo que podía hacer.

"Famous" by Naomi Shihab Nye. Illustrated by Lisa Desimini. Wings Press. 2015. Used by permission of the author. Translated by Julie Flores Lizarraga.

Strawberries in Watsonville

Putting family and student knowledge at the center of the curriculum

BY PEGGY MORRISON

DAVID BACON

"¡M*aestra, Maestra!*" Lorena, a feisty and energetic 6-year-old, rushed to catch up with me. She was brandishing *Strawberries in Watsonville*, the book she was writing in class. "Teacher! I taught my cousin and her friends about the cycle of the strawberry!"

"Lorena, that's great!" I answered. "Tell me, what did you talk about?"

"Spring and autumn," Lorena replied, smiling. "Luz said that the plant life cycle starts when you plant seeds in the spring, but the strawberries are different. I showed her the part about autumn." I knelt down on one knee to be at Lorena's eye level, and she opened her book to show me the page as she explained, "For the strawberries we don't plant the seeds in the spring. We plant baby plants in November so the roots can grow strong with the winter rain, and then the strawberry fruits will grow in spring."

Lorena was writing her book about strawberries during a multiday lesson that was still in progress. When our team of six 1st-grade teachers collaboratively planned this lesson on the life cycle of the strawberry, our goal was for the students to form a conceptual understanding of what is meant by a cycle, that a cycle is a repeating sequence where the end comes back to the beginning in a circular or spiral form. We also wanted them to see the connection between the life cycle of the strawberry and the annual cycle of the seasons. In our school's early literacy program, language and literacy were taught in the context of meaningful content, so along with the content goals, our lesson sequence was designed to support next steps in literacy development for each child. Just as important, we wanted students to see themselves and their families as producers and owners of knowledge that is valuable in school and in the larger world. Our 1st-grade teaching team did not want to replicate the inequities of the society at large, where the knowledge and potential of working-class Mexican immigrant communities was little respected or validated. We tried to challenge the monopoly of knowledge by engaging students and families as co-constructors of the curriculum.

> **"I can ask my cousin tonight; he works in the strawberries."**
> **—Javier, a student**

Lorena saw herself as a person with knowledge. During recess, she had taken the initiative to share her learning with her cousin and friends. Lorena's sense of agency was nurtured by our curriculum approach. We designed the School-Home Interactive Curriculum Development process over several school years. We intentionally included perspectives and knowledge of our students' families and community. We constructed the curriculum by cycling the content between school and home. There were five basic steps in the process:

1. Students gather information at home and in the community.
2. Home knowledge is shared, organized, and synthesized at school.
3. Students create a literacy product. Home knowledge is incorporated into academic work.
4. Students take home their academic work to share and families respond.
5. Family responses become part of and extend classroom learning.

The team co-planned and prepared the curriculum that each of us implemented in our individual classrooms. I taught the lesson about the life cycle of the strawberry during the third and fourth weeks of the six-week thematic, interdisciplinary unit "From the Field to the Table." I taught the lesson during the Spanish part of the dual-language immersion school day, so the instruction, all the materials used, and the student work were in Spanish.

Students Gather Information at Home and in the Community

The students clustered on the carpet as I reviewed the weekly newsletter and homework assignments they would take home in their Monday folders. I explained that this week, students would interview neighbors or family members to collect information about the life of the strawberry during each season of the year.

Displaying the organizer provided in the folder, I explained, "This week, we are going to be learning more about the seasons of the year, and about strawberries in each season."

After asking students to name the four seasons with a partner, I continued: "I'd like you to talk to your parents and other people you know to research and find information about strawberries in each season of the year. Ask 'What happens in the strawberry fields in autumn?' and write the information on these lines and draw it in this box. Ask about each season. Here are the box and the lines for winter, spring, and summer. Here you will write the names of the people to whom you've asked questions."

Andrés knew that his uncles come every year to work. The work cycle impacted his family.

The Monday homework folder, containing the week's homework assignments, the newsletter for parents, and a comment log for parents and teacher to stay in touch, was a well-established routine in our classroom. I knew that most of the students were excited to do the homework, and that they would have it ready on Friday morning. There were small-print bilingual instructions for adults on the edge of the organizer. There was also a note in the bilingual parent newsletter explaining the goals of the lesson:

> This week we'll continue our studies of the agricultural industry: the process of planting, cultivating, harvesting, packing, transporting, and preparing our food. We will study strawberry production. Please help your child with the homework about strawberries by talking about what happens to strawberry plants and strawberry fields at different times of the year. Our goal is for the students to understand that the plants have a life cycle related to the seasons.

On Friday morning, I gathered all the completed homework papers in preparation for our morning lesson the following Monday.

Home Knowledge Is Shared, Organized, and Synthesized at School

During circle time the next Monday, I passed the completed homework papers back to each student. I showed the students four chart papers I had prepared, each labeled with one of the seasons of the year. As we passed the talking stick around the circle, some students read from their homework papers; others participated orally even if they had not brought the written homework.

Esteban had collected information from his mother, his father, and his aunt. He read aloud from his homework paper. "Cultivation begins in the spring. The plants produce a lot in the summer and finish producing in the fall."

I went to the "Spring" chart and wrote Esteban's sentence: "Cultivation begins in the spring." Then Esteban wrote on the "Summer" chart: "The strawberry plants produce a lot in the summer."

Esteban passed the talking stick to Lupe and she read aloud from her homework. "I asked about the harvest and they answered that the harvest is when the fruit is mature, and the best fruit is selected. Also, we fertilize the soil to improve the quality of the fruit." Lupe shared that her mother had given her this information as I wrote it on the "Summer" chart.

There was some discussion about when the soil was fertilized, and we agreed to research further before adding this information to the chart. Javier promised, "I can ask my cousin tonight; he works in the strawberries." As the students continued to share the information they had collected, I scribed their words and also shared the pen with students to record the information on the charts. We kept the four charts displayed in the classroom throughout the week and added information to them as we learned more.

Planning the lesson, I had visualized that it would focus on the plant life cycle and the weather in each season, but as I listened to the students share their research from home, I realized that for many of the children and their families, the social and economic cycles of their lives were linked to the strawberries and the seasons. Andrés shared: "In spring, my uncles come from Mexico to live with us." He explained that his father's brothers came to work in the strawberry fields, and they would live at his house until work ran out in the fall and they returned to Mexico. Another student shared that her family moved into multifamily shared housing during the winter when there is less work.

The voices of my students and their families expanded my thinking about our curriculum. We've heard a hundred times that learning must be relevant to our students' lives and connected to "prior knowledge." In this context, Andrés knew that his uncles come every year to work. The work cycle impacted his family. His personal connections helped him to understand the concept of a cycle. This knowledge was more than a memorized definition; it was his own.

Home Knowledge Is Incorporated into Academic Work

Each day after morning circle, the students rotated through language and literacy centers in small groups or with partners. This was organized so that each group would have a turn with me in the teacher center, where I would do the model and guided practice components of a lesson. The group would continue their work independently in the next rotation.

I started the small-group session by reviewing the season charts the class had created. Then I introduced the writing activity they would do during the week. Each student would make his or her own book about the strawberry cycle. I gave each student a six-page template with a title page, a page for each season, and a concluding page. Each page had a space for a picture and lines for words. I explained, "In your book, you have one page for each season. You'll write and illustrate that page with information about strawberries in that season. You can read our charts to get ideas. Now, think about where you want to start. What page will you do first?"

Sara said: "I'm going to do summer. I'm going to write: 'The workers harvest the fruit.'"

"Yes, lots of workers in our community harvest strawberries in the summer," I said, as Sara began to write. "José, what page will you do first?"

"Autumn," he answered. "In autumn, the earth is cold and dark."

"I see that you're drawing a barren field," I replied. He read what he had already written: "In autumn." I prompted, "In autumn, the earth is" and he began to write: "the earth."

Then, I asked Sara to read me the sentence she had written: "The workers harvest the fruit." Reading aloud, she noticed and corrected a word omission. Then she told me, "Teacher, it's hard work. My mom has back pain when she's working in the harvest. She has to crouch down all day." The other children in the group joined in the conversation. One said, "My uncle has back problems, too." We added this information about the workers to the "Summer" chart. At the end of the small-group time, each student read and showed his or her writing to the group. They took their books to continue writing during their next rotation.

Many of the children had firsthand knowledge about working conditions and socioeconomic status of agricultural workers.

Like Sara, many of the children in the classroom had firsthand experience and knowledge about working conditions and socioeconomic status of agricultural workers. During the six-week unit, we discussed these issues both at home and at school. The children interviewed family and community members who had worked in agriculture, explicitly asking about work conditions and the workers' knowledge and experience with the UFW or other labor movements. Children asked their parents about justice and injustice, and we grappled with understanding these deep ideas in class and small-group discussions.

Building Knowledge Throughout the Week

During Tuesday morning circle I shared Alma Flor Ada's *Mi mamá siembra fresas* (*My Mother Plants Strawberries*) as an interactive read-aloud. We added a couple of pieces of information from the book to our charts. On the "Summer" chart we added: "Work in the strawberries is hard. The fields are hot and dusty." On the "Autumn" chart we added: "The roots of the baby plants are delicate and they have to be planted carefully."

When the class went to the school library on Wednesday, students navigated informational texts to find facts that interested them. We added more information to our season charts. Each day, the students continued to work on their individual books. The classroom hummed with the energy of collective inquiry.

During morning circle on Thursday, the students and I arranged our four charts into a cycle pattern. Later, the children made their own diagrams of the life cycle of the strawberry. We compared their diagrams to a textbook diagram of the life cycle of a sunflower. One student commented, "The cycle starts over again and again; it's a circle."

Carolina, José's mom, joined us for a couple of days to support students working at literacy centers. A second-generation immigrant and daughter of farmworkers, Carolina communicated her deep respect for the workers through thoughtful conversation. She asked each group of students: "Why is this work important?" Peter, a native English-speaking student whose mom was a RN, wrote: "Melinda's father's work is important. He works so that all of us can eat." Cristina wrote: "The farmworkers are very important, because if they were not here, I and the world and the animals would not have food." Carolina's collaboration enriched the students' learning with a community perspective and values that I alone could not represent.

> **Carolina's collaboration enriched the students' learning with a community perspective and values that I alone could not represent.**

By the end of the week, each student had written and illustrated a unique book based on the collectively generated information. Some students focused on the plant life cycle; others focused on the seasonal changes for the workers. The text of Esteban's six-page book described the seasonal cycle of work and the delight of eating strawberries in summer:

Las fresas de Watsonville
por Esteban

En el otoño, algunas personas no trabajan. Algunas personas
  plantan las nuevas plantas de fresa.
El el invierno, se congelan las plantas, y nadie trabaja en la fresa.
En la primavera, las plantas comienzan a florear.
En el verano, se cortan las fresas. Todos trabajan.
A mí me gusta comer pastel de fresas.

The Strawberries of Watsonville
by Esteban

In the autumn, some people don't work. Some people plant new
  strawberry plants.
In the winter, the plants freeze, and nobody works in the
  strawberries.
In the spring, the plants begin to flower.

In the summer, the strawberries are picked. Everyone works.
I love to eat cake with strawberries.

Susana's text focused on descriptive details:

El ciclo de la fresa
por Susana

*En el otoño, plantamos las fresas. Se les crecerán raíces fuertes
    durante los meses del invierno.*
*En el invierno, hay frío. Las plantas de fresa son pequeñas y no dan
    fruta durante el invierno.*
*En la primavera, las plantas de fresa florecen y despues las frutas
    crecen rojas y grandes. El clima es cálido.*
*Durante el verano caluroso, todo el mundo trabaja en la fresa. ¡Hay
    miles de fresas en los campos y los jardines!*
¡Me encantan los licuados de fresa! ¡Las fresas son deliciosas!

The Strawberry Cycle
by Susana

In the autumn, we plant the strawberries. They will grow strong
    roots during the winter months.
In the winter, the weather is cold. The strawberry plants are small
    and there is no fruit during the winter.
In the spring, the strawberries flower and then the fruit grows big
    and red. The weather is warm.
In the hot summer, everyone works in the strawberries. There are
    thousands of strawberries in the farms and gardens!
I love strawberry smoothies! Strawberries are delicious!

During the writing process, I structured opportunities for students to share their work in progress with different audiences in small groups, with partners and with the whole class. Some, like Lorena, took their books out to recess to read them to more friends.

Students Take Home Their Academic Work to Share and Families Respond

At the end of the week, the students took their books home with a new homework assignment: Read the books to at least three people in your home or neighborhood and have a conversation with them about your book. We wanted the families to see how the information they shared had become part of the children's academic work and literacy development at school.

When the students came back with the completed homework, we shared again in morning circle. David told us that he shared his work with two neighbors, LaLa and Miguel, and with his parents. David was clear that, if he wanted to learn more about strawberries, his grandfather and his Uncle Pedro would be his primary sources of information. Anita said she would do further research with "people who work in the strawberries."

Family Responses Become Part of and Extend Classroom Learning

After reading her daughter's book, Janet's mom, Dolores, stopped by the classroom one afternoon on her way home from work in the fields and offered, "*Maestra*, if you like I can bring seedlings for the school garden."

A few days later, Dolores came with seedlings and spent the afternoon with the class. Dressed for work, she explained that the wide-brimmed hat protected her from the sun and that the long sleeves, scarf, and gloves protected her arms, face, and hands from dust and from direct contact with agricultural chemicals. In the classroom, she showed

> "Am I teaching for empowerment and transformation or for confinement and containment?"
> —Enid Lee

and explained the parts of the plant to the children while I drew and labeled a picture of a seedling, a reference chart for the classroom. Dolores answered the students' questions and showed how the strawberry is propagated.

Then the class went out to the school garden and Dolores patiently guided each child in planting a strawberry plant. As each child took a turn, some of the other children observed. Meanwhile, other children clustered with me to talk about the parts of the plant, how the plants reproduce, how they plan to care for the plants, and what growth they predicted they might see. As we planted strawberry plants in the garden, I hoped that, for these children, school and home no longer felt like completely separate worlds.

Enid Lee (2000) suggests that teachers ask themselves this each day as they walk into the classroom: "Am I teaching for empowerment and transformation or for confinement and containment?" This was one of the questions at the center our 1st-grade team's collaborative planning. Working with us as our curriculum coach, Enid guided us to critically examine our own perspectives and sources of knowledge. We recognized that our society and our school system are infected with the mistaken idea that knowledge only belongs to privileged ethnic, economic, social, and linguistic groups and that this knowledge should be "transmitted" to the "others." What might a more democratic society and schooling look like? Lorena teaching her cousin about agricultural cycles, Andrés noticing the economic forces that made his uncles migrate, or Dolores volunteering to share her knowledge about planting strawberries with her daughter's classmates give us a glimpse of what is missing from the textbooks. ☼

Peggy Morrison is a bilingual and multicultural education consultant and writer based in San Francisco. She taught 19 years in K–12 classrooms in Watsonville, California, and 15 years in professional development and university teacher education. Instruction described took place in Spanish during the Spanish portion of the dual-language-immersion school day. Student names have been changed.

Note from the author: The curriculum described in this article was developed by Alianza School 1st-grade teachers and coaches—Liliana Barrios, Patricia Casillas, Lorie Contreras, Bryce Fifield, Elsi Hernandez, Enid Lee, Peggy Morrison, Diana Muñoz, Graciela Olivar, Maria Rocha, Margaret Rosa, Judy Stobbe, and Jenna White.

Resources

Ada, Alma Flor. 1995. *Mi mamá siembra fresas.* Macmillan/McGraw-Hill.

Lee, Enid. 2000. *A Million Moments for Equity: A Professional Development Manual for Teachers and Administrators in Schools with Immigrant Students.* Center for Language Minority Education and Research.

González, Katia and Rhoda Frumkin. 2016. *Handbook of Research on Effective Communication in Culturally Diverse Classrooms.* IGI Global.

"When Are You Coming to Visit?"

Home visits and seeing our students

BY ELIZABETH BARBIAN

BEC YOUNG

"*Está diciendo gracias por venir*" (She's saying thank you for coming), Juan interpreted from the Trique language to Spanish as he stood beside his mom on the concrete kitchen floor at the migrant work camp. It wasn't the easiest address to find—before I followed the school bus down the dirt road, I hadn't even known Camp Sealy existed.

"When are you going to come visit?" Juan kept asking. I'd tried to stop by to meet the family once before. I couldn't call to schedule a visit; the family had no phone. The notes I sent home were in Spanish; Juan's parents mostly spoke Trique, an Indigenous language of the Oaxaca region of Mexico. The family hadn't come to conferences. Juan wanted to attend 4th-grade swimming lessons with the class the following week, and I still needed a signed permission slip. I wanted to update the family on Juan's progress, let them know how much he was learning, how hard he was working. And so I parked my car, made my way between the concrete buildings of dorm rooms with bunk beds, and asked those I passed where I might find Juan's family.

The visit was short and, to me, appeared to be effortlessly interpreted from Spanish to Trique and back to Spanish by Juan as we stood beside the pot of boiling milk on the stove in the communal kitchen. In those 10 to 15 minutes, my perspective on Juan's life expanded from simple to complex.

Social justice curriculum is grounded in students' lives. Yet what are our students' lives? How do we know them? How can we push beyond our own unspoken norms and assumptions—for me, white and middle-class—to see and listen and learn and create space to understand the lives of students?

My visit to Juan's home in the migrant work camp was one facet of an effort to better understand his life. In the classroom, students shared their lives in many ways: writing journals, narratives, and poetry; making personal connections to literature and class content; interviewing and surveying family members; choosing research projects that they were passionate about. Yet home visits expanded my perspective in new ways. Home visits invited me to ask and wonder instead of label and assume. I didn't invent home visits, but they did transform my perspectives and my teaching.

> Home visits invited me to ask and wonder instead of label and assume.

First, I Hesitated

The process that led me to home visits was a gradual one. I sensed that on the other side of the bus ride home, students' lives were much richer and more varied than could be taken into account by classroom conversations, curriculum, and conferences. As I talked with colleagues about the possibilities of home visits, my interest grew. But I also hesitated. There is a long history of dominant culture institutions intruding on the privacy and lives of people who are part of nondominant groups. I did not want families to feel that my visit was an obligation.

I had lots of questions: Would it be appropriate to invite myself to a student's home? Would families be uncomfortable? Would I be uncomfortable? How would I structure the visit? Would families feel obligated to prepare food or clean the house? Could I find time for visits at the beginning of an already busy school year?

I topped off my hesitations with some carefully constructed rationalizations: I lived in the largely Latina/o community where I taught; I had a sense of the apartment complexes, streets, and neighborhoods that my students' families called home; I saw students crossing streets with siblings, buying ice cream from a bicycle vendor, checking out library books at the public library, and jumping into the local pool. I told myself I knew my students' lives.

And, besides, 25 homes is a lot of visits.

"I am definitely doing home visits," my good friend and colleague Jillian Perez informed me. Did she not understand all the complications? Where would she—a first-year bilingual kindergarten teacher—find the time? As we talked about logistics and the potential of home visits, however, I realized that the best way forward was to begin—with more questions than answers, and a willingness to learn.

Then, I Leapt

And learn I did. While conversing on couches, at kitchen tables, soccer game sidelines, and front porches, I learned how much I still had to learn.

I learned that Jesús and Ale had been next-door neighbors their whole lives. I learned that Alberto's family spoke Tarasco, an Indigenous language of the Michoacán region of Mexico—which I hadn't realized, despite teaching two of his older brothers in previous years. I learned that quiet José was the responsible oldest of five, and that Carolina's family was thinking about moving back to Mexico. I learned that Alejandra was affectionately known as Ale, Miguel went by Junior, and Fernando was called Nando. I met babies and sisters and grandparents and pet birds. I learned that Diego's mom was too sick to work, Antonio's yard was full of trees, Erica's family had a garden, and Luis' mom spoke a secret language.

Now, more than ever, family involvement at schools is typically driven by school agendas. Whether families come to school for a game night, a young authors celebration, or 10-minute conference slots, school-based family interactions are filled with agendas, information, and activities. My hope was that home visits would create space to listen.

Although I often carried public library card applications, extra reading material, or an overdue permission slip to home visits, listening was my priority. I remember Erick's dad standing on the front porch, asking, "Do you have any questions to ask me?" When I assured him that my purpose was to introduce myself and learn more about his hopes for his son, the conversation opened up. I learned that Erick was expected to clean his own room, and that his dad was concerned that Erick was getting into trouble with neighborhood friends. When I got to school the next day, Erick, who had been at his grandmother's the evening before, immediately asked: "Did you meet my cats?"

In my bilingual classroom, 80 to 90 percent of my students were native Spanish speakers. Their families sometimes had roots in parts of Mexico where Indigenous Mixtec and Zapotec languages were spoken, so I often asked the question: Do you speak other languages?

The language question became pivotal as it turned parents into experts and me into learner. As I struggled, my students and their parents guided and scaffolded my learning, re-pronouncing sounds and syllables until I could somewhat successfully produce a word or phrase in Amuzgo, Tarasco, or Trique. I asked parents and students to teach me at least a few words or phrases, and wrote down as much as I could.

At the end of the visit, I'd often reference the paper in my hand, and attempt a "thank you." I kept the scraps of paper with the phonetic phrases and translations on them, and then occasionally used them during classroom transitions with students (explaining the language and translation) and again with families at conferences.

As I learned more about the linguistic diversity of my students, I changed the way I discussed bilingualism in the classroom. In monolingual classrooms, English becomes the measure of language progress, with no credit or recognition given to students for fluency in other languages. In the same way, Spanish and English acquisition had become the definitions of bilingual in my teaching. By defining bilingual as Spanish and English, I'd inadvertently missed the opportunity to recognize parents—many of whom spoke little English—as bilingual. When I failed to recognize the Indigenous languages spoken by students' families in my class discussions about being bilingual, I unintentionally diminished their value.

Home Visit Logistics

My approach to home visits is just one of many. Here are a few ideas that helped me manage logistics:

- Printing out a calendar for the month of September allowed me to note possible home visit slots one or two days each week. By preselecting the days and time slots, I could balance home visits with other responsibilities and commitments.

- There are always a few parents who drop their students off on the first day of school. As I met parents in the classroom or during open house at the beginning of the school year, I took a moment to share the home visit calendar. If they were willing, I asked them to sign up for a time.

- I printed out a list of addresses for the class so I could code home visit groups (i.e., all students who lived in a particular neighborhood or apartment complex). Once I had a parent sign up, I'd send notes home to the others who lived in close proximity to try to schedule a visit for the same evening.

- When I scheduled home visits for parents I did not see at school, I sent a note home suggesting times that fit with nearby home visits. (I always asked the student what time parents got home from work.) The note stated that the visit would last 10–15 minutes, and that the family did not need to cook, clean, or prepare anything for the home visit.

- If visits were hard to schedule, I'd make a few attempts to contact parents by note or phone call. Sometimes I'd see parents at a soccer game or schedule a home visit at a parent conference.

Through the discussions about language during home visits, I began to understand the cognitive complexity involved as students like Juan wove their way through the world in three languages. I hoped that by naming, using, wondering about, and valuing Indigenous languages, I was empowering students to respect the knowledge of their families and the communities around them. We spent more time discussing language, talking about the benefits of being bilingual and speaking other languages, the occasions and situations when we use one or another language. By occasionally asking, "How do you say that in Trique?" I offered Juan the power that comes with being an expert, being a teacher. I was reminding him that he was smart, that he was lucky, that he could learn, that Indigenous languages—and the people who speak them—are of great value. And I was reminding myself how little I really knew.

Making Connections

As I learned more about student lives, I also found myself searching for ways to shake the invisible lines that snaked through our community. Visiting the various apartment complexes and neighborhoods, I started to sense the subcultures within them and the lines between them. Students socialized with family and neighbors who were often of similar socioeconomic, linguistic, and cultural backgrounds. I sensed that the experience I was having—the intimate experience of visiting in homes—was not one my students were regularly experiencing outside of their own neighborhoods.

Home visits made me even more aware of the need to provide opportunities for students to learn about each other's lives in the classroom. Although I wanted to honor students' affinity groups, I also wanted the classroom to prompt students to step outside of social comfort zones. I became more intentional about student grouping: assigning partners, groups, and reasons for students to interact more often than I had in the past.

> **Home visits made me even more aware of the need to provide opportunities for students to learn about each other's lives in the classroom.**

Writing—and sharing—our lives through poetry, narratives, and essays became even more central to our classroom curriculum.

By far, the most powerful outcome of home visits was trust. Meeting parents at their homes instead of on school turf seemed to create a willingness to call, visit, and communicate during the school year. Ana Maria's mom came to teach the class how she designs and embroiders a *huipil*; David's mom came to reading workshop to work one-on-one with students. And there was something almost magical about being able to exchange a meaningful look with a student and refer to home visits—Ale's pet care responsibilities or Jesús' homework routine—in the middle of teaching.

Over and over I heard students proudly announcing, "She's coming to my house tomorrow." Parents remarked: "We've never had a teacher come visit before. Thank you."

When I think I'm done learning, that I have a good enough label or assumption to work with, I stop asking questions. Home visits taught me that, although students may live in the same apartment complex or neighborhood, and may share a demographic like Latina/o or working class or native English speaker, their individual lives are incredibly complex and nuanced. Home visits taught me humility. They taught me to wonder. ☼

Elizabeth Barbian (formerly Schlessman) has taught bilingual students and worked with teachers in the United States, Bolivia, Tanzania, and South Africa. She currently lives in the Denver area. Student names have been changed.

"Aren't You on the Parent Listserv?"

Working for equitable family involvement in a dual-immersion elementary school

BY GRACE CORNELL GONZALES

BEC YOUNG

When I visited my current school in San Francisco to do a demo lesson in a dual-immersion classroom, I was excited by the diversity that I saw. The bilingual Oakland school I had worked in before had been anything but diverse, either racially or socioeconomically—98 percent of the students identified as Latina/o, 95 percent were eligible for free or reduced lunch, and about 86 percent were classified as English language learners. Everywhere it seemed that segregation in public schools was becoming more entrenched. Yet here I was, awkwardly clutching my bag of demo lesson materials, facing a sea of kindergarten faces that seemed to buck this trend. There were Latina/o students, African American students, white students, all chattering away in Spanish. I was elated. Could I have found a place where the interests and needs of many different populations converged—a public school that worked for everyone?

Then, in September, after starting my new job as a kindergarten teacher, I went to a PTA meeting. The parents at the meeting were excited to be there and dedicated to making the school a place that would serve their children. They were also almost entirely white, and—as I would learn as I got to know parents personally in our small school community—almost entirely middle- or upper-middle-class native English speakers. On paper, our school was about 50 percent Latina/o and 20 percent African American. Yet, in that first PTA meeting, with about 40 people in attendance, I saw only a handful of Latina/o parents. There were no African American families present. Later in the year, one African American family did frequently attend, but the number of Latina/o parents who came and used the interpretation services quickly dropped to zero. In addition, most of the parents involved came from the Spanish immersion track. The general education track, composed largely of students of color, was essentially unrepresented.

At my previous school, where the majority of families were recent immigrants, I had seen the positive impact of parents who were empowered to advocate for their children, although most were not native English speakers and many were unfamiliar with the structures of the local school system. The English Learner Advisory Committee (ELAC) and School Site Council (SSC), the two required decision-making bodies with parent members, were run in Spanish by parents. The idea that there would be low family involvement due to the demographics of the community seemed ridiculous. Parents felt at home and knew that neither their native language nor unfamiliarity with the school system would be barriers to participation. Where were these families at my current school?

As I watched the PTA set fundraising goals, choose art enrichment programs, fund teaching positions, allocate money for books, determine what technology would be purchased, and select what types of paraprofessionals to hire, I became more and more concerned about whose voices were being heard and whose children were being advocated for.

I quickly began to see these inequities play out in my own classroom. The three mothers who signed up to be room parents were middle-class professionals, all white native English speakers. They all knew each other because their children had gone to the same bilingual preschool. The majority of families at Back to School Night were also white and English speaking. In the first two weeks, emails were sent, Google docs created, and listservs were joined, all in English. One half of the classroom parent community got to work, humming right along on rails that missed the other half by miles.

This was worrisome for a number of reasons. At my school, the stakes for parent participation are high because of the sorts of decisions the parent groups are responsible for. The PTA and SSC manage the budget, and the PTA brings in more than $100,000 a year. These groups work together to decide everything from whether or not there should be combination classes to what types of after-school intervention are available to struggling students, from field trip budgets to whether there are art enrichment classes and for whom.

I was also concerned about this pattern for another reason: As teachers we see the direct impact of parent involvement on our students—families who feel comfortable with and included in the school community can advocate for their children's needs, check in about their progress, get tips on how to help them at home, and stay informed about programs and opportunities that will be beneficial to their family. Attendance goes up and children benefit from seeing their parents as involved in their school community. When parents and teachers talk, children's behavior and motivation improves as they begin to understand the ways their home and school worlds are connected. I was going to have to do something quickly or risk losing those benefits for many of my students, and instead see my classroom duplicate the same sort of inequitable parent involvement that I saw at that first PTA meeting. The story of how I attempted to shift those dynamics is one of tiny victories, but it also shows how what we do in our own classrooms to address equity in parent participation can ripple out to affect the school as a whole.

Overcoming Communication Barriers

From the first week, when emails began to fly around in English asking parents to volunteer for important school roles, it became clear that communication was the key. Out of my class of 19 kindergarteners, 11 were Latina/o, two were African American, and six were white.

Right away, assumptions about both language and technology use created dividing lines. For example, five of my Spanish-speaking families had limited to no English, yet most parent-to-parent communication was happening without translation. This was especially ironic at a dual-immersion school where ostensibly everyone had committed to elevating the status of Spanish and making it the primary language. The other key problem related to the medium of communication. Only about half of my families regularly used email and at least one family did not have an email address at all, yet nearly all parent communication was happening via electronic means. I asked the advice of other teachers and talked to my room parents, and we started to negotiate some guidelines:

> I became more and more concerned about whose voices were being heard and whose children were being advocated for.

All communication must be bilingual, and Spanish always goes first. This applied to emails, letters home, handouts, homework packets, and sign-up sheets. This rule was championed by the most experienced bilingual teacher on my grade-level team, and we helped each other stick to it. For my room parents, it meant asking a bilingual parent or myself to translate or, in desperate situations, using Google translate and hoping someone could give it a quick look-over. Putting Spanish first was of symbolic as well as practical significance—it served to remind us all that we are committed to a bilingual environment, and that means that native English speakers have to get used to not having their language always come first. Also, it helped to elevate the status of Spanish in our school community, which is essential because children are sensitive to issues of language and power and will sometimes be resistant to learning and speaking languages that they perceive to be low-status.

Important communication cannot just be through email. As convenient as sending out notes through email may be, important communication must also go home in paper form in the weekly homework folders. This included invitations to classroom events, field trip notifications, notices about school or class policies, and invitations to volunteer. Often this meant that I used the same text, reformatted, for both an email and a letter attached to the homework packet. I also usually printed these out and taped them to the classroom door.

Sign-up opportunities have to be fair. This is especially important because there are usually limitations on how many parents can go on the bus or enter a field trip location for free. I had to think a bit about the best way to give parents equal chances to sign up for those spots. I settled on this routine: I would create a paper sign-up sheet and hang it on the door of the classroom. The sign-up sheet would have spots for parents who needed to ride on the school bus and spots for parents who volunteered to drive and pay for themselves. Then, at the morning circle, I specifically approached families I thought might not see the sign-up sheet on the door (because they didn't pick up their kids in the afternoon) and who I knew didn't use email. If they wanted to go, I signed them up on the sheet myself. Then I sent out an email advising parents that there was a sign-up sheet on the door. I also told parents that the spots that guaranteed free transport and entrance were reserved for families who needed them.

Teacher-to-parent communication needs to fit the family. I spent a good deal of time figuring out the best way to communicate with the families in my classroom, both by asking parents what they preferred, and through trial and error. For some families, email really did work best. For others, the best way to get a hold of them was a call home. For still more parents, text messages were the most effective. This can be tricky because not all teachers give out their personal cell phone numbers. Although it worked for me, other teachers might choose to use parent liaisons to text the families more easily reachable in that way. Also, services like Google Voice and some smartphone apps enable teachers to make calls or send group texts without giving out their personal information. By creating a profile in my mind of how to communicate best with each family, I was able to reach out in appropriate ways and ultimately get more families involved.

Determine which families require more concerted effort. Over the course of the year, I identified a couple of families who were trickier to loop into classroom communication in traditional ways, either because of work schedules or because home language literacy levels made reading print notices a challenge. So I tried to catch up with these families frequently in person—snagging them at any opportunity to just check in about how things were going, to personally invite them to important events, and to help, if necessary, with filling out forms and permission slips.

These strategies paid off in visible ways. Some of my native Spanish-speaking parents were the most involved, chaperoning all of the field trips and consistently coming to classroom events like writers' celebrations, birthdays, and family reading parties. This was also the case for my two African American families. In fact, one of those families never missed a classroom event all year, and four generations showed up for our promotion ceremony.

However, when it came to the room parents, the parents who participated in the PTA or SSC, and the parents who came in weekly to volunteer in class, the majority were still from the same affluent group who dominated the schoolwide parent committees. Although that represented significant missed opportunities, it did fuel some interesting interactions that helped begin to shift the tone of parent dialogue.

Building Awareness

Throughout the year, I tried to be as explicit as possible about the reasons why I communicated with parents the way I did. I talked with my room parents about the importance of bilingual communications and about the necessity of sending paper copies of announcements home in the homework folder. When I wrote emails about the field trip sign-up sheets, I explained that I posted them on the door in order to give access to families who did not use email. As I worked through issues of equitable parent participation myself, I tried whenever possible to include parents in those conversations, even when I myself was not sure I was doing the right thing.

Near the end of the year, something interesting started happening. The parents in my class who were most explicitly involved in the operations of the school—the ones who were room parents, PTA members, and committee leads—started to bring up issues of equity themselves. One mom who was a fluent Spanish speaker approached me, wondering how she could help get more Spanish-speaking parents in to volunteer in the classroom. One of my room parents asked about how I thought she could best utilize phone trees and texting to reach the parents who were hard to get by email. Several parents who were active in the PTA wanted to talk about recruitment and retention of Latina/o families in the immersion program.

> **One half of the classroom parent community got to work, humming right along on rails that missed the other half by miles.**

These conversations extended out into interactions with other parents as well. For example, during the last room parent meeting of the year, one of the room parents from the other immersion classroom suggested that we coordinate the potluck on the last day of school through a Google Doc sign-up sheet. One of my room parents replied: "I don't know about your class, but in our class we have a lot of families who don't use email. Let's print out a sign-up sheet to hang up on the doors as well, and also send something home in the folders. We want to make sure everyone can participate. I can volunteer to do the translation into Spanish, as long as someone will look it over." I was so happy that the same parent who hadn't thought twice about communicating entirely through English emails at the beginning of the year was now advocating for the diverse communication needs of the families in our class.

I came to realize that many of these parents had come to our school because they wanted a diverse environment for their children, but they didn't necessarily know how to navigate within that environment themselves. The insensitivity to issues of equity wasn't necessarily intentional. Sometimes it didn't occur to the parents involved that their way of doing something might be alienating to other families. The conversations that we had in my classroom were a step, albeit a small one, toward opening up wider dialogues about these issues at the school level.

Missed Opportunities

Looking back on the year, I wanted to celebrate the victories without losing sight of the things that I would choose to do differently in the future. For instance, I had learned from other teachers that in many dual-immersion schools all classrooms must have a room parent who is a native Spanish speaker to partner with an English-speaking room parent. This simple expectation would have made an enormous difference in my classroom. It would have facilitated translation and made the classroom parent community feel more inclusive to a wider range of families. It also would have made it easier to do volunteer outreach to Spanish-speaking families and bring in more Spanish-speaking classroom volunteers to work directly with the kids. Especially in a bilingual program, there is so much need for students to have Spanish-speaking role models, and it is even better if they are from the parent community. It's also important for these parents and their children to understand what an asset their language skills are in our classroom.

But, most importantly, I was acutely aware that the majority of those vital conversations I had with parents about equity happened with my room parents and a few other regular classroom volunteers, most of whom were from white middle-class families. Here I realized I was swayed by my own issues. As a white teacher, I felt more comfortable bringing up equity issues with the more privileged parents, particularly white parents, and those parents felt more comfortable bringing them up with me. If real changes were going to take place, however, everyone would need to be involved in the conversation.

New Beginnings

Armed with the knowledge of what had gone well and what had gone wrong during that first school year, I entered the current school year with a different set of priorities. My first priority was to find room parents who were native Spanish speakers. My second priority was to begin to have the conversations that I had avoided the previous year.

Instead of waiting for parents to volunteer for the room parent slots, I approached a couple of Spanish-speaking parents individually before Back to School Night and asked if they would be room parents. One accepted; the other politely declined and offered to volunteer in another way. At Back to School Night, I asked for volunteers and got one native Spanish speaker and one English-speaking parent. Thus, I had my team of three: one mother from Argentina and one from Mexico, both bilingual native Spanish speakers, and one white parent who spoke some Spanish.

That night I also sent around a list asking parents to specify how they wanted to be contacted—phone, text, or email. Then, my room parents and I set up contact lists and divided them up. One room mother would send bilingual emails, one would text, and the third would call the families who requested to be contacted by phone, all of whom happened to be Spanish speaking.

Mercedes, my room parent from Mexico, has been an extraordinary resource. Because she is willing to call the Spanish-speaking families to ask for volunteers, I've ended up with many Spanish-speaking volunteers doing classroom work—three who read with children during reading workshop and two who help out during art class. Thus, my students have Spanish language models from their community during the school day, and the Latina/o parents in my classroom are getting to know my room parents and each other through phone calls and working alongside each other in the classroom.

This system—that of divvying up the task of contacting families among my room parents—has led not only to increased involvement but also to a model of family engagement that is more sustainable for me as a teacher. When I need to get a piece of information to parents, whether it's an invitation to a class party, a call for volunteers, or a reminder about parent conferences, I simply contact my room parents and they reach out to the others through phone calls, emails, and texts. As teachers, we have enough on our plates already, and finding a system of parent involvement that is both equitable and sustainable is a real boon. Partnering with bilingual room parents is even more crucial for teachers who are not bilingual themselves but work in communities where many families speak other languages.

> **I started to have explicit conversations with parents of color about equity and involvement at our school.**

Beginning with my own room parents, I started to have explicit conversations with parents of color about equity and involvement at our school. One of my Spanish-speaking room parents suggested creating a network of PTA/ELAC parent volunteers who could call Spanish-speaking families to invite them personally to the meetings. With the help of other bilingual parents, we were able to coordinate this before the first PTA and ELAC meetings of the year for about half of the classes in the school. There is talk about expanding this in the future to include all classes and also to reach out to African American families in a similar way. I also recently began attending a series of morning meetings with parents about increasing family involvement, hosted by my principal. That has given me the chance to talk to Latina/o and African American parents about how both the teachers and the parent community could be more welcoming; they have shared ideas that range from making sure that the Wednesday folders go home consistently, alternating PTA meeting times between morning and afternoon, advertising translation at meetings, and reminding teachers how important it is to smile and say hello to parents when they see them in the mornings.

Ripples of Change

Although we have a long way to go, these conversations with parents across our school community seem to be bearing some fruit. At the end of the first year, a parent from my classroom volunteered to head a committee focused on recruiting and maintaining Latina/o families at our school. Another made a presentation in Spanish at our new kindergarten family orientation appealing to Spanish-speaking families to volunteer in classrooms and join the PTA. I committed to presenting at a staff meeting to share with other teachers the strategies I had used for parent communication and engagement. This year, parents are talking about holding some PTA meetings in Spanish with English translation, and about changing the structure of the PTA meetings to allow for small-group breakout sessions to foster more participation. Also, as I have become more involved with the SSC, I have been able to connect and brainstorm with parents of older students who have been thinking and talking about these issues for a while.

There is still a lot to be done, both in my classroom and at the school level, to rectify the exclusive patterns of parent participation I observed at the beginning of last year. As long as the PTA focuses exclusively on fundraising and pressures parents to make large personal donations, many families will continue to feel alienated and decide not to participate. As long as the SSC has no African American members and includes mostly parents from the school's immersion track, many of the students at our school will have no one to advocate for their needs. And, although it is important to reach out to Spanish-speaking Latina/o families, it is essential that we also focus time and attention on including and empowering African American families and other families of color.

It's not easy, but I think that substantive change is possible if we begin to talk about these issues instead of leaving them unexplored. At the beginning of the year, a friend of mine who is also a public school parent reminded me that, especially in elementary school, teachers train parents what to expect when it comes to how they should and should not be involved in their children's schools. Those lessons shape how parents interact with future teachers and future school communities. This serves as a constant reminder to me that we are always communicating, through the phrasing of every note home, through the positioning of every sign-up sheet. We are communicating about who we expect to be involved and how. We are either opening up dialogues with parents or closing them off. And all of those decisions, both the small ones and the large ones, reach beyond our classrooms. If we want equitable schools, we need to be as intentional about how we involve parents as we are about how we educate their children. ☼

Grace Cornell Gonzales is an editor for Rethinking Schools and has worked for nine years as a bilingual elementary school teacher in California and Guatemala City.

*A Spanish translation of this article is available at on the Rethinking Schools website at rethinkingschools.org/articles/no-estas-registrado-en-la-lista-de-correos-electronicos.

Tellin' Stories, Changing Lives

How bilingual parent power can complement bilingual education

BY DAVID LEVINE

JILL WEILER

When parent organizer Doris Watkins started at Washington, D.C.'s Bruce-Monroe Elementary School in 2000, she was troubled by the racial tension that divided parents. She would walk into a room and notice that the Black parents were sitting on one side and the Latina/o parents were on the other. Since the 1980s, the historically Black Columbia Heights community in which the school was located has become the new home of many immigrants from Central America. Although incidents of open hostility were rare, this demographic shift meant many residents perceived competition for jobs and community resources. Black and Latina/o parents rarely interacted with each other at school events, and, occasionally, angry words were exchanged.

Watkins realized that the small group of parents she was working with were vulnerable to these tensions, and faced language barriers as well. The Black parents did not understand Spanish and most of the Latina/o parents understood little English, and neither set of parents was familiar with the cultural traditions of the other. Drawing from her own Black heritage, Watkins hit upon food as a universal language to overcome these communication and cultural barriers. One morning she took the group to the Union Market on 5th Street to purchase "all the items that an African American family would cook for a festive occasion in their home: sweet potato pie, collard greens with ham hocks, potatoes for Southern-style potato salad, chicken for Southern fried chicken, pigs feet. . . ."

Under her guidance, the parents cooked at her son's home nearby, and they communicated. "We talked about the food. We expressed why we served these foods in our homes and how we prepared them. Now, grant you, we had limited language but we had gestures we could use. We had such a wonderful time." The next day, the group shared the leftovers with other parents at the school and explained the recipes. A week later, they convened at the home of a Latino parent, where the Latina/o parents showed the Black parents how to make pupusas, a traditional Salvadoran tortilla that can be filled with cheese, pork, and refried beans. According to Watkins, these two cooking events helped bridge the cultural divide: "We could not have a long conversation [because of the language barrier], but we had hugs and gestures. And we were now sitting together."

The *Tellin' Stories* Approach to Parent Organizing

Watkins and her colleague Jill Weiler were part of the D.C.-based parent organizing project *Tellin' Stories*. They were invited to initiate work at Bruce-Monroe by assistant principal Marta Palacios. Palacios, a Salvadoran immigrant herself, had joined the school as an assistant principal in 1999. Her long-term vision was to convert Bruce-Monroe into a bilingual program. In addition to assembling a strong and supportive staff for such a program, she knew it would be important to address the racial tensions at the school and the challenges it faced around parent involvement.

In contrast to traditional models of parent involvement that often sideline working-class parents and parents of color, *Tellin' Stories* uses the power of story to help traditionally excluded parents organize collective action and get involved in the decision-making process at a school. Weiler and Watkins began working with Ramiro Acosta, a Bruce-Monroe paraprofessional who became its parent coordinator, to build parental involvement and bonds of trust between Black and Latina/o parents. They formed the Parents and Friends of Bruce-Monroe, a group of Black and Latina/o parents that met weekly. Typically attended by 15 to 20 parents, all the meetings were bilingual—with Weiler interpreting the remarks of the Latina/o parents into English and Acosta interpreting the remarks of the Black parents into Spanish. (When Acosta went on to become a pre-K teacher at the school, he was replaced by Lillian Hernandez, whose son attended Bruce-Monroe.) The group came to provide an emotional home to parents within the school, through baby showers, birthday celebrations, and occasionally collecting money for a parent who couldn't make a rent payment. As Weiler explained, "For the first time many parents felt connected to each other and to the school. We shared stories. It's very different from coming to a PTA meeting where parents sit in rows, receive reports, and go home without even knowing the name of the person they sat beside. It made the school the kind of place parents wanted to be."

An early episode of trust building involved the parents taking turns reaching into a "story fortune bag." The bag was filled with side-by-side bilingual story prompts: "My first day at school," "A time my mom/dad made me proud," "A time I felt I had no voice." As parents shared stories over the next few weeks, they built bonds of empathy through discussing life-changing events, child-rearing challenges, and positive and negative experiences at the school.

Parents also shared stories through *Tellin' Stories'* signature quilting project. Each parent designed and completed a quilt square that included an image and written message, in Spanish or English, embodying a crucial life story. Parent Rodney Mc-Daniel recalls, "Through the quilt, you would take a little part of your experience and make it into art . . . [the quilt] told a piece of everybody's life. One Black parent had a child who died, the victim of a violent attack. A Hispanic parent had a child who was also killed through a violent act. Even though they didn't speak the same language, they were brought together because of the common ground they shared. They couldn't really hold a long conversation, but they were able to identify with one another through the tragic episodes that took place in their lives."

> **"Even though they didn't speak the same language, they were brought together because of the common ground they shared."**
> **—Rodney McDaniel, parent**

As trust started to grow through shared stories, the group was able to talk about racial and cultural tensions. During one "fish bowl" activity, Latina/o parents gathered in the center of the room. Encircled by the Black parents, they talked with each other about three questions: What makes us proud to be Latina/o? What do we find challenging? What don't we ever want people to say about us? The Black parents responded to what they heard, and then answered the same questions as they were encircled by the Latina/o parents.

Latina/o parents spoke about hardships and hopes: "We want you to understand that we have to feed our families. If we get offered the opportunity to get a job, we're going to take it. We are in the same boat you are in. We want what is best for our children. We want to be able to provide for them, and we have to take whatever job we can get. Often times, those are the same jobs you are pursuing: the house cleaning, the office work."

Black parents also reflected on their hard work to provide for their families and their commitment to their children. Watkins recalls that some also articulated their desire to escape the crippling effect of powerful stereotypes: "What I don't want people to say about me was that I am a welfare recipient and that I don't care about work. I don't want you to say that I let my kids run wild and that my parenting skills are terrible."

Addressing School Problems

After completing the quilt project and listening to each other's hopes and challenges, Bruce-Monroe parents began to discuss and prioritize their concerns about the school. The parents shared their perceptions about school dynamics and issues, asked the teachers and the principal about what they saw as crucial problems, and visited other schools with successful academic programs. *Tellin' Stories* helped parents develop the skills needed to document problems, organize activities, and exercise leadership.

Concerned about the state of the building, the group conducted a dismaying tour. Garbage cluttered a front entrance that lacked permanent trash cans, water fountains needed replacement, and mice and roaches infested some rooms. Ceilings were

JILL WEILER

blackened near inadequate ventilation ducts that posed a danger for children, especially those with asthma. A hallway was closed because of exposed asbestos. Children reported bladder problems because they couldn't use bathrooms that lacked doors on the stalls and functioning toilets. Lack of exterior lighting made the school dangerous at night. A broken gate allowed outside adults selling drugs to enter the playground where they verbally and physically harassed students.

In spring of 2001, the parent group embarked on a six-year struggle to compel District of Columbia Public Schools (DCPS) to address the host of physical problems that plagued the school. The parents petitioned public officials and testified at several school board, city council, and mayoral meetings. In January of 2004 they wrote the new superintendent about their anger after encountering "a series of rotating DCPS officials delivering an endless string of broken promises." In May of 2004 they demanded that the DCPS chief building operations officer "correct these violations to create a school you would be proud to send your own children to." The next month, more than 40 Bruce-Monroe parents and students conducted a demonstration in front of the school demanding that the "learning pods," in which three classes were only separated by temporary barriers that were not soundproof, be converted to classrooms.

Eventually, the parents were able to win significant, if partial, victories. The clanking DCPS bureaucracy implemented several repairs—new windows, new playground equipment, functional bathrooms, improved exterior lighting, and a renovated auditorium. And in 2003 the school board finally appropriated $1.4 million to build walls for one of the dysfunctional "learning pods."

Perhaps the most important lesson that Bruce-Monroe parents learned through these battles was to remain insistent that school officials deliver on promises made. Weiler recalls that at the start of the struggle for building improvements, most parents believed, "There is nothing we can do." But five years later, when a DCPS official said there were no additional actions the parent group could take to move the process along, a parent said, "Don't you ever tell us that!"

A Bilingual Program to Match Bilingual Parent Engagement

In 2001, the Bruce-Monroe principal was promoted and, at the emphatic request of a group of parents, assistant principal Marta Palacios became the school's new principal. As principal, Palacios arranged to have Ramiro Acosta pilot a pre-K bilingual class. Over the next several years, under Palacios' persistent leadership, bilingual instruction advanced grade level by grade level and eventually became the comprehensive program of instruction for the entire school. According to Weiler, the work of the bilingual parent group helped create a more receptive climate for building a bilingual instructional program: "The parents who had built relationships across race and culture were generally more open to innovation, to the bilingual program."

The bilingual climate of the school was also enhanced through visits by the *Tellin' Stories* Roving Readers, pairs of Latina/o and Black parent volunteers from Bruce-Monroe and other schools. The Roving Reader pairs gave dramatic readings of children's literature in both English and Spanish. As Weiler notes, the Roving Readers modeled a key goal of bilingual instruction: "To build this bridge between culture and people and language, and to really appreciate each other."

Even though the work of the parent group helped lay the groundwork for the development of a bilingual program, there was struggle and discomfort among the staff as this substantial instructional change was implemented over several years. Part of the challenge was that Black and Latina/o teachers had to work

> Black and Latina/o teachers had to work through stereotypes and preconceived notions that in some ways mirrored divisions among parents.

through their own stereotypes and preconceived notions that in some ways mirrored divisions among parents. As the proportion of Latina/o students increased, some Black teachers struggled with a sense that they were losing their school. In the teacher's lounge, some Black teachers were uncomfortable that a group of Latina/o teachers sat together and spoke in Spanish.

In addition to these tensions, some teachers were skeptical that bilingual education was appropriate for students who struggled academically, no matter what their first language was. Katarina Brito, bilingual program developer with the D.C. Public Schools, recalls, "[They argued] 'when we are working with poor, underperforming kids who we can barely get to read in one language, why in the world would we be bringing in a program that is going to be asking them to read in two languages?'"

In 2006, Brito began working regularly with the Bruce-Monroe staff. She and Palacios arranged for panel discussions through which teachers could directly raise their concerns and learn about the extensive research demonstrating that a well-implemented bilingual education can accelerate learning for struggling students, whether their first language is English or Spanish. Through voluntary study groups that met before school and workshops with Brito, staff members of the D.C.-based Center for Applied Linguistics, and faculty from Columbia University, the teachers acquired new instructional ideas in several subjects.

Equally important, the teachers took on the arduous task of designing a program from the ground up. Through experimentation, the staff fashioned a model in which students received all their instruction for all subjects from one teacher in Spanish on one day, and all their instruction in English from a partner teacher on the next day. This approach depended on close teamwork by the teaching pairs, and the staff insisted that new teachers joining the school be committed to the labor-intensive teamwork it involved.

The implementation of this model helped the bilingual program begin to flourish, as did demographic neighborhood changes that made Latina/o students the majority and the arrival of new teachers committed to bilingual instruction. But Brito notes the process was never painless. Some teachers pushed back hard: "At a certain point, I remember Dr. Palacios saying, 'We want to accommodate you, but this is going to be our model and it is not negotiable.'"

> **The successful bilingual instruction program and parent empowerment program complement each other.**

According to Weiler, Brito, and Palacios, persevering through this difficult process of conflict and professional development has enabled the staff to develop an exemplary bilingual program. Brito also emphasizes that, in contrast to many other schools, a vital part of the Bruce-Monroe approach has been "a shared leadership model, in that a teaching assistant's opinion was as important as the assistant principal's opinion. Everybody's voice was listened to, and it was understood that everyone was bringing a perspective, and all of those perspectives together painted a more complete picture of what was happening at the school."

Persevering Through a Stormy Transition

In 2007, shrinking enrollments landed Bruce-Monroe on a list of schools to be closed, launching the parent group on a path of lobbying and demonstrations to save the school. Then-Chancellor Michelle Rhee offered a compromise plan to consolidate the school with the nearby Park View Elementary for a three-year period, as the Bruce-Monroe building was rebuilt. Bruce-Monroe students were transferred to the Park View building, but DCPS eventually reneged on its promise. The Bruce-Monroe building was demolished and replaced by a park. Re-emerging as a school with a combined population—now known as "Bruce-Monroe at Park View"—the school had to incorporate 100 former Park View students in an English-only instructional strand and survive the disruption of being located in a new building in poor shape in a new neighborhood. Building on their years of forging and nurturing a resilient school community, the teachers and parents endured and re-grouped. Today Bruce-Monroe at Park View has a well-respected bilingual program. And with ongoing support from *Tellin' Stories*, the parent group continues to act as a strong advocate for the school community.

At Bruce-Monroe, the successful bilingual instruction program and parent empowerment program complement each other, and mirror some shared attributes: respect and nurturance of home culture, creativity and experimentation, and constant attention to school dynamics so that all students and parents are embraced by school staff. The synergy between the two brought powerful benefits to the school's students and their families. Through sharing food and sharing stories, seeing themselves in each other's eyes, organizing to nudge a recalcitrant school bureaucracy, and acting as respected partners and guardians of their children's school, Bruce-Monroe parents demonstrate how bilingual/bicultural parent power is a natural ally for effective bilingual instructional programs. ☼

David Levine is a Rethinking Schools editor and retired teacher educator interested in U.S. educational history and policy. He lives in Columbus, Ohio.

Note from the editors: This article was adapted from a previously published piece by David Levine, "Tellin' Stories, Finding Common Ground" (*Rethinking Schools* magazine, Spring 2009).

Rethinking Family Literacy in Head Start

BY MICHAEL AMES CONNOR

DAVID McLIMANS

Two dozen mostly immigrant parents of Head Start children settled into elementary school desks. Holding cheese and crackers in one hand and wiggly infants in the other, the parents gathered for an annual event: Family Literacy Night. Over many years of Head Start teaching, I'd sat through a handful of these presentations, and I knew what we were in for: A nice person from the public library would talk for 45 minutes, in English, about how parents need to read more with their children at home. The parents would listen attentively via translation for the first few minutes, and then realize that the message would simply repeat and amplify. They knew a finger wagging when they were getting one. I knew things could be different, but I didn't know how.

Discovering Family Literacy

To be fair, the librarians had a good point: Reading at home with young children brings all sorts of benefits, from literacy to language development to building attachment. Parents and early educators alike know the almost-indescribable wonderfulness of snuggling in with a youngster and diving into a book, talking and laughing and wondering and repeating, discovering hidden images, puzzling over new words.

At the time of the family literacy event, I worked as a Head Start teacher, meeting frequently with parents who expressed desire to read more effectively with their children at home. Their ideas and frustrations prompted me to consider what family literacy might entail if a workshop built on parents' strengths, capitalized on their experiences, and honored their family cultures. Instead of a lecture, where a white, English-speaking professional would explain what parents should be doing, I wanted to create a workshop where parents' ideas would contribute to new understandings, and where obstacles and fears could be addressed collectively. With this in mind, my colleagues and I developed a new family literacy workshop over the course of a year. I implemented the workshop more than a dozen times in rural and suburban Head Start districts outside of Portland, Oregon.

The parents who participated in our workshop comprised two main groups. The majority were immigrants from Mexico and Central America who spoke mostly Spanish or sometimes an Indigenous language at home. These parents often worked in fields, orchards, construction, and the lower levels of retail. The other group included white, English-speaking families who were working class or impoverished. These two groups coexisted but rarely interacted—another dynamic I thought worth challenging.

Highlighting What Parents Already Know

Language barriers and cliques can sabotage the best-intentioned learning groups, and I was determined not to let that happen. For several days before the workshop, I sought out bilingual parents. I asked these parents to take on a special role in the workshop as bilingual table captains, and many agreed. Before we settled into the initial small groups, I reshuffled the parents, playfully asking them to line up shortest to tallest. This technique, which some call a *human array*, produced some grins, but the parents were game.

Then I invited the bilingual table captains to distribute themselves throughout the room. With each table anchored by a bilingual peer, I asked groups of four parents, alike only in height, to join tables. Some spouses were now seated at different tables. Many grinned and joked at being separated. But having moved around, the parents knew things would be different. As a warm-up, I challenged each table group to learn each other's names and the names of their Head Start children. Groups relied on peer translation for the introductions.

To begin, I wanted to highlight and celebrate what parents already knew. I knew that for many, their own parents and grandparents had told stories much more frequently than they read books. In order for this family literacy workshop to be genuinely cross-cultural, I wanted to start with an expansive understanding of parents' early literacy activities. I offered some prompts for parents to discuss in their small groups: "Who told stories in your families? Who shared books with you?"

Parents recalled their own early experiences, writing down notes and drawing pictures on a large piece of paper. Desi, a parent working nights in a restaurant, recalled an older sister pointing out street signs and connecting these to family names. Andrea, whose two children both participated in Head Start, recalled her grandpa telling history stories of the Mexican Revolution: "We learned about all those adventures, all those important battles and dramas." When one parent shared an experience, others related their own memories—involving books or stories, or sometimes both.

After this reminiscing, I asked them to discuss their booksharing experiences as parents: "How often do you read with your children? What works for you at home? What obstacles do you encounter? What solutions have you tried?" Each table responded slightly differently, with many sharing stories and frustrations. One parent spoke about the special feeling of snuggling with a child and a book: "I feel like the worries I have in the day can go away for a bit." Another parent expressed exasperation at wanting to read with the kids but having to cook and clean after a long day of work: "They want to read, I know, but I just don't have time." Other parents nodded in agreement.

"They want to read, I know, but I just don't have time."

Each table, peer-facilitated by a bilingual parent, tackled the challenge of two languages in different ways: Some leaders provided simultaneous translation, others summed up. Some peer interpreters wrote key words in both languages. For the parent who recalled an older sister pointing out street signs, the facilitator wrote "*hermana*/sister, *letreros de calles*/street signs." Some drew pictures representing key ideas or stories.

After these small-group discussions, I invited each table to analyze their own early literacy experiences by identifying commonalities and differences. Then I brought the groups together to review ideas. Parents reported that older siblings played a big role in learning to read, with street signs, Bibles, and "big kid" books from school as important objects of study. Alicia recalled an older brother's picture dictionary providing hours of stimulation: "I would look at something in my room, the bed for example, and then I would try to find it in the dictionary; I remember being really frustrated sometimes, but then I would find it and shout." Participants also recalled grandparents and great-grandparents telling stories—either firsthand memories or significant history lessons that youngsters are expected to know. As each table shared in turn, we saw both common themes and sharp differences.

As we shared current family literacy practices, the wisdom of the whole group helped expose challenges and identify solutions. Many parents spoke of lack of time, of exhaustion from work, school, and the care of younger siblings. Pat, whose daughter will enter kindergarten in the fall, said that, after delivering food all day, "I just don't have the energy I need to really pay attention." Tentatively, but with growing confidence, some parents spoke of their own marginal reading abilities, or the perceived expectation that they read in English. "I don't read to my son because I don't speak English," Marisol said, and many agreed. "I feel that my child is not attracted to reading in Spanish," said Luz, prompting other parents to speak with anguish about how they see older siblings shunning the home language. Someone else commented that when grandparents visit, they are concerned that the grandkids speak so little Spanish at home.

When I shared research showing that reading in one language with children helps them read in another language, many recognized how their children borrow skills learned at home and transfer them to school. A mother whose three children have attended Head Start said that the oldest child loves to show off when a Spanish cognate gives insight into a new English word.

By now parents were openly expressing frustrations, offering each other solutions, asking questions to the group and getting answers. For each challenge mentioned, parents frequently offered two or three possible solutions.

Booksharing Styles

After parents shared past and present literary practices, I introduced the concept of booksharing style. Margaret Caspe (2009) examined how Latina mothers share books with their children, finding that these parents are more likely to have defined roles of narrator and listener. This contradicts the assumptions of other family literacy models, which encourage questions and prompts to the child. I knew that for many families, the dialogic style of booksharing favored by schools contradicted their own family style. I needed to find a way to encourage booksharing that did not begin with the implicit message "You're doing it wrong."

I invited parents to think about two very different styles of storytelling and booksharing. The first style I called "Grandpa tells a story": The adult talks or reads, holding the book, and the child's job is to listen with attention, and remember. The opposite style I labeled "Let's chat about a book": In this method, the child and adult talk together about the book, "reading" whatever the child recalls, asking questions, and describing the pictures. I gave quick demonstrations of each style, exaggerating the differences for clarity.

Then I turned to the human array activity again, this time asking parents to stand along a continuum showing how books and stories were shared when they were young. Parents moved to places along a line, either toward the right end ("Grandpa tells a story"), or the left ("Let's chat about a book"), or somewhere in the middle.

Some parents playfully suggested that they be allowed to move so far right as to be in the next room. "Mom talks, you listen," one parent said, "no interrupting."

Another parent recalled, "When Grandma tells a story, you have to listen."

Another commented, "When we were little, we had to listen to the grown-ups as they read. We were not allowed to talk; it was a way to show respect."

Other parents shared from the other end of the spectrum, recalling how, as children, they would insist on reading to their parents or older siblings.

Next, I invited parents to rearray themselves, this time based on how they currently shared books and stories as a parent. Some parents moved, some held fast. Some of those on the far right moved more toward the middle, explaining that they like to give their children more control than they themselves had as a child. "I don't have to be so rigid," said one. Another parent said the opposite: "I tell them we do it one way at home, and they can do it the school way at school."

I Do, We Do, You Do

As parents rejoined their tables, I introduced the final part of the workshop, a Vygotskian booksharing strategy: "I do, We do, You do." For Vygotsky, supporting children meant providing just enough support so that the child moves to higher independent ability. I demonstrated this style with a book, and I asked the parents to play along as young children. In "I do," the adult begins by reading a book with authority and animation, sticking fairly close to the text. This initial reading sits pretty far toward "Grandpa tells a story," though with flexibility and playfulness. I read the book more or less straight through, telling the parents I wanted them to listen and remember.

Next, I asked parents: "When you read a good book well, what do your children ask next?" Parents smiled and called out, "Read it again!" I did so, but in this second reading ("We do") I invited them to help me: I began sentences but did not finish them, waiting for them to chime in. I asked questions and modeled finding out the answer or soliciting theirs. I asked them what might happen next, before turning the page to find out. At this point, we were sharing authority for reading. In the second go-round, we read the book again, but together.

> **I needed to find a way to encourage booksharing that did not begin with the implicit message "You're doing it wrong."**

At last, we reached the "You do" stage. At this stage, the child re-reads the book to the parent. For younger children, this may involve retelling from memory or reading the pictures. Physically handing the book to the child helps reinforce the shift in control. By now the parents saw the pattern, noticing how much of the reading they were doing (as mock children), with my role (as mock adult) limited to asking questions and encouraging the child.

I mentioned to parents that re-reading books multiple times word-for-word can be tiresome for adults, and they ruefully agreed. "I get so tired of *Brown Bear,*" said Kim, and many parents laughed and nodded. However, the "You do" phase can be repeated nearly effortlessly by parents, moving beyond comprehension to critical thinking together. "What happens next?" for one page. "Why do you think she did that?" for another. "What else could he do?" for a third.

"I do, We do, You do" is a parenting/teaching approach familiar to many participants. From toileting with toddlers to helping an elementary schooler learn to ride a bike, many times as adults we give maximum support at the beginning and then fade our support as the child moves toward independence. This style of interaction incorporates both "Grandpa tells a story" and "Let's chat about a book," which means that multiple culturally embedded styles can be validated, while at the same time adding to each parent's toolbox. I made the point that as parents we want our children to be adept at both kinds of engagement as they transition to elementary school. There are times, after all, when children need to be able to listen with attention and remember. And there are other times when they will need to work with peers or adults to construct meaning together.

At the end, I asked parents to think about the problems they had listed earlier. Could this style of booksharing help with some of those barriers? Parents brainstormed together. Andrea asked, "I wonder if when I'm doing things in the house, if I read it once and then asked the kids to read it to me, would that work?" Alicia said, "I think this could help at bedtime, because I can read it once, and then we can read it together, and then I can tell the kids they can read to themselves until they feel sleepy." Several parents pointed out that reading the book first felt more natural. Some Spanish-speaking parents talked about how the method could work even if the children often responded in English.

"I Got the Idea from Another Parent"

Immediately after the workshop, parents reported that they found booksharing more enjoyable—even compared to how they felt an hour previously. During conversations at school and in home visits after the workshop, many parents spoke to me about their new appreciation for family booksharing. A mother of twins in one classroom said, "We used to read just like you said—just the parent talking. Now we tried it, and the kids are asking questions." The twins' father eagerly agreed: "Even if we read a book just once, when we are done, the kids say they want to read it. They invent their own story. My son is over in the corner, reading! I can finish cooking and listen to him, just asking questions." Another mom said she had increased her conversations with her daughter during booksharing: "I like the reminder to do that critical thinking part with her." One father advised, "You have to make it fun, something fun for both of you."

In a survey I conducted later, many parents reported more confidence reading in their first language. On average, they said they used two solutions offered by other parents to logistical problems of booksharing. "My kids read to me every day while I cook," said Luz. "I read it the first time like I always did, but now they kind of take over." Pat reported that bedtime had become more enjoyable: "I got the idea from another parent to take turns choosing books, and the kids like to have that choice. But I still pick sometimes. And we both do some reading."

For early childhood teachers and parent educators interested in borrowing from this experience, taking parents' home languages into account during planning is essential. Organizers must carefully assess participant language differences and then develop conscious strategies to facilitate conversation across barriers. Without careful arrangement, bilingual groups will devolve into two parallel monolingual groups. Our strategy of anchoring small groups with a competent bilingual peer may not be adequate for polylingual groups; for communities with three or more languages, educators will need to develop different tactics.

In our society, approaches to adult learning often mimic and mirror competitive and individualist assumptions. Lectures predominate, with talking and listening roles preordained by social class and organizational position. Building participatory learning communities that tackle real issues requires so much more than arranging for a guest speaker and setting up chairs. For early educators stressed by workload and time, taking on an active facilitator role, rather than introducing an outside expert, demands time and energy—both in short supply.

But, as this experience illustrates, parents' experiences, motivation, and expertise are abundant. By inviting multiple solutions for every problem, parents came away with more tools and strategies for reading with their children at home. Parents built on what they brought, felt confident in their own skills, and incorporated new approaches to the challenges of family literacy. ☼

Michael Ames Connor (Michael.Connor@mhcc.edu) has worked as an early educator for 20 years, as a Head Start teacher, college instructor, coach, and trainer. His article "Straight Talk with Kids About War" appeared in Rethinking Schools *(Summer 2003). Parents names have been changed.*

References

Caspe, Margaret. 2009. "Low-Income Latino Mothers' Booksharing Styles and Children's Emergent Literacy Development." *Early Childhood Research Quarterly* 24.3:306–24. doi: 10.1016/j.ecresq.2009.03.006.

Our Language Lives by What We Do

An interview with Hawaiian educator Kekoa Harman

BY GRACE CORNELL GONZALES

Na Kihapai Nani Lua 'Ole O Edena a Me Elenale (The Beautiful Unequaled Gardens of Eden and of Elenale), Hawaiian cotton quilt, before 1918, Honolulu Museum of Art

The number of native speakers of the Hawaiian language was in sharp decline for the first half of the 20th century, but an organized revitalization effort has made a huge difference over the last three decades. The first Pūnana Leo immersion preschools opened in 1984, and were followed by a system of public Hawaiian immersion schools that now span kindergarten to 12th grade. The University of Hawai'i offers bachelors, masters, and doctoral programs in Hawaiian, and, in

1998, founded a training program to certify Indigenous teachers to teach in Hawaiian-medium schools.

Kekoa Harman is currently working on his doctorate at Ka Haka 'Ula O Ke'elikōlani College of Hawaiian Language, and he and his wife, Pele, a Hawaiian-medium mathematics teacher, are raising their three children in Hawaiian. He took time to talk with us about the importance of the Hawaiian language revitalization movement and the impact that it has had on him and on his family.

Grace Cornell Gonzales: Could you tell us a little bit about your background with Hawaiian language education?

Kekoa Harman: I started my undergraduate education at Ka Haka 'Ula O Ke'elikōlani College of Hawaiian Language at the University of Hawai'i in 1998. Later I entered the masters in Hawaiian Language and Literature and then the doctoral program in Indigenous Language and Culture Revitalization. My wife, a graduate of the Kahuawaiola Indigenous teacher certification program and the master's program in Hawaiian Language and Literature, teaches at Ke Kula 'O Nāwahīokalani'ōpu'u (Nāwahī for short), the K–12 Hawaiian-medium school our children now attend.

> **Without the language we miss a major connection to our *kūpuna*, to our elders, and to the land that we live on here.**

In 2001, when our first child was born, we decided that our household would be a Hawaiian language household. We have three children. Our eldest daughter is 15, our son is 11, and our youngest daughter is 10. All three of our children attend Nāwahī—our two younger ones actually started attending the Pūnana Leo infant/toddler program when they were 6 weeks old. In many ways, these Hawaiian language sites are also a second home for our children.

GCG: What role have schools played in the movement to revitalize Hawaiian?

KH: The number of native Hawaiian speakers has dwindled since the early 1900s. The private Kamehameha Schools, for example, banned Hawaiian from being spoken, a policy begun by the school's first principal, William Oleson, in 1887. Hawaiian was forbidden in the classroom and on the playing fields, and the boys were punished if they were heard speaking the language of their families. By the end of the century, children in the remotest public schools were also being punished for speaking Hawaiian on school grounds.

By the 1980s, the number of Hawaiian speakers had dwindled—there were only about 1,500 native Hawaiian speakers. But there was also a greater awareness of revitalizing the Hawaiian language and culture. After almost a century of being excluded as a school language, the Pūnana Leo preschools were set up as part of a last-ditch effort to save the Hawaiian language.

'Aha Pūnana Leo (the organization that founded the language nest preschools) was established in 1983. Since its formation 'Aha Pūnana Leo has been a key force in changing legislation in Hawai'i, and also at the federal level. In 1986, the Hawai'i state legislature removed a ban that had been placed on Hawaiian-medium education in 1896, three years after the overthrow of the monarchy.

Schools have been a powerful tool in systematizing the use of the language. It started with the preschools, and then at each level the parents and families fought to create another grade level. There was an urgency—with the elders passing on—and we're lucky that, at that time, there were still native speakers living who helped develop the preschools. The result of that struggle is that now, from infancy all the way up to the doctorate level, you can be educated in Hawaiian.

The preschool's curriculum intertwined language, culture, and academic areas. The school kind of woke everybody up to the importance of Hawaiian language, especially native Hawaiians—we began to realize that the knowledge of our ancestors, the knowledge of our families, is still very important for our future. In Western education, we place all this emphasis on looking for knowledge elsewhere, outside of your family, outside of your community. But creating Hawaiian language schools helped us understand that knowledge we take from our ancestors, from our families, from the land that we come from is important as an academic subject area. And if we have that as a foundation, we will be able to seek out information from other areas, from other people, from other cultures.

GCG: How many Hawaiian-medium schools are there today?

KH: There are 21 public Hawaiian immersion schools in the state. Some of the schools exist within a larger English-speaking school.

GCG: Could you tell me a little bit more about the school that your children attend?

KH: The Hawaiian language program goes from infancy all the way to 12th grade. All instruction is in Hawaiian, with the exception of Japanese as a subject area from 1st to 6th grade and English from 6th to 12th. We have students from all different ethnicities; it's not only native Hawaiian students who are interested in the program. As we move to strengthen our school, the hope is that everyone—from the janitors and office staff to all the teachers—will speak only Hawaiian on this campus. That's the goal for what we call Hawaiian-medium education: Every activity on the campus is conducted in Hawaiian. Of course, it's quite a challenge to make sure that you have sufficient staff that speaks Hawaiian.

GCG: How does the school deal with the issue of staffing, both in terms of hiring teachers and the kind of support staff that you mention?

KH: It is sometimes challenging to find qualified Indigenous teachers who are skilled in a specialized academic area and fluent in the Hawaiian language. We currently have faculty and staff members who do not speak Hawaiian, although the majority of those employed by the school are highly fluent. It's a challenge. There's an understanding that faculty cannot stay in their positions without learning the language. A lot of our office and grounds staff are conversational Hawaiian speakers. But the beauty of it is that we have a lot of parents who went through the Indigenous teacher certification program. They teach at the school and their children go through the school. There is also a culture of understanding that Hawaiian is the language of the school and everyone needs to contribute to its survival and perpetuation.

GCG: Tell me a little bit about the Indigenous teacher certification program.

KH: It's a specialized program through Ka Haka ʻUla o Keʻelikōlani College of Hawaiian Language at the University of Hawaiʻi at Hilo that was established in 1997. The program is different from the traditional teacher education program of the university in that it's conducted in Hawaiian and uses Indigenous pedagogies and methodologies.

GCG: Can you give me an example of what Indigenous pedagogies might look like with children?

KH: When we look at Indigenous methods of teaching for Hawaiian children, especially at the kindergarten level, the first skill that the child needs to be able to learn is to observe, hoʻolohe (listen), shut the mouth, and hoʻolohe lawena (control his or her behaviors) so that the child can learn. The idea in Western education is often that the child needs to be able to talk all the time and ask questions, which sometimes is very different from our Indigenous way of thinking and imparting information on a child.

Our actions need to align with the language of instruction that we are using. Much of the Hawaiian pedagogy is coded in the language. Continual strengthening of the language skills of teachers is key to holding on to this Indigenous way of thinking. On a systematic level, this comes in the form of weekly staff meetings conducted in Hawaiian. As we identify issues that embody a Western style or foreign style of learning, it is important to discuss them together to affirm the Indigenous perspective through the language.

My wife teaches mathematics in Hawaiian from an Indigenous perspective, and works to connect Indigenous knowledge with traditional knowledge. For example, students can look at our taro fields and see the function of math in daily life. They can measure how many taro plants you can plant within a particular area. Our kūpuna, our elders, used math in many different ways for their livelihood. We can also use the concept of ratio and proportion to decide how much greenery is necessary to make a lei, thereby honoring the Hawaiian value of mālama ʻāina, or taking care of the land and not wasting or taking more than is necessary. It's powerful for students to make the connection that mathematical knowledge was very important to our elders, even before math was seen as an academic subject.

Another example of how cultural practices inform pedagogical practices is the syllabic reading method used at the early elementary level. This method is based on a cultural practice of learning to read that comes from the 19th century. So, as parents, we see that there is this connection to the way in which Hawaiians learned to read more than 100 years ago, and the way that our children started learning in the Pūnana Leo and in 1st grade. It's something that our elders did that's still used today.

GCG: What is at stake with the revitalization of Hawaiian, for you personally and for the Hawaiian people?

KH: Language is what binds all aspects of our culture. Without the language we miss a major connection to our *kūpuna*, to our elders, and to the land that we live on here. We miss a crucial link to understanding our landscape, where we come from, and who we are. We're fighting to validate Indigenous knowledge today. We're fighting to help people see how important it is.

GCG: Do you encounter resistance to the emphasis on Hawaiian language in the immersion schools?

KH: Hawaiian-medium education is a lot more popular today than it was in the early '80s, or when many of the native speakers were passing away at the end of the '70s. But even within our own families and our native Hawaiian community, people have doubts about the importance of this work.

Some parents are worried their children won't learn to read and write in English because of the immersion model. Our school focuses on exclusive Hawaiian language instruction up to 6th grade, because, for most of our families, school is the only environment where they are exposed to Hawaiian. Although there are families with one or two parents who speak Hawaiian, like ours, most of the children come from families with English-speaking backgrounds.

> To have this understanding, to have this connection to the land, to know where you live, and to know the language of Hawai'i—that is unique.

We didn't speak English to our daughter at home, but she was exposed to English literacy in other ways, outside of the school environment. We'd watch movies in English and sometimes we'd read books in English. Also, most of our relatives only speak English. When we were driving, she would see signs in English and would try and sound them out. Even though our daughter was immersed in Hawaiian at home and at school, she was able to read English by the time she reached the 4th grade, despite never having been formally instructed. I think sometimes we fail to acknowledge the power of English as a dominant language and the organic development of English literacy.

When I talk with people who doubt the program, I emphasize how this type of education connects your child to this place, to Hawai'i . To have this understanding, to have this connection to the land, to know where you live, and to know the language of Hawai'i—that is unique. And the confidence that comes from that, from knowing who you are, where you come from, where you were raised—those are things that you hold on to for your whole life.

And you can see how Hawaiian immersion benefits our students. Since 1999, there has been a 100 percent graduation rate and 95 percent of the graduates have been going into postsecondary education.

GCG: Has there been resistance to the standardized tests that are being used to evaluate schools?

KH: About 90 percent of students and their families protested taking the Hawai'i state assessment because English isn't even introduced until the 6th grade. It isn't fair to students and their families to subject them to a test that does not measure, and is not even written, in the language they're instructed in. It's important to be sure that the test content also reflects what's being taught. Philosophically, it's just wrong—to be tested on something when you're not instructed in that language.

GCG: What is the role of the home in maintaining the Hawaiian language?

KH: We believe, even from the Pūnana Leo level, the language nest level, that if we can't take the language back into the home, the language cannot live. That's at the core of this type of schooling. The hope is that our children are going to use the language within their own households one day.

It's not an easy thing. Neither my wife's nor my parents speak Hawaiian. We were both exposed to the Hawaiian language in high school, but it wasn't until our college years that we were able to become fluent because of the Hawaiian language community here in Hilo and because of employment opportunities at 'Aha Pūnana Leo and Nāwahī where we were able to use the language.

> **The hope is that our children are going to use the language within their own households one day.**

A few years ago, I participated in a swim on the other side of the island, and my wife and I were pretty shocked when our youngest daughter and our son asked us, "Why is everyone here speaking English?" Of course, now that they're getting older and playing sports with English-speaking friends and teammates, they realize that there is a different world outside of this Hawaiian-medium education world.

From an early age, my children have had a strong belief that this is *our* language, and I don't think my wife and I could have foreseen that. That's the kind of impact we're making on our children. They know this is a language we can use anywhere to speak to each other, and our language will continue to live by what we do.

But we haven't experienced the high school years yet. We've heard they may have a little rebellion in them, as teenagers do, but in the end they come back to you.

GCG: What would you say has been the biggest challenge so far in raising your kids in Hawaiian?

KH: I think, especially as educators, it's realizing that this system isn't perfect. And we're not perfect either. As a family, as parents, and as educators, we need to play a role in understanding some of the flaws this system has. And we need to work together, without getting frustrated or irritated or giving in to disappointment. We can't give up.

During our firstborn daughter's preschool years, Pele and I were pretty frustrated with the rigor of the preschool level; we were frustrated by the lack of structure. We had to take that role as parents and understand that when you bring up an issue, especially in this type of education, we're all in this together. It's one thing to complain about it, to feel that it's not really up to par, but it's another to get involved. We ended up joining committees to look at ways in which we could make this better with some of the other

> **You've got to get involved, you've got to play a part in making it better if you see something that needs improvement.**

educators and the administrative staff of the preschool. It was an opportunity for us, as parents, to learn how this should be done, rather than just sitting on the side and complaining about it.

We've recognized throughout the years that that's really how you go about making an impact as a family within this type of educational system. You've got to get involved, you've got to play a part in making it better if you see something that needs improvement. We need families like that. Even with our daughter entering 10th grade this fall, we realize there may be things about high school that we didn't know about. But that same way that we got involved when she started preschool, that may be the same way we have to participate and play a part in making it stronger at the high school level.

GCG: What do you think the biggest rewards have been so far in raising your children in this way?

KH: The biggest reward has been the relationships that we've had with so many people that have been a part of this type of education. I don't think I would have experienced this anyplace else—to be a part of a unified effort with our family and children. Some of the children have grown up with our children, and really, in so many ways, they're like our own. We're all part of this movement together.

We used to sometimes get questioned in a sort of condescending way when the kids were younger: "What good is knowing Hawaiian going to be for your kids?" Now people don't stop and stare as much when we cheer for our kids in Hawaiian at a volleyball game or converse at the supermarket. Instead, we experience overwhelming support and a lot of questions about when school registration opens up.

These are questions that bring me joy because it means that people are seeing something—in our family, in our schools and community—that they want to be a part of and support. ☼

Kekoa L. Harman is an associate professor at Ka Haka ʻUla O Keʻelikōlani College of Hawaiian Language at the University of Hawaiʻi at Hilo. He has taught from the infant level at the Pūnana Leo (language nest) up to the collegiate level in Hawaiian-medium education.

Grace Cornell Gonzales is an editor for Rethinking Schools and has worked for nine years as a bilingual elementary teacher in California and Guatemala City.

Chapter 6

POLICY AND ADVOCACY

RICARDO LEVINS MORALES

Introduction

In the deepest reaches of my brain, there is a boy who speaks Spanish.

He calls his mother and father "*Mamá*" and "*Papá*." One of his favorite expressions is "*qué lindo*" (how nice, or how sweet). He's proud of the Mexican slang he's learned: for instance, "*no hay pedo,*" which means "no problem," though its literal translation is "there is no fart."

California nearly killed that boy.

T his is how Héctor Tobar begins his op-ed for the *New York Times*, "The Spanish Lesson I Never Got at School," where he reflects on what it meant for him to grow up as the child of Guatemalan immigrants in California at a time when quality bilingual education was not available to him. "Like millions of Latino kids educated in California public schools, I never took a class in Spanish grammar or Spanish literature, nor was I ever asked to write a single word with an accent or a squiggly tilde over it." He knew he had lost something priceless when he realized he was losing his Spanish. He also describes the wave of English-only legislation in the late 1990s and early 2000s—which essentially guaranteed that more children would be cut off from their home languages—as a "form of cultural erasure" and a "cruel, shortsighted act, born of ignorance and intolerance."

His story reminds us how personal policy is, and how deeply our own histories intertwine with larger histories of struggle, litigation, legislation, repression, loss, and triumph. The articles in this chapter seek to give a window into some of the history of bilingual education—from local activists in Milwaukee fighting for maintenance bilingual programs to student teachers in California uncovering the ways their own K–12 educations were shaped by Proposition 227.

Today bilingual programs around the country face many types of adversity, often much more subtle than English-only legislation. Schools and teachers are under tremendous pressure to focus on standards that make no mention of bilingualism and thus push programs toward English-only instruction. High-stakes standardized testing undermines the integrity of bilingual programs by forcing teachers to teach more English, sooner. From Connecticut to California, we see bilingual programs face obstacles ranging from school closures and intolerant leadership, to local adversity and district inaction.

Salvador Gabaldón sums up the resistance to bilingual education succinctly:

> To learn more than one language, to gain a broad understanding of history, to study about other cultures and more deeply understand

our own: Who could find fault in that kind of curriculum? "*Solo los ignorantes*," my mother might say. Only the ignorant.

Whether attacks on bilingual education occur because of ignorance, intolerance, or xenophobia, the authors in this chapter remind us to stand up and speak out. ☀

Are *You* a Subject or an Object?

BY CARLOS LENKERSDORF

Excerpted by Norm Diamond with introduction by Bill Bigelow

MICHAEL DUFFY

Introduction

The war against the world's Indigenous peoples has been long-standing. In our hemisphere, it began when Columbus arrived in 1492, and "discovered" the Taínos, declaring on his third day in the Americas that "with 50 men we could subjugate them all and make them do whatever we want." He also wrote that he would bring some Taínos back to Spain so that they could "learn to talk." Of course, the Taínos could already talk, but he needed them to know the language in which he could issue commands, and have those commands passed along to others.

The Taíno language now remains mostly in single words, like *huracán*, hurricane; *amaca*, hammock; and *barbicú*, barbecue. Columbus' policies toward the Taínos were genocidal—a fact admitted even by his affectionate biographer Samuel Eliot Morison. Countless Taínos lost their lives; the world lost the Taínos' language.

These days, the war against Indigenous peoples continues. One manifestation of this war is climate change. The so-called developed world has filled the atmosphere with heat-trapping gases, putting at risk the homes of Indigenous people from Pacific islands like Kiribati and Tuvalu to communities from Bolivia to Louisiana to sub-Saharan Africa. And like Columbus' war on the Taínos, this war is not only a war against the homes and bodies of Indigenous peoples, but also their languages—languages with root metaphors profoundly different from Western languages. When climate change displaces and disperses Indigenous peoples from their lands, it endangers the integrity and future of their languages.

Too often, languages are regarded merely as collections of words. But languages embed a worldview, as Norm Diamond—drawing on the work of his friend Carlos Lenkersdorf—describes in this article about the Tojolabal language of Chiapas, Mexico. For the Tojolabales, everyone and everything is a subject, acting on and with other subjects. So the Earth, animals, and plants all have agency. Nothing is merely "done to." If a language encodes this kind of mutuality and equality, its implications extend beyond a cultural group's view of humanity. When all life is interrelated, the Earth is more than inert stuff, more than a "natural resource." It's more difficult to commodify something that your language invests with consciousness. So when we lose a language, we may be losing the kind of worldview that is essential for the survival of humanity.

—Bill Bigelow, *curriculum editor of* Rethinking Schools *magazine, co-director of the Zinn Education Project, co-editor of* A People's Curriculum for the Earth: Teaching Climate Change and the Environmental Crisis.

Are *You* a Subject or an Object?

(1) You [created an experience where] I loved.
(2) You [created an experience where] I saw.
(3) I spoke. You heard.

Before you read any further—who is the subject of the sentences above? Who is the object?

Answer: There are two subjects to each of these sentences—and no object. Everyone is an active participant. These are just a few sentences translated from the language of the Tojolabal people who live in the southeastern part of the Mexican state of Chiapas, near the Guatemalan border. They are descendants of the Maya civilization of Central America. Their territory includes forests, valleys, and mountainous highlands. Some of the settlements require a full day's difficult hike from the point where the rutted dirt roads give out.

How would we make these same statements in English? Or in any other Indo-European language? What does this tell us about the different ways in which we view the world? The grammatical structure of the Indo-European languages shows us a divided world. Some people are subjects. They are the ones who rule, plan, and make the decisions. Others are objects. Their lives are planned for them. It is not up to them to make decisions, because the subjects make their decisions for them, without asking their opinion.

We can study language to see how people relate to each other, to nature, and to the larger society. The Tojolabal language is a living connection to the pre-Columbian way of thinking. In this Mayan language, as in others of this language family, there are no objects; rather there are two classes of subjects.

Let's analyze the three sample sentences. In sentences (1) and (2), we have two subjects: you and I. We notice that the *you* is creating or has an experience equal to the actions or emotions achieved by the *I*. That is why we can say that these sentences have two subjects.

The Tojolabales do not view personal relationships to be situations where someone takes action toward or for a passive recipient. Quite the contrary: Experiences and perception cause the Tojolabal to speak of two participants coming together to achieve their purpose or participate in some event.

In sentence (3), the structure is different. Two subjects join to create a single event composed of two actions. In Spanish or any other Indo-European language, only one action is mentioned: "I told you." We can expand the sentence to make it more complete—for example, "I told you the word." The expanded sentence corresponds to the Tojolabal phrase: "The word created an experience where I was speaking and also an experience where you were hearing."

All these examples suggest something that is as typical and fundamental to the behavior of the Tojolabales as it is to their language. This is their way of understanding and dealing with reality, which may be summed up as: "No person or thing is an object, because we are all subjects." In the Tojolabal language, we and the world around us are all subjects, related and not isolated. From this, we can see why the Tojolabal people insist that we are all equals and we are all interrelated. We don't act alone—we interact in a mutual relationship.

On a philosophical level then, the Tojolabal believe that we live in a world that is not simply a product of our making, nor of our collaboration. Instead it is that totality of our interrelationships that makes possible our actions. We are all children of this whole; part of the total cosmic dimension that gives us life and sustains us. ☼

Note from the editors: This article excerpt—based on the studies of Carlos Lenkersdorf, who lived among the Tojolabales for more than 20 years—was published in *Rediscovering America/Redescubriendo América* (Teaching for Change, 1992). It was originally excerpted by Norm Diamond from Lenkersdorf, Carlos. 1992. "El Quinto Centenario de Ignorancia" (The Fifth Century of Ignorance). Centro de Estudios Ecuménicos. Translation by Dave Edelstein.

Reflecting on My Mother's Spanish

BY SALVADOR GABALDÓN

MELANIE CERVANTES

My mother, a gifted storyteller, nourished a love of language in all her children. Even before we began school, she would read to us from the Spanish translations of such classic works as Jules Verne's *Twenty Thousand Leagues Under the Sea* and Victor Hugo's *The Hunchback of Notre-Dame*. Mexican music from the radio filled our house in Los Angeles, and my mother taught us to hear the words as well as the melody. She managed to stretch my father's small paycheck to include a daily Spanish-language newspaper and a subscription to a children's magazine. Books from the local library filled our home, and she corrected the Spanish we used in writing letters to our family in Chihuahua. With the wisdom of a young mother, she realized that the foundation of a good education is a love of language.

Knowing the importance of English in the United States, she made sure we would learn it. Her contribution to that end was to enroll us in the local public school while also giving us an appreciation for the language she knew best and for the culture of her native land—Mexico. She expected us to be proud of our Mexican heritage: We were not Spanish. Though she studied English along with us, she had the good sense to realize that literacy is a skill that crosses language barriers. She realized that by enriching our minds with literacy in one language, we'd be better prepared for a second.

Perhaps inevitably, all five of her children became bilingual and several of us went on to work in education. As teachers in our nation's public schools, we saw the evidence for interlanguage literacy again and again: Students who were strong readers in their native language invariably became strong readers in English. Literacy in two languages is a treasure. If more politicians had the good sense to realize this, our schools would be better off.

But, around the turn of this century, Spanish seemed a convenient scapegoat, blamed for the educational struggles of the children of immigrants. The logic behind Proposition 227 in California, Proposition 203 in Arizona, and Question 2 in Massachusetts was simple: If we could rid our schools of Spanish, then all children would acquire English "in a period not normally intended to exceed one year."

The reality turned out to be something very different. California launched its experiment with English immersion in 1998. In the first few years after their immersion programs began, school officials bragged about test score improvements. They insisted that immersion programs were working, and that children were acquiring English with amazing speed. Then, slowly, the exuberant reports from California began to fade away.

The results were exactly what specialists in language acquisition had been saying all along. "English in one year" is a fantasy. Unfortunately, by promoting harsh English-only policies, many states continue to squander the valuable linguistic and cultural contributions that ethnically diverse groups of students can provide.

And now, my own state of Arizona has gone to great lengths to devalue its rich multicultural heritage, even instituting a law intended to criminalize the teaching of ethnic studies classes in our public schools. Elected officials have openly declared that such classes are seditious. They warn against the dangers of Mexican American novels, the threat of African American poetry, the menace of inclusive historical accounts. They root out song lyrics and passages taken out of context from supplementary materials as proof of a conspiracy to indoctrinate students with an Anglophobic ideology.

Is this country's Anglo-Saxon and Eurocentric heritage so fragile that it might be weakened by a deeper examination of other cultural influences? We do our students a great disservice by denying them information about our nation's multicultural roots. After all, in the Southwest, people of African and Mexican descent lived, worked, and died on this land for centuries, long before the first English speakers arrived. And our schools have always taught courses focused on particular cultures, traditionally including French language classes, Greek and Roman history, and British literature. Ethnic studies courses add immeasurably to those options.

To learn more than one language, to gain a broad understanding of history, to study about other cultures and more deeply understand our own: Who could find fault in that kind of curriculum? "*Solo los ignorantes,*" my mother might say. Only the ignorant. ☼

Salvador Gabaldón has served in a number of positions in the Tucson Unified School District and currently provides inservice support to teachers as part of the Department of Culturally Relevant Pedagogy and Instruction.

Note from the editors: This article was adapted from a previously published piece by Salvador Gabaldón, "My Mother's Spanish" (*Rethinking Schools* magazine, Winter 2004/2005).

The Struggle for Bilingual Education

An interview with bilingual education advocate Tony Báez

BY BOB PETERSON

Tony Báez at the "Fulfill the Promise" march in Milwaukee.

SUSAN RUGGLES

Dr. Tony Báez is a longtime teacher, organizer, administrator, and advocate for bilingual education. When he was a child, his parents moved regularly between New York City and Puerto Rico as migrant garment workers. After 6th grade, he remained in Puerto Rico until his early 20s, when he moved to the United States and became involved in political movements in the Chicago and Milwaukee areas. Over several decades, Báez has worked as a community organizer, expert on bilingual education litigation, university instructor, and high school principal. He has also served as vice president of the Milwaukee Area Technical College and as executive director of Centro Hispano Milwaukee. In the following interview by Rethinking Schools editor Bob Peterson, Báez talks about the history and current state of bilingual education, and describes how parents and educators successfully fought for a maintenance K–12 bilingual program in the Milwaukee Public Schools.

Bob Peterson: How did bilingual education start in the United States?

Tony Báez: In modern times it started in the 1960s, as people in the Southwest of the United States and Cuban immigrants in Miami pushed for bilingual education to retain their home languages and improve the academic situation for their children. It emerged in the midst of the Civil Rights Movement. These were communities in battle, communities fighting for improvements in services. For example, in New York City, there was the community control movement. Evelina López Antonetty, a parent leader who was involved in improving schools, gradually began talking about bilingual education and about creating parent universities to prepare families to fight for bilingual education. Chicano leaders like Rodolfo "Corky" Gonzales in Colorado connected Latino and Chicano cultures to the notion that bilingual/bicultural education is something we all deserve.

It wasn't only people in the streets demanding bilingual education from school systems and elected officials. Litigation on language issues goes back to the 1940s. The push for bilingual education at the local level encouraged organizing at the national level as well. This led to Congress adding Title VII to the Elementary and Secondary Education Act (ESEA) when it was reauthorized in 1967. Title VII became known as the Bilingual Education Act of 1968 when President Johnson signed it in January of that year; it recognized multicultural education and bilingual education, and led to instructional programs that helped students whose home language was not English. But it was permissive, not mandatory. That meant that if you could get people together to write a proposal to the federal government and get a school district to submit it, you could draw on a little pot of money. Many of the communities fighting for bilingual education were not satisfied with the permissive nature of the legislation. People kept on organizing, and a lot of new litigation emerged between 1968 and 1974.

BP: How did that litigation affect the course of bilingual education?

TB: The case *United States v. State of Texas* in San Felipe in 1970–1971 was groundbreaking. Judge William Wayne Justice ordered that two segregated districts be integrated. It's an amazing case in which the judge mandated bilingual education and adequate bilingual staffing. He basically said that this country had to recognize the growth of the population that speaks a language other than English, and that it behooves us to learn their language.

However, the 1974 U.S. Supreme Court *Lau v. Nichols* decision, which dealt with Chinese students in San Francisco, brought that all down. Although it defended the civil right of national-origin minority students to not be discriminated against because of their language, the suggested remedies were transitional—ESL classes or transitional bilingual education classes that moved children into all-English classes as soon as possible. This ruling became a precedent. The *Lau* lawyers didn't insist on real bilingual education as a remedy, even though this was what parents and communities all over this country were asking for. By real, I mean "developmental" or what some call "maintenance" bilingual programs. The goal should be for children to maintain and develop their home language and build on their skills in their first language to learn English. In fact, research shows if students are strong in their home language, they will more rapidly learn a second language.

In another way, *Lau* was not really a good decision for us because it put the brakes on movements that combined community organizing and litigation. It was also near the end of the Civil Rights Movement and people were getting tired. This included lawyers, particularly those arguing for cases in court; they'd go to communities and say, "Look, after *Lau* you can't win. You have to accept on precedent."

That's what happened in New York City with one of the most important cases, *Aspira v. the New York Board of Education*. My colleague Ricardo Fernandez and I had discussions with the lawyers and told them it was crazy to accept a transitional bilingual program. Sure, it was better than monolingual classrooms, but the lawyers represented 250,000 kids and should have demanded more. They said they had to accept the transitional program because the Supreme Court had spoken [*Lau v. Nichols*]. That deflated community efforts to organize for more robust bilingual programs.

After the 1974 *Lau* decision, the struggle for bilingual education was reduced to promoting transitional programs in most places. Latino communities had been driving the struggle for bilingual education up until then. After *Lau*, school districts were usually the ones making the decisions. Cities like Chicago that were in the midst of discussions or litigation accepted transitional bilingual education as a remedy.

There were many other things going on at that time—issues of unemployment and access to housing, community services, healthcare—so community organizers said, "OK, this is the best we are going to get for education."

BP: In that climate, how were the Latino community and its allies in Milwaukee able to win a maintenance (developmental) bilingual program?

TB: People organized. In the late 1960s, Latino parents whose kids were "graduating" from a Spanish-language Head Start Center on Milwaukee's near south side were concerned about where their children would go to school. They worked with teacher Olga Schwartz—who, a few years later, became director of bilingual education in the district—and applied for a federal grant from the Bilingual Education Act; it was funded.

That started bilingual programs at Vieau Elementary, Kosciuszko Middle School, and South Division High School in 1969. But Olga also recognized that the grant would end. She went to the parents and said, "We have a problem here. What if we write for another grant and we don't get it?" So we all got involved in committees and started organizing. Parents at Vieau School, under the leadership of Mercedes Rivas, organized the Citywide Bilingual Bicultural Advisory Committee.

The committee decided that the best way to secure the program was to get the school board to assume funding. The parents were against the compromise of a transitional program, and decided to fight for a developmental program with bilingual classes from kindergarten through high school.

BP: How did you organize?

TB: The committee held a parent meeting and a community meeting, and then we went to the school board en masse in 1972. After a couple of years, we worked out an agreement with the Milwaukee Public Schools (MPS). It wasn't easy. This all happened about the same time as the *Lau* decision, so some administrators argued that the MPS program should be transitional. We went before the school board and made the case that they should embrace language instruction differently from how people were doing it all over the country, and support developmental programs. Privately, we told them, "We don't want to sue you, and we won't if you give us bilingual education that allows our children to maintain our language."

I was involved in organizing students to support bilingual education at that time. Actually, most of the concerns of parents and students at the high school level were about excessive suspensions of Latino kids, to the point that we had to create alternative schools for the dropouts. We told the school officials, "You could change the high push-out rate if you develop the capacity to deliver good bilingual programs at the high school level—not only at the elementary level." And they said, "We don't have the resources." So we helped students organize walkouts at South Division, Lincoln, and Riverside high schools.

> It wasn't just about language, but about helping Latino students develop a positive identity for themselves.

The Citywide Bilingual Bicultural Advisory Committee demanded any agreement with the school board be put in writing. An agreement was finalized in 1974 that called for increasing bilingual programs and implementing culturally relevant curriculum that respected the language and culture of students. It was intended to reduce the push-out factor in high schools. It wasn't just about language, but about helping Latino students develop a positive identity for themselves.

BP: What about organizing on the state level?

TB: We mobilized and got the first bilingual act passed in 1975 in Wisconsin. That act funded the maintenance programs, but subsequent amendments to the act created transitional programs, where students were expected to "exit" the program once they became "proficient" in English. This was a problem, but we were at least able to solve it in Milwaukee. Even though kids were officially "exited" from the program, they would continue in the maintenance bilingual program unless the parent said, "Take them out." So the MPS bilingual program remained a maintenance one; that helped us down the line. Many of the people working in bilingual education today in Milwaukee—teachers, principals, and other administrators—went through the Milwaukee bilingual program. Because of that, they are bilingual.

BP: How did the struggle for bilingual education in Milwaukee relate to the struggle for ethnic studies?

TB: In 1969, the same year the bilingual program started in MPS, there was a protest at the University of Wisconsin–Milwaukee (UWM) over treatment of Latinos. In

November 1970, Latino student leaders took over the chancellor's office and refused to leave. They weren't demanding bilingual education, but rather ethnic studies classes and a Latino student center. Some of the same people involved in that struggle also fought beside the parent activists in the community for bilingual programs. In 1970, the Spanish Speaking Outreach Institute at UWM was founded. One of the actions of that center was to increase the number of ESL classes at UWM (and simultaneously at Milwaukee Area Technical College), with the hopes of raising the enrollment of Latino students.

BP: Returning to the national scene, presently there is a rapid expansion of dual-language bilingual programs in which native English speakers and native Spanish speakers learn in the same classrooms. What do you think of those programs?

TB: The dual-language programs are a "growing up" of what we had before. With the large increase in the Spanish-speaking populations in the United States and the growth of movements for immigrant rights, people have started once again to more forcefully argue for maintaining their native languages. In some communities where bilingual programs have, in the past, been politically untenable, dual-language programs are a way to make sure children have access to a developmental program. In other places, such programs draw support and interest from families of all races who don't speak the language that is the focus of the program.

> **Dual-language programs have the effect of getting people engaged in transforming public education together.**

The schools go by a variety of names—dual language, two-way bilingual, dual immersion. Different names, but the same goal: biliteracy and bilingualism, not the swift transition of language learners into all-English classes. La Escuela Fratney in Milwaukee is a good example of such a school, even though at the same time we have long-standing developmental bilingual education programs here as well.

Many advocates of bilingual education go the route of dual-language programs because then we are not fighting white parents; we are uniting with them to get what we need. We are bringing white parents and people of privilege into the process to recognize and fight for bilingualism for everybody.

It brings other communities in as well—in some communities in Texas, for example, the Black and Latino parents work closely together because of the dual-language programs. In Miami, North Carolina, New York, New Jersey, and Massachusetts, too. Parents from different ethnic backgrounds talk to each other; they participate together in committees and councils. Dual-language programs have the effect of getting people engaged in transforming public education together.

BP: Why is it important for a teacher who believes in social justice to promote bilingual education?

TB: Teaching a language well requires that teachers build a certain level of multiculturalism, tolerance, and connection to the world, to another part of humanity. Paulo Freire argued that a key to education is to listen and learn from the learner—that means their language. His theories and work showed that an education leading toward peace and humanity is an education that values the language and ethnicity of a child.

BP: What does the future hold for bilingual education? What are some of the challenges?

TB: Bilingual education is on the rise. In 2000, the U.S. Department of Education estimated there were around 260 dual-language schools in the nation and called for an increase. Now some estimates put the number at over 2,000, almost a tenfold increase. What we need for people in the United States to recognize is that learning a second language should be part of what constitutes quality education in this country. We need to keep increasing the number of dual-language schools.

We also need to promote the preservation of Indigenous languages—and one of the best ways to do that is through quality bilingual programs.

There are serious challenges, such as finding enough qualified and fully bilingual teachers. We also need to figure out appropriate forms of assessment for bilingual programs, and fight against the over-testing that is hurting all kids. And, in the United States, we need to teach children not only to speak more than one language, but also to do so with a certain humanity. A good school instills in kids the sense that we are not the policemen of the world and that it's not good to exert the arrogance of power. Rather we are joining with people around the world through learning their languages; as we do so, we can come together to deal with our planet's serious problems. ☼

Tony Báez is a longtime community organizer, scholar, and advocate for bilingual education. He is a former university instructor and high school principal, and has served as vice president of the Milwaukee Area Technical College and executive director of Centro Hispano Milwaukee.

Bob Peterson (bob.e.peterson@gmail.com) is a founding editor of Rethinking Schools and a founder of La Escuela Fratney. He taught 5th grade for 30 years in the Milwaukee Public Schools and served four years as president of the Milwaukee Teachers' Education Association.

English-Only to the Core

What the Common Core means for emergent bilingual youth

BY JEFF BALE

Among bilingual educators, there has been much debate about the Common Core State Standards (CCSS). Some of the most respected scholars of bilingual education have endorsed the Common Core and are working hard to make it relevant for English learners. Others have been more suspicious. Not only do the standards focus on English-only, critics note, but they were bankrolled by the Gates Foundation, pushed on states in a way that amounts to bribery by the Obama administration, and promise to worsen the impact of high-stakes standardized testing.

In fact, the genesis of the Common Core stands in direct contrast to how bilingual education programs were won, namely through grassroots, explicitly anti-racist organizing by students, parents, teachers, and community allies. The standards thus raise a key question: Given the history of bilingual education programs in the United States, is it possible to expand social justice for emergent bilingual youth through the Common Core?

Addressing that question has been challenging, given the inconsistent responses of professional and civil rights organizations to the standards. The National Association for Bilingual Education (NABE) issued a position statement in January 2013 with mixed messages. Although NABE's membership passed a resolution opposing the Common Core, the statement explains that the group is "working collaboratively with policymakers, school administrators, and teachers" to ensure that implementing the Common Core does not negatively impact English learners. The TESOL (Teachers of English to Speakers of Other Languages) International Association issued a policy brief endorsing the standards.

Civil rights organizations—including the Mexican American Legal Defense and Education Fund (MALDEF), the National Council of La Raza (NCLR), and the National Association for the Advancement of Colored People (NAACP)—have endorsed the standards while calling for equitable implementation. The NCLR, for example, has used Gates Foundation money to apply the standards to English-language education and to develop tool kits supporting parent advocacy on behalf of the Common Core. The League of United Latin American Citizens (LULAC) posted resources on its website to help parents make sense of the Common Core.

However, the Common Core isn't just a set of standards. Instead, new standardized tests accompanying the standards promise to deepen the impact of high-stakes accountability measures in place since No Child Left Behind (NCLB) took effect in 2002. On this count, civil rights organizations have wavered. In October 2014, MALDEF and LULAC joined nine other civil rights organizations in issuing a letter to President Obama protesting the negative impact of high-stakes testing, and calling for more equitable resources and multiple measures (i.e., not just test scores) to define accountability. This letter clearly fit the mood of growing resistance by students, parents, and teachers to high-stakes testing. And yet, not three months later, many of these same organizations issued a letter to Arne Duncan endorsing the practice of annual, high-stakes standardized testing.

Their stance is significant, if unfortunate: When NCLB was first proposed, support from leading civil rights organizations gave enormous political cover to its high-stakes testing policies. The main argument was that accountability measures would "shine a light" on how poorly many schools were educating youth of color, including emergent bilinguals, and thus lead to positive change. Fifteen years later, we know how misguided that hope was. As Wayne Au has argued in *Unequal by Design: High-Stakes Testing and the Standardization of Inequality*, and as the many contributors to *More Than a Score: The New Uprising Against High-Stakes Testing* have documented, high-stakes testing has had a devastating effect on many schools, but especially on schools that primarily serve Black and Brown youth. And yet, mainstream civil rights organizations continue to pursue this strategy for education reform.

If the response to the Common Core by scholars, professional organizations, and civil rights groups has been inconsistent, then it is no wonder that bilingual educators and teachers of English learners have struggled to make sense of the standards. If the standards can't just be adopted, is there a way to adapt them and make them relevant for English learners? Is it enough to create a bilingual Common Core, that is, to translate the standards to guide bilingual instruction of language arts and math? If not, then what is the alternative?

To help address these questions, this article looks at CCSS in three ways: against the backdrop of the history of bilingual education and anti-racist struggle, on their own terms, and in light of the current status of bilingual education. Each perspective suggests that the Common Core will further erode bilingual education and linguistic justice in the United States.

A History of Successful Community Organizing

Usually, when the story of bilingual education in recent U.S. history is told, that story tends to focus on the actions of Important People like President Lyndon Johnson and Sen. Ralph Yarborough. The narrative tracks formal policy, including the Bilingual Education Act of 1968 and the *Lau v. Nichols* Supreme Court case in 1974 as key plot points.

However, this approach to history distorts as much as it reveals. Actually, it was the actions of Chicana/o, Puerto Rican, Native American, and Asian American activists in the 1960s and '70s that brought about bilingual education in the first place. As these activists focused on schools, they combated segregation and a lack of resources, and demanded bilingual and bicultural programming. They built strong social movements from the ground up, which compelled policymakers to heed their demands and either create or expand bilingual education. But the dominant historical perspective takes our attention away from grassroots activism and focuses instead on the actions of "key players" and/or policies.

It also reduces struggle to "advocacy." That is, it narrows the definition of political activism to lobbying this or that politician, or testifying before this or that committee. This sort of advocacy can matter, to be sure. But it takes place on terms set by those with power. The politicians in their offices and the committees in their hearing rooms are able to set the boundaries of the discussion and debate, while advocates are left to adapt to it or be shut out of the conversation altogether. What gives this sort of advocacy any real weight is whether students, teachers, parents, and community allies have built movements that are strong enough to change the terms of the conversation.

In fact, it was local struggles—often school by school and district by district, led by students in concert with parents, sometimes teachers and teacher organizations, and radicals—that provided the necessary momentum to make advocacy effective. Without the blowouts in East Los Angeles in 1968; without the student boycotts in Crystal City, Texas, in 1969; without the Third World student strike in San Francisco in 1968 (where the lawyers for the Lau family cut their political teeth), it is difficult to imagine bilingual education becoming formal policy at the district, state, or federal level.

Finally, the dominant approach to bilingual education history completely misidentifies the source of hostility to bilingualism and bilingual education from the 1980s on. It focuses, accurately, on the election of Ronald Reagan as a turning point, a moment when all the gains of the civil rights movements came under attack. The Reagan administration backtracked on the *Lau* remedies, a series of measures flowing from the 1974 Supreme Court case that strengthened bilingual education. There was also a concerted campaign to declare English the official language, federally and in several individual states. But when it comes to explaining why this conservative shift happened, the story runs into trouble—it lays the blame at the feet of the very civil rights activists who pushed for bilingual education in the first place. Their activism is described as too confrontational, the demands for meaningful bilingual education as too radical.

According to the terms of the dominant view of the history, which ignores or denigrates community demands and organizing, I guess it's logical to rely on official channels and Important People to reform schools. But the actual history of bilingual education in the United States suggests something quite different. It was the conscious, ambitious, and collective actions of anti-racist activists that brought real change to schools for emergent bilingual youth. The CCSS are neither the product of, nor will they contribute to, the creation of such movements.

Emergent Bilingual Education and the Common Core

Bilingual education scholars who support the Common Core, and even some who don't, have acknowledged the significant shift it represents in understanding the relationship between language and content. How language and content are connected has been an enduring dilemma for language educators.

One traditional, but prevalent, model claims that English learners must first "master" the language (i.e., use grammar and vocabulary accurately) before they can engage in meaningful, age- and grade-appropriate content. The most extreme version of this model is Structured English Immersion (SEI) in Arizona. In 2000, Arizona voters overwhelmingly passed Proposition 203. This measure not only severely restricted bilingual education, but also required the state to develop a new model of English-only education. The state responded with SEI. English learners are grouped by proficiency level—and segregated from their English-proficient peers—for up to four hours per day in English-language development classes. This model includes no content instruction or cultural components. Contrary to what some 40 years of applied linguistic research have taught us about language learning, SEI assumes that students can develop enough language "skills" to be successful in mainstream classes within one year.

> The Common Core amounts to another English-only policy.

This approach to language education is consistent with the twin logics of standardization and accountability that have deformed our schools. Skills and facts are broken down into discrete parts; it is assumed that these parts can be measured and that those measurements reflect real learning. Students are then "prepped" on those parts ad nauseum. Under the SEI model, student progress is tracked on what is called the Discrete Skills Inventory. This stranger-than-fiction document contains a series of tables that literally break down the English language into grammatical units. Teachers are then expected to use the inventory as a checklist to track student "mastery" of English: Student uses past tense of *to be* accurately—check! Student uses past negative of *to be* accurately—check! Student uses past simple negative accurately—check!

Other models have tried to unify language development and content knowledge in so-called sheltered environments. Here, academic language is scaffolded to facilitate student engagement with content. Prominent examples of this model include the Sheltered Instruction Observation Protocol, widely adopted by school districts across the country; the Specially Designed Academic Instruction in English model, first developed in California; and the Cognitive Academic Language Learning model. Although there is much value in these models, it is an ongoing challenge to prevent scaffolded or sheltered instruction from becoming watered-down instruction.

Part of the support for the Common Core among bilingual educators and teachers of English language learners (ELLs) is rooted in the potential they see in CCSS for moving away from these models toward an academically robust environment for emergent bilinguals. Scholars and practitioners working with the Understanding Language project at Stanford University have made this case most clearly. For them, the Common Core assumes that English learners can learn the language through rigorous content. The standards focus literacy instruction simultaneously on text (processing individual letters, words, etc.) and discourse (overall meaning). That is, it shifts literacy instruction away from mere decoding skills and instead gives English learners access to instruction using academic language for a variety of complex, critical tasks. Emergent bilinguals don't just learn about language through explicit instruction on grammar items or isolated vocabulary. Rather, they use language to engage academic content and to collaborate with others (with native-speaker, English-only, and multilingual peers, and with teachers who do and don't share their home language) on academic tasks. The math standards also support language development by focusing on the language of math, namely, the language of explanation, reasoning, and argumentation associated with mathematical functions. Finally, the standards reinforce the idea that every teacher is a language teacher, not just the ELL or bilingual ed specialist.

> **Bilingual education is above all a question of *politics*, not of *evidence*.**

This shift in orientation to the language-content connection reflects perspectives that many bilingual and English-language educators have long held. It is certainly refreshing to see these ideas taken up so broadly in policy briefs and curriculum guides. My sense is that for this reason alone many bilingual educators (practitioners and academics alike) have gotten on board with the Common Core.

However, the Common Core only makes this connection between language and content in English. The CCSS make no reference to linguistic diversity, to culture and its relationship to language, or to the linguistic and cultural resources that emergent bilinguals bring with them to the classroom. Worse still, the standards make no room for applying the language-content model to any language other than English.

The standards invoke all the opportunity represented in sociocultural approaches to language learning, only to foreclose on it by focusing on English only.

The authors of the Common Core do explicitly address English learners in a brief addendum to the standards, but the addendum is inconsistent in its perspective. On the one hand, it acknowledges the linguistic, cultural, economic, and academic diversity of emergent bilinguals and states clearly that these students are capable of engaging rigorous content. However, it uses a medical model for defining effective instruction as that which "diagnos[es] each student instructionally." It also labels students as *English learners* (i.e., defining them by what they do not yet know) rather than as the *emergent bilingual* youth they are. Moreover, the cultural knowledge that emergent bilingual students possess, and how teachers might leverage that knowledge, is left entirely unaddressed.

Most revealing, though, is how the addendum talks about students' home languages. In the very few instances where they are mentioned at all, home languages serve merely as tools for learning English and English language content. In the section on English language arts, for example, "first languages" are mentioned only as a resource to learn a second language more efficiently. In the section on mathematics, "all languages and language varieties" are identified as resources for learning about mathematical reasoning. But home languages are never described as worthy of further academic development themselves. This stance continues the long tradition in the United States, even within some bilingual education models, of using home languages just long enough to learn English, and then leaving them behind.

On their own terms, then, the CCSS amount to another English-only policy. This severely undermines whatever curricular or pedagogical advances they might contain.

Bilingual Education Under Attack

Of course, the Common Core does not exist in isolation from other education reforms. In fact, the standards are part of a doubling down on the test-and-punish approach to reform that has had disastrous consequences for all students, but especially for schools serving students of color and multilingual communities. In addition, the standards appear at a moment in which bilingual education has long been in decline as a legitimate model for emergent bilingual youth.

There are several factors that account for this decline. One is an open political assault on bilingual education that reached its highpoint at the turn of this century. Four state-level ballot initiatives attempted to restrict bilingual education; three of them (in California, Arizona, and Massachusetts) were successful. These initiatives were part of a larger wave of anti-immigrant racism that had grown significantly by the 1990s. At first, anti-immigrant activists focused on denying undocumented immigrants access to public services, as with Proposition 187 in California in 1994. Although voters approved that measure, it was overturned by a federal court. In some ways, measures like Prop. 187 were seen at the time as too radical. Anti-immigrant forces quickly regrouped and focused instead on attacking bilingual education. Here, they found greater success—and greater legitimacy for their ideas. Bilingual education has long been low-hanging political fruit for anti-immigrant racists (Bale, 2012).

Beyond these explicit attacks, shifts in education policy have further undermined bilingual education. Most significantly, NCLB abolished the Bilingual Education Act of 1968 and all mentions of bilingual education and bilingualism were replaced with English-only terminology. NCLB's high-stakes accountability measures have had direct and disastrous consequences for emergent bilingual youth. Kate Menken has documented this trend in two important studies in New York City public schools. Her work shows that the pressure exerted on schools to perform on high-stakes literacy exams in English has led to a significant decline in bilingual programs—even though both city and state policies still formally support bilingual education (Menken, 2008; Menken and Solorza, 2014).

One glimmer of hope in this otherwise dismal situation is the modest growth in dual-language programs. Different from compensatory bilingual education models, in which all students are English learners, dual-language programs have a more balanced mix of students. Some students are proficient speakers of English, and some are proficient speakers of the other language. This balance between speakers of dominant and minoritized languages is designed to build equity into dual-language programs: Each set of students acts as a linguistic and cultural resource for the other. However, language educators have long raised concerns that dual-language programs are often created either at the behest of or to attract (upper-) middle-class, white families and they tend to function more to the linguistic and academic benefit of English-speaking children. Language scholar Nelson Flores recently referred to this dynamic as "columbusing"—the "discovery" by white families of the benefits of bilingual education programs that in fact were fought for and won through the activism of communities of color.

The standards function as the culmination of more than a decade of attacks on bilingual programs and emergent bilingual youth.

Moreover, dual-language programs are not necessarily more exempt from racism than other bilingual programs. Consider the experience of the Khalil Gibran International Academy, an Arabic/English dual-language program that opened in Brooklyn in 2007. As Brooklyn is home to the largest number of Arabic speakers in the United States, it is a logical site for such a school. The Arabic language curriculum it initially adopted was developed by researchers at Michigan State University and Arabic language teachers in that state. Their work was funded by the Department of Defense, which supports Arabic language learning in the name of national security. Neither logic nor the shroud of national security protected the school from a hateful campaign of anti-Arab and anti-Muslim racism. Although the school managed to weather the storm, its potential was severely undermined. Its founding principal was forced to resign, and the school has changed locations several times.

Given this political context, whether the next generation of education standards sets bilingualism and biliteracy as explicit goals for all students is not a neutral question. And clearly, the Common Core has taken sides. By focusing on English only, the standards function as the culmination of more than a decade of attacks on bilingual programs and emergent bilingual youth.

Politics, Not Evidence

From every perspective, then, it's clear that the CCSS promise to further erode bilingual education and linguistic justice in the United States.

This conclusion underscores a point that has long been acknowledged, even by bilingual educators who support Common Core: Bilingual education is above all a question of *politics*, not of *evidence*. We have no shortage of evidence about the cognitive, personal, and social benefits of bilingualism. And, as difficult as it has been to come by, given the ups and downs of research funding and changing models of language education, we even have significant evidence of the benefits of bilingual education models themselves (Baker, 2006; García, 2009; García and Baker, 2007).

To be clear, as linguistic diversity in U.S. schools continues to increase, we need much more research on educational models for multilingual as well as bilingual settings. Also, there is much work to do in developing standards and curriculum that support and sustain students' home languages while they learn academic English. This is the goal, for example, of the Bilingual Common Core Initiative in New York, a welcome response to the English-only assumptions in Common Core. But even here, "translating" the standards misses the point because the Common Core isn't just a set of standards, but part and parcel of the test-and-punish paradigm. A bilingual version of Common Core may be pragmatic, but it does not move us away from the high-stakes testing that has so disfigured public schools. In short, adapting to the Common Core, rather than challenging it, does not help progressive educators change the conversation about real school reform.

Although challenging the Common Core may seem like a daunting task, the good news is that we already know a lot about what makes for high-quality and equitable bilingual education. In their book *Educating Emergent Bilinguals: Policies, Programs, and Practices for English Language Learners*, Ofelia García and Joanne Kleifgen describe the most effective practices for emergent bilinguals organized around four key strands: tailoring educational programs to the specific linguistic and academic needs of English learners; implementing fair assessments, especially assessments that decouple language from content proficiency; providing equitable resources, especially age- and grade-appropriate curricular resources in both home language(s) and English; and involving parents and communities at school. An important advance in the ideas they describe is moving away from a traditional approach to bilingual education that strictly separates the two languages and privileges only academic/standard varieties of language, and instead moving toward classroom practices that help students become conscious and critical users of the full language repertoire they bring with them to school, that is, both standard and non-standard varieties of English and home language(s).

History also tells us that challenges to the Common Core can't come from just inside the classroom. Although many teachers and language scholars were working on models of bilingual education in the 1950s and early '60s, it wasn't until that work connected with a radical and grassroots civil rights movement that those models were widely implemented. The same holds for us today: If we are to transform schools into more equitable places for emergent bilinguals, then we need to rebuild social movements of students, parents, teachers, and community allies to make that change happen. The coalition building of the Chicago Teachers Union before their successful strike in 2012; the ongoing coalition work by groups such as the Grassroots Education Movement or the biannual Free Minds, Free People conference; the dramatic and rapid growth of opt-out and other anti-standardized testing activism across the country; the potential of deepening the #BlackLivesMatter movement to include education issues—all offer compelling and promising models for what this work looks like moving forward.

Not only did the CCSS not emerge from these educational and activist spaces, their vision of "reform" stands in direct opposition to grassroots, anti-racist democracy. If we are to transform schools into places that foster linguistic equity, the Common Core will not be the vehicle of that change. The burden, then, is on us—as supporters of linguistic and social equity for emergent bilingual youth—to organize against the Common Core politically, and to be part of building social movements that force open social space at school and beyond for bilingual education and practice. ☼

Jeff Bale (jeff.bale@utoronto.ca) is associate professor of language and literacies education at the University of Toronto's Ontario Institute for Studies in Education. Previously, he taught English to newcomers in urban secondary schools in Washington, D.C., Chicago, and Phoenix for a decade.

References

Au, Wayne. 2009. *Unequal by Design: High-Stakes Testing and the Standardization of Inequality.* Routledge.

Baker, Colin. 2006. *Foundations of Bilingual Education and Bilingualism* (4th ed.). Multilingual Matters.

Bale, Jeff. 2012. "Linguistic Justice at School." *Education and Capitalism: Struggles for Learning and Liberation.* Eds. Jeff Bale and Sarah Knopp. Haymarket Books.

García, Ofelia. 2009. *Bilingual Education in the 21st Century: A Global Perspective.* Wiley.

García, Ofelia, and Colin Baker. 2007. *Bilingual Education: An Introductory Reader.* Multilingual Matters.

García, Ofelia, and Joanne Kleifgen. 2010. *Educating Emergent Bilinguals: Policies, Programs, and Practices for English Language Learners.* Teachers College Press.

Hagopian, Jesse, ed. 2014. *More Than a Score: The New Uprising Against High-Stakes Testing.* Haymarket Books.

Menken, Kate. 2008. *English Learners Left Behind: Standardized Testing as Language Policy.* Multilingual Matters.

Menken, Kate, and Cristian Solorza. 2014. "No Child Left Bilingual: Accountability and the Elimination of Bilingual Education Programs in New York City Schools." *Educational Policy* 28.1:96–125.

What Happened to Spanish?

How high-stakes tests doomed biliteracy at my school

BY GRACE CORNELL GONZALES

RICARDO LEVINS MORALES

ndrés, normally high-energy and jittery, was shaking so hard he could barely hold his pencil. Oscar, who used to come into the classroom smiling and who wrote me love notes in his student-teacher journal, was rhythmically banging his head on his desk. Geovanny would barely sit down; he walked in circles around his desk, slamming into people or furniture that got too close, muttering angrily to himself.

Looking around, I couldn't believe these were the same 3rd graders I had started the year with. On the first day of school they had been so eager to learn.

All my students at our Oakland, California, bilingual K–5 school were English language learners. Most came from families that had emigrated from Mexico relatively recently, and I had two newcomers, one from Mexico and one from Peru. Until 3rd grade, these kids' school days had been primarily in Spanish, with English language development for two blocks in the afternoon. Our program was designed to value Spanish and promote literacy in students' home language first, with the ultimate goal of biliteracy. In 3rd grade, we switched to English instruction for language arts and math. It was a somewhat abrupt change, but my class had been enthusiastic about tackling more English time. And the year had been full of exploration and questions about our world. We went to Alcatraz Island to learn about the native birds. We mucked about in tide pools and explored local sea life at the aquarium. We had a pet crayfish that hatched a ton of tiny translucent crayfish babies. We studied the solar system and tracked the phases of the moon. We made dioramas to show the structure of an Ohlone village. Yet now, in April, we found ourselves silent, everyone staring at a test in English that would take up a month of our instructional time.

I was at least as anxious as the kids. I walked around behind them, peering over their shoulders, terrified by every wrong answer I saw. I wanted so badly to remind them about the time we learned that one trick in math class, or how we reviewed what that particular word meant last week and compared it to its Spanish cognate. Of course, I knew that I couldn't.

I also knew that my job was on the line. It was my second year in the classroom. I was still two months away from finishing my teaching credential, still two years away from tenure. I began teaching with no meaningful training or experience, right out of college, through a teaching fellows program. My second year was better than my first, but I was still a long way from being a confident, experienced teacher. My principal didn't hesitate to let me know just how aware she was of my failings.

The message was loud and clear: When the tests roll around, English is the only important language.

There was no fair way to talk about this test to the kids. We wouldn't get the results back until the fall, so it wouldn't affect moving on to the next grade. But it would affect our school's Academic Performance Index (API) score. In year 5+ of Program Improvement Status under No Child Left Behind (NCLB) rules, that was a big deal. It could also affect my job. My principal looked carefully at how our students had improved from the previous year. Every fall, she prepared certificates for each teacher, stating how many of their students had moved from "far below basic" to "basic," from "basic" to "proficient." She presented them in front of the whole staff, so it was clear who had "moved" 10 students and who had "moved" only four. Everyone was expected to clap and look happy to receive the certificates and the accompanying dose of public praise or shaming.

Looking at Andrés, I wasn't surprised that he was shaking. His dad was an intimidating man, and I could almost imagine the conversation at his house the night before: "Andrés, you better do your best on that test or they won't let you go to 4th grade!"

We had tried to explain to our parents that this test wouldn't affect their children's report cards or whether they were promoted. But it wasn't that surprising that they didn't believe us. It didn't make sense that the test their children would cry over and struggle through for a full month was irrelevant to the kids. And, to be fair, the STAR test results would be looked at in aggregate, over several years, to determine whether our students could be reclassified as Fully English Proficient by middle school. In middle school, if they were still classified as Limited English

Proficient, they would enter a tracked system that might limit their opportunities in high school and beyond.

Testing English learners, some of them newcomers, in English always leads to a host of problems. But in our bilingual program, which was designed to value and make space for Spanish, it seemed like a particular betrayal of trust. Over the four years that I worked at my school before moving to another district, I saw just how confusing and damaging high-stakes standardized testing can be to both bilingual kids and to bilingual programs themselves.

Biliteracy Succumbs to Testing Panic

From kindergarten through 2nd grade, we spent a lot of time telling our kids how important Spanish was. We worked hard to make a separation between the languages—students spoke only Spanish with their homeroom teacher and only English with the teacher who taught the two English blocks in the afternoon. During Spanish time, we provided high-quality literacy and math instruction: We highlighted academic vocabulary in Spanish, focused on reading comprehension and writing skills, and taught phonics and conventions. This was all in accordance with our program's philosophy. Our school was dedicated to helping students develop their Spanish for the long term. We started with a 90/10 ratio of Spanish to English and worked up to about 50/50 by 3rd grade, which was the ratio the program was meant to maintain through 5th grade. Students were supposed to graduate bilingual and biliterate, proud of their identities and connected to their communities.

But in California at that point, annual high-stakes standardized testing started in 2nd grade. By April of 2nd grade, our students had received exactly zero language arts or mathematics instruction in English. Our transition to English instruction in these subjects began in 3rd grade. How is it fair to evaluate kids, teachers, and programs based on a test taken in the wrong language?

The solution, at least according to our administrators, came in the form of a test prep boot camp. Second-grade teachers were expected to carve daily time out of their Spanish instructional blocks for a month or so before the test. During this time, they would switch to English and teach transferability and test prep strategies. The idea was that, with enough willpower, they could make up for the fact that these kids' entire educational lives so far (as far as language arts and math were concerned) had been in their home language. Instead of gently transitioning into English language arts instruction at the beginning of 3rd grade, the students were thrust into it through test prep boot camp.

This sent the message loud and clear, starting at the end of 2nd grade: When the tests roll around, English is the only important language. Your teacher, who had spoken to you only in Spanish before, suddenly switched to English and started talking to you in that language about how to compose a friendly letter or the rules for quotation marks. This new information in a new language was so important that it interrupted and supplanted all the work that you had been doing so far in Spanish.

The problems started in 2nd grade, but they didn't end there. In the 4th and 5th grades, students were supposed to have social studies and science in Spanish. The idea was that they would continue expanding their academic vocabularies and their literacy skills in their home language during these blocks. However, during my second year at the school, 4th grade switched its science blocks into English because of concerns about student scores on a standardized science test given at the end of that grade. This rippled up to 5th grade. Suddenly, our bilingual program wasn't looking so bilingual anymore. By the time I left the school, 4th and 5th grade were de facto English-only, and our maintenance bilingual program had essentially become a transitional program ending in 3rd grade.

Double Testing and Double Standards

Another thing that hit us hard as a bilingual school was double testing. At that point, bilingual elementary school teachers in California were expected to test in both languages. However, our principal hinted to us that the Spanish test results wouldn't really count. Since the kids would be exhausted after the first round of testing, we were asked to test them first in English, and then in Spanish. We never looked at or analyzed the Spanish scores, even though they were probably a better indicator of how much students had learned.

To emphasize the fact that the Spanish test was a throwaway, non-bilingual homeroom teachers were not required to give it to their classes. Our school had two such teachers. In both cases, they were paired with a partner teacher who was bilingual and taught their students during the Spanish blocks. For example, in 3rd grade, my partner teacher and I switched classes daily—she taught my students math in English and I taught her students science in Spanish. Her students were in the same program as mine and had received the same amount of Spanish instruction from kindergarten to 3rd grade. However, because she didn't have a bilingual credential, her students didn't take the Spanish standardized test.

Of course, language isn't the only problem with these tests. Some states allow students to choose the language in which they are tested for language arts, and others provide side-by-side translations of the tests. However, testing students in their home language does nothing about issues of cultural bias in standardized tests. It does little to help newcomers and other students who may not have had access to formal schooling or literacy instruction in their home language. It doesn't take into consideration the generally poor quality of translations, and the fact that regional variations in vocabulary in a language like Spanish can be extremely confusing for students of diverse backgrounds.

> **Our bilingual program, with its goal of lifelong biliteracy, had become a transitional program ending in 3rd grade.**

It also doesn't recognize that bilingual students can't be treated like two monolingual students rolled up into one: Their oral language and literacy development in both languages necessarily proceed at a different pace and along different axes from those of their monolingual peers. Most importantly, it doesn't factor in the reality that the messy, joyful work of learning to think, create, and reason—in one language or two—can never be captured by clicking a multiple-choice response on a computer screen or by bubbling in an A, B, C, D, or E with a No. 2 pencil.

As for my students, they were required to take the full standardized test, language arts and math sections, in both English and Spanish. We tested Tuesday, Wednesday, and Thursday, for two hours every morning, for about a month. As can be imagined, not a lot of high-quality instruction happened afterward on those days. Our administration wanted us to "make it fun." We had pep rally assemblies and special snacks each morning of testing. But there's no quantity of granola bars that can make 8- and 9-year-olds tolerate that much testing and that much tension for that long without starting to crack.

> You don't need to pass laws banning bilingual education in order to eradicate programs. A system of standardized testing that punishes schools for teaching native language literacy is enough of a deterrent.

What Are the Consequences?

Our district said it supported bilingual programs. So did our administrators. It's easy to say that you want kids to be bilingual and biliterate. But when you encourage schools and teachers to do something and then punish them for doing that very thing, there's a problem with your system.

We know bilingual education leads to academic achievement in the long term; kids in bilingual programs will, by middle school, often perform at higher levels than their peers in monolingual programs (Thomas and Collier, 2002). But that doesn't mean that 2nd and 3rd graders, who have barely begun to practice reading and writing in English, will do as well on English standardized tests as students in an English-only program. How could they?

Expecting the impossible sets bilingual programs up for failure. At the end of the day, you don't need to pass laws banning bilingual education in order to eradicate programs. A system of standardized testing that punishes schools for teaching native language literacy is enough of a deterrent by itself.

I don't think Andrés, Oscar, or Geovanny ever forgave me for that month that I made them sit quietly in their seats and bubble in answers with No. 2 pencils. Why should they? Third grade ended on a sour note, for them and for me. We never recovered the joy that we had felt at the beginning of the year when we created crayfish habitats or measured our shadows in chalk on the playground.

The systems in place during my second year of teaching—NCLB, program improvement status, California's API scores and STAR tests—are giving way to new standards, new tests, and new ways of ranking and punishing schools. Under the surface, nothing has changed. The English tests are still the tests that count, and kids still know that. Bilingual schools still pay for trying to implement bilingual programs.

But these days, more families, students, and teachers are speaking out and opting out. For many of these advocates, the needs of English language learners are an important consideration. During the MAP boycott in 2013 in Seattle, teachers specifically cited the negative effects on emergent bilingual students as one of many reasons they believed the tests were doing harm. At International High School in Brooklyn, teachers banded together in 2014 to boycott the New York State English Language Assessment exam, citing how inappropriate the test was for their student population—majority English language learners. These are just two of many instances of teachers standing up for their emergent bilingual students. As advocates for bilingual education and as teachers in bilingual programs, it's important that we join with these educators and make our voices heard. We need to talk about how these tests don't and can't show what our kids know or what we are capable of teaching. We need to call districts out when they say they support bilingual schools and then punish them for "underperforming." Otherwise we risk seeing more and more of our bilingual programs go down without a fight. ☼

Grace Cornell Gonzales is an editor for Rethinking Schools and has worked for nine years as a bilingual elementary teacher in California and Guatemala City. Student names have been changed.

*A Spanish translation of this article is available at on the Rethinking Schools website at rethinkingschools.org/articles/que-le-paso-al-espanol.

Reference

Thomas, Wayne, and Virginia Collier. 2002. *A National Study of School Effectiveness for Language Minority Students' Long-Term Academic Achievement.* Center for Research on Education, Diversity, & Excellence, UC Berkeley.

Advocating for Arabic, Facing Resistance

An interview with Lara Kiswani

BY JODY SOKOLOWER

RAMSEY EL-QARE

n San Francisco, there are a variety of different ways that non-English languages are taught, including dual-immersion programs, other bilingual programs, and pull-out programs. Taken together, these are called language pathways. A few years ago, the Arab Resource & Organizing Center (AROC), Vietnamese Youth Development Center, and Arabic- and Vietnamese-speaking parents in San Francisco successfully organized a campaign to advocate for the addition of Arabic and Vietnamese language pathways. Despite unanimous board approval of the resolution, the San Francisco Unified School District has stalled implementation.

Lara Kiswani, executive director of AROC, talked with Rethinking Schools editor Jody Sokolower about the successful organizing effort and the ways that the Jewish Community Relations Council (JCRC), racism, and xenophobia have so far kept the Arabic and Vietnamese language pathways from being rolled out.

Jody Sokolower: What is your own history with Arabic?

Lara Kiswani: Arabic is written in my history, identity, and culture. I was the first of my siblings to be born in the United States, and I was raised speaking both Arabic and English. I went to English-only schools, and I was put in English language learner classes because of my knowledge of Arabic and because I spoke Arabic at home.

I learned a lot about my family history and our Palestinian culture in Arabic from my grandma, who lived with us as I was growing up. On Friday evenings I attended a community-run Arabic school, and on Sunday mornings I attended a community-led Islamic school to learn to read and recite the Quran. Since then, I have continued learning on my own. I can speak, read, and write Arabic, although not as well as I would like to.

JS: Did you learn enough academic Arabic to study at a university in an Arab country?

LK: No. Although I did learn classical Arabic, most of my Arabic is conversational. I can read classical Arabic, I can understand some, and speak and write even less. I don't have a formalized knowledge of the language.

JS: Is that fairly typical of second-generation Arabic speakers in the United States?

LK: Most Arab American youth understand conversational Arabic, but can't communicate in Arabic. Then you'll meet those who can communicate in Arabic, but can't write or read Arabic. Others can read and write, but only conversational Arabic. They aren't able to understand classical Arabic, so watching the news or reading a novel would be really difficult.

JS: Why is learning Arabic important, not just for kids from Arabic-speaking families?

LK: It's obvious that the Arab region is of great interest to the world for political and economic reasons. This perpetuates the hyper visibility and invisibility that Arabs face in the United States. What is known about Arab people, history, and culture is often based on stereotypes and racist understandings of Arab people as the "other." Otherwise, we as a people with a history and a living culture are not seen at all. What is seen is the devastation of our region, often at the hands of the United States and Israel, or the relationship of Westerners—the military, politicians, or service workers—to our region. U.S. warmongering has led to a growing population of international organizations dealing with the devastation on the ground in many Arabic-speaking areas of the world. All this amounts to little understanding of the sociopolitical landscape of the Arab region. Understanding Arabic is one window into that landscape. And it is a window into the Arab world from the viewpoint of those who live and breathe it.

And, of course, we know it's good for children to learn more than one language. That's not specific to Arabic. There's lots of evidence that knowing more than one language supports cognitive and academic development. Although Arabic is often viewed as a difficult language to learn, it has a long history that is visible in current subjects taught in U.S. classrooms such as math and science. It's also unbelievably beautiful and rich. There are multiple words in Arabic to describe one word in English. There are ways to describe feelings that you don't have in English or other languages. When you read, write, or hear Arabic, you are learning and engaging with a deep history. You see a lot of Arabic in Spanish, French, and other languages.

JS: What do Arab American students and their parents say about the lack of Arabic language in San Francisco schools?

LK: The way that Arab American students and parents relate to the lack of Arabic language is a broader issue, one that goes beyond not being offered Arabic language instruction. It's about feeling isolated, marginalized, and invisible. It's about living in a city where racist anti-Arab and Islamophobic ads drape the buses you and your children ride each day, where your people and family are vilified on a daily basis in mainstream media. And it's about the deep desire to maintain your culture and live a dignified life despite that.

If parents want their children to progress beyond conversational levels in their home language, it's extremely challenging to do that. And it can be very difficult for Arab-speaking family members to communicate with the school district or with their children's teachers. There have been some efforts at Arabic interpretation, but they are totally inadequate in reaching the growing Arabic-speaking population in San Francisco. Like other immigrant parents, Arab parents are particularly concerned because, in an environment that denigrates their home language, there's a breakdown in communication between them and their children as their children rely increasingly on English and don't keep up their Arabic. This breakdown in communication often leads to the further criminalization of Arab youth.

> **Arabic is unbelievably beautiful and rich. When you read, write, or hear Arabic, you are learning and engaging with a deep history.**

There's also a fear of losing the heritage, the culture, and the history that are transferred through language. Often after kids come home from school, their parents make them study Arabic or read the Quran. Or they are sent to volunteer-run weekend schools, as I was, at a mosque, perhaps, where there is some Arabic instruction. But these programs are informal and not as effective as they could be.

When Arab parents realized that San Francisco has a commitment to world language pathways and that 10 languages are offered, these families were excited. They are happy to have their children learn Spanish or French, but they would much rather have them advance in their native language as well. When the idea emerged that there was a way to implement an Arabic language pathway, similar to all the other language pathways in San Francisco, parents felt a sense of relief. They also felt empowered. They said they felt that they had a place in San Francisco—they were being seen and heard. Their experiences were being validated, and it brought them closer to a point that they could trust their kids to the school district. It created a sense of belonging for these parents in terms of decision-making in the district and the city more broadly.

Once they realized they could fight for an Arabic language pathway and win, it became something they were very committed to.

JS: How did the campaign for teaching Arabic in the San Francisco schools begin?

LK: One of AROC's ongoing programs is working with Arab youth. Back in 2009, the youth decided to do a research project on what it was like to be Arab American in the San Francisco schools. They interviewed hundreds of teachers and students, and surveyed them on the representation of Arabs in high school curricula. They came out with a report and one of the recommendations was to have interpretation available for Arabic-speaking families. As an extension, a group of mother leaders decided to advocate for interpreters in the district because they were having a difficult time communicating with teachers and administrators. And rather than trying to bridge the gap, teachers and administrators were labeling these families as hard to work with or inaccessible. We fought for interpreters and eventually two part-time Arabic-speaking interpreters were hired. That's been tremendously helpful. It hasn't resolved the tensions or lack of accessibility to resources and information, but it has helped.

Then, about two years ago, one of the teachers from San Francisco's Teachers 4 Social Justice (T4SJ), Jeremiah Jeffries, was thinking about the large Arab population at his elementary school in the Tenderloin neighborhood of the city. He

> **Ultimately what's coming to the surface is that there continues to be racism in the school district and xenophobia in San Francisco.**

wondered: Given all the language pathways the district is implementing, why isn't Arabic being taught? Jeremiah approached AROC to see if it was something we'd work on, and we said absolutely yes, it's in line with our strategy and definitely in line with the concerns of our community.

In the same area in the Tenderloin, we noticed there was also a need for Vietnamese. It's a growing population—larger than the Arab population in San Francisco—and there was no Vietnamese being offered. So we began collaborating with the Vietnamese Youth Development Center.

Together we advocated for Arabic and Vietnamese language pathways in San Francisco. A couple of members of the board of education co-authored the proposal and worked with us. Some members of the board of supervisors were also advocates.

The resolution passed unanimously. It was obvious, with the several dozen community members who mobilized to the board of education meetings, that our families were visibly in support, and there seemed to be no reason to say no to something that would benefit Arabic-speaking and Vietnamese-speaking families, as well as other families in San Francisco who might be interested in learning one of these languages.

JS: You looked at different models for language pathways, right? What did you decide to recommend and why?

LK: Since the resolution passed, we have been working with the district to develop models to roll out. We had to weigh a number of factors: how to best support the development of Arabic fluency and literacy, what is realistic politically, and what is realistic in the face of a shortage of credentialed Arabic-speaking teachers. We decided to suggest a model similar to the way Japanese is taught here. An important strength of the Japanese model is that, although the principal teachers are credentialed, there are opportunities for Japanese-speaking members of the community to participate and help teach the students. There is also an emphasis on Japanese culture as well as language acquisition. Because this is a grassroots effort, we want to involve the community in helping teach Arabic and cultural aspects of the Arab world as much as possible. So this seemed like a good place to start.

This will start as a small program, and we don't want kids to be separated out from the rest of the children in the school. So children enrolled in the Arabic language pathway would be with other classmates most of the day; about 30 to 45 minutes a day they would go to Arabic class. And anyone who wants to enroll will be welcome, of course, so it won't only be Arab American children. In middle school, one subject would always be taught in Arabic so the children develop more academic language. In high school, it would be offered as a foreign language. That's the model we are currently advocating for and we think will work best for the number of Arab students we have and the current resources in terms of Arabic-speaking teachers.

JS: Are there Arabic language pathways in other parts of the country?

LK: Not similar to this. We looked at what is being done nationally because we wanted to learn from what has worked elsewhere. Arabic is taught in some charter and private schools, and some schools in Michigan teach it as a foreign language. There have been attempts to open schools focused on Arabic, including the Khalil Gibran School in New York, which was based on a dual-language grades 6–12 model, but Khalil Gibran School was systematically destroyed by the mayor and New York Department of Education in the face of racist and Islamophobic attacks. So there are resources around curriculum and approaches, but no similar public K–12 programs.

JS: Why do you think some languages are privileged over others in schools?

LK: In general, education in this country doesn't reflect the needs of families, communities, and neighborhoods; it's more about what's politically expedient and what fills business needs and projections.

The situation with Arabic is complicated because there are a lot of expensive private institutions that teach Arabic to adults for military and political reasons. Many non-Arabs are learning Arabic because it's useful for U.S. foreign policy. But no one is making Arabic language and culture part of K–12 education. That would mean reaching out to a population that is being labeled as other, validating our place in society, and relating to us as part of the fabric of life in the United States.

JS: What has happened since the Arabic and Vietnamese language pathways were approved by the board?

LK: It's been stalled time and time again, but we have managed to move it forward. The Jewish Community Relations Council (JCRC), a wealthy private institution that's pro-Israel, has led an effort to kill the plan, specifically because AROC is listed as a partner and has been one of the main champions of the effort.

JS: Why is the JCRC opposed to AROC being connected with the pathway?

LK: This is a period when Zionist organizations are escalating their efforts to isolate pro-Palestinian organizations anywhere. In the Bay Area, JCRC tries to ensure that any criticism of Israel is attacked and marginalized. They want to make it impossible to be critical of Israel and still be a community organizer. They have threatened the funding of nonprofits that held workshops or took positions in solidarity with Palestinian human rights, they succeeded in getting the Museum of Children's Arts in Oakland to cancel an exhibit of artwork by children in Gaza, they destroyed the economic base of a community newspaper that printed articles questioning Israeli policies. There's a long list going back many years.

AROC is a community-based organization. We provide legal help to Arab immigrants, we work with youth, we advocate for Arabic interpretation in education and healthcare, we work in coalitions around police violence. But we are unapologetically anti-racist and anti-Zionist, and our work reflects those values. The JCRC saw how much the language pathways mobilized our community and the force

> **They haven't succeeded in crushing the commitment of the Vietnamese and Arab families and communities. That's not going away; it won't dissipate.**

that it showed. They also have seen the impact of our work over the years, and the strength of cross-movement building in raising awareness about the struggles of Arabs, the role of Israel in our region, and the ongoing systematic racism we face here. As an institution committed to maintaining Israeli apartheid, supporting the occupation, and dehumanizing Arabs and Palestinians, they saw our work as a threat—they don't want the Arab voice to be heard and definitely don't want it to be impactful.

They used our criticism of Israel as a basis for us not to be allowed to work in the schools or to be a partner in the languages pathways. They tried to get the board of education to take a new vote on the resolution, removing the community partners from the proposal. That has never happened before for any of the other language pathways. But we got a lot of support from the community and from allied social justice organizations, and after months of organizing to challenge JCRC's attack on AROC, the board decided not to revote but to move forward.

But since then, the process has been stalled. This never happened before—not for Spanish, Latin, Japanese, Chinese, Hebrew, or any of the many languages taught in San Francisco. Once a pathway's resolution gets passed, there's an internal process working with community partners to decide on an approach and assess which schools to place the languages at. Those recommendations come back to the board and, within a year or so, there's staffing, the program is implemented, and it's rolled out.

But that hasn't happened with Arabic and Vietnamese. Now we have teachers sending petitions to the district saying they don't want this language at their school, that it will bring more immigrant families, who are harder to work with and already behind in their learning, thus making the teachers' jobs more difficult. They say they don't want to change the demographic of their school by attracting more Arab or Vietnamese families.

This has put the district in a difficult position. They are committed to the language pathways. On the other hand, there is this campaign by powerful forces. And we don't have as much political power as other communities. The district still says it's committed to seeing the language pathways implemented in schools by 2017. And we are committed to working with them to see this program through.

JS: How has the Arab American community responded to the lack of motion on the pathway?

LK: This is having a huge impact on our community. Hundreds of parents were so excited. Families mobilized to come to the board of education meetings, to speak up and let the district know we want this. When we won, it was extremely empowering and inspiring. People felt motivated to fight for what they believe in ways they hadn't before.

This is an immigrant community escaping from war-torn home countries, coming to the United States and feeling marginalized, feeling they don't know how to communicate with people in power. Then to see they can exert themselves, be heard, challenge power, and win something for their children—especially working alongside the families from the Vietnamese Youth Development Center—it was a transformative experience.

For that to be followed by attacks smearing the community-based organization they're a part of, attacks by teachers questioning the need for and legitimacy of having Arabic taught in San Francisco at all, to find themselves pitted against teachers who don't want them, their families, their children, and their language in the school—that experience has been extremely demoralizing. Particularly in this political moment where the way in which the district has invisibilized the community in the implementation process, and stalled the process as a whole, has mirrored the lack of concern and respect for Arabs and Muslims by people in power.

JS: Is the Vietnamese pathway facing similar obstacles?

LK: At this point, yes. We don't know if it would have been similarly stalled had they done it on their own. But we do know that the same case is being made against Vietnamese. Our suggested schools for the two languages are different, and at the schools we're looking at for Vietnamese pathways, the teachers are similarly saying we don't want these families at our schools, we don't want to change the demographic of our school, we don't need to have youth who are having difficulty learning pulled out of the classroom for 30 to 45 minutes a day to learn Vietnamese.

Ultimately what's coming to the surface is that there continues to be racism in the school district and xenophobia in San Francisco—a reflection of society at large and also our history as a city, even though we don't always want to remember that. And in times like these, it is easier for people to express it.

JS: How has the teacher union responded?

LK: The union hasn't taken a position. I will say that many teachers and union leaders have spoken up and been advocates for the language pathways. Teachers, administrators, community members, faith leaders, unions, youth, parents, and Jewish allies—all have written endless letters and testimonies to the board about the need for this, and the impact of the attack on the pathways.

JS: How do you see this in the overall context of the anti-Arab, Islamophobic atmosphere in the United States?

LK: Although there is an upsurge in resistance to racism and state violence in the United States, we're also seeing the reaction to that. Suddenly something like language pathways are controversial, or AROC, which has a long history of working with the city of San Francisco providing services for immigrants and organizing our community against war and racism. Now suddenly it's a question of whether or not we're a legitimate organization.

We have been in the schools since 2009. The district has acknowledged that they need us; they need every community to have a way to address racism in the schools. AROC plays that role for the Arab community. We create a place for Arab youth to talk about issues that matter to them, to unpack things they're experiencing, and to come up with ways to address them. That's an important aspect of the social and political development of youth, and it's also part of helping them feel connected and committed to their schools and their education.

So our work is necessary and critical. But the political climate has made it OK to question our legitimacy. A white-led, wealthy, political organization like JCRC, who are they to say that an Arab organization can't work with Arab youth?

It's unfortunate we're up against these huge forces, but at the same time it's been inspiring to see the ways we're able to develop our own force and power and resistance through community—through solidarity and a commitment to social justice. We've been meeting with families over the past months to find out how they would like to move forward. And they want to fight for this, to do whatever they can.

But the antagonism that's been created as a result of the tension and opposition has changed things. Families no longer feel that the city and the school district are partnering with them to make this wonderful thing happen. Now, it's the Arab community fighting to make our case. There's no longer a clear partnership, and that's exactly what the opposition wanted.

But they haven't succeeded in crushing the commitment of the Vietnamese and Arab families and communities. It's so deep and so grounded in their lived experiences, rooted in their values. That's not going away; it won't dissipate.

And despite all the delays and problems, the school district still has a commitment to diversity, and to the values of language and world language pathways. They haven't been able to navigate the racism that still exists—or its impact. I think they're struggling to figure out a way to address it.

I believe these different aspects will ultimately lead to a positive outcome. It's just unfortunate that the process has been so difficult and challenging for people who are already facing mounting challenges because of who they are. Yet it is inspiring to see the outpouring of support that AROC, the Arab community, and the struggle to fight for the dignity of Arab families in San Francisco has received from people all across the country. This has become a fight against anti-Arab racism, Zionism, and Islamophobia. And it has brought together movements and people from all walks of life, who, as people struggling against all forms of oppression, understand this fight as their own. ☼

Lara Kiswani is the executive director of the Arab Resource & Organizing Center (AROC) in San Francisco, which organizes Arab and Muslim communities to challenge militarism, racism, and repression. A Palestinian born in the San Francisco Bay Area, she has worked as a youth and adult educator and is a member of Al-Juthoor of the Arab Shatat, a local Palestinian folkloric dance troupe.

Jody Sokolower is a political activist, teacher, writer, and editor. She is the managing editor at Rethinking Schools.

Language Wars

The struggle for bilingual education in New Britain, Connecticut

BY JACOB WERBLOW, ARAM AYALON, AND MARINA PEREZ

CT MIRROR

"We want to have the right to speak Spanish and to be able to do our work in both languages," said Yasmin, a Puerto Rican middle school student. Her words were met with applause as she turned from the microphone and returned to her seat in the overcrowded school board room. Nearly 100 students, teachers, and parents had joined Yasmin in advocating to save the dual-language program at DiLoreto Dual-Language Magnet School in New Britain, Connecticut. Yet after two hours of public testimony in support of the program, one of only six in the state, it became clear that the school board had made up its mind to immediately dissolve the dual-language program, along with bilingual education across the district.

Around the turn of this century, legislation banning bilingual education was passed in California, Arizona, and Massachusetts. Even though no such law was passed in Connecticut, the story of DiLoreto shows that there are subtler ways to dismantle bilingual programs in the current political climate—particularly in the name of raising test scores, closing "underperforming" schools, and effecting budget cuts.

Dual Language Rises and Falls

New Britain is a small, racially and ethnically diverse, postindustrial city. Once referred to as the thriving "hardware capital of the world," New Britain's economic history is similar to countless other cities scattered across the Northeast: In the last 50 years, the local economy has been nearly decimated by globalization.

> **It became clear that consolidating bilingual programs across the district was the first step in eradicating the community's bilingual programs altogether.**

In the late 1990s, a group of local administrators, educators, and parents lobbied the school district to implement a Spanish-English dual-language school, which eventually became the DiLoreto Dual-Language Magnet School. DiLoreto enrolled approximately 50 percent native English speakers and 50 percent native Spanish speakers. Students spent half the school day learning their academic subjects in English and the other half learning in Spanish. The school had a long waiting list of applicants. In 2007, Marina Perez became principal and expanded DiLoreto by adding grades 6–8. The school thrived. In 2009, local newspaper *Hispanic Trending* described DiLoreto as "one of the district's most sought-after [public] schools because of its dual-language curriculum."

Despite DiLoreto's success, the superintendent began to undermine the integrity of the dual-language program and other bilingual programs in the district. In the summer of 2010, the superintendent closed four of the transitional bilingual education programs in elementary schools across the district and relocated the students to DiLoreto. Although the relocation gave more emergent bilingual students access to the dual-language program, the quality of the program began to suffer. DiLoreto's 50/50 English-to-Spanish speaker ratio shifted; the number of emergent bilingual students outnumbered English speakers three-to-one. Average class size grew from under 24 to more than 33, with no paraprofessional support.

Consolidating transitional bilingual programs across the district and relocating the children into DiLoreto was a way for the superintendent to artificially inflate standardized test scores in the four other elementary schools by shrinking or removing the emergent bilingual population. Later it became clear that this was the first step in eradicating the community's bilingual programs altogether.

Mr. Cooper Comes to Town

In 2012, after repeated years of flat funding and rumors of a state takeover, New Britain was desperate to hire a strong superintendent. When the board of education narrowed the search to three finalists, several were impressed with Kelt Cooper, from Del Rio, Texas. He was the only candidate to reach out to the Latina/o community and many were excited about the possibility of the district hiring someone who could speak Spanish.

A few local educators, however, found some disturbing news about Cooper on the internet. In 2009, Cooper made national news in his previous superintendent's position for assigning his staff to videotape and threaten expulsion warnings to more than 200 children and their families at a border checkpoint outside of Del Rio, Texas. Cooper also testified in the *Flores v. Horne* Supreme Court case (2009) claiming that it is not the state's responsibility to provide adequate funding for emergent bilingual students. Cooper also played a role in passing Arizona's legislation mandating that all emergent bilingual students study English only, instead of bilingual education. Despite these controversies, the majority of the school board members voted to hire Cooper.

Given Cooper's claims to support bilingualism, Perez reached out to him to share research about the benefits of dual language and to ask for his help in strengthening the integrity of the DiLoreto's dual-language model. Cooper responded: "I do not believe in all of this research. . . . Anyone can manipulate the numbers to prove their point. I've seen it all. I've read it all, and I don't believe it!"

Cooper started a radio campaign in Spanish, telling the community that he wanted what was best for its kids. He wanted students to learn English, so they could get good jobs. According to Cooper, New Britain's schools were failing because bilingual education wasn't working, and he was going to get them "out of the ditch" with his new plan.

Kevin Clark's English Language Development

During his tenure in Del Rio, Cooper had implemented Kevin Clark's highly controversial version of English Language Development, a program widely implemented in Arizona and California under the term "Structured English Immersion" (SEI). Clark's model, which involves replacing daily instruction in core subject areas with a 3.5-hour block of discrete grammar skills in English, does not include instruction with textbooks or children's literature. Research on the model found that the program has an adverse effect on student learning: UCLA's Civil Rights Project has found that it contributes little to closing the achievement gap, increases classroom segregation of emergent bilingual students, and negatively affects academic performance (see References).

Cooper hired Clark's consulting company. In September 2012, two of the company's consultants submitted a report summarizing their findings of a two-day site visit:

> Programs referred to as "bilingual" or "dual language" create a negatively skewed bell curve distribution pattern with large numbers of students who can best be classified as "bi-illiterate." . . . The sheer complexity of trying to implement and manage such bulk and

largely theoretical bilingual and dual-language designs . . . [gives] rise to site-level redundancy and minutiae in the form of Byzantine amounts of paperwork.

In less than six months on the job, without formal input from parents or teachers or even a vote by the school board, Cooper told Perez that the dual-language program would be replaced immediately by Clark's ELD model. In a November 2012 memo to the school board, Cooper defended his decision:

> DiLoreto is no longer a Dual Language School, but rather a regular K–8 school which provides Spanish as a foreign language. Our desire is that it becomes a high performing school with acceptable [standardized test] scores; that ultimately the school provides the best instruction possible and that students learn Spanish [as a foreign language] in the process.

Teachers, Parents, and Students Fight Back

Perez called for an emergency parent meeting to inform parents of what had happened and encourage them to speak out. At the next school board meeting, a huge crowd of DiLoreto parents, students, alumni, and teachers came to defend the dual-language program.

Myriam Vázquez, a DiLoreto parent, spoke during the two-hour public testimony: "Listen to me and the other parents. Do not change the dual-language program at our school. I am proud to tell my family in Puerto Rico that my daughter is attending DiLoreto where she can learn and speak two languages." Several DiLoreto teachers also spoke out. They argued that the program should be improved, not replaced, and that the district's decision-making process should be more transparent.

> **"I am proud to tell my family in Puerto Rico that my daughter is attending DiLoreto where she can learn and speak two languages."**
> **—Myriam Vázquez, parent**

Most school board members defended Cooper's plan and argued that those in the audience were misinformed. "Dual language is not being eliminated at DiLoreto Magnet School," stated Sharon Saavedra, chair of the school board. "The proposal made by the superintendent is to change the instructional practices on how to deliver that language, not to eliminate Spanish culture or the Spanish language." Equating dual-language instruction with instruction in Spanish as a foreign language muddied the debate, confusing and infuriating many parents in the audience.

Aram Ayalon was the only member of the school board to side with the parents. He called for the board to respect voices of parents and students by establishing a task force to take a look at DiLoreto and the education of emergent bilingual students across the district. Instead of heeding the request of Ayalon and all those who were in attendance, the board passed the resolution 7-1 to hire Clark's company to implement his model of ELD districtwide.

After the school board meeting, Perez gave her two-week notice, announcing her retirement as principal of DiLoreto School.

Many DiLoreto teachers and parents turned to the School Governance Council as a formal mechanism to challenge the decision to terminate the dual-language program. Parent involvement at the meetings, however, soon dropped after the district appointed Mark Fernandes, a non-Spanish speaker, as interim principal of DiLoreto. Some of the first changes made by Fernandes included removing "Dual-Language" from the school name on the school's website and materials, discontinuing Spanish translation at the parent meetings, and enforcing Cooper's mandate to remove all Spanish textbooks and children's literature from classrooms. As a result, half of the educators at DiLoreto School, many of whom were experienced bilingual teachers, left the district by the end of the year. As one teacher stated: "The morale of the school was at an all-time low. Instead of teaching this absolutely racist curriculum, I decided that I had to leave."

Advocating for Bilingual Programs

In the five years that have passed since the termination of bilingual programs in New Britain, the authors of this article, along with a small group of other parents, educators, and students in the community, have continued to organize to bring bilingual education back to the district. Highlights of our efforts include:

- Filing a formal legal complaint. Ayalon filed a legal complaint to the U.S. Office of Civil Rights (OCR) against the school district's implementation of Clark's ELD program. After doing a site visit in June 2014, OCR opened a full investigation of the New Britain school district, but has not yet released a report.

- Telling our story in the national media. We reached out to various media outlets and presented this story at national educator conferences. In July 2013, PBS NewsHour featured a 10-minute exposé, "Language Wars," highlighting the ELD controversy. According to the exposé, Cooper's previous school district (Del Rio, Texas) abandoned Clark's ELD program shortly after Cooper left for the position in New Britain. PBS found that Clark's program in Texas had an overall negative effect on student achievement: Students' English proficiency scores increased slightly, but their math and science scores decreased by 15 percent.

- Educating teachers and students across the state. A group of students, parents, educators, and academics came together to organize a statewide workshop called "Dos Días Para Transforming Bilingual Education in Connecticut." This workshop involved breakouts led by teachers, students, and academics. More than 200 teachers attended. The workshop also led to two front-page articles in the local newspaper slamming Clark's ELD program.

- Writing letters. After the conference, a small group of parents and educators conducted a two-month long letter-writing campaign, which included five op-ed articles to local newspapers about the controversial termination of the dual-language school at DiLoreto and promoted a vision of bilingualism as an asset, not a deficit.

- Promoting student voice in local media. Bilingual advocates within New Britain High School helped identify teenagers who had attended DiLoreto and were willing to speak with the local media about the importance of being bilingual and the bilingual program at DiLoreto. In April 2015, Fox 61 News broadcast the students' perspectives in an exposé about the language controversy.

All of these efforts, as well as other controversial decisions made by the superintendent, eventually led to the school board voting 7-1 not to renew Cooper's contract after the 2015–2016 school year.

The struggle for bilingual education in our community has helped us realize the importance of fighting for bilingual education across the state. Many of those involved in DiLoreto activism joined other parents and educators from across Connecticut in testifying to the Latino and Puerto Rican Affairs Council, a state legislative commission, which was able to leverage important legislative changes in bilingual education. At the end of the 2015 legislative session, bilingual services for emergent bilingual students were extended

> **"Instead of teaching this absolutely racist curriculum, I decided that I had to leave."**
> **—Former teacher, DiLoreto School**

from a maximum of 30 months to 60 months and funding for bilingual education significantly increased. These changes now make it easier for communities to develop bilingual programs in Connecticut.

Despite our efforts to organize locally, the dual-language curriculum at DiLoreto has not been reinstated. Clark's consulting company continues to provide professional services for the ELD program in the district. The DiLoreto story shows that it isn't just legislation that can shut down bilingual schools—budget cuts, pressure to improve test scores, and district politics can also do the trick. It is only in losing a dual-language program that we learned the importance of joining bilingual education advocates beyond our local community; we will continue to fight for the programs that all our kids deserve. ☼

Jacob Werblow is an associate professor in educational leadership at Central Connecticut State University and the 2016 Harber Fellow in Education at Wesleyan University. Aram Ayalon is a professor of educational leadership at Central Connecticut State University. He is a former high school science teacher and recently served as board member in a local school district for six years. Marina Perez is a dual-language education consultant and Massachusetts Association for Bilingual Education board member representing Connecticut. She is the former principal of two multilingual and multicultural schools in Connecticut.

References

The Civil Rights Project/Proyecto Derechos Civiles. 2010. "Language Minority Students." Retrieved May 19, 2014. civilrightsproject.ucla.edu/research/k-12-education/language-minority-students.

del Bosque, Melissa. 2009. "Child X-ing: Del Rio's Controversial Crackdown on Border-Crossing Students." *Texas Observer.* Dec. 10. texasobserver.org/child-x-ing.

Horne v. Flores. 2008. Supreme Court of the United States. No.08-289. supremecourt.gov/opinions/08pdf/08-289.pdf.

"Language Wars: Should Spanish-Speaking Students Be Taught in English Only?" *PBS NewsHour.* December 2013. pbs.org/newshour/bb/education-july-dec13-language_07-18.

"Superintendent with Controversial Language Program Staying in New Britain" (video). 2015. *Fox 61 News.* April 10. foxct.com/2015/04/10/superintendent-with-controversial-language-program-staying-in-new-britain.

Zehr, Mary Ann. 2007. "Arizona's Tom Horne Hires 'Super Cooper.'" *Education Week*, April 11. blogs.edweek.org/edweek/learning-the-language/2007/04/arizonas_tom_horne_hires_super_1.html.

Bilingual Against the Odds

Examining Proposition 227 with bilingual teacher candidates

BY ANA M. HERNÁNDEZ

DAVID BACON

Note: English translations are provided in summarized form immediately preceding or following Spanish text.

As we settled into a new semester, Sandra, a bilingual teacher candidate in our Spanish Bilingual Authorization Program, walked into my office and handed me a set of papers that required my signature to drop out of the program. "I don't think I have the Spanish skills needed to meet the program requirements and become a bilingual teacher," she said.

I, too, had begun to wonder if some of the candidates had the Spanish skills necessary to become bilingual educators. Although 26 out of the 35 students were Latinas/os who had grown up speaking or being exposed to Spanish at home, I was surprised that most of the teacher candidates struggled with the readings in Spanish. Their written assignments often contained grammatical errors and lacked the Spanish academic language needed to pass a graduate-level course. I noticed group discussions revert to English, as candidates searched for appropriate terms in Spanish. Even though the candidates spoke of their lifelong dreams to become bilingual educators, some wondered if they had the necessary Spanish language skills to continue with the classes.

Sandra was not the only teacher candidate who came to my office to discuss dropping out of the program. As I spoke with students and learned more about their histories, I realized that many of these future bilingual teachers were products of California's Proposition 227.

Reflecting a nativist hostility toward Latina/o immigrants, Prop. 227 was passed in 1998 to ban bilingual education in California's public schools. As elementary, middle, and high school students, many of these bilingual teacher candidates had not had the opportunity to learn content in their primary language, read a textbook in Spanish, or have their identities affirmed in their schools. Only two teacher candidates had attended dual-language programs—because their parents had applied for bilingual education waivers.

Even though many of the candidates had been denied the benefits of bilingual education, they felt a calling to become the bilingual teachers they never had. Yet I knew passion was not enough. In addition to rigorous teaching methodology courses and Spanish language development, I knew these teacher candidates needed to have opportunities to explore and reflect on their own bilingual histories and identities within the political and sociocultural contexts that had shaped them.

Some members of the class had heard about the politics surrounding Prop. 227, but the majority had not made the connections to their own schooling. I wanted to explore the political context and instructional ramifications of the proposition at the time of the teacher candidates' own schooling experiences. I wanted students to have conversations about the racial and cultural oppression of Prop. 227, and reflect on the ways their families resisted this oppression. By exploring patterns of injustice, my hope was that the teacher candidates would find liberation and empowerment that they might apply in their practice as teachers.

Talking Back to Prop. 227

We had previously discussed the history of bilingual education and the rapid decline of bilingual programs in California following the passing of Prop. 227. However, it wasn't until we began to study the demographics of the most affected students and program types that teacher candidates started to recognize the dominant white-class ideology imposed through such restrictive language policies. Politically charged racism was at the core of the proposition and motivated its proponents.

We began by examining the 1998 California's voters' guide for Prop. 227. We read that the proposition was designed to destroy bilingual programs by stipulating that English learners receive instruction "overwhelmingly in English." English learners were to be placed in structured English immersion programs for one year or less, and then transferred to mainstream English-language classrooms. The mandate sanctioned parent/guardian lawsuits against teachers or administrators who refused to comply with the policy.

As students examined each of the major articles of the proposition in small groups, they began to reflect on their own schooling experiences. "I can't believe this part about the lawsuits!" stated Kyle, a native English speaker who attended a dual-language program.

Micaela commented, "Now, I understand why my teacher always whispered in Spanish when we didn't understand an aspect of the lesson in English. She must have been terrified of losing her job."

> **"Now, I understand why my teacher always whispered in Spanish when we did not understand an aspect of the lesson in English. She must have been terrified of losing her job."**
> **—Micaela, teacher candidate**

In their weekly response journals on readings and class discussions, the teacher candidates recalled the dismantling of bilingual programs in their communities. Many shared emotional accounts of confusion at school and at home with their parents. Some shared stories of falling behind in their English classes. Yolanda vividly recalled the passing of Prop. 227 during her schooling:

> *Me afectó personalmente cuando los votantes de California decidieron aprobar la Proposición 227. Soy hispanohablante y asistí a un programa bilingüe hasta el tercer grado. Cuando se aprobó la ley, me pusieron inmediatamente en una clase que me iba a preparar para las clases de inglés. Recuerdo que estaba muy confundida porque tuve que cambiar el idioma de mi educación. Como era una niña que no entendía el significado social de estas legislaciones, no sabía que estas leyes tenían una agenda xenófoba y discriminatoria. Hoy en día me pregunto cómo hubiera sido el desarrollo de mi bilingüismo si esta proposición nunca hubiera tomado efecto en California.*

In this journal, Yolanda recalled feeling very confused when she was suddenly placed in English-only instruction soon after the passing of Prop. 227 during 3rd grade. She also wrote of a lost opportunity to fully develop her bilingualism in school due to a xenophobic and discriminatory legislation. She wondered what could have been the level of her bilingualism had this proposition not been instituted in California.

Raquel also shared feelings of confusion. Arriving in the United States as a 4th grader, Raquel explained how she lost two years of schooling when she could not understand the teacher or books shared in class. She felt devalued as an individual. "*Recuerdo que durante cuarto y quinto año no aprendí nada porque mi maestra solo hablaba inglés. Recuerdo haberme sentido confundida y que no era valorada.*"

Although Raquel was not given access to curriculum in her native language at her school in California, she maintained her Spanish skills through much hard work at home. Now, her younger siblings benefit from Raquel's bilingualism. She helps them with homework in English and translates complex texts into Spanish. Her siblings look forward to Raquel's daily English and Spanish lessons.

Bilingual Against the Odds

The political and personal contexts of Prop. 227 set the background for a series of reading assignments related to language and identity. María de la Luz Reyes' book *Words Were All We Had: Becoming Biliterate Against the Odds* is a collection of auto-biographical narratives from a generation of Latina/o students whose early schooling was marked by attempts to stifle their bilingualism. The authors describe how they triumphed over school systems that suppressed Spanish. The stories recount literacy events created at home, at church, or in the community that helped the young Latinas/os access rich linguistic and cultural resources. For example:

> It was the mid-1960s and Maria Lydia had recently come to San Diego from Sinaloa, Mexico, my mother's home state, to work as a housekeeper for a white American family. On weekends, she typically visited us. Part of the socializing ritual included trading and discussing *novelas*, also known as *historietas*, featuring comic style-like illustrations and text. My mother typically kept a large grocery paper bag filled to the brink with these books.

Many of my Latina/o students connected to these personal stories of Spanish literacy experiences at home despite having been forced to choose English over Spanish at school. In conversations and journals, students recalled parents taking on the task of teaching Spanish reading and writing at home during the era of Prop. 227. Many of my students described their mothers' persistence in teaching them the Spanish alphabet, combining syllables to create words, and helping them read and write simple sentences in their home language.

In one journal entry, Carla recalled how her mother taught her how to read and write in Spanish at home even though her schooling was all in English. She described how her mom would buy her Spanish textbooks and would make Carla read them aloud to her. Afterward, Carla would copy sentences straight from the book. By the time Carla started high school, she was able to write paragraphs in Spanish:

> *Desde pequeña mi mamá me enseñó a escribir y a leer en español aunque no lo estudié en la escuela. Me compraba textos y me hacía escribir como si yo estuviera en su clase. Me acuerdo que mi mamá hacía que yo leyera con ella en voz alta para asegurarse que yo estaba pronunciando las palabras bien. Me daba libros y me hacía copiar oraciones para practicar mi escritura. Cuando entré a la escuela secundaria ya podía escribir oraciones y párrafos en español por los esfuerzos que hizo mi mamá.*

Josefina wrote about her gratitude that her mother always spoke to her and her siblings in Spanish. She described how she would read Spanish magazines left at the lunch tables by farmworkers as she waited for her mom to finish work in the fields. *"Le doy las gracias a mi madre porque siempre nos hablaba en español, nos llevaba a trabajar con ella en el campo. Allí pasábamos las tardes en el campo leyendo revistas que conseguíamos en las mesas donde comían el almuerzo los trabajadores."*

Micaela connected her story to similar ones in Reyes' book, where children became brokers of languages for their own parents and families. Micaela shared how she maintained her Spanish by translating for her mom who was a seamstress. As a child, Micaela learned the sewing terms related to making alterations to articles of clothing in both languages, so her mom could keep her job. She learned to write and read messages for her mom and for clients. Micaela was frustrated when she did not know how to accurately translate, fearing that her mother would misinterpret the clients' wishes. Micaela described how during this stressful time she felt ashamed of her faulty English and her family's poverty.

Micaela also shared how these early experiences of learning and using Spanish affected her later commitment to advocacy for bilingual education. She described identifying with other Mexican American students in secondary school because they were also bilingual and bicultural; joining the La Raza Club; and becoming an activist for social justice in protests against Proposition 187 (California's anti-immigration measure) in 1994, and later Prop. 227 in 1998.

> *Me identificaba más con otros estudiantes mexicoamericanos porque hablaban dos idiomas y entendían las dos culturas al igual que yo. Formé parte del Club de la Raza y gracias a la proposición 187 en 1994, empecé a ser activista de la justicia social. Luego en 1998, formé parte de las protestas en contra de la proposición 227.*

The nine students in the class who were not Latina/o—all of whom were white, native English speakers—did not have these personal experiences of linguistic and racial marginalization. Their efforts to learn a second language had been celebrated at home and by their teachers and peers. In their cases, reading the narratives and listening to their classmates' stories made them more aware of the marginalization of linguistically diverse students, and made it easier for them to recognize discrimination at local schools while student teaching.

Linguistic Confusion at Home

Not all my students' parents affirmed use of their native language at home. Prop. 227 instilled uncertainties in parents' beliefs about the language of success and status in the United States. Many Latina/o parents quit speaking Spanish at home to advance their children's proficiency in English. Some students told me that their parents had older siblings translate messages into English for younger children, thereby breaking down their means of communication within their own families.

For some of my students, English was outlawed both at home and at school. Laura came to the United States at age 14 and was placed in English-only classrooms. She talked about succeeding in her mainstream English math classes because she could problem-solve using computational skills, not because she understood the teacher's lectures. Laura spoke of alienation and stigmatization at school that caused her to feel shame for her cultural identity and language. She would hear her teachers tell her, "If you keep speaking Spanish, you will never learn English. English only!" Laura explained how her parents also scolded her when she used Spanish at home, demanding she communicate with her brothers only in English so she could master the new language quickly and also provide her parents with exposure to English at home.

Cuando apenas llegamos a los Estados Unidos, mis papás casi me forzaron a abandonar mi idioma español. Me regañaban cuando usaba el español en casa. Mis papás querían que solo usara el inglés y que lo practicara con mis hermanos. De esta manera, ellos pensaban que yo iba a aprender mejor el idioma e iba a poder hablarlo más. A su vez, ellos hacían que mis hermanos y yo habláramos solo el inglés para que ellos pudieran escuchar también el idioma y aprender a hablarlo.

Throughout the semester, I encouraged the bilingual teacher candidates to link their own past experiences to their present and future work with their own students. When Laura was assigned to a clinical practice experience in an English language development (ELD) class with students labeled as long-term English language learners, she described how these students struggled to learn rigorous content in English under the Common Core Standards, which lacked connection to students' cultural and linguistic identities. Laura recognized similarities to her secondary schooling in California, and described how she identified with the ELD students in her clinical practice. She talked about the benefits of knowing two languages and invited the students to share how they learned their languages. She spoke about her renewed pride in her roots, culture, and language: "*Cada día me siento más orgullosa de mis raíces, de mi cultura, y de mi idioma.*"

Politically charged racism was at the core of the proposition and motivated its proponents.

Alex also shared how the past limits placed on his bilingualism shaped his future. When he was young, Alex's Mexican father refused to speak Spanish at home so his children could become proficient in English and succeed in school. When Alex was 14, he realized he could not communicate with his grandparents; he decided to learn Spanish in high school so that he would be able to talk with his family in Mexico. He continued his studies through college, where he realized that he could become a Spanish teacher and help other students learn the language. Alex wrote that although his father has passed away, his dad must be happy that at last he is able to speak and teach in such a beautiful language.

Loopholes in the Law

Of the 36 teacher candidates in the Bilingual Authorization Program, two of them were privileged to participate in a dual-language program because of the waiver process. The waiver process was a loophole in the law that allowed bilingual education to still function in California even though it had been deemed illegal in public schools. Districts with strong bilingual education programs—and those where white, middle-class parents advocated for dual-language programs—could support parents' rights to request waivers for primary language instruction. Under these waivers, the only restriction on language policy was to instruct the students solely in English during the first 30 days of a new school year. After this "quarantine period" programs could continue their content instruction in full bilingual mode, and some districts ignored the 30-day language restriction or found ways to circumvent the regulation.

Both Kyle, a white, middle-class student, and Omar, an immigrant from Guatemala, received their core content instruction in Spanish and English dual-language programs through 8th grade. However, their experiences differed greatly. Prop. 227 required that Omar's parents attend a mandatory district meeting to learn about the new regulations and sign a waiver on a yearly basis. Yet Kyle's parents were not mandated to attend the meetings or sign yearly waivers to register or maintain their child in a dual-language program; the law unfairly discriminated against linguistically diverse students and families.

Kyle described his schooling as an additive process—he learned Spanish as a second language while maintaining and developing his first language, English. Although Kyle celebrated his biliteracy, he understood that his enriched experience was unlike that of others who suffered the injustices of Prop. 227. He knew that his future students might see him as privileged and part of the dominant culture. In his journal, he clarified his obligation to raise the prestige of Spanish, as the mother tongue that connects his students to their culture.

In contrast, Omar described his experience as a challenging one, since his primary language was Q'anjob'al, an Indigenous language from Guatemala. Even though learning Spanish as a second language and English as a third was challenging, Omar felt he benefited greatly from the bilingual program. However, he experienced marginalization from other students for being a Latino, and discrimination from Latina/o students for being of Indigenous background. He described acts of violence against his family and how he felt the need to fight others or clown around in school to be accepted.

> *Mi familia ha sido discriminada por mucha gente. Hemos sido víctimas de violencia por ser guatemaltecos. Hemos escuchado muchas palabras negativas que fueron dirigidas hacia nosotros. Como niño, quería pelear o hacerme el chistoso en la clase para que otros me aceptaran, pero ahora, camino con el rostro hacia arriba y marcho adelante para educar a muchos sobre la presencia indígena en esta sociedad. Podemos ser líderes comunitarios como antes fuimos.*

Omar wrote how he now walks with his head held high because he knows he can educate others about the presence of Indigenous groups in society and their power to become leaders in their communities. Omar works with various nonprofit organizations that provide educational supplies to Indigenous schools in rural Guatemala. He also mentors young Guatemalan students in soccer leagues and academic programs. He is invited to speak at community events and parent meetings at local schools. He is truly a trilingual and multicultural leader.

Toward the Future

We culminated our unit by examining Sen. Ricardo Lara's initiative under California Senate Bill 1174, which included an amendment to revoke English-only education as outlined in Prop. 227. To quote the bill:

> This bill would amend and repeal various provisions of Proposition 227: delete the English immersion requirement and waiver provisions, and would instead authorize school districts and county offices of education to determine the best language instruction methods and language acquisition programs to implement by consulting experts in the field, parents, and engaging local communities. The bill would authorize parents to choose the education model that best suits their child, as provided.

There was a feeling of elation in the classroom as we read newspaper articles on Lara's proposal to restore bilingual education in California and learned how the bill would give parents of English learners the right to select the appropriate language acquisition program for their children. Someone shouted, "At last, our parents will have a voice!" Students were excited to learn that the bill had been signed by the governor and was slated to make its way to the California voters in 2016. The bill, Proposition 58, was approved by voters on Nov. 8, 2016.

> The teacher candidates are fueled by their commitment to transform the system that wrongly denied their right to learn in two or more languages, particularly in their native tongue.

I wanted my students to tell their own stories of becoming bilingual against the odds. Each teacher candidate created their own photovoice project to explain the "Story of My Languages," with narratives, family photographs, music, poems, and videos that explored their identities through their life experiences, including their schooling and their challenges and successes in becoming bilingual. We celebrated their accomplishments and resiliency against the powerful political storm of restrictive language policies that had swept through their schools and communities.

As I watched my students present their final projects, I realized they represented an era of struggle in California schools. They symbolized the thousands of children who have been denied the legitimate recognition of their home languages in instructional programs. They also stood for the resistance of bilingual communities to those restrictive language policies. These future teachers knew the hardships of linguistic discrimination and the power of families to maintain the vitality of a home language.

Although many had felt unsure of their language abilities at the beginning of the program, the teacher candidates demonstrated a transformation in self-image and academic progress. Those who had difficulty with Spanish proficiency at the onset of the program practiced Spanish grammar through class essays, rewrote papers, took Spanish classes, or received peer tutoring to advance their proficiency. All 36 candidates completed the program. Many now have jobs as bilingual/dual-language educators. Nine candidates have continued to advance their studies: Four earned their Special Education Advanced Credentials and five went on to complete a Master of Arts in Education degree with a concentration in Multilingual and Multicultural Education, while also completing a Dual-Language Certificate.

As I read their final reflections on their experiences in the Bilingual Authorization Program, I saw students' identities reawakened by their passion to become bilingual educators. They believe in breaking the cycle of prejudice and discrimination by becoming change agents in bilingual programs. They are fueled by their commitment to transform the system that wrongly denied their right to learn in two or more languages, particularly in their native tongue. In their reflections, the candidates' voices resonated in affirmation of a long struggle for cultural and linguistic equity. Alex described what he nearly lost as a child and how he will fight to help his children and students maintain their identities:

> *Nadie podrá jamás robarme de mis lenguas ni de mi cultura, y lucharé para el futuro de mis hijos y estudiantes. Ser bilingüe es algo que siempre mantendré y haré lo posible para que mis estudiantes logren y mantengan su bilingüismo también.* (No one will ever steal my languages or my culture, and I will fight for the future of my children and students. Being bilingual is something I will always maintain and I will do what is possible so that my students achieve and maintain their bilingualism as well). ☼

Ana M. Hernández is an associate professor of multilingual and multicultural education in the School of Education at California State University San Marcos. Previously, she taught for 32 years as a K–8 bilingual teacher in California public schools. Student names have been changed.

Resources

Reyes, María de la Luz, ed. 2011. *Words Were All We Had: Becoming Biliterate Against the Odds.* Teachers College Press.

Senate Bill No. 1174, California Legislative Information, retrieved on April 26, 2014 from leginfo.legislature.ca.gov/faces/billNavClient.xhtml?bill_id=201320140SB1174.

Recommended Resources

. . . .
Aram Ayalon recommends:

Foundations of Bilingual Education and Bilingualism
Colin Baker
Multilingual Matters, 2006
A basic introductory text from a cross-disciplinary perspective for people new to
bilingual education.

Second Language Acquisition
Susan M. Gass and Larry Selinker
Routledge, 2008
blogs.umass.edu/moiry/files/2015/08/Gass.Second-Language-Acquisition.pdf
A cornerstone text on how children acquire a second language.

. . . .
Elizabeth Barbian recommends:

Nal'ibali
nalibali.org
A South African literacy campaign that supports multilingualism and home
language literacy through an array of resources that include printable stories
(available in all 11 of South Africa's official languages), book clubs, bilingual
newspaper supplements, and multilingual audio stories.

Radio Ambulante
radioambulante.org
A Spanish-language podcast with great quality narratives, fiction, and interviews
from the United States and Latin America.

Zinn Education Project
zinnedproject.org
A joint project of Teaching for Change and Rethinking Schools with a wealth of
materials and resources (including some in Spanish) for the teaching of U.S. history
from a social justice perspective in later elementary, middle, and high schools.

. . . .

Grace Cornell Gonzales recommends:

De Colores: The Raza Experience in Books for Children
decoloresreviews.blogspot.com
A blog that reviews children's books about the Latina/o experience through a critical, social justice lens.

Lenguas Indígenas: Una Red de Activistas Digitales en América Latina
rising.globalvoices.org/lenguas
A network of Indigenous activists in Latin America who are using digital media to support their language revitalization efforts.

When We Were Young/There Was a War
centralamericanstories.com
A bilingual resource for teaching and learning about the civil wars in Guatemala and El Salvador—people who lived through the wars as children share their stories.

. . . .

Jessica Singer Early recommends:

Choice Literacy
choiceliteracy.com
A collection of web-based resources for literacy educators across all grade levels and disciplines, which includes tools, guides, literacy lessons, teacher research projects, and examples of student writing and reading.

Creating Welcoming Schools: A Practical Guide to Home-School Partnerships with Diverse Families
JoBeth Allen
Teachers College Press, 2007
A guide that supports teachers and administrators in building lasting and productive partnerships with families to enhance student learning.

School's Out: Bridging Out-of-School Literacies with Classroom Practice
Glynda Hull and Katherine Schultz, Editors
Teachers College Press, 2001
A valuable resource on models for bridging literacy practices in formal school settings with literacy practices beyond the school walls.

Pilar Mejía recommends:

Guía para padres y maestros de niños bilingües
Alma Flor Ada and Colin Baker
Multilingual Matters, 2001
An easy-to-access question and answer format of everything you ever wanted to
know about raising bilingual children.

*Life-Enriching Education: Nonviolent Communication Helps Schools
Improve Performance, Reduce Conflict, and Enhance Relationships*
Marshall B. Rosenberg
PuddleDancer Press, 2003
A guide to nonviolent communication in school settings.

Linguistic Human Rights: Overcoming Linguistic Discrimination
Tove Skutnabb-Kangas and Robert Phillipson, Editors
De Gruyter Mouton, 1995
A collection of papers describing what linguistic human rights are, and how and
why many groups are deprived of these rights.

. . . .
Peggy Morrison recommends:

Beyond the Bake Sale: The Essential Guide to Family-School Partnerships
Anne T. Henderson, Karen L. Mapp, Vivian R. Johnson, and Don Davies, Editors
The New Press, 2007
A book that helps educators examine their own beliefs and practices in relation
to culturally and linguistically diverse families and communities, evaluate their
schools' "welcome quotient," and respectfully collaborate with the parents of their
students.

*Beyond Heroes and Holidays: A Practical Guide to K–12 Anti-Racist,
Multicultural Education and Staff Development*
Enid Lee, Deborah Menkart, and Margo Okazawa-Rey, Editors
Teaching for Change, 2008
A book that provides both conceptual frameworks and practical examples of anti-
bias, culturally responsive educational practice from researchers, teachers, poets,
and cultural elders.

Dual Language Education for a Transformed World
Wayne P. Thomas and Virginia P. Collier
Fuente Press, 2012
A research-based book that makes the case for dual-language education to become
the standard for all schools.

Through Indian Eyes: The Native Experience in Books for Children
Beverly Slapin and Doris Seale, Editors
Oyate, 1998
A resource that helps educators understand and recognize the difference between subtle forms of discrimination and disrespect in published literature and respectful and authentic depiction of cultural perspectives.

. . . .

Michelle Nicola recommends:

Black in Latin America [book, film]
Henry Louis Gates
New York University Press, 2011
Also available as a DVD from PBS, 2011
Both a book and a DVD that provide valuable insights regarding the history and present-day realities of Afro Latinas/os living in the Caribbean and Latin America.

¡Sí! Somos latinos
Alma Flor Ada and F. Isabel Campoy, David Díaz (Illustrator)
Alfaguara, 2014
Yes! We Are Latinos [English edition]
Charlesbridge, 2016
A collection of poems and informative texts that beautifully captures the multiplicity of identities with Latina/o culture.

. . . .

Marina Perez recommends:

Center for Applied Linguistics (CAL)
cal.org
An organization that provides research, resources, and links to current events regarding emergent bilinguals, particularly in the areas of bilingual and dual-language education.

. . . .

Bob Peterson recommends:

The Natural Approach: Language Acquisition in the Classroom
Stephen D. Krashen and Tracy D. Terrell
Alemany Press, 1983
A teacher-friendly book that looks at the theory and practice of 2nd language acquisition, highlighting the need for students to obtain comprehensible input and for teachers to focus on communicative goals (not grammar) and to use methods that lower students' affective filters.

Language, Power and Pedagogy: Bilingual Children in the Crossfire
Jim Cummins
Multilingual Matters, 2000
A comprehensive exploration of key issues confronting educators who teach students a second language, including both theory and practice in the classroom as well as broader issues of social class and power.

. . . .

April S. Salerno and Amanda K. Kibler recommend:

Speaking in Tongues [film]
Marcia Jarmel and Ken Schneider, Directors
PatchWorks Films, 2009
A documentary following four K–8 students through their experiences in U.S. dual-language programs, this resource gives insight into the complex public and personal dialogues surrounding bilingual education.

Teaching for Biliteracy: Strengthening Bridges Between Languages
Karen Beeman and Cheryl Urow
Caslon Publishing, 2012
A research-based resource for designing instruction that helps students bridge or transfer knowledge between languages.

The Translanguaging Classroom: Leveraging Student Bilingualism for Learning
Ofelia García, Susana Ibarra Johnson, and Kate Seltzer
Caslon, 2016
A guide that helps teachers create translanguaging classrooms where students are free to use their "full linguistic repertoires" instead of only the official classroom language(s).

. . . .

Jacqui Stanford recommends:

"The Patois/Patwa Wars" [blog post]
newsandviewsbydjmillerja.wordpress.com/2012/09/12/the-patoispatwa-wars
Broadcaster Dionne Jackson Miller summarizes debates about the Patwa language.

"Saluting Miss Lou: Aunty Roachy Online Party" [video]
livestream.com/FlowLive/MissLou/videos/135045053
Jamaica Cultural Development Commission (JCDC) 2016 celebration of Miss Lou, with performances of her work by Jamaican schoolchildren and leading artists.

Talking Tongue(s) Blog
icclr.wordpress.com
Engaging articles on Patwa in Jamaica.

. . . .

Rita Tenorio recommends:

The Anti-Bias Curriculum: Tools for Empowering Young Children
Louise Derman-Sparks and the A.B.C. Task Force
National Association for the Education of Young Children, 1989
Perhaps the best book for early childhood teachers to learn about all forms of bias
and how to teach about it.

Creative Resources for the Anti-Bias Classroom
Nadia Saderman Hall
Delmar Publishers, 1999
A comprehensive guide for teachers that contains developmentally appropriate
activities for elementary children.

. . . .

Joanne Tompkins recommends:

Negotiating Identities: Education for Empowerment in a Diverse Society
Jim Cummins
California Association for Bilingual Education, 2001
A great overview of bilingual education that offers clear information on power
relationships in bilingual education; illustrations and concept maps provide
educators and communities with the research and theory that they need to advocate
for the creation and maintenance of bilingual programs.

. . . .

Jacob Werblow recommends:

Dual Language Schools.org
duallanguageschools.org
A national directory of PK–12 dual-language schools in the United States that
includes helpful resources about them.

The Dual Language Program Planner: A Guide for Designing and Implementing Dual Language Programs [report]
Elizabeth R. Howard, Natalie Olague, and David Rogers
Center for Research on Education, Diversity, & Excellence, 2003
researchgate.net
A step-by-step plan for parents, educators, and community members to follow if they are interested in establishing a dual-language school in their community.

From English Language Learners to Emergent Bilinguals [report]
Ofelia García, Jo Anne Kleifgen, and Lorraine Falchi
Campaign for Educational Equity, Teachers College, 2008
files.eric.ed.gov/fulltext/ED524002.pdf
An excellent overview of the needs of ELLs, the history of bilingual education, and the research on different programs for emergent bilingual students.

Index

Page numbers in *italics* indicate illustrations

A

Athabaskan language, 100, 106
Attention-Deficit/Hyperactivity Disorder
    (ADHD), 182–184
Australia, boarding school system in,
    102–103
Au, Wayne, 281
Ayalon, Aram, 307–308, 310, 321
    "Language Wars," 304–310

B

Babino, Alexandra, 199
    "Making Space for Spanish," 193–199
Baca, Jimmy Santiago, 114
Bacon, David, *170, 187, 220, 311*
Báez, Tony, xvi, *274,* 274–279
Baker, Colin, 321, 323
Bale, Jeff, 288
    "English-Only to the Core," xvi,
        280–288
Banks, James, 158
Barbian, Elizabeth, 71, 169, 234, 321
    "Aquí y Allá," 64–71
    "Building Bilingual Communities at César
        Chávez Elementary," 163–169
    "When Are You Coming to Visit?," 229–234
basal reader program, 32–33
Bean Soup (Argueta), 64–65
Beeman, Karen, 325
Bell, Alexander Graham, 54–55
Bennett-Coverley, Louise, 129, 134–135
Berdan, Robert, 124–125
Beyond the Bake Sale (Henderson, Mapp,
    Johnson, and Davies), 323
"Beyond Bilingual" (Durán, Hikida, and
    Martínez), 186–192
Beyond Heroes and Holidays (Lee, Menkart,
    and Okazawa-Rey), 323
Bigelow, Bill, 269–270
Big L, 117
"Bilingual Against the Odds" (Hernández),
    311–319
bilingual education
    attacks on, 267–268, 285–287, 304–308
    and Common Core State Standards,
        280–281, 283–285, 287–288
    decline of. See English-only laws
    developmental (maintenance) programs,
        xii, 31, 154, 165, 276, 277
    future of, 279

history of, xvi–xvii, 274–278, 282–283
multiple language program, 163–169
resources for, 321–327
school libraries, 200–204
and social justice. *See* social justice in
    bilingual education
standardized testing of English learners,
    289–294
transitional programs, xii, 165, 276, 277,
    305
types of programs, xii–xiii
See also dual-language programs;
    immersion programs
Bilingual Education Act of 1968 (Title VII),
    275, 282, 286
Bilingual Education Act of 1974, xvi
Bilingual Education Project, in Jamaica,
    131–132
biliteracy, x, xii–xiii, xvii, 32, 132, 137, 141,
    164, 165, 278, 286, 289, 291–292, 317
Black English. *See* Ebonics
Black in Latin America (film), 84, 324
Black in Latin America (Gates), 324
Black Lives Matter, 169
Blacks. *See* African Americans
boarding schools
    in Australia, 102–103
    Deaf schools, 53–55
    Native American, 49–53, *97*, 98, 101–102
Bonnin, Gertrude (Zitkala-Sa), 51–52
book project, bilingual, 139–140
books. *See* children's books
booksharing, family, 253–255
brainstorming, 66, 176, 212
Brewer, Jake, *127*
Brewer, Jan, 210
Brito, Katarina, 247–248
Brooklyn (New York)
    Arabic-English program in, 286
    standardized test boycott in, 294
Bruce-Monroe Elementary School,
    Washington, D.C., 207, 243–249
"Building Bilingual Communities at César
    Chávez Elementary" (Barbian and Cornell
    Gonzales), 163–169
"Building Bridges" (Salerno and Kibler),
    136–142

C

CABE (California Association for Bilingual Education), 169

California
anti-immigrant law in (Proposition 187), xvii, 285, 315
English immersion programs in, 306, 312–313
English-only law in (Proposition 227), xvii, 176, 267, 273, 304, 312–318
repeal of English-only law, xvii, 318–319
school libraries in, 202
standardized testing in, 289–294
waiver process for bilingual programs, 317
See also Oakland (California); San Francisco (California)

California Association for Bilingual Education (CABE), 169

California School Library Association (CSLA), 202

Campoy, F. Isabel, 324

Canada, Mi'kmaq immersion program in, 57–63

Cantonese language, 108, 110, 165, 167

Carlisle Indian Industrial School, 53, *97*, 101

Caron, Roscoe, 148
"Ganas Means Desire," 143–148

"Carrying Our Sacred Language" (Paul, Paul-Gould, Murray-Orr, and Tompkins), 57–63

Caspe, Margaret, 253

Cassidy, Frederic, 128

Cazden, Courtney B., 122, 123

CCSS (Common Core State Standards), impact on bilingual education, 280–281, 283–285

Celestino, Catherine, 69

Center for Applied Linguistics, 40, 248, 324

Centre of Excellence, 59–60

Cervantes, Melanie, *11, 17, 193, 272*

César Chávez Elementary School, San Francisco, 151, 163–169

Chair for My Mother, A (Williams), 46

charter schools, 161
Asian American, 109–110

Chavez, Cesar, 25–26

"Chicago Stole My Mother's Yesterdays" (Smith), 16–18

Chicago Teachers Union, 288

Chicanas/os. *See* Latinas/os; Mexican Americans

Chicano Student Movement of Aztlán (MEChA), 143, 145–148

children's books
on African history, 75
on bilingualism, 174
creating bilingual books, 139–140
on family traditions, 46
on farmworkers, 25–28, 224
on immigrants, 37
by Latina/o authors, 33
Latina/o culture-free, 32–33
on linguistic diversity, 121
on Native American boarding schools, 50–51
poetry, 64–65
resources for, 322, 324
on skin color, 78–79

Chinese language
Cantonese, 108, 110, 165, 167
Fujianese, 110
Mandarin, 109–110

Chinn, Karen, 46

Choice Literacy, 322

Christensen, Linda, 107, 118
"Putting Out the Linguistic Welcome Mat," 113–118
"Uncovering the Legacy of Language and Power," xiii, 91, 97–107

Clark, Kevin, 306, 308, 309

climate change, and Indigenous peoples, 270

Cloues, Rachel, 204
"El corazón de la escuela/The Heart of the School," 200–204

code-switching, 115, 121–122

Cognitive Academic Language Learning model, 284

Colato Laínez, René, 31, 33

college students, Latina/o, in middle school after-school program (Ganas), 143–148

Collier, Virginia P., 323

colonialism, effect on Indigenous languages, 97–106

"Colonization in Reverse" (Bennett-Coverley), 129, 134–135

"Colonizing Wild Tongues" (Arze Torres Goitia), 3, 5–7

Colors of Us, The (Katz), 78

Common Core State Standards (CCSS), impact on bilingual education, 280–281, 283–285, 287–288

communications with parents, bilingual, 237–240, 242

community-building conversations, 138

computer-based testing, in school libraries, 203

Conklin, Marijke, 30
"Cultivando sus voces," 21, *23*, 23–30

Connecticut, termination of bilingual education in, 304–309

Connor, Michael Ames, 256
"Rethinking Family Literacy in Head Start," 250–256

contractions, concept of, 198

Cooperative Children's Book Center, 33

Cooper, Kelt, 306–307, 308, 309

Cordioli, Bruno, *8*

Cornell Gonzales, Grace, 112, 169, 242, 264, 294, 322
"Aren't You on the Parent Listserv?," 235–242
"Building Bilingual Communities at César Chávez Elementary," 163–169
"Language Is a Human Right," 108–112
"Our Language Lives by What We Do," 257–264
"What Happened to Spanish?," 289–294

Council on Interracial Books for Children, 156

Creating Welcoming Schools (Allen), 322

Creative Resources for the Anti-Bias Classroom (Hall), 326

cross-language groups, 138, 139, 140

Cruz Carretero, Sagrario, 85

"Cuentos del corazón/Stories from the Heart" (Flores and Early), 209–219

"Cultivando sus voces" (Conklin), 23–30

culture, as component of language instruction, x

Cummins, Jim, 183, 185, 325, 326

Cunningham, Patricia, 123

D

Davies, Bronwyn, 173

Davies, Don, 323

Day of the Dead event, 138

Deaf education classroom, in multiple language bilingual school, 165

Deaf President Now movement, at Gallaudet College, 56

Deaf schools
American Sign Language (ASL) in, 48, 51
comparison with Native American boarding schools, 50–53
cultural consciousness in, 48
history of, 53–55
oral education in, 49, 53–54
resistance to assimilation policies, 55

"Death of My Mexican Name, The" (Treviño), 11–12

De Colores: The Raza Experience in Books for Children (blog), 322

De La Salle North school, Portland, Oregon, 81–88

Del Norte al Sur (Colato Laínez), 34

Delpit, Lisa, 125
"Ebonics and Culturally Responsive Instruction," 119–126

Denny, Ida, 59, 60

deportation issue, in social justice curriculum, 31–32, 34–37

Derman-Sparks, Louise, 326

developmental (maintenance) bilingual programs, xii, 31, 154, 165, 276, 277

dialects, 120–121

Diamond, Norm, 270

Díaz, David, 324

dictionaries, linguistic diversity in, 121

DiLoreto Dual-Language Magnet School, New Britain, Connecticut, 304–310

Discrete Skills Inventory, 283–284

drawings
in family writing project, 212–213
metaphorical, 104–105
self-portraits, 44

drumming, in Mi'kmaq immersion program, 60

Dual Language Education for a Transformed World (Thomas and Collier), 323

Dual Language Program Planner, The (Howard, Olague, and Rogers), 327

dual-language programs, xii, xvii
collaborative, 161–162
English preference of students, 193–194
equity for non-dominant language/ culture, x–xi, 151, 155–156, 172–174, 286
establishing (La Escuela Fratney), 153–154

expansion of, 278, 279

extracurricular high school, 137–142

integrated curriculum, 159, 161

language imbalance in, 174–175, 194–196

and multiculturalism, 154, 156–158

multilingual students in, 186–192

one-language/one-teacher model, 194

poetry curriculum (here/there), 64–71

rethinking pedagogy/curriculum, 39–47

schoolwide themes in, 159, 160

site-based hiring in, 161

Spanish supports in, 193–199

termination of, 304–309, 312, 313

waiver process for, 317

See also family involvement

Dual Language Schools.org, 326

Duffy, Michael, *113, 269*

Dumas Lachtman, Ofelia, 33, 174

Duncan, Arne, 281

Durairajan, Geetha, 15

"Some Languages Are More Equal than Others," 13–15

Durán, Leah, 192

"Beyond Bilingual," 186–192

E

Early, Jessica Singer, 216, 322

"Cuentos del corazón/Stories from the Heart," 209–219

early childhood education

bilingual approach in, 155, 247

Hawaiian immersion schools, 257, 258–259, 263

Mi'kmaq immersion school, 57–58, 59–63

welcoming of non-dominant cultures, 93–96

EBD (Emotional Behavior Disorder), 178, 179–181

"Ebonics" (song), 117

Ebonics (Black English)

code-switching, 115, 121–122

and conformity to Standard English, 119–120

and group identity, 119, 120–122

in language diversity curriculum, 121–122

in language and power curriculum, 115–118

linguistic roots of, 116

in multiple language bilingual school, 163, 165–166

negative effect of correction, 114, 120, 123–124

prejudice against, 98, 115, 117

and reading development, 123–125

and writing, 125

"Ebonics and Culturally Responsive Instruction" (Delpit), 119–126

Educating Emergent Bilinguals (García and Kleifgen), 287

Educators' Network for Social Justice, 159, 161

ELAC (English Learner Advisory Committee), 236, 241

El camino de Amelia (Altman), 27

"El corazón de la escuela/The Heart of the School" (Cloues), 200–204

El Salvador, teaching resource on, 322

ELD (English Language Development) classroom, 210–211, 306–309, 316

elementary schools

after-school family writing project, 209–219

Asian American, 108, 109–110, 112

basal-based reading instruction in, 32–33

equality concept in dual-language programs, 154–155

family involvement in, 210–216, 227, 243 249

farmworkers curriculum in, 23–30

home visits in, 229–234

immigration/deportation issues in curriculum of, 31–32, 34–37

literature-based discussions in, 26–28, 33–38

maintenance (developmental) program in, xii, 31, 32

Mi'kmaq immersion program, x, 57–58, 59–63

multicultural/multiracial teaching in, 73–76, 79–80, 156–158

multi-language students in dual-language programs, 186–192

multiple language programs in, 163–169

non-dominant language privileged in, 151, 155–156

pedagogy/curriculum for dual-language programs, 39–47

poetry writing (here/there), 64–72

Heart," 209–219

Flores v. Horne, 306

Folk Arts-Cultural Treasures Charter School (FACTS), Philadelphia, 108, 109, 112

Fought, Carmen, 194

Foundations of Bilingual Education and Bilingualism (Baker), 321

Francis, Bernie, 57–58

Free Minds, Free People conference, 288

Freire, Paulo, 279

From English Language Learners to Emergent Bilinguals (García, Kleifgen, and Falchi), 327

From North to South (Colato Laínez), 31

Fujianese language, 110

Fully English Proficient classification, 290

G

Gabaldón, Salvador, 267–268, 273
  "Reflecting on My Mother's Spanish," 272–273

Gallaudet College, Deaf President Now movement at, 56

Ganas after-school program, middle school/college student, 143–148

"Ganas Means Desire" (Caron), 143–148

García, Ofelia, 287, 325, 327

Gass, Susan M., 321

Gates, Henry Louis, 84, 324

Gates Foundation, 280, 281

Gonzales, Grace Cornell, *See* Cornell Gonzales, Grace

Gonzales, Rodolfo "Corky," xvi, 275

Gosse, Marcus, 57

Goudvis, Anne, 214

Grassroots Education Movement, 288

Grauert, Christiane, *13*, *39*

Guatemala
  Indigenous languages of, 317–318
  teaching resource on, 322

Guía para padres y maestros de niños bilingües (Ada and Baker), 323

Guzman, Mario, 81

H

Hall, Nadia Saderman, 326

Hamanaka, Sheila, 73, 78

Hamilton High School, Virginia, 137–142

Harman, Kekoa, 207, 258–264

Harré, Rom, 173

Harris, Wendy, 56
  "Kill the Indian, Kill the Deaf," 48–56

Harrison, David, 98

Harvey, Stephanie, 214

Hawaii
  immersion schools in, 257–264
  Indigenous teaching methods in, 260–261
  standardized tests in, 262

Hawaiian language
  in home, 258, 262
  revitalization of, 207, 257–264

Heath, Shirley Brice, 121

Henderson, Anne T., 323

heritage language programs, xii–xiii, 81–88, 109–111, 295–303

heritage language speakers, xii–xiii, 82, 110–111, 186

Hernández, Ana M., 319
  "Bilingual Against the Odds," 311–319

Hernandez, Lillian, 244

Herrera, Juan Felipe, 33

high schools
  African American literature in, 115–116
  bilingual education in, 277
  curriculum about language and power, 97–107
  dual-language extracurricular program in, 136–142
  Patwa language in (Jamaica), 128–133
  Spanish heritage language class in, 81–88
  teaching about Ebonics in, 113–118

Hikida, Michiko, 192
  "Beyond Bilingual," 186–192

Hispanics. *See* Latinas/os; Mexican Americans

Hollins, Etta, 121–122

home knowledge curriculum development, 220–228

home languages
  Asian, 110–112
  discrimination against, 8–10, 13–15, 113, 171, 172
  erasure of, 97–99
  heritage language speakers, xii–xiii, 82, 110–111, 186
  as human right, ix, x, 110, 154
  maintaining use of, 110–111, 186, 199
  of multilingual students, 187–188, 191
  valuing, 189–191

language dominance. *See* English dominance

"Language Is a Human Right" (Cornell Gonzales), 108–112

language pathway, Arabic, 295, 297–303

Language, Power and Pedagogy (Cummins), 325

"Language Wars" (Werblow, Ayalon, and Perez), 304–310

Languages Across Borders (LAB), 136–142

Lara, Ricardo, 318

Latin American Teachers Association (LATA), 169

Latinas/os

    after-school program, middle school, college students in, 143–148

    Americanization of names, 11–12

    authors of children's books, 33

    booksharing styles of, 253–254

    and deportation, 31–32

    ethnic studies classes for, 277–278

    family literacy practices of, 251–252

    home language exclusion of, 113, 137, 171

    invisibility in curriculum, 32

    as language models in dual-language classroom, 171

    parental involvement in schools, 236, 237, 240–241, 244–249

    racial tension with African American parents, 243–244

    See also Mexican Americans; Spanish language; Spanish language, in dual-language program

Latinx community, 164, 165

Lau v. Nichols (1974), xvi, 275–276, 277, 282–283

Lazore, Dorothy, 62

League of Latin American Citizens (LULAC), 281

Lee, Enid, 158, 227, 323

Lenguas Indígenas, 322

Lenkersdorf, Carlos, 271

    "Are You a Subject or an Object?," 269–271

letter-writing campaign, advocacy, 309

Levine, David, 249

    "Tellin' Stories, Changing Lives," 243–249

Levine, Ellen, 37

Li Shuyuan, 109

libraries, school, 200–204

Life-Enriching Education (Rosenberg), 323

Limited English Proficient classification,

290–291

Linguistic Human Rights (Skutnabb-Kangas and Phillipson), 323

literature discussion groups, 26–28, 33–38

Living Tongues Institute for Endangered Languages, 98, 100

Lowry, Judith, 50

LULAC (League of United Latin American Citizens), 281

M

Mahmoudi, Nessa, 47

    "Questioning Assumptions in Dual Immersion," 39–47

maintenance (developmental) bilingual programs, xii, 31, 154, 165, 276, 277

"Making Space for Spanish" (Babino and Wickstrom), 193–199

MALDEF (Mexican American Legal Defense and Education Fund), 281

Mandarin language, 109–110

Mapp, Karen L., 323

La mariposa (Jiménez), 21, 27, 174

Marshall Islands/Marshallese language, 94–95

Martinez, Esther, 106

Martínez, Ramón Antonio, 192

    "Beyond Bilingual," 186–192

"Las maravillas de la ciudad" (Argueta), 72

Massachusetts, English-only law in (Question 2), xvii, 171, 273, 304

mathematics, 260, 291

Mayan language, 271

Mbalia, Ahmed, 151, 156–157

McDaniel, Rodney, 245

McLimans, David, *250*

me pockets activity, 76–77

MEChA (Chicano Student Movement of Aztlán), 143, 145–148

media, bilingual advocacy in, 308–309

Mejía, Pilar, 163–169, 323

Memín Pinguín, 86–87

Memoir upon the Formation of a Deaf Variety of the Human Race (Bell), 54

Men in Black (film), 103

Menkart, Deborah, 323

Menken, Kate, 286

Menominee language, 55

metaphorical drawings, 104–105

Metro Deaf School, St. Paul, Minnesota, 48,

49, 56

Mexican American Legal Defense and Education Fund (MALDEF), 281

Mexican Americans
    and Afro-Mexican history curriculum, 81–88
    bilingual/multilingual, 187–188, 198–199, 272–273
    home visits to, 229–230
    student union (Chicano Student Movement of Aztlán), 143, 145
    See also Latinas/os; Spanish language; Spanish language, in dual-language program

Mexico
    Afro-Mexican history curriculum, 81–88
    Indigenous languages of, 187, 190, 229, 231–232, 270–271

"Mexico & Peru: The Black Grandma in the Closet" (film), 84

"Mi Love di Way Mi Chat" (Stanford), 127–135

Michaels, Sarah, 122

middle schools
    Afro-Mexican history unit in, 81–88
    after-school program, Latina/o, college students in, 143–148
    Deaf students, 48–56

Mi'kma'ji'j (Francis), 57–58

Mi'kmaq community, in Canada, 58–59

Mi'kmaq immersion program, x, 57–58, 59–63

Milwaukee (Wisconsin)
    bilingual education in, 276–277
    dual-language school in, 74–80, 151, 153–162
    ethnic studies in, 277–278

Milwaukee Area Technical College, 278

Miner, Barbara, *119, 153,* 162

Minnesota, deaf education in, 48–56

Minnesota School for the Deaf, *49,* 54

Miss Lou's poetry, 129, 134–135

Mixtec language, 231

Morales, Ricardo Levins, *1, 19, 89, 149, 205, 265, 289*

Morison, Samuel Eliot, 269

Morrison, Peggy, 228, 323–324
    "Strawberries in Watsonville," xi, 220–228

Morrison, Toni, 114

Movie in My Pillow, A (Argueta), 65

Mufaro's Beautiful Daughters (Steptoe), 75

multicultural education
    anti-racist curriculum, x, 74–76, 79–80, 156–158
    in dual-language program, 154–155
    opposition to, xvi–xvii, 273
    welcoming of non-dominant cultures, 93–96, 114, 157

multilingual students, 186–192

Munson, Derek, 188

Murray-Orr, Anne, 63
    "Carrying Our Sacred Language," 57–63

Musgrove, Margaret, 75

music, in Mi'kmaq immersion program, 60

My Mexico poetry anthology, 187

My Mother Plants Strawberries (Ada), 224

N

NAACP (National Association for the Advancement of Colored People), 281

NABE (National Association for Bilingual Education), 280–281

Nal'ibali literacy campaign, South Africa, 321

National Association for the Advancement of Colored People (NAACP), 281

National Association for Bilingual Education (NABE), 280–281

National Association of the Deaf, 55

National Council of La Raza (NCLR), 281

National Language Project, 106

Native Americans
    in boarding schools, 49–53, 55–56, 97–98, 101–102
    and colonial legacy, 61
    and language extinction, 98–100
    and language restoration, 106
    Mi'kmaq bilingual immersion program, x, 57–58, 59–63
    Mi'kmaq community, 58–59
    teacher education, 61–62

Natural Approach, The (Krashen and Terrell), 324

NCLB (No Child Left Behind), 281, 286, 290

NCLR (National Council of La Raza), 281

Negotiating Identities (Cummins), 326

Negri-Pool, Laura Linda, 96
    "Welcoming Kalenna," 93–96

New Britain, Connecticut, termination of bilingual program in, 304–309

New York City
    Arabic-English school in, 286, 299
    Bilingual Common Core initiative in, 287
    bilingual education in, 275, 276, 286
    standardized test boycott in, 294
Nicholas, Andrea Bear, 62
Nicola, Michelle, 88, 324
    "Rethinking Identity," 81–88
"Niños campesinos," 23, 28, 30
Nobisso, Josephine, 37
No Child Left Behind (NCLB), 281, 286, 290
No, David! (Shannon), 95
No English (Jules), 37
nonverbal communication, with bilingual
    special education students, 180
"Not Too Young" (Tenorio), 73–80
Nye, Naomi Shihab, 213, 218, 219

O

Oakland (California)
    dual-immersion school in, 39–47
    Ebonics instruction in, 98, 115, 121
    farmworkers curriculum in, 23–30
Obama, Barack, 280
Office of Civil Rights (OCR), U.S., 308
Okazawa-Rey, Margo, 323
Okinawa, Uchinaaguchi language in, 8–10
Olague, Natalie, 327
Oleson, William, 258
oral history, in Philadelphia Chinatown, 110
Oregon, 113
    African American literature curriculum
        in, 115–116
    Afro-Mexican history curriculum in,
        81–88
    Ganas Latina/o after-school program,
        143–148
    Indigenous languages in, 100, 106
Osorio, Sandra L., 38
    "Qué es deportar?," 31–38
"Our Language Lives by What We Do"
    (Cornell Gonzales), 257–264

P

Palacios, Marta, 244, 247, 248
Palmer, Deborah, 176
    "Why Are We Speaking So Much English,"
        xi, 170–176

parent involvement. *See* family involvement
"Patois/Patwa Wars, The" (blog post), 325
Patwa Bible, 128
Patwa language (Jamaica), 127–128
    bilingual program for, 131–132
    Miss Lou's poetry, 129, 134–135
    prejudice against, 128–129
    recognition/validation of, 129–130,
        132–133
    Shakespeare instruction in, 130–131
Paul, Elizabeth, 59
Paul, Starr, 63
    "Carrying Our Sacred Language," x, 57–63
Paul-Gould, Sherise, 58, 62, 63
    "Carrying Our Sacred Language," 57–63
peer coaching, 169
Pennsylvania
    bilingual programs in, 111–112
    Folk Arts-Cultural Treasures Charter
        School (FACTS), 108–112
Pepita habla dos veces (Dumas Lachtman), 33
Pepita Talks Twice (Dumas Lachtman), 174
Perez, Marina, 305, 307, 308, 310, 324
    "Language Wars," 304–310
Peterson, Bob, xi–xii, xvi, 151, 162, 279,
        324–325
    "La Escuela Fratney," 153–162
    "The Struggle for Bilingual Education,"
        274–279
Philadelphia (Pennsylvania), Folk Arts-
    Cultural Treasures Charter School
        (FACTS), 108–112
Phillipson, Robert, 323
phrase scripts, 181, 182
poetry
    in family writing project, 213–214,
        218–219
    here/there poems, 64–72
    "I am" poems, 189–190
    Jamaican, 129
    in multiple languages, 112
    read aloud, 187
Portland (Oregon)
    African American literature curriculum
        in, 115–116
    Afro-Mexican history curriculum in,
        81–88
Potowski, Kim, 194
PRAESA (Project for the Study of Alternative
    Education in South Africa), 106

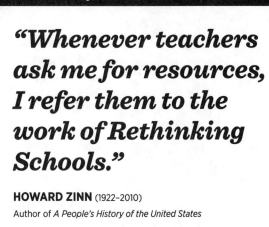

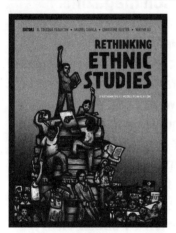

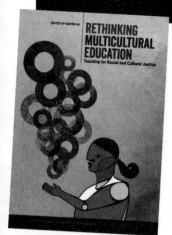

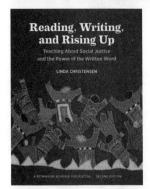

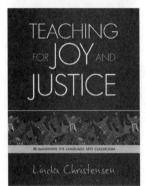

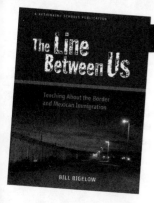

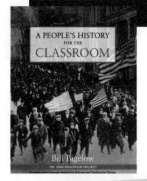